STOPPING THE SPIES

STOPPING THE SPIES

Constructing and resisting the surveillance state in South Africa

JANE DUNCAN

WITS UNIVERSITY PRESS

Published in South Africa by:
Wits University Press
1 Jan Smuts Avenue
Johannesburg 2001

www.witspress.co.za

First published 2018

http://dx.doi.org.10.18772/12018052156

978-1-77614-215-6 (Print)
978-1-77614-216-3 (Web PDF)
978-1-77614-217-0 (EPUB)

Copy-editor: Russell Martin
Proofreader: Inga Norenius
Indexer: Marlene Burger
Cover design: Fire and Lion
Typesetter: Integra
Typeset in 10 point MinionPro-Regular

CONTENTS

ACKNOWLEDGEMENTS

would like to thank my colleagues and comrades in the MPDP, especially Julie Reid and Viola Milton, for their unstinting support of the work that led to this book. The Department of Journalism, Film and Television at UJ acted as a host for the project, and for that I would like to thank the former head of department, Ylva Rodny-Gumede, and the current head, Dumisani Moyo, as well as the departmental administrator, Amy Maphagela, and her predecessor, Emmerentia Breytenbach. The OSF-SA provided funding for the research project that informs this book, and I thank them profusely for that. The OSF-SA continues to be an unstinting supporter of work that seeks to strengthen the quality of our democracy, even if this work puts them on the wrong side of power, and I thank them for their courageousness and their foresight. In particular, I would like to single out the following OSF staffers for their support: Fatima Hassan, Allan Wallis and Leonie Sampson. Although they have now left the OSF-SA, Vinayak Bhardwaj and Michael Moss were instrumental in ensuring that the OSF-SA supported the project, and I thank them for that too.

My thanks to the *Mail & Guardian*, *Daily Maverick*, *Sunday Times* and openDemocracy for having carried opinion pieces I have written on surveillance and privacy in South Africa. I remain indebted to Fazila Farouk, former owner and publisher of the South African Civil Society Information Service (SACSIS), which provided a platform for my early writings on these issues; these opinion pieces formed the basis of this manuscript. I must also acknowledge the contribution of Ronnie Kasrils, a former Minister of Intelligence, who acted as a respondent to my inaugural lecture, which is incorporated into this manuscript. I thank the APC's executive director, Anriette Esterhuysen, for the opportunity to undertake a research project into journalists and communications surveillance, and to allow me to incorporate some of this research material into this manuscript, as well as Stephan Hofstatter and Mzilikazi wa Afrika, for having contributed as interviewees to this research.

Avani Singh, Dale McKinley and Nora Ní Loideain conducted research for the MPDP for the Privacy International project on privacy in South Africa. The Privacy International team were unwavering in their assistance when I asked for it during the writing of this book (and that was often). The Legal Resources Centre also assisted with information on aspects of the book. I would also like to thank the following people for agreeing to be interviewed for the book, or for providing information in response to requests: Gus Hosein, Scarlet Kim, Tomaso Falchetta and Caroline Wilson Palow, Claire Lauterbach, Matthew Rice, Edin Omanovic and Alexandrine Pirlot de Corbion from Privacy International; Eric King and Javier Ruiz from Don't Spy on Us; James Welch from Liberty; former RICA judge Yvonne Mokgoro; Sam Sole, Stefaans Brümmer and Karabo Rajuili from the amaBhungane Centre for Investigative Journalism, Ant Brooks, special advisor to the Internet Service Providers' Association (ISPA), Thulani Mavuso from the Department of Home Affairs, Charles Nqakula, the chairperson of the parliamentary Joint Standing Committee on Intelligence; Stephan Hofstatter from the *Sunday Times*; and Wayne Minnaar and Gert van der Berg from the Johannesburg Metropolitan Police Department (JMPD), who took me on a guided tour of the JMPD closed-circuit television (CCTV) control centre. I have also included previously unused interview material with Dennis Dlomo, then co-ordinator for government intelligence and head of the National Intelligence Coordinating Committee, conducted at the end of 2013 at the SSA offices. There are also many interviewees who contributed to the research and journalism through agreeing to semi-structured interviews or focus groups, and who cannot be acknowledged by name as they were granted confidentiality as part of the interview process. They know who they are. I thank them for their courage in speaking out, and hope that in time to come, it will become easier for people to speak out about the issues touched on in this book, without fear of retribution. Only once they can do so, can we really say that we live in a robust democracy.

I would also like to thank SAHA for filing information requests to the City of Johannesburg, the South African Parliament and the Civil Aviation Authority. The records these bodies released in response to these requests are useful, although they were not as comprehensive as they could have been. Lasse Skou Andersen, a journalist with the Danish publication *Dagbladet Information*, was also extremely helpful and I thank him for making some of his records available, released in response to a series of information requests to the various European Union (EU) governments.

I would also like to acknowledge the R2K, of which I am a member, and which has provided me with such a rich intellectual climate for this work. The collaboration between the MPDP and R2K has been an extremely important one, as the MPDP provides research resources for the activist work of R2K, which strengthens the work of both organisations: R2K uses the research to undertake informed advocacy, and the MPDP's research is put to use, rather than gathering dust on the shelves of university libraries. In particular, I would like to acknowledge the support of the Secrecy and Securitisation Focus Group, and especially its convener, Murray Hunter, who has been unwavering in his support and his willingness to act as a sounding board. Both he and Heidi Swart read and commented on several chapters, and I thank them for their attentiveness.

The team at Wits University Press have been extremely supportive of this book from the moment I approached the press with the initial book idea. I would like to thank publisher Veronica Klipp, commissioning editor Roshan Cader, project manager Julie Miller and editor Russell Martin, the two anonymous peer reviewers who reviewed the manuscript, as well as the entire team that contributed towards the production of this book.

Sadly, but not unexpectedly, there are those whom I cannot thank as they failed to respond to interviews or requests for information. For most of 2017, I attempted to secure an interview with the Minister of State Security, but to no avail. Eventually, I asked the ministry to delegate the request to a suitable person in the SSA, but still did not receive a response. They have only themselves to blame if their voices are not included in this book. The Department of Justice and Constitutional Development and the office of the Inspector General of Intelligence refused interviews at the time of request, on the basis that the amaBhungane Centre for Investigative Journalism had filed a constitutional challenge to sections of RICA, and as they were cited as respondents, they did not want to grant interviews until the case was concluded. I appreciate their responses, but my position on this matter is that the *sub judice* rule is largely an anachronism, in that they would have to prove substantial and demonstrable threats to the administration of justice for the rule to apply. In any event, there was no reason not to grant interviews once the respondents had filed their responding papers as their positions were known publicly, which was the case with the SSA. I also tried to secure an interview with the National Conventional Arms Control Committee (NCACC), but was unable to before the book went to print. Telkom turned down an interview request on the basis that company policy did not allow its officials to speak on behalf of the company with regard to legislation affecting the sector, and referred me to the Department of Justice: a bit odd for a company that is meant to operate at arm's length from the government. A request for them to reconsider went unanswered. An interview request to Vastech yielded a bland statement, and my follow-up request for an interview went unanswered. While writing this book with little official information was difficult, it was not impossible. Happily, surveillance researchers are not dependent on official sources of information anymore; more investigative journalists and whistleblowers are shining a light into this dark and murky area of government, providing us with unprecedented amounts of information about its inner workings. Governments are losing control of the flow of information about how, why and when they spy on their citizens. This book would not have been possible without the important work of the whistleblowing site WikiLeaks and the people who provided it with information, and the incredibly principled actions of Edward Snowden, who made huge personal sacrifices to bring evidence of surveillance abuses to public attention. I remain indebted to them.

LIST OF FIGURES AND TABLES

IMAGES FROM LEAKED DOCUMENTS AND OTHER SOURCES

There are several references in the text and the footnotes to images that are in the public domain which are from leaked sources such as the National Security Agency and surveillance technology manufacturers. The publisher has chosen not to print these images, but they are available from the websites referred to in the notes. There are also references to images that come from other sources, but that could not be reproduced as they were not available in high-resolution formats. These are also available from websites, which are cited in the notes.

LIST OF ACRONYMS

ACLU	American Civil Liberties Union
AFIS	Automated Fingerprint Information System
AMCU	Association of Mineworkers and Construction Union
ANC	African National Congress
ANPR	Automatic number-plate recognition
APC	Association for Progressive Communications
APF	Anti-Privatisation Forum
CAA	Civil Aviation Authority
CALEA	Communications Assistance for Law Enforcement Act
CBD	central business district
CCTV	closed circuit television
CIA	Central Intelligence Agency
CID	Crime Intelligence Division
COSATU	Congress of South African Trade Unions
DA	Democratic Alliance
DSM	Democratic Socialist Movement
DSO	Directorate of Special Operations
EFF	Economic Freedom Fighters
EFF	Electronic Frontier Foundation
eNATIS	Electronic National Administration Traffic Information System
EPIC	Electronic Privacy Information Center

EPIC	Emergency Policing and Incident Control Programme
ETSI	European Telecommunications Standards Institute
EU	European Union
FBI	Federal Bureau of Investigation
FIC	Financial Intelligence Centre
FISA	Foreign Intelligence Surveillance Act
FISC	Foreign Intelligence Surveillance Court
GCHQ	Government Communications Headquarters
GILAA	General Intelligence Laws Amendment Act
HANIS	Home Affairs National Identification System
ICANN	Internet Corporation for Assigned Names and Numbers
ICTs	information and communications technologies
IMSI	international mobile subscriber identity
INTERPOL	International Criminal Police Organisation
IP	internet protocol
IPCC	Independent Police Complaints Commission
IPT	Investigatory Powers Tribunal
IRIS	incident registration information system
ISIS	Islamic State for Iraq and Syria
ISP	internet service provider
ISPA	Internet Service Providers' Association
ITS	intelligent transport systems
JMPD	Johannesburg Metropolitan Police Department
JSCI	Joint Standing Committee on Intelligence
KZN	KwaZulu-Natal
LRC	Legal Resources Centre
MK	Umkhonto we Sizwe
MPDP	Media Policy and Democracy Project

NAT	Department of National Intelligence and Security (also National Security)
NATO	North Atlantic Treaty Organisation
NC	National Communications
NCACC	National Conventional Arms Control Committee
NCC	National Communications Centre
NGO	non-governmental organisation
NIA	National Intelligence Agency
NICOC	National Intelligence Coordinating Committee
NIS	National Identity System
NIS	National Intelligence Service
NSA	National Security Agency
NUMSA	National Union of Metalworkers of South Africa
OCR	optical character recognition
OECD	Organisation for Economic Co-operation and Development
OIC	Office for Interception Centres
OSF-SA	Open Society Foundation for South Africa
PIN	personal identification number
POPI	Protection of Personal Information
R2K	Right2Know Campaign
RICA	Regulation of Interception of Communications and Provision of Communication-Related Information Act
RIPA	Regulation of Investigatory Powers Act
RGA	Regulation of Gatherings Act
SADF	South African Defence Force
SAHA	South African History Archive
SANDF	South African National Defence Force
SANRAL	South African National Roads Agency
SAPS	South African Police Service

SARS	South African Revenue Service
SASS	South African Secret Service
SASSA	South African Social Security Agency
SIGINT	signals intelligence
SIM	subscriber information module
SSA	State Security Agency
SSC	State Security Council
TRC	Truth and Reconciliation Commission
UN	United Nations
UJ	University of Johannesburg
UK	United Kingdom
US	Unites States of America
USSR	Union of Soviet Socialist Republics
WASP	Workers and Socialist Party
WAU	Worker's Association Union

PREFACE

In 2013, the former National Security Agency (NSA) contractor Edward Snowden leaked secret documents revealing that various state spy agencies, notably the NSA and the UK Government Communications Headquarters (GCHQ) and other allied intelligence agencies, had spied on the communications of millions of innocent citizens. Many were outraged that their privacy was being violated, and rightly so. They objected to the fact that these governments had used the war against terror – launched in the wake of the 11 September 2001 attacks on the United States and the 2005 attack on London – as a pretext to expand state surveillance capacities far beyond what was actually needed to fight this war. The spy agencies scooped up the communications of millions of people into their dragnet, including those of lawyers, journalists and academics, who are under professional obligations to protect their sources of information. But the Snowden revelations revealed only the tip of the surveillance iceberg; apart from insisting on their right to tap into communications, more and more governments introduced surveillance technologies to track people's movements and transactions with public and private institutions (such as banks). As a result, the state is becoming like a one-way mirror, where it can see more and more of what its citizens do and say, while citizens see less and less of what the state does, owing to high levels of secrecy around surveillance.

In this book, I assess the relevance of Snowden's revelations for South Africa, and in doing so, I ask to what extent South Africa is becoming a surveillance society governed by a surveillance state. How concerned should we be about the ever-expanding surveillance capacities of the state, and the uses to which they are being put? Are they being used for the democratic purpose of making people safer, or for the repressive purpose of social control, to pacify citizens and to target those considered to be politically threatening to ruling interests? What forms of collective action are needed to ensure that unaccountable surveillance does not take place, as the secretive nature of these activities makes them very difficult to organise around. What works and what doesn't when it comes to developing organised responses?

These questions should concern all those who care about our democracy, and we have a democratic responsibility to demand the information necessary to answer them properly.

I started engaging with issues relating to surveillance in the early 2000s, when I directed a non-governmental organisation (NGO) called the Freedom of Expression Institute (FXI). At the time, 9/11 had just taken place, and the world (including South Africa) was considering what contributions should be made to fight the war against terror. While South Africa has not been a terrorist target, it faced its own internal challenges, too, including a massive crime wave that threatened social stability. These factors led to its reviewing its communications surveillance capacities, and resulted in the passing of the Regulation of Interception of Communications and Provision of Communication-Related Information Act (RICA). A few years later, evidence emerged of these capacities being abused to spy on politicians, business people and journalists, in the context of a bruising succession battle for the presidency. Also, a new wave of social movements against various aspects of neoliberal service delivery was formed, and evidence emerged of their being placed under surveillance, too. I documented some of these incidents in a 2014 book called *The Rise of the Securocrats: The Case of South Africa*. Through my involvement in the FXI, it became apparent to me that all was not well with our spy agencies. More recently, my involvement in the Right2Know Campaign (R2K) has taught me that these unhealthy practices continue. Consequently, when the Snowden documents were released, and South African journalists and ordinary residents began asking what the implications were for our own society, I became interested in developing researched responses to these questions.

In writing this book, I drew on research funded by the Open Society Foundation for South Africa (OSF-SA) into communications surveillance policies and practices in South Africa. The research was commissioned by the Media Policy and Democracy Project (MPDP), a joint project of the Department of Journalism, Film and Television of the University of Johannesburg (UJ) – where I am based – and the Department of Communication Science at the University of South Africa. The MPDP promotes participatory, public interest media and communications policy-making, and to that end has collaborated with a range of organisations in South Africa to ensure a more bottom-up approach to policy-making. I conceptualised and managed the research for the MPDP. The overall purpose of the research was to assess the extent to which South Africa measures up to international human rights principles when it comes to communications surveillance. The research methodology was qualitative in nature, and consisted of policy and legislative analysis and interviews with constituencies that are particularly vulnerable to surveillance by virtue of the fact that they handle sensitive information – namely, lawyers, journalists, academics, political and social activists, and trade unionists – to assess to what extent they are adapting to and resisting surveillance or the threat of surveillance. Admire Mare undertook the analysis and interviews, and I have incorporated some of the key findings into this book.

The research also included investigative journalism into surveillance practices in South Africa. Journalist Heidi Swart undertook this work, and she produced a technical report on actual communications practices, as well as a range of newspaper articles on the technical capacities of those undertaking surveillance, the uses to which these capacities are being put and what needs to change about surveillance practices. These stories were published in the *Mail & Guardian* newspaper and the *Daily Maverick* online news site. I draw on Swart's pathbreaking journalism for the book.

It could be argued that surveillance in South Africa is too secretive a topic on which to write a book, but this is not so. By combining this research with information available in the public domain, including leaked documents about the operations of the various branches of South Africa's civilian intelligence service, the State Security Agency (SSA), and South African surveillance companies, available through WikiLeaks, the global news network Al Jazeera and the Snowden documents, as well as industry information collected by the London-based international non-governmental organisation Privacy International, it is very possible to build up a picture of surveillance practices in South Africa and to subject them to a 'health check'. I have also drawn on a series of articles I have written on these questions for local publications, notably the *Mail & Guardian*, *Daily Maverick* and the *Sunday Times*, some of which have been republished on the UK-based site openDemocracy.

I have also incorporated into the manuscript my inaugural professorial lecture, which dealt with the question whether South Africa was reverting to a repressive state, as well as the main findings of a research project I undertook for the Association for Progressive Communications (APC) on the impact of communications surveillance on journalists. Furthermore, during the course of this research, I represented the MPDP in a global network of privacy researchers and advocates, set up by Privacy International and including organisations from across the global South. Privacy International also raised funds from the International Development Research Centre to map the state of the right to privacy in several countries, including South Africa, and the MPDP undertook the research for this project. I have also drawn on this research, especially a monograph on privacy written by MPDP researcher Dale McKinley. The South African History Archive (SAHA) assisted with information requests to various state entities, leading to records being released by the Civil Aviation Authority, the City of Johannesburg and the South African Parliament.

There is much more to be done on this particular topic. I realise that many gaps exist in our understanding of the issues it addresses, including my own, but I hope that this book provides a basis for future explorations.

Jane Duncan

November 2017

Introduction

'I saw my final hour unfurl before me, I thought this was the end. I thought I'm finished, I'm finished. I was terrified. We must all have thought the same.'[1] Julian Pierce, a journalist for the French radio network Europe 1, was inside the Bataclan theatre in Paris in November 2015, watching a live music show, when gunmen claiming to support the Islamic State for Iraq and Syria (ISIS) stormed the theatre and shot indiscriminately into the crowd. Eighty-nine people died in that attack, and a further 41 people were killed in other co-ordinated attacks around the city that night.[2] It must be many people's worst nightmare: becoming a victim of a terrorist attack simply for being in the wrong place at the wrong time.

Terrorist attacks have swept Europe in the past few years, with France being attacked repeatedly. I will discuss the politics of naming particular acts as 'terrorist' later in the book; for the moment, suffice it to say that I do recognise forms of violent political action that could be legitimately considered terrorist. Fearful citizens have looked to their governments to protect them from terrorist violence, and these governments have responded by increasing their intelligence and policing powers. In fact, intelligence work has become increasingly important to governments seeking to thwart terrorist threats, as it allows them to identify the culprits of these attacks and even prevent future attacks from taking place. They can also profile possible 'persons of interest', who might become terrorists in future. Gathering intelligence from human sources (or human intelligence, as it is known in the intelligence community) is expensive, time-consuming and often dangerous, as terrorist organisations could uncover spies in their midst, or these spies may provide unreliable information, or even be recruited as double agents. Given the drawbacks of human intelligence, more governments are turning to the surveillance of communications networks to acquire intelligence on terrorist activities and plans (what is called signals intelligence).

Yet, government surveillance programmes may not be motivated purely by the noble objective of protecting public safety. We have all become familiar with terms that describe a government that spies indiscriminately on its people in order to maintain its grip on power. George Orwell's terse novel *Nineteen Eighty-Four* painted a chilling picture of an authoritarian society dominated by pervasive surveillance, and his character 'Big Brother' came to symbolise the horrors of such a society.[3] Writing several decades later, Michel Foucault drew on the nineteenth-century British philosopher Jeremy Bentham's plan for a 'panopticon' – a building that allows a single watchman to watch large numbers of people – as a metaphor for a modern society in which its subjects are made to practise self-discipline through the threat of constant surveillance.[4] These terms have endured in the public imagination as descriptors of the power of surveillance and the dangers of its being undertaken on an unaccountable basis. In spite of the real and present danger of terrorist attacks in some countries, more people have become concerned about the dangers of unaccountable state surveillance and the impact that it may have on the fundamental human right to privacy. According to Article 12 of the United Nations (UN) Declaration of Human Rights, 'No one shall be subjected to arbitrary interference with his privacy, family, home or correspondence, nor to attacks upon his honour and reputation. Everyone has the right to the protection of the law against such interference or attacks.'[5] Clearly, arbitrary surveillance would threaten this right. However, opinion polls suggest that public opinion remains sharply divided on whether privacy is more important than national security.[6]

'The idea that they can lock us out and there will be no change is no longer tenable. Everyone accepts these programmes were not effective, did not keep us safe and, even if they did, represent an unacceptable degradation of our rights.'[7] Whistleblower Edward Snowden made these comments two years after leaking thousands of NSA documents about secretive mass communications surveillance programmes. The NSA is the United States government agency responsible for communications surveillance for intelligence purposes. These leaks, drip-released in collaboration with journalists such as Glenn Greenwald and Laura Poitras, led to the journalists blowing the lid on secret government spying programmes that had moved far beyond their original stated purpose of fighting terrorism and violated the privacy of millions of innocent people in the process. While the Snowden documents focused mainly on US and UK government programmes, they also revealed information about the close co-operation with other 'Five Eyes' countries. Referring to a coalition of countries co-operating with one another to fight terrorism and other national security threats, and dating back to the post-World War II period when Western hostility to the Union of Soviet Socialist Republics (Soviet Union or USSR) was at its height, the Five Eyes coalition consists of the US, UK, Australia, New Zealand and Canada. While little is known about the nature of their co-operation, what is known is that they co-operate around the sharing of intelligence, including the interception and analysis of signals intelligence.[8]

The Snowden revelations created a huge public outcry, and pressure from privacy advocates forced the US government to concede reforms of some of its programmes. Yet, critics have argued that these reforms are not as significant as they appear, as they leave most of the surveillance programmes revealed by Snowden intact. According to Privacy International and Amnesty International, many governments are continuing or even expanding their mass surveillance capabilities.[9] The intractable nature of mass surveillance is unsurprising: it has become big business. State and consumer surveillance programmes have converged to the point where it has become difficult to separate the two. The state relies on private security companies to store huge datasets in the cloud, while the private sector commercialises these datasets for profit by selling them to other companies, mainly advertisers. The state and the private sector operate in a charmed circle, where intelligence is used to advance countries' commercial interests, especially for imperial powers that risk losing their dominance in global affairs; as a result, more governments are including the protection of commercial interests in their definition of national security.[10]

As the importance of signals intelligence has evolved, regulatory regimes have developed to give this form of surveillance a semblance of public accountability, but these regimes are often inadequate. For instance, in 1978 the US government established the Foreign Intelligence Surveillance Court (FISC), set up in terms of the Foreign Intelligence Surveillance Act (FISA), to hear applications for communications surveillance warrants for the interception of communications between foreign powers and agents of foreign powers operating in the US, which may include US citizens too. The surveillance of foreign communications is authorised under Executive Order 12333, which is not subject to judicial review and which may also involve the collection of communications records of US citizens in contact with overseas targets. While the existence of the FISC suggests that due process is followed in the interception of foreigners' communications, court proceedings are secret and the vast majority of applications are approved. This is largely because the application process is not adversarial in that the grounds for application are not interrogated by counsel for the defence, as would usually be the case in open court. Furthermore, the grounds for the issuing of warrants in FISA are less stringent than those required for ordinary criminal warrants (or Title III warrants), even when it comes to the interception of US citizens' communications. More seriously, though, the FISC has authorised the establishment of mass surveillance programmes in terms of the amendments to FISA by the Amendment Act, and, according to the Snowden documents, the court had used a controversial section of the Patriot Act to approve the collection of the phone metadata records of Americans in bulk. In authorising the procedures for mass surveillance programmes, FISC had no concrete knowledge of their actual functionings, and as a result deferred to the intelligence agency applicants rather than second-guess them. Under these circumstances, it is hardly surprising that the FISC has been a poor check on official surveillance abuses.[11]

WHY WORRY ABOUT SURVEILLANCE?

Why should we be worried about surveillance? After all, governments argue, if people have nothing to hide, then they have nothing to fear: a saying whose origin is unclear, but which has been attributed to Orwell and, before him, the Nazi Minister of Propaganda, Joseph Goebbels. The problem with this argument is that it assumes that government motives in undertaking surveillance are pure: that is, they will not misuse these powers to spy on their political opponents and others whom they consider to be politically inconvenient, like investigative journalists intent on holding governments to account. Governments the world over have justified surveillance to their citizens as a necessary evil to counter criminal activities and threats to national security, especially those posed by terrorists. Yet, even in the wake of the terrorist attacks on the US on 11 September 2001, the 'war against terror' never remained a pure war against those who were responsible for their acts and their supporters. Some countries seized on the heightened global security measures to place political activists under surveillance. In fact, the expansion of security powers was under way even before 11 September. In New Zealand, for instance, the country's definition of national security was extended to include the country's economic and international well-being as far back as 1996.[12] The UK government spy agencies MI5 (the domestic intelligence agency) and MI6 (the foreign intelligence agency) have spied on social movements calling for nuclear disarmament and trade unions, clearly considering them to be an 'enemy within', in spite of scant evidence of illegality.[13] There are many well-documented cases of states, under the political direction of government officials, using their surveillance capacities to spy on activists who posed no real threat to national security; these practices have cast a pall on the supposed political neutrality of state surveillance practices and the uses to which they are put.[14] These cases point to a broader truth about surveillance – namely, that it is not being used simply to fight crime and terrorism but to stabilise social relations more broadly by collecting information on those who may expose or challenge how society is currently organised. The purpose of surveillance in this broader context is to make people who are considered to be problem subjects legible to public and private power, for the purposes of determining their risk profiles, managing them as risks and even acting against the most extreme risks. This is particularly the case in relation to intelligence work, where broad definitions of what constitutes threats to national security are coupled with technologically advanced forms of surveillance, leading to state spies claiming the right to access more and more personal information.

There are many forms of intelligence-gathering, but the two that are of concern in this book are human intelligence and signals intelligence. Human intelligence (or HUMINT) is intelligence gathered by physical means, such as the infiltration of organisations, tailing of suspects or espionage, while signals intelligence (or SIGINT) is intelligence gathered from the surveillance of electronics networks, including telemetry intelligence, electronic intelligence and communications intelligence (or COMINT).[15] Globally, intelligence agencies are being tempted to shift away from human intelligence and towards signals intelligence. Why is this so?

Technological advancements have reduced the cost of surveillance using electronic signals, making it easier for governments to place whole populations under surveillance. Previously, if governments wished to spy on their citizens, they would need to place them under physical surveillance – which could also be uncovered, possibly at great political cost to the government concerned – or need to use costly telephone-bugging equipment that could be detected if people knew what to look for. However, new information and communications technologies (ICTs) have allowed governments and private companies to gather vast amounts of information about people at a small fraction of the previous cost. They are able to collect and analyse huge databases detailing people's travel habits, banking details, personal interests and reading habits, who their closest friends and associates are, and what they communicate about. For instance, cellphones can provide huge amounts of information about whom people communicate with, as well as location information about where they have travelled. Internet and communications companies are also busy storing information about people's locations, search habits and communications with other people, to mine it for commercial uses. This information is called metadata, as it provides information about a person's communications, but not the actual content. However, metadata can provide such rich information about a person's habits, personal preferences and associations that it can be as revealing as, if not more revealing than, communications content. Yet there are few legal protections for metadata.

Other data-driven technologies are being used increasingly to monitor public spaces, for a range of national security, criminal justice and commercial reasons.

CCTV cameras can monitor people's movements, and increasingly these cameras are fitted with invasive technologies such as facial recognition, which allows a computer to identify a person from his or her facial features from a photograph stored in a facial database (known as 'smart' CCTV, which is something of a misnomer as once the data is transmitted over the internet to another location, the television system no longer operates on a closed circuit). Electronic tolling systems track drivers' movements for the purpose of billing them for road usage. These schemes usually include automatic number-plate recognition systems, allowing tolling companies to recognise vehicle licence plates and match them to a database of vehicle owners. Biometric identifiers – or digital impressions of fingerprints, irises or voices – can also be used to identify people for surveillance purposes; this is a particularly invasive form of identification as it involves a person's body. While many countries use biometrics for border control, some have attempted to use them to establish national identity systems. In countries like the US and the UK, these attempts have been met with mass opposition on the ground that they threaten privacy on a massive scale. More governments are also using unmanned assistance vehicles – colloquially known as 'drones' – to conduct surveillance of borders and monitor crime scenes and disaster areas. Drones can also be loaded with lethal payloads to kill opponents, and, controversially, lethal drone strikes became a distinctive feature of the Barack Obama administration.

These surveillance devices can gather vast datasets, or 'big data', which can be analysed using computer algorithms, or sets of rules or methods for the processing of data and for the purpose of establishing patterns. Search engines like Google mine people's internet searches to analyse personal interests, and then on-sell this information to advertisers. But big data is being used increasingly by intelligence agencies as well. One of the challenges of living in the digital age is that we are not necessarily who our data suggests we are: we can develop 'data doubles', or digital identities that may bear little, if any, resemblance to who we really are and what we really think.[16] These identities can then be used to profile people as terrorists or criminals, even if they are innocent. So, intelligence analysts may tell computers to analyse datasets for individuals who have searched for information on how to buy a gun, have spent time in Syria or Iraq recently – where ISIS established its strongholds – and have made enquiries about travelling to Paris. Such an individual could match the profile of a terrorist. Yet, he or she could also match the profile of a researcher seeking to understand ISIS as an organisation, its criminal networks and its reach into Western countries. Or the individual may simply have travelled to the Middle East for personal reasons, have an interest in collecting guns and wish to take a holiday in Paris, with no underlying motive linking these actions and interests together.

Big data analysis is meant to bring a measure of objectivity to intelligence-gathering, profiling possible suspects on the basis of clear criteria. In the process, analysts assume that they can eschew the subjective assumptions (even prejudices) to which analysis undertaken by humans is susceptible. Intelligence agencies like GCHQ have argued that mass surveillance does not violate privacy as there are no (or limited) human interventions in the process given that surveillance is a machine-driven process. The automated nature of the process means that the vast majority of data that is intercepted is discarded without human beings ever having looked at it. Once data of interest is identified, then an examination warrant is needed before the examination can be undertaken.[17] However, the reality of big data analysis is somewhat different. There are six stages in the surveillance process: initial interception of the signals, often from cables as they enter the country; extraction, the stage where the signals are converted into an intelligible format; filtering, where analysts identify particular information of interest; storage, where this information is retained for further analysis; analysis, where the stored information is queried or examined; and dissemination, where the information is sent on to the relevant agencies.[18] Spy agencies are reluctant to admit that privacy is interfered with at all stages of the surveillance process, while data is being diverted from its original and intended path, but this impacts on communications privacy even if it is an automated process.[19] The most glaring privacy invasion occurs at the level of filtering, though. Analysts need to identify the search terms (known as selectors) for the processing of the raw data, and this involves subjective decisions about what matters and what doesn't; so, clearly, there is human intervention at this stage, even if the selectors are used to undertake an automated filtering process.

Analysts may use hard selectors (such as email addresses or telephone numbers), a combination of selectors (such as an Internet Protocol address combined with a name), or what Eric King, director of Don't Spy on Us, an organisation campaigning for surveillance reform in the UK, has referred to as 'fuzzy selectors that can easily be critiqued' (such as 'all Muslims living in the city of London').[20] Once analysts have the data, they may become so overwhelmed with the volume that they may bring their own subjective lenses to bear on the analytical process. As a result, agencies have a vested interest in being as precise as possible, but the dangers of overbreadth remain, nonetheless. According to King:

> Mass surveillance and targetted surveillance aren't adequately precise. This doesn't do justice to agency practice, which is to collect on a very large scale but in a targeted manner. Sometimes they overcollect. They may be going after a group, then may collect far more than they need … Targetted and

mass surveillance are functionally hard to separate … What I take umbrage with is the limiting of people's rights in the process. Where I have a problem, is the gathering of information of a whole country. Intrusion occurs when data is filtered out of the cable, irrespective of how much. There are a number of cases where communications have been intercepted when they were the target and where they weren't the target.[21]

US attorney Brandon Mayfield is a real-life example of just how wrong big data-driven intelligence work can go. In 2004, he was falsely linked to the Madrid train bombings after his fingerprints were matched incorrectly to those found at one of the scenes of the crime. His fingerprint had found its way into an International Criminal Police Organisation (INTERPOL) database for an arrest two decades earlier on a charge that was subsequently dropped. In addition to his matched fingerprint, Mayfield became a prime suspect because he had converted to Islam and, as an attorney, had represented a person accused of attempting to assist the Taliban. Another suspect who did not fit this profile was ignored.[22] Yet, in spite of the real dangers of falsely accusing people of a crime through big data analysis, and using the analysis to confirm already existing prejudices against social groups (Muslims, for instance), intelligence agencies are relying more and more on intelligence gleaned from big data.

ICTs have made contemporary life much more convenient; but they have also created new mechanisms of potentially anti-democratic social control. Is it really desirable for the state and private companies, sometimes working together, to regulate the most private actions and even thoughts of its citizens? The concerns about powerful institutions having such intimate knowledge about us have led to many becoming concerned that we are living in a surveillance society, where the collection, retention and analysis of vast quantities of data for the purposes of controlling human behaviour become central to our social fabric. Even more worryingly, we may be living under a surveillance state, in which the state uses this information to control citizens more effectively than in the past, because it has access to their most intimate details.

The surveillance society and state did not come out of nowhere; they have been under construction for many years. David Lyon has warned about the dangers by referring to what he calls 'the slow cooker of surveillance', in which the practices and technologies that are being deployed now have evolved over several decades,[23] but such warnings have been confined largely to the arcane forums of academic publishing, rarely spilling over into public debate. The 'slow cooker' effect becomes apparent only when people understand the full extent of the surveillance architecture and how different elements of the surveillance assemblage link together. This bigger picture allows active citizens to anticipate what the state's capacities are likely to be, and how the corporate sector bolsters these capacities: information which, in turn, can be used to anticipate when the state is becoming too powerful.

Surveillance creates mistrust between governments and citizens, leading to a reluctance to speak out on controversial issues of public importance, and even self-censorship. Being watched, or the fear of being watched, has a chilling effect in that it may dissuade people from expressing their innermost thoughts, and, when they do, they may alter what they have to say to please those who they think may be watching. In this regard, a distinction needs to be drawn between targeted surveillance and mass surveillance. Targeted surveillance involves the observation and gathering of information about individuals and groups where there is a reasonable suspicion that they have been involved in a crime, or where there are strong reasons to believe that they may be intending to commit a crime. This form of surveillance has also become known as 'lawful interception', as communications service providers are usually required by law to assist with such interceptions for the purposes of surveillance. Governments generally prescribe certain standards that communications companies must meet in making their networks surveillance-capable for lawful interception purposes: standards that originated from the Communications Assistance for Law Enforcement Act (CALEA), passed by the US Congress in 1994 to respond to law enforcement concerns that their ability to monitor networks was declining (or 'going dark') as more networks were digitised. The Act required network operators to use digital switches or handover interfaces that have surveillance capabilities built into them: a requirement that was subsequently incorporated into EU regulatory frameworks as well, according to standards set by the European Telecommunications Standards Institute (ETSI), subsequently known as ETSI standards.[24]

CALEA and ETSI standards have become internationalised as the surveillance standards for many countries.[25] According to the communications security expert Susan Landau, while these standards have made surveillance of digital networks easier, they also introduced security vulnerabilities that have been exploited by intelligence agencies and criminals alike. Between 2004 and 2005, still-unidentified individuals exploited the inherent weaknesses in these interfaces to intercept the communications of senior Greek government officials for ten months, until the vulnerability was discovered. Over six thousand Italians, including judges, politicians and celebrities, also had their communications intercepted by criminals over a period of a decade.[26] In 2012, in the wake of massive abuses of internet freedom by regimes desperate to cling to power in the Middle East and North Africa, the Directorate-General for External Policies of the European Parliament called for a reconsideration of some ETSI standards, as they were simply too vulnerable to abuse and enabled mass surveillance.[27] Yet in spite of these problems, South Africa adopted CALEA and ETSI standards in 2005, including some of the very standards about which the European Parliament expressed concern.

Before we proceed with this discussion, it is necessary to add a terminological note on the differences between monitoring, surveillance, interception and equipment interference, as these terms are difficult to distinguish from one another, and at times some are used interchangeably. Monitoring involves the intermittent observation of communications over a period of time without specific pre-defined objectives. Surveillance, on the other hand, involves much closer continuous and systematic observation for analysis with specific objectives in mind, and may involve the collection and retention of communications for these purposes. Needless to say, I am more concerned with the surveillance of communications, rather than its monitoring, as surveillance carries with it greater potential for harm if unregulated than monitoring. In order for surveillance to take place, the communications need to be intercepted, or diverted from the intended recipient and captured, collected or acquired by a third party. A human being does not have to divert, collect or analyse the communications for the action to constitute surveillance: a machine can do so, too.[28] However, not everyone agrees that machine surveillance constitutes surveillance at all; intelligence agencies have argued that machines cannot violate privacy, only humans can.[29] This disagreement is not purely semantic: it goes to the heart of whether mass surveillance can be considered a privacy violation at all, and consequently whether societies should tolerate such conduct by their security services. I take the position that as the basis for machine interception, collection or analysis is determined by humans, an act of surveillance occurs even if machine analysis is involved, and privacy stands to be violated in the process. Surveillance can occur through the monitoring of communications traffic, such as internet traffic, the interception of mobile phone communication content and data about those communications, the interception of fixed-line communication content and data about those communications, and the planting of intrusion equipment on communications devices, as well as through the use of data-driven surveillance tools like CCTV.

On the whole, though, targeted surveillance through lawful interception has been less controversial than mass surveillance, which is often referred to as 'suspicionless surveillance'. The latter involves the tracking of individuals or organisations where there is no suspicion of wrongdoing, but where information about their communications may be stored just in case the law enforcement or intelligence agencies need it to detect suspicious activities in future. While lawful interception generally requires human intervention in order to intercept the communications of specific individuals, and communications service providers have to 'switch' the communications to a monitoring centre, mass surveillance is generally automated, and may be conducted through network probes that transmit communications directly to a monitoring centre. Communications service providers may not be involved in this form of surveillance, as the data can be copied off the backbone of the communications infrastructure. Once it is copied, then an agency can conduct searches for specific terms, names or numbers in the intercepted communications to narrow them down to more manageable levels. They may also choose to look for associations between various individuals in order to map contacts. The Snowden documents revealed how the NSA is allowed to travel three 'hops' from the communications of a person of interest: that is, they can examine the people who spoke to that person and the people who spoke to those people. As a result of the 'three hops' policy, the communications of large numbers of people, many of whom are likely to be innocent of any crime, can be examined.[30] However, surveillance affects different social groups differently, and can be used for the purposes of discriminatory social sorting: selectors can be developed on the basis of populations (Afghanis, for instance), and the tendency to profile what the agencies consider to be problem populations is particularly pronounced with mass surveillance.[31]

Surveillance provides the state with a politically low-cost form of social control, as abuses are very difficult to detect, and it can use such surveillance, or the threat of surveillance, to create fear that organised violence will be used against perceived opponents. To that extent, and when used inappropriately, surveillance could be considered a form of violence. At the same time, the fear of being watched may force people to self-police their own behaviour, as Foucault argued.[32] Such a society is not one that we should want to live in, or to allow our children to inherit, as it will be premised on fear and insecurity.

Perhaps even more controversial than mass surveillance, which involves passive monitoring of networks, are more active forms of communications interception using equipment interference, such as hacking. Increasingly, law enforcement and intelligence agencies are arguing that encryption is making it more and more difficult to conduct communications surveillance, and this is pushing them to resort to more extreme measures such as infiltrating a communications device like a computer remotely, using malware that delivers surveillance software through an email attachment, taking control of the device and opening any document or application as though it was the device owner. Hacking can even alter or delete a person's communications, which not only renders the communications and the device pretty useless for evidentiary purposes, but presents grave threats to the security of communications networks as a whole.[33]

In spite of the widespread public outrage about the expansiveness of the programmes exposed by Snowden, and in spite of ongoing controversies about the effectiveness of mass surveillance relative to more traditional intelligence efforts, the UK responded by not only defending its existing bulk powers in terms of the Regulation of Investigatory Powers Act (RIPA) and the Data Retention and Investigatory Powers Act (DRIPA), but also seeking new powers through a controversial new Investigatory Powers Act, which was passed in the dying days of 2016. Bulk powers target people outside the country, with less privacy-invasive surveillance ostensibly being reserved for UK nationals. As a result, the Act subjects non-nationals to weaker privacy protections, and thus discriminates against them, thereby flying in the face of attempts to universalise human rights. The most controversial elements of the Act are the executive's bulk powers to intercept, store and even hack communications on a massive scale. The debate about the Act did put a spotlight on the UK government's use of hacking. Up to that point, the UK government had never admitted its use of bulk hacking of the computer equipment of non-nationals, until several NGOs brought a case before the Investigatory Powers Tribunal (IPT), which confirmed GCHQ's use of this surveillance practice.[34] This form of surveillance is possibly the most intrusive and dubious of all, as it allows the intelligence agencies, on a mass scale, to access address books, track every keystroke, email and internet search on communications devices, and even turn on a computer's camera and microphone, using it as a surveillance device against its owner.

WHY SHOULD THE GLOBAL SOUTH BE CONCERNED?

But should countries in the global South, like South Africa, even be concerned? The southern African region has largely escaped the terrorism problem plaguing countries like France, the UK and the US, and African countries further north, like Nigeria and Kenya. No southern African country has its own version of al-Shabaab or Boko Haram, responsible for terrible atrocities in East Africa and Nigeria respectively. South Africa faces no significant threats to national security, especially terrorist threats, although the presence of terrorists in the country has been an enduring source of speculation. So, it could be assumed that the region should have little reason to invest in the building of surveillance states. Evidence is emerging that suggests this assumption is incorrect.

Even though South Africa is not a terrorist target, growing social discord over inequality means that the temptation is there for less principled members of the security apparatus to abuse the state's surveillance capabilities to advantage the ruling group in the ruling party and disadvantage their perceived detractors. This possibility is not far-fetched. In 2005, the state's mass surveillance capacities were misused to spy on perceived opponents of Jacob Zuma, then contender for the presidency. Journalists have also had their communications intercepted, and several politicians and activists have alleged that their communications were intercepted. The *Mail & Guardian* has quoted sources inside the police and the SSA alleging that security personnel often do not even bother to obtain directions to intercept communications.[35] In 2013, it emerged during a trial that the Crime Intelligence Division of the South African Police Service (SAPS) had placed members of the extreme Afrikaner militia, the Boeremag, under surveillance while in prison, which included intercepting communications between the accused and their lawyers, in violation of attorney–client privilege.[36] While it is extremely difficult to establish the extent of the problem, these incidents make the case for reforms to ensure that the state's surveillance capacities are not abused.

South Africa has a law, RICA, that governs lawful interceptions for policing and national security purposes. In spite of the fact that its drafters attempted to strike a balance between the interests of justice and national security, on the one hand, and civil liberties such as privacy, on the other, it ignores many of the most basic international human rights protections. Even worse, the available evidence points to mass surveillance being grossly under-regulated in South Africa, and, as Snowden has shown, where there is a lack of accountability, abuses are almost inevitable. The centre that undertakes this form of surveillance is the National Communications Centre (NCC); the centre has no founding statute and its interceptions do not require a warrant. In fact, the available evidence points to its operating on an entirely separate but parallel track to the targeted, lawful interception process of RICA. In 2005, abuses of the NCC's surveillance capacities were confirmed by the statutory intelligence watchdog, the Inspector General of Intelligence, who found that the country's bulk scanning facilities had been used to keep South Africans under surveillance during the country's bruising presidential succession battle, including senior members of the ruling party, the opposition, businessmen and officials in the public service.[37] So, the organ of state that has the greatest capacity to conduct mass surveillance is also the one that is least regulated by law. This capacity is so intrusive that its use should be authorised by primary legislation. WikiLeaks has also revealed how South Africa manufactures and exports mass surveillance equipment to authoritarian regimes such as Libya. Privacy International has also publicised the fact that the South African government has provided funding to the local technology company Vastech for the manufacture of one of its surveillance products, and that the problem of taxpayers' money being used to fund mass surveillance equipment which was exported to a repressive regime has not been addressed.[38]

There has been little public controversy in South Africa about the implications of other potentially privacy-invasive, data-driven surveillance technologies, such as the use of CCTV in more and more public spaces. The government intends biometrics to become the technology of choice in its transactions with citizens. It is establishing centralised biometric databases for its social security system and identity cards, in spite of major concerns globally about the wisdom of establishing such databases. In 2015, the state entity responsible for airspace safety, the Civil Aviation Authority (CAA), passed regulations authorising the flying of drones, but the privacy protections contained in its regulations are weak. South Africa is also experimenting with electronic tolling of drivers who use certain freeways, which allows their movements to be tracked for the purposes of billing. However, the relationships (if any) between these various forms of surveillance, and the way they relate to police and intelligence surveillance activities, remain largely unexplored. While South Africa has a data protection law in the form of a Protection of Personal Information (POPI) Act, at the time of writing the information and privacy regulator that the Act envisages was still in the process of being set up, which meant that some of the most privacy-invasive technologies were being rolled out in the absence of enforceable privacy protections. In fact, South Africa has been sleepwalking through some of the most significant privacy issues of recent times, ones that have made people elsewhere take to the streets in protest. This book is an attempt to change that situation by linking the current global debates about surveillance and privacy to South Africa, and asking how concerned we should be. Could the widespread abuses of the right to privacy that we have seen in the US, the UK and elsewhere in the North, and as revealed so dramatically by Snowden, take place here too? And if so, what are the implications for the quality of South Africa's democracy?

OBJECTIVES OF THE BOOK AND THEORETICAL OUTLOOK

In this book, I attempt to answer the following key question: to what extent is South Africa becoming a 'surveillance society' governed by a 'surveillance' state, in which data-driven surveillance becomes a key instrument of social control? The book is motivated by a growing concern that contemporary societies are starting to experience unacceptably high levels of surveillance, and that South Africa may be no exception to this general rule. But there is little understanding of how surveillance is being practised in South Africa, the extent to which it is being routinised, and the implications of all this. In this book, I seek to establish patterns in the way surveillance is practised in the country, and attempt to explain the phenomenon in the context of the country's post-apartheid political economy. I will focus particularly on the extent to which political surveillance is being used to stabilise social relations – which have become increasingly fractious since the 2008 global recession – and on the relationship between political surveillance and the economic expansion of the industry. In order to maintain this focus, I do not delve deeply into the social or cultural aspects of data-driven surveillance (or 'dataveillance'). The commonsense understanding of these issues is that the surveillance state is expanding and that privacy is dead. But the workings of the world of surveillance are not self-evident, which is hardly surprising as so many surveillance practices are still shrouded in secrecy.

I consider the relevance of Snowden's revelations for South Africa, which does not face any major terrorist threats, and yet inexplicably still engages in mass surveillance. Drawing on a wealth of surveillance studies literature, I look at what is driving the worldwide assault on the right to privacy by state surveillance practices, and how these problems are manifested in South Africa. In exploring these issues, I will focus particularly on those who are most vulnerable to abusive forms of state surveillance because they challenge how power is organised in society, namely political activists, as well as those who write about and defend these change agents, namely academics, journalists and lawyers.

In mapping the growth of 'surveillance state' practices in South Africa, I look not only at the globally controversial issues of surveillance of communications, but at more 'benign' data-driven tools developed in the North to enable the state to track its subjects, such as bulk personal datasets recording people's banking transactions, location data and biometrically based identity systems, and the growing use of invasive technologies like CCTV and drones in public spaces. After having mapped the nature and extent of the problem, I seek to answer the following questions: What concepts are needed to mount successful resistance to these practices? What resistance practices have succeeded or are likely to succeed, what social forces and actors are most likely to mount successful resistance, and under what conditions are they most likely to succeed? To what extent are companies pushing back against state surveillance, or are they complicit in the problem? What kind of society do we want to live in? Should this be a society where every movement is tracked, and where there is no such thing as private space anymore?

A key challenge to mounting successful resistance to surveillance is that so much of it is mobile and invisible; people may not even be aware that their movements are being tracked through their cellphones, for instance. In exploring these questions, I seek to contribute to a growing body of literature on privacy, surveillance and resistance, but from a Southern perspective and with a particular bias towards working-class political and social movements as actors. So much of the literature on these questions focuses on the global North and the middle-class NGO activists who campaign against unaccountable surveillance. These questions are important because – in spite of significant gains – the public outrage in the wake of the Snowden revelations has not translated into game-changing collective action against mass surveillance, and this has exposed some of the limits of NGO-led privacy advocacy. South Africans are likely to become much more sensitive to privacy issues as the country's information or privacy regulator is being established. A comprehensive analysis of how worried we should be about these problems should hopefully set an agenda for this regulator in the years to come. While this book uses developments in the global North as a touchstone – which is necessary given that the Snowden revelations were largely about surveillance abuses in the North – it is focused on South Africa, and should therefore be considered a single case study of surveillance in South Africa, rather than a comparative study of several countries.

My outlook is critical in nature, and I embrace a critical political economy approach to explore the above-mentioned questions. Political economy focuses on the structures of control in capitalist society and the production of wealth needed to reproduce that society.[39] In relation to communication studies, political economy examines power relations in the functioning of communications systems and embeds this analysis in the social context in which communications take place.[40] Political economy can provide the conceptual tools to examine the relationship, if any, between political, economic and communications power and to analyse the impact of commodification of communications on the ability of people to receive and impart information. Furthermore, political economy's emphasis on engaged research is of relevance in that the theoretical insights offered by such analyses can be used to develop effective intervention strategies in the real world, to solve real social problems.[41] In other words, this book is premised on the need to transform power relations and ensure a more just and equal society. It assumes that under capitalism, communications systems are structured to reproduce and reinforce elite interests; but, equally, communications systems are key sites of struggle and communications tools are important assets in that struggle. However, it does not assume that the capitalist economy determines communications content in any simplistic, deterministic way. Communications messages are not mere reflections of the capitalist base. Whether these systems are used in the service of the ruling class or the working class is determined by real-world struggles. That is why I use the word 'critical'.

While critical political economy is a fairly well-developed approach to communications studies generally, and media specifically, it is not as well developed in relation to surveillance studies, which itself is an emerging field that studies how the collection, storage and processing of information have become integral to the functioning of contemporary society.[42] A world in which privacy is truly respected will be impossible without successful struggles for justice and equality, as the ability to enjoy rights such as privacy will remain the preserve of a select few. Owners of the means of production will continue to define the conditions under which this right is enjoyed on a widespread basis. We must not resign ourselves to thinking that a world where privacy is invaded on a routine basis is the way things necessarily are, and cannot be changed. We must not accept unquestioningly the statement made by Steve Rambam that 'privacy is dead – get over it'.[43] What is needed to mount an effective fightback is a thorough understanding of why the world looks the way it does at this current conjuncture. This requires not just analysis, but theory.

The problem, though, is that some of the key concepts that have been used to describe the surveillance state have not been particularly empowering. The panopticon, for instance, does not encourage people to identify the agents involved in surveillance. Theories of resistance to surveillance are underdeveloped, which makes it more difficult to see the world differently from how it currently operates. While surveillance has always been a feature of the capitalist system, its importance as a mechanism of social control has grown massively over the past two decades. This means that there are still many people who have experienced a world where pervasive surveillance was not such a problem. As a result, we are challenged to identify the particular political-economic and technical conditions that have given rise to the forms of surveillance being experienced today. Through an examination of surveillance in South Africa, this book seeks to address some of these broader theoretical questions.

THE RESEARCH PROCESS AND ANALYTICAL FRAMEWORK

The collection and analysis of information amassed through the research and journalism incorporated into this book have been guided by an analytical framework based around the following organising concepts: actors, interventions or actions, relationships, and outcomes or impacts. A series of sub-questions were then posed in relation to each concept. The frame directed the researchers to collect information about the different surveillance actors and their roles and responsibilities, the relationships between these different actors and how they were changing over time, and relationships between these actors and the broader political environment. The questions that guided the research process were as follows:

Interest groups
- The different actors: the main state surveillance 'clients' (the police, military and intelligence, and other state agencies), surveillance oversight bodies, communications companies, surveillance subjects, civil society and social movements. Who are the main actors, and what are their roles and responsibilities? Is there any evidence of other actors becoming active in relation to surveillance?

Interventions or actions
- The surveillance perpetrators: Who is undertaking surveillance and how often? What is motivating the surveillance? What forms of surveillance do they use (including the technologies), and are these changing over time? Are the organisations and individuals that are being placed under surveillance changing over time, and why? Where do they stand in relation to key power-holders in the state and society? Are some organisations or individuals more likely to be subjected to surveillance than others, and why? How much surveillance is warranted in that it is legal and pursues a legitimate aim, and how much is not?
- The surveillance oversight bodies: What interventions do they engage in to keep the perpetrators under review? How are they set up, and how independent and accountable are they? How effective are they at holding perpetrators to account if there are abuses?
- The surveillance subjects: How are surveillance subjects chosen? How do subjects respond to surveillance? Are particular social groups more likely to become subjects of surveillance, and, if so, who are they and why are they groups of interest? Do different categories of victim respond differently to surveillance? Under what conditions do subjects resist surveillance, and how?
- Communications companies: What are the roles of these companies in relation to surveillance, and are there shifts in their roles over time, and why? If they themselves engage in surveillance, what technologies do they use and how is this changing over time? Under what conditions do they enable surveillance, and under what conditions do they resist it?
- Civil society and social movements: What are the roles of these actors in relation to surveillance, and are their roles shifting over time? Under what conditions do

they take up advocacy in relation to surveillance, what are the main organising concepts they use, and how successful have they been in resisting surveillance abuses?

Relationships

- The relations between these different actors: What are the relationships, if any, between private and state surveillance? Is decision-making among these different actors static or is it changing over time, and why? Are roles and responsibilities of these different actors clear? Which actor or actors seem to hold the power in relation to decision-making about surveillance? How are surveillance practices impacting on relationships among the different actors? Why do different actors support or resist surveillance? Do they act alone, or do they build coalitions of interest around this issue?
- Relationships between actors and the broader political environment: What are the relations of different surveillance actors to the broader political environment, and how are they impacting on this environment? What do the uses of surveillance tell us about broader political shifts?

Outcomes and impacts

- Outcomes and impacts of surveillance: How have different actors responded to surveillance or the threat of it? What are the impacts and consequences of surveillance? What are the impacts and consequences of resistance to surveillance? What forms of resistance work, and what concepts are the most empowering? What is the broader political significance of surveillance, and how does this significance (or lack of it) impact on civil society and social movement responses? If surveillance is being used for positive purposes, are positive impacts evident, and, if so, what are they? If surveillance is being used for negative purposes, are negative impacts evident, and, if so, what are they?

These sub-questions are then used to answer the overall question. These key elements of the analytical framework allowed me to develop an answer to the broader question of whether South Africa is becoming a surveillance society governed by a surveillance state, to construct some general explanations or theories about the contributions of surveillance to social control, and to propose some theoretical points about elements of resistance to surveillance.

1

Theorising the surveillance state

This chapter examines possibly the most important concept used in this book, namely surveillance. It identifies some of the ways in which surveillance has been conceptualised and theorised, and how these theorisations have changed over time. As Alan Sears has argued, theory is not a mere neutral tool, but a guide to action. The value of theory is that it helps us to ask and answer causal questions that cannot be answered at the level of fact alone.[1] If the problem – to the extent that there is one – is not correctly understood, then it becomes more difficult to craft effective intervention strategies. There can be little doubt that technological developments associated with computerisation have made surveillance easier, but does this automatically mean that these recent developments are negative in nature? Surely, surveillance can also have positive effects? Given the extent to which surveillance has become pervasive, how do the different elements of surveillance relate to one another? Are we really looking at a 'Big Brother'-type scenario, where different surveillance actors combine their efforts to track and control people from the cradle to the grave? Or are the more benign elements of surveillance really nothing to worry about, with the threats being overstated by more paranoid elements of society? This chapter focuses on theoretical debates about these specific questions, as they impact on what we define as surveillance, and how we mark it out from other forms of information collection and analysis. Such questions matter, as answering them will help us answer the broader question of how worried we should be about these developments.

FOUCAULT AND THE PANOPTICON

It is impossible to discuss the concept of surveillance without invoking Michel Foucault and his appropriation of Jeremy Bentham's panopticon as a metaphor for the kind of surveillance being undertaken by the NSA and its UK counterpart, GCHQ, and other state surveillance actors in the present time. In his book *Panopticon*, Bentham defined surveillance as 'a new mode of obtaining power of mind over mind, in a quantity hitherto without example'.[2] Bentham's definition is significant, as it links surveillance directly to social control. In other words, it is not aimed only at satisfying curiosity or meeting a voyeuristic need to peep into someone's personal affairs; rather, it is aimed at obtaining information about a person to coerce that person to change his or her behaviour.

Bentham designed a panopticon, or a building that relies on surveillance, to achieve control of particular populations. The building design was meant for a variety of purposes, such as hospitals, schools and prisons, but Bentham was particularly interested in putting the design to use for penal purposes. Consisting of a circular building with an observation post at the centre, and cells radiating out from the centre, this design allowed a single guard to maintain watch over all the inmates in the cells. While it was physically impossible for the watchman to observe everyone at the same time, inmates never knew when they were being watched or not, and as a result they internalised disciplinary behaviour.[3]

While few panopticons have been built, the concept has found currency as a metaphor for the growth of surveillance in contemporary society. Foucault, who has probably done more than anyone else to popularise the concept, argued that the panopticon was the perfect surveillance tool, as it allowed the enforcers of discipline to observe their charges with a single gaze; while the supervisor is invisible, the inmates are visible to the supervisor at all times. For Foucault, this arrangement allowed for 'the automatic functioning of power'[4] by making the actual exercise of power unnecessary: a boon, especially in a society where governments perceived to be tyrannical faced the risk of rebellion by their subjects. This was because inmates were more inclined to alter their behaviour of their own accord because of the awareness that they could be observed. The technical possibility of constant surveillance also turned them into more knowable subjects, which was likely to make them more docile. This internalisation of discipline made the need for more overt forms of control through physical confrontation less necessary, and reduced the number of those exercising power, while potentially increasing the number of those over whom power was exercised. At the same time, power became dissociated from a particular governing individual: rather, it became a deindividualised regime of rules and mechanisms.[5]

The panopticon has become a metaphor for a state that keeps its citizens under constant surveillance to create the feeling of being watched – what Foucault has referred to as a disciplinary society. Such a society can be governed at a distance, allowing for more dispersed forms of social control that do not necessarily require a monolithic and homogenising state with a huge bureaucracy; instead, control is exercised through a variety of administrative systems, institutions and even discourses. Technologies of surveillance allow the activities of the state to become invisible, and its existence enters the realm of abstract ideas.[6]

Foucault elaborated on his conception of surveillance and the power that it produces in later writings, where he identified surveillance as being central to both liberalism and neoliberalism. For him, the panopticon was central to liberal government in that it disciplined individuals by subjecting them to constant visibility, which made overt violence unnecessary because they policed themselves. In other words, power was exercised in a 'polite' fashion. Government intervened only when individuals did not function according to established modes of behaviour.[7] This form of surveillance is biopolitical in the sense that the body is controlled not through physical violence but through observation and classification, to enforce a liberal mode of governance. Biological features of the human body – such as people's fingerprints and irises – as well as their movements, viewing and internet browsing habits, have become the stuff of surveillance, and are used to manage populations by analysing their present habits, identifying problem populations, and predicting future ones.[8] This exercise of power is not exclusive to the state, however, but can be used by any institution that gathers and processes personal information. Google, for instance, can be considered an incredibly powerful biopolitical tool, as data generated from users' internet searches is mined algorithmically and their profiles are sold to advertisers.[9]

The enormous value of Foucault's conception of power is that it departs from monolithic, state-centric conceptions, which fail to explain adequately how social order is maintained in nominally democratic, non-authoritarian societies. Also, Foucault did not necessarily see power as a negative force in society; it could also be productive. Furthermore, by recognising the dispersal of power, he opened up the possibility that multiple sites of resistance to power might develop. However, the problem with Foucault's conception of power is that it goes too far in depersonalising and decentralising power, in that it is everywhere and nowhere: this makes power infinitely more difficult to challenge. It also tends to ignore the ideological purposes of surveillance as a means of controlling those rendered surplus by neoliberal capitalism. This is not to say that Foucault did not have a concept of resistance; for him, resistance became possible only if one recognised the interests embedded in a variety of social practices. Simply pointing fingers at a single authority such as a government did not help one to understand how modern social orders actually worked.[10]

Another issue that Foucault's conception of surveillance tends to ignore is that the surveillance capacities of the state have not necessarily replaced more overt forms of repression: on the contrary, at times both have been rolled out together and in fact they complement one another.[11] Surveillance may be used to identify populations that need to be contained by the use of more overt methods; for instance, policing decisions about protests may be either facilitative or militarised depending on the extent of the threat that the police identify through surveillance.[12]

THE POSTMODERN TURN IN SURVEILLANCE STUDIES

There are others who have argued that the panopticon is not an appropriate metaphor for contemporary societies. Drawing on the insights of postmodern studies – which problematise theories that advance one-sided narratives of how societies function – some theorists have pointed out that surveillance now takes place on a much more distributed basis than in the past, and that a state-centric approach to surveillance studies is no longer appropriate in societies where there is a huge diversity of surveillance actors. In fact, Kevin Haggerty has argued that the panopticon has been overused in surveillance studies, and has even called for the panopticon to be demolished metaphorically, to remove its grip on the field. He has pointed out that since Foucault's groundbreaking book, surveillance has come to serve a variety of different functions, not just to police the activities of problem subjects. Surveillance is being used in education and medical treatment, too, so it cannot be said that surveillance serves the single purpose of social control. This means that a less negative, more neutral definition of surveillance is now required.

Surveillance is not necessarily directed at the poor or marginalised to maintain social hierarchies, either; it has become much more widespread. Surveillance is also being directed at non-human subjects, a development that unsettles the control argument, and this form of surveillance has even brought social benefits. Different social actors are also using surveillance, not just the state. The democratisation of surveillance technologies has also meant that ordinary citizens can use inverse surveillance, turning these technologies against the powerful and exposing their abuses of power: practices that have become known as 'sousveillance'.[13] Protesters, for instance, can use video cameras to record police violence. These capacities, when put in the hand of citizens, problematise the view that all surveillance is necessarily bad. Other examples of neutral definitions abound in surveillance literature.[14] Haggerty has argued that surveillance scholars tend to avoid studying positive examples of surveillance, as their immersion in critique makes them blind to these phenomena.[15]

Different and even alternative metaphors to the panopticon have also been offered, based on the argument that Foucault did not foresee computerisation and the rise of consumerism, which have greatly expanded the scope for surveillance.[16] These developments mean that there is not one single point where surveillance takes place, but multiple points. Thomas Mathiesen's term 'the synopticon' – where the many watch the few by using the mass media – has become popular in surveillance studies, as it recognises these more recent developments. In other words, mass audiences are able to peer into the lives of celebrities and other public figures, placing them under unprecedented levels of scrutiny to which audiences themselves are not subjected.[17] However, Mathiesen did not necessarily propose the synopticon as an alternative to the panopticon; in fact, the two are interlinked in that both are still structures of domination, and he was not necessarily optimistic about the mass media's effects in society.

Surveillance in contemporary society has even been described as a surveillant assemblage, where surveillance practices do not take place in one part of society only, but where information is gleaned from multiple sources and locations.[18] Drawing on the work of Gilles Deleuze and Felix Guattari, Kevin Haggerty and Richard Ericson have argued that discrete surveillance systems have converged, leading to a rhizomic levelling of surveillance. No longer is it conducted on a top-down basis and primarily by states – as the panoptic metaphor suggests – but diverse media can be connected to pursue surveillance for multiple purposes, and human surveillance efforts can be augmented by computers. Scattered centres of calculation, from police stations to banks, undertake surveillance, and as a result surveillance transcends the boundaries of separate institutions.[19] Zygmunt Bauman and David Lyon have termed such surveillance 'liquid surveillance', or a form of surveillance that relies on the body being encoded by data and tracked through multiple data flows.[20] Deleuze himself recognised the fact that surveillance practices had changed from the early modern period about which Foucault wrote, in that computerisation had made constant surveillance possible at a reduced cost, allowing for continuous control rather than periodic examination. As a result, Deleuze argued, contemporary societies should not be described as disciplinary societies, but as societies of control.[21] In other words, power over individuals is not necessarily exercised through fixed institutional structures, but through mobile and rapid ICTs, which enable control 'on the go': a form of control that is perfectly suited to societies defined by flexibility. At the same time, electronic tagging still allows surveillance to take place, to ensure that individuals are in a permissible place.[22]

Other theorists have argued that Foucault's ideas still remain highly relevant to today's surveillance society, and that he would not have been surprised by recent attempts to universalise surveillance using the internet and other technologies. Far from being a technology linked to societies of control – which, according to Deleuze, have replaced disciplinary societies – the cellphone can be understood as a portable panopticon, in that it allows users to be tracked and monitored invisibly.[23] In fact, the Snowden revelations have brought Foucault back to the fore, with an emerging group of scholars arguing for his continued relevance. They maintain that there has been an unfair dismissal of his work, even though the panopticon may not describe the functioning of the internet with precision.[24] For instance, Gilbert Caluya has argued that what he terms the Deleuzian turn in surveillance studies – with its influential metaphor of the rhizomic surveillant assemblage – does not necessarily represent a significant break from Foucault, who recognised that a myriad forms of surveillance characterised modern society and rejected state-centric conceptions of power.[25] Furthermore, while the internet is a distributed medium, it is inherently surveillant in that in its current state it allows for the invisible filtering of information as an exercise of power. Its surveillant potential enables governments to shift their interventions from direct enforcement of the law to more invisible, decentralised, technologically based forms of enforcement. This fits Foucault's conception of power very well. However, contemporary surveillance operates vertically, horizontally and diagonally, and people also participate in their own surveillance. This added dimension has led David Lyon to insist that researchers should take the cultures of surveillance seriously, as they need to understand the circumstances under which people willingly participate in surveillance activities through their social media and internet usage.[26]

POLITICAL ECONOMY AND MARXIST THEORIES OF SURVEILLANCE

Political economy theorists have also argued that while contemporary surveillance takes place undeniably on a far more distributed basis than in the period Foucault wrote about, the means of surveillance are much more centralised than is often acknowledged. The internet – and the applications and infrastructure it relies on – is dominated by a few major companies, such as Google, Microsoft and Facebook.[27] They have co-operated with NSA surveillance through the surveillance programme known as PRISM, handing over internet data based on selectors that the NSA provided. The programme was apparently directed at foreigners in the main, but US nationals were caught in the dragnet too: a fact that the NSA denied initially, but was subsequently forced to admit.[28] Capital has an insatiable desire to control every aspect of human existence, to open up new vistas of profit-making and to minimise resistance to commodification: that is why it has moved into so many areas of life previously considered private, such as personal information. While the capitalist state incorporated elements of surveillance in earlier periods in history, technological developments associated with computerisation have allowed an unprecedented expansion of the surveillance capacities of the state. Since the 9/11 attacks on the US, public and private institutions have poured resources into enhancing their surveillance capabilities, while relaxing laws governing these capabilities on the pretext of national security. Surveillance has also been used to track groups that powerful interests feel threatened by, such as political activists and journalists. To this extent, the growth in surveillance technologies could be considered a surface manifestation of a deeper capitalist crisis, and surveillance has become integral to neoliberal state formation.

However, political economists have not paid sufficient attention to the fact that the relationship between the state and business is not one of straightforward co-operation, and the relationship between the political and the economic cannot be seen in narrow deterministic ways. Communications companies have begun to recognise that there is a business case for privacy; they have become more willing to push back against state surveillance practices. For instance, Apple has fought back against Federal Bureau of Investigation (FBI) attempts to make it unlock the cellphone of a criminal suspect.[29] However, the convergence of interests between the surveillance industry and governments is strong enough for Ben Hayes to refer to the existence of a surveillance-industrial complex.[30] Hayes argues that – far from being deployed in a sporadic fashion – surveillance technologies have become central to population control through policing, intelligence work, border control and other forms of population management. The industry and government are linked through security specialists shifting from the one to the other, leading to what has become known as the 'revolving door' syndrome. Governments also outsource key surveillance tasks to the private sector and may even fund the development of surveillance technologies from innovation funds, while the private sector relies on governments for contracts. The fact that both the military and the police have turned inwards and focused increasingly on domestic security – to the point where military, policing, and intelligence logics and technologies have converged – has opened up new domestic markets for surveillance. For instance, policing has become increasingly intelligence-led, with the result that intelligence is used not just to solve crimes reactively, but to anticipate likely crimes pre-emptively. 'National secu-rity' has become the legitimising discourse for these practices, which the security industry has a vested interest in talking up to expand markets. Key companies have expanded globally to provide surveillance equipment in markets other than their home market, and in consequence the globalisation, privatisation and securitisa-tion of surveillance have become mutually reinforcing trends.[31]

DEFINING SURVEILLANCE

Having explored briefly some of the key theoretical trends in surveillance studies, we can now attempt a definition of surveillance. Needless to say, as befits an increas-ingly complex field, there are competing definitions of the word. The most signifi-cant differences of opinion turn on whether surveillance is an inherently negative phenomenon, or whether a less judgemental or more neutral approach should be taken to defining it.[32] Thomas Allmer has even divided scholars into two schools of thought on the 'problem' of surveillance: non-panoptic and panoptic.[33] Proponents of the first approach have argued that surveillance can have positive benefits too. David Lyon has, for instance, identified watching over a child or taking care of a patient as positive examples of surveillance. Banks, too, put their customers under surveillance to identify suspicious transactions and prevent fraud. CCTV can be used to identify criminals and even deter crime. No one would argue that sur-veillance in these contexts is bad for democracy: on the contrary. In view of these examples and others, Lyon had defined surveillance as the many contexts in which information is gathered, stored and processed by a variety of state, commercial and administrative agencies.[34]

Others have supported Lyon's view that surveillance is not inherently bad. For Gary Marx, for instance, surveillance is about having regard to a person or to fac-tors presumed to be associated with a person; an individual may be subjected to non-strategic surveillance – where information is gathered about him or her on a routine basis – or to strategic surveillance, where information is gathered con-sciously for particular ends, often negative.[35] Roger Clarke sees surveillance as the systematic monitoring of one or more persons through the collection of informa-tion about them, their activities and their associates.[36] By using such broad defini-tions, these theorists lean towards arguing that surveillance is an inevitable feature of modern bureaucracies. In fact, the practice has existed to different extents since time immemorial. In other words, it is impossible to conceive of societies that do not involve surveillance, neither is it desirable to do so.

Proponents of the second approach include scholars from more critical traditions, including critical political economy and Marxism, who have argued that surveillance is an inherently negative phenomenon: that is, it is about the collection and analysis of information primarily for repressive purposes. As a result, surveillance must be rejected because it impedes human emancipation. They argue that to portray surveillance as a neutral phenomenon depoliticises the problem. This portrayal is made possible by the fact that non-surveillant theorists tend to expand their definitions to include forms of information collection that should not be understood as surveillance practices at all. However, not all scholars who think like this are necessarily political economists or Marxists; that is, they do not necessarily take their analyses further and relate them to broader questions of class domination and capitalism.[37]

One theorist who does is Christian Fuchs, a Marxist who argues that surveillance is linked inextricably to class domination, coercion and even violence. For him, an emancipated society must necessarily be a society that frees itself from surveillance: a struggle that should be linked inextricably to the struggle against capitalism and for socialism.[38] Benign forms of information collection (such as the collection of information about a person's heart rate to monitor that person's health or the usage of smog or air pollution early warning detectors) cannot be considered as surveillance as they are geared towards providing social benefits.[39] In response to assertions that surveillance can be (and is being) practised by a broader array of social actors – in other words, surveillance is being 'democratised' – Fuchs points out that the state and large corporations still dominate the surveillance terrain, which means that surveillance does actually manifest a panoptic character. In fact, the Snowden revelations pointed to a dangerous concentration of executive power. While surveillance technologies may have advanced and become cheaper and hence more accessible, to infer democratisation from these developments is technologically determinist and ignores questions of how capitalism's unequal power relations continue to structure surveillance practices. While political and economic surveillance may appear to serve different purposes, ultimately their objectives converge on making citizens available for exploitation. The Snowden revelations have also shown how internet companies and the state collude to conduct mass surveillance, although their immediate interests may diverge at different moments in history. Fuchs considers the stretching of the definition of surveillance to include non-coercive information-gathering as dangerous, as it normalises surveillance, making it less possible to mount effective resistance to it, as even benign practices are included in its remit.[40]

THE RIGHT TO PRIVACY AS AN ORGANISING CONCEPT

Much of the resistance to surveillance has been couched in rights-based terms, and more specifically as a violation of the right to privacy. The Snowden revelations caused outrage while they were being drip-released, as they showed just how much privacy Americans, and in fact many other citizens, had lost. The revelations triggered a huge amount of activism in defence of human rights, especially privacy. However, notwithstanding the din of outrage, a growing number of citizens appear to have become resigned to the idea of a surveillance state, arguing that privacy has become impossible to achieve in an increasingly digitised era: a phenomenon that Linna Dencik and Jonathan Cable have termed 'surveillance realism'. This adaptation to the 'reality' of surveillance has been much more apparent in the UK than in America or other European countries such as Germany, where thousands of people staged mass protests in the wake of the revelations.[41] 'Surveillance realism' has also been driven by the fact that more public and private companies are storing highly sensitive personal information in databases and mining it for a range of different uses; in fact, it is becoming increasingly impossible to transact with many institutions without being willing to part with such information. Many give up their right to privacy by handing over huge swathes of personal information to private technology companies like Facebook and Google, which then quarry this data for commercially useful information. As a result, the challenge has moved far beyond state-based forms of control. Over-sharing of personal information online has become a habit, one that feeds the surveillance beast even more. The selfie has become the leitmotif of a generation of internet users obsessed with constructing self-regarding, even narcissistic, digital identities. These practices have come to form an integral part of what David Lyon has termed 'surveillance culture', where people have come to accept, and even be complicit in, the collection and analysis of information about themselves.[42] Until activists understand how deeply surveillance is embedded in everyday meaning-making practices of more and more people, it will be difficult, even impossible, to develop effective resistance strategies. This is because these strategies tend to focus on the legal or political dimensions of surveillance, without addressing the pay-offs that people receive for making themselves more visible (such as satisfying their need for connectedness and recognition in a world where social fragmentation has become more of a reality), and what they can do to change these practices to lessen the potential for abuse of their data.[43]

Given the pervasiveness and seeming inevitability of surveillance, privacy sceptics have asked why, after all, one should worry about protecting privacy if one has not done anything wrong and has nothing to hide. The problem with this argument is that citizens will never know when they need the right to privacy. Privacy violations are also irreversible. Once something is known, it cannot be un-known. Change agents, such as political activists, are in particular need of the right to privacy, as they are more likely than most to challenge how power is organised in society. As a result, they are more likely to attract the wrath of the authorities, who may be very tempted to use the surveillance capacities of the state to track their activities.

While the definition of privacy is contested, the dominant conception that has found its way into legal instruments has been influenced by natural rights theory and positivism. This conception has been heavily influenced by Samuel D. Warren and Louis Brandeis's claim that privacy is the 'right to be let alone'.[44] The influence of this definition can be found in the UN Declaration of Human Rights, which protects the individual from 'arbitrary interference with his [sic] privacy, family, home or correspondence, [or] to attacks upon his [sic] honour or reputation'.[45] Even the 1996 South African constitution includes a right to privacy that emphasises the individual's right to his or her personal autonomy, free of intrusions or interferences in his or her private life. It also includes an informational right to privacy, where disclosure of information is prevented without the express and informed consent of the individual.[46]

Elaborating on Warren and Brandeis's asocial (even anti-social) definition, Alan Westin defined the right to privacy as 'the voluntary and temporary withdrawal of a person from the general society through physical or psychological means, whether in a state of solitude or small group intimacy or, when among larger groups, in a condition of anonymity or reserve'.[47] This definition pivots on the right of the individual to be an individual *sans* social interactions. In this definition, Westin identified four dimensions of privacy: solitude, where an individual can be free of observation by others; intimacy, where a person has a right to form and enjoy close social bonds; anonymity, where an individual can refuse to be identified by others; and reserve, where personal information about the individual is limited as he or she sees fit.[48] Westin was particularly vocal about the informational aspects of the right to privacy, and his views influenced a great deal of public policy work on privacy and data protection work, both of which came to equate privacy with the protection of personal information.[49] Charles Fried also offered an individualised, but much more truncated, definition of privacy, namely '[the] control we have over information about ourselves'.[50]

These views can lead to the conclusion that privacy should enable a person to control information about himself or herself to achieve independence, self-reliance and, ultimately, self-determination. In fact, privacy can be said to have various functions, in that it allows a person to act autonomously, it allows for spaces in which a person can manage stresses away from the hurly-burly of the world's pressures and engage in self-reflection about his or her relations with the world, and it allows for the protection of personal information so that the individual can decide what to share, and under what conditions.[51] Privacy can also be said to involve four elements: bodily privacy, where a person has a right to decide what happens to his or her body; information privacy, where a person has a right to decide what information is released about him or her, and how; privacy of communication, where people should be guaranteed the right to communicate without fear of having their communications intercepted; and territorial privacy, where a person has a right to enjoy the privacy of his or her own home or personal space.[52]

What unites these scholars is that they see individuals as the main rights-holders, a view that is based on the moral stance that emphasises the worth of the individual above that of the group. To that extent, their conception of privacy could be said to rest on liberal-democratic conceptions of the individual. Scholars from a variety of perspectives have critiqued this individualised concept of privacy for separating the public and private realms artificially, and playing down communitarian values such as sharing and other forms of social solidarity. Furthermore, this concept of privacy fails to see the right as a social right, or one that is mediated by questions of power. Articulating the right as an individual right is also self-defeating, as it opens up the right to limitation on the basis that it competes with other rights, and, when it clashes with rights that are more important to the collective, then the individual right must give way. On the other hand, if the defence of the right was embedded in broader questions of democracy and human rights (such as the right to form opinions free from state interference, or to participate in shaping a society's political life), then it would be less vulnerable to limitation, as its broader societal value would be clearer.[53] As a result, more recent conceptualisations of the right to privacy have evolved from focusing on the individual to focusing on its social necessity, as a lack of privacy erodes trust in relationships, including those between individuals and organisations.

Rather than abandoning the right entirely, some have conceptualised the right to privacy in social terms – as being a common need – and have even argued for a sociality of privacy.[54] All individuals experience a need for minimum levels of privacy. In fact, democracy could not function without privacy, as people would become fearful about speaking out and holding the powerful to account, in case their words or deeds were being tracked. The boundaries between the self and society are also much more porous than Westin has made out, as the individual is defined through interactions with others, and privacy in its various forms is negotiated through these interactions. Furthermore, the problem should not be understood as being about protecting the privacy 'bubble' around a person from invasion, but rather about managing relationships between individuals and organisations in the realm of information: in other words, in this worldview a social relationship is assumed.

The growing problem of unwarranted surveillance, and the need to have a common instrument to fight it, have spurred scholars such as Colin Bennett to articulate a collective conception of privacy. In any event, he has argued, privacy has become a matter of public policy and has been recognised for its societal value for several decades now.[55] Even David Lyon, previously a privacy sceptic, has come to recognise the need for a common uniting concept in the struggle against surveillance, and privacy provides just such a concept.[56] If privacy is not reinvigorated, then societies could see surveillance grow relatively unchecked in spite of the right to privacy's existence, as surveillance advocates would merely need to point to a social problem for the right to wither into insignificance.[57]

But will emphasising the right to privacy's sociality be enough to rescue it from irrelevance in the real world, weighed down as it is by concerns about terrorism and public safety, on the one hand, and unaccountable surveillance, on the other? What does policy need to look like to roll back attempts to turn societies into 'surveillance societies', where people cannot act or even think without the fear of being watched by powerful actors that may not have their best interests at heart? Social conceptions of privacy may still be deficient, as they may not focus on the social justice aspects of surveillance, such as social sorting on discriminatory grounds.[58] Privacy may even enable surveillance, as it can lead to organisations ticking privacy boxes while largely continuing with their practices unhindered: a problem that will be explored in more detail later on when the work of privacy regulators is discussed.[59] While emphasising the social content of the right strengthens the ability of privacy advocates to defend it against limitations on national security grounds, the problem with the 'turn to the social' in privacy studies is that it can be depoliticised. That is, it lacks a political perspective on the problem, and more specifically on power relations in society, and how the right will continue to be attacked, both as an individual and as a social right, unless the political interests at work in doing so are identified and addressed. A critical political perspective, including a Marxist perspective, is particularly important in this regard, as it is orientated to progressive social change; such a perspective should also address the limitations of a rights-based analysis. In other words, challenging unaccountable surveillance is not just about asserting a right to privacy, but also about changing how surveillant forms of power are organised in society. In this regard, Zachary Bruno has detected an absence of critique in the face of the massive expansion of the surveillance state: even the Snowden revelations did not cause US citizens to revolt en masse against violations of their rights.

The sheer pervasiveness of the surveillance machinery, coupled with the absence of any critique of its dangers, means that alternatives remain difficult to imagine.[60]

From a Marxist perspective, the concept of a 'natural individual' vested with pre-political rights is a historical product of capitalist property relations and forms of production. Under these conditions, these freedoms have been developed mainly within the relationships of the ruling class.[61] In other words, in unequal societies the ability to individuate is available to a select few. In outlining the conditions for freedom of the working class, Marx and Engels recognised a difference between negative freedom and positive freedom. Negative freedom means the lack of forces which prevent individuals from doing whatever they want. Positive freedom is the capacity of people to determine the best course of action and the existence of opportunities for them to realise their full potential. For Marx, negative freedom was a bourgeois concept, as it is the freedom primarily of those who own the means of production. Positive freedom comes about through working-class struggles, which create opportunities for the class to develop as human beings. However, in spite of his critique about negative freedom, Marx argued that both negative and positive freedoms need to be advanced, as the former creates spaces for the latter to be advanced. When applied to privacy, this means that activists need to protect privacy as a negative freedom – that is, as a freedom to protect and control individual and collective spaces for reflection, discussion and debate from intrusive interference – while advancing conditions for the enjoyment of the right by the broader society.

Henry Giroux has made some interesting arguments about shifting the terrain on which the struggle for privacy is carried out, onto a more outrightly political terrain. According to Giroux, recent resistance strategies to the surveillance state have individualised the problem by reducing it to a struggle for privacy. He argues that this approach is limited, in that it fails to address the bigger context in which the surveillance state is expanding, which is the growth in the exercise of arbitrary power. To this extent, the surveillance state is linked intimately to other techniques to increase social control, such as the militarisation of policing, the arrest and harassment of activists, the stretching of the definition of terrorism to include acts of political dissent, and the growing use of prisons to control marginalised social groups, who are disproportionately working-class and black. Citing Ariel Dorfman, Giroux argues that surveillance is about increasing power and control, and not just about violating privacy. He also argues that resistance must move beyond resistance to surveillance as such, and be channelled into the building of popular movements that have the capacity to engage in collective struggles to challenge abuses of power and, ultimately, change how power is organised in society. This may well include the establishment of an anti-capitalist party, which politicises surveillance as a systemic feature of neoliberal capitalism, and which organises to end a system that has come to rely so heavily on surveillance to achieve social control of increasingly restive populations.[62]

Another theorist who has grappled with how to conceptualise privacy from a Marxist perspective is Christian Fuchs. According to Fuchs, while it is important to defend privacy as a negative right, an alternative conception of privacy also needs to recognise the relations between privacy and private property, such as the use of the right to prevent the release of personal information revealing income differentials and prevent abuses of power. In order to understand these relations, Fuchs argues that it is necessary to consider privacy as a historical concept linked to the separation of social life into public and private realms. The private realm has become a realm of leisure and consumption, which creates demand for more goods and services and allows for a more effective reproduction of labour. Based as it is on liberal underpinnings, the dominant conception of privacy is highly individualistic. In order to develop the radical content of privacy, it is necessary to reconceptualise it as the right to resist surveillance by dominant groups, thereby strengthening the collective strength of subaltern groups. But in order to do so, privacy activists must emphasise the privacy rights of those at the bottom of the power structure, and they should not allow those who exercise power to conceal themselves.[63]

CONCLUSION: DEFINING SURVEILLANCE AND PRIVACY

Based on this foregoing discussion, my working definition of surveillance is the collection and analysis of information and the accessing of a person's physical characteristics for the purposes of social control. Other forms of information collection and storage do not, to my mind, qualify as surveillance. Separating out these two practices is important, as it allows a more focused analysis of the problem, which is necessary for the development of appropriate resistance strategies.

When it comes to defining privacy, Fuchs's orientation towards those aspects of privacy that allow workers, the unemployed and other subaltern groups to exercise their agency and gain social power is important, as it provides a conceptual basis for developing strategies and tactics for effective resistance, as these will move beyond addressing privacy violations as the end point of activists, to regarding them as problems epiphenomenal to a whole system of exploitation and oppression that needs to be changed if privacy is to be realised. Requiring privacy activism to occur within the context of an anti-capitalist party – as suggested by Giroux – is rather restrictive, and even dogmatic, as it prescribes the organisational form that struggles for privacy should take. Anti-capitalist parties are also few and far between in the current political period. Instead, these struggles should be waged wherever existing struggles against oppression and exploitation are taking place, and in the organisational forms that make the most sense to those engaged in them: in other words, privacy work should be 'mainstreamed' into these struggles. Privacy activists also need to identify the social forces that are most likely to challenge oppressive and exploitative systems successfully, and prioritise their collective efforts as the most important agents of change.

2

Is privacy dead? Resistance to surveillance after the Snowden disclosures

'I think it's important to recognise that you can't have 100 per cent security and also then have 100 per cent privacy and zero inconvenience.'[1] This was how US President Barack Obama responded to questions about the Snowden revelations of the NSA's spying activities.[2] Politicians have used the supposed trade-off between privacy and security as a means of legitimising privacy-invading national security measures, including communications surveillance. Never in modern world history have there been so many violations of the right to privacy. Yet, never in modern world history have there been so many privacy protections. How should this seeming contradiction be explained? This chapter will examine this issue and, in doing so, will consider the range of actors involved in resisting unaccountable surveillance, their organising concepts, strategies and tactics, and will ask whether they are 'fit for purpose'.

THE FALL AND RISE OF MILITARY TECHNOLOGIES, PRACTICES AND LOGICS

Four per cent of companies which feature in Privacy International's Surveillance Industry Index are also major arms producers, including BAE Systems (UK), Boeing (US) and Elbit Systems (Israel). Arms manufacturers have expanded into cybersecurity, which has proved to be a hugely lucrative area: a boon for companies that are seeing their profits decline due to governmental budget cuts on conventional arms.[3] While the US ramped up its military spending in the wake of the 9/11 attacks, its withdrawal from 'theatres of war' like Iraq impacted negatively on arms manufacturers, as did the reduction in military spending of other governments in the wake of the 2008 global recession.[4] In an attempt to adapt to this changing global situation, some of the major arms manufacturers increased their involvement in the lucrative and ever-expanding surveillance market. A case in point is BAE Systems, which expanded the intelligence and cybersecurity aspects of its business from the late 2000s onwards, acquiring existing businesses in this area. The company intensified this focus when it experienced declining revenues owing to the falling demand for conventional armaments.[5] Arms manufacturer Lockheed Martin has expanded its activities to include providing intelligence-gathering and analysis capacities to the Central Intelligence Agency (CIA) and other US government agencies, and even to commercial retail giant Walmart to spy on critics of its corporate practices.[6] The French company Thales, traditionally a conventional arms manufacturer, also branched out into the communications surveillance business, but it was less agile in creating much-needed local partnerships, which assisted other companies to develop local security solutions for country-specific needs, rather than expecting them to purchase off-the-shelf technology. Arms companies saw the partnership approach as essential for survival in 'developing country' contexts in the face of cutbacks to armaments spending by Western governments.[7]

As is well known, war is good for economies, because it creates demand for armaments and industrial output more generally – an industrial strategy that has become known as 'military Keynesianism'.[8] However, what does a permanent warfare state do when the number of wars decline? It finds other markets by creating demand for related technologies. Surveillance is an excellent alternative. Wars involve bodies, which raises the cost of involvement in theatres of war, politically and socially. Ordinary citizens may begin to push back against warfare economies as the true human cost becomes visible. On the other hand, the lack of visible victims of surveillance makes it a much more difficult problem about which to raise public consciousness and, consequently, around which to organise. Small wonder that key arms-producing countries have begun to orientate their economies away from traditional industrial capitalism to what Robert McChesney and John Bellamy Foster have called surveillance capitalism, a form of capitalism that has new, distinct characteristics.[9]

These characteristics include the creation of huge but unstable financial surpluses, generated by financial speculation, which need to find investments but cannot turn to a favoured outlet like arms. Financialisation has also created a huge appetite for data, and these databanks themselves have offered new revenue streams to companies that can profile and target potential customers with products. More intense public–private collaboration in an industry that was traditionally dominated by governments cannot be underestimated as a key factor: as Snowden himself has observed, surveillance is the business model of the internet.[10] This model has allowed unprecedented co-operation between communications companies and governments, as the former have the resources to develop and maintain huge databanks that the latter can plunder at will (at least until recently).[11] The turning inward of military technologies, practices and logics through, for instance, police militarisation has also facilitated the expansion of the industry, as it has allowed governments and arms manufacturers to create new domestic markets for arms. But this expansion has required governments to blur distinctions between internal and external security, and to shift the way violence is organised in society.[12] This shift would not be possible without a discursive reframing of who are considered to be 'enemies', which requires an expansion beyond the traditional targets of warfare (such as hostile countries) to non-traditional ones (such as internal populations that threaten existing social 'orders'). These new state concerns have led to the importation of practices used in external intelligence-gathering, such as excessive secrecy, into internal policing. The nature of enemies has shifted – no longer are they whole nations, but fuzzier constituencies that are profiled as threats. Law enforcement concerns are being cast increasingly as national security concerns, which suggests that a less overtly violent and more disciplinary surveillance state is under construction.[13] Forms of social control have shifted from who has the most tanks and guns to who has the most intelligence. These factors have created conditions for the development of an industrial base for surveillance, allowing for its rapid expansion and even universalisation.[14]

The increasingly powerful surveillance industry has a vested interest in keeping these new markets for its products alive, creating powerful commercial incentives to expand the trade in mass surveillance equipment. The possibility of losing massive public spending on weapons has established powerful incentives for manufacturers to shift production from military to civilian uses: hence the rise in the number of dual-use technologies. Producers of mass surveillance also play an important consultancy role for government, creating revolving doors between industry and government that are potentially replete with conflicts of interest:[15] a case in point being former NSA director Mike McConnell, who later became vice chairman of Snowden's former employer, Booz Allen Hamilton.[16]

Given the powerful forces at work in promoting the expansion of surveillance, individuals and organisations seeking to resist unaccountable surveillance are going to have a tough fight on their hands. They will need to have a deep understanding of the factors that have driven this expansion, a keen sense of how to create public awareness about the dangers, and highly developed advocacy skills to be able to mount an effective pushback. This chapter will explore some of the key strategies and tactics used by anti-surveillance activists, the underlying concepts they work with and the effectiveness of their activism.

CONTEMPORARY PRIVACY STRUGGLES: ACTORS, STRATEGIES AND TACTICS

Resistance to surveillance can take place at the individual and collective levels. At the individual level, tactics may range from more passive forms of resistance to more active ones. For instance, people can resist invasions of their right to privacy by engaging in what James C. Scott has termed everyday forms of resistance, where less well-organised, weaker and more peripheral citizens may use 'foot-dragging, evasion, false compliance, pilfering, feigned ignorance, slander and sabotage' to express their discontent.[17] When applied to the digital world, internet users may refuse to use privacy-invading applications or hardware, resist providing their voice prints or fingerprints to the authorities or 'spoof' fingerprints to fool biometric systems, provide no, false or misleading information, or refuse to register their subscriber information module (SIM) cards or register them under false names. For instance, in Mexico, a SIM card registration process was resisted by over seventeen million subscribers. In an act of civil disobedience, over five thousand people protested by subscribing their SIM cards under the name of the President.[18]

Increasingly, individual acts of resistance also include encrypting communications to make surveillance more difficult, using tools that anonymise browsing, such as TOR (software that allows users to browse anonymously on the internet), and not using company hardware or applications that take cavalier approaches to their users' privacy. However, the use of these tools is purely voluntary and at the discretion of the individual, who may not have the technical knowledge to be able to use them or even know that they exist. While the relevant authorities may be irritated by these tactics, they are unlikely to result in substantive challenges to broader surveillant forms of governance, which would require more organised responses. Nevertheless, there are signs that more users are changing their communications practices in the wake of the Snowden revelations, with more people taking steps to hide their communications from the government.[19]

At the collective level, privacy advocacy has traditionally been based mainly in the US, where many of the well-funded groups are to be found (such as the Electronic Frontier Foundation, or the EFF; the Electronic Privacy Information Center, or EPIC; and the American Civil Liberties Union, or the ACLU).[20] The problem civil society faced in mounting organised opposition in the wake of the Snowden revelations was that while they could appeal to the internationally recognised right to privacy, they lacked clarity on what this right meant when applied to communications surveillance in the digital age. In an attempt to reach such clarity, they developed a set of thirteen principles called the International Principles on the Application of Human Rights to Communications Surveillance, otherwise known as the Necessary and Proportionate Principles. At their launch in 2013 at the UN Human Rights Council, over four hundred organisations worldwide endorsed them. The initiating organisations also broadened the range of anti-surveillance actors beyond those of the 'usual suspects', drawing support from organisations and individuals from around the world, although with a bias towards the US and Europe. While the signatories represented a broad range of actors, there was a clear bias towards media freedom and civil liberties organisations, as well as technology, digital rights and legal organisations and experts. The challenge this new movement faced was to translate this spurt of energy into an organised form and to sustain it.

The Principles were updated in 2014, to ensure that communications surveillance practices would adhere to international human rights law. The Principles state that any surveillance law needs to comply with the principle of legality, must serve a legitimate aim and be adequate for the fulfilment of this aim. It must also be necessary, proportional to the level of threat faced by a country and determined by a competent judicial authority following due process. Users have a right to be informed that their communications have been surveilled, and public oversight involving transparency must apply to communications surveillance. States should not compel communications service providers to build surveillance capacities into their systems, and they should also put in place safeguards against illegitimate access to these systems and the information that flows through them. Where mutual assistance from other states is sought, the available standards with the highest levels of protection should apply.[21] These standards provided a useful framework for advocacy against unaccountable communications surveillance, and allowed for a generalisation of grievances against these practices. At the same time, while it made the establishment of the broadest possible coalitions possible that did not alienate groups who might not share the political perspectives of privacy activists, it also risked depoliticising the problem, as it failed to locate the problem within the broader context of the growth of surveillant capitalism and inequality.

In this regard, many in organised civil society have argued for stronger privacy protections for people's personal data through laws protecting informational privacy. For instance, Privacy International has argued that data protection laws are needed to protect personal information from abuse by governments and commercial companies.[22] To this end, many countries have set up data protection or privacy commissioners to ensure privacy protections are upheld by public and private actors. Some countries began to enact data protection laws in the 1970s and 1980s, and by November 2016 over a hundred countries had passed data protection laws, and over forty countries were developing draft legislation.[23] Many of these laws incorporate the basic principles of data protection outlined in the Fair Information Practice Principles (FIPPs), which emerged from the US government in the 1970s, and which were incorporated into the Organisation for Economic Co-operation and Development (OECD) Guidelines on the Protection of Privacy. These principles limit the collection and processing of personal data, and require the consent of the person whose data is being collected, who also has the right to know that data is being collected about him or her. They also commit data controllers to use the data only for the purposes for which it was collected, unless the data subject has granted permission for other uses, and they require the data processor to be responsible for complying with these principles.[24] Other Fair Information Practice Principles have been developed, which range from minimalist to maximalist, but the ones aligned to the OECD Guidelines have become the most prominent as foundational principles for data protection or privacy commissioners tasked with enforcing privacy and data protection laws.

However, when put into practice, these principles have not necessarily served the struggle for privacy very well, as they have prioritised individual control over personal data, while failing to address broader societal pressures exerted on the right. In doing so, these principles have individualised the problem and reduced it to sets of narrow, technical formulae that may not work well, and may even become dysfunctional. The activities of privacy commissioners tend to be premised on the control theory of privacy – as articulated by Alan Westin – that emphasises the right of individuals to exercise control over their personal information. In terms of this theory, individuals are asked to make choices (and often very few at that) about what happens to their data, but with little understanding of the real issues at stake, as data controllers skilfully bury them in legalese. However, as the underlying theory is premised on individual behaviour to enforce privacy safeguards, the principles fail to consider the massive obstacles that individuals face when attempting to enforce this right. For instance, very few people are able to understand the increasingly complex privacy notices that companies provide; this skews individual decision-making towards those with more resources or higher levels of education, and who can access legal advice, which in turn makes this form of privacy one that only a select few can and do enjoy. Consumers are also unlikely to know if information in the possession of a data controller has been misused; this calls into question the effectiveness of complaints mechanisms. By creating the impression that individuals do, in fact, have control over their own data, the principles ignore the power differentials between institutions and individuals that may make the exercise of this control difficult. They also fail to consider whether particular forms of surveillance should be taking place at all. Broad-ranging exclusions on grounds such as national security render data protection principles all but useless in the most controversial areas of data governance, where protections are often most needed. When these factors are taken together, it is hardly surprising that an overemphasis on procedural protections for privacy, rather than substantive ones, has made little difference to the overall protection of the right. In fact, it could be argued that privacy commissioners create the illusion of information control, rather than actual control.[25]

The most serious flaw of data protection laws is that they often fail to hold governments to account for data breaches in the same way that private sector companies are held accountable. A former adviser to Canada's Privacy Commissioner, Michael Geist, has argued that the Canadian government shared intelligence with other governments that went far beyond what was needed to investigate terrorism or other serious crimes, and that the government lacked the political will to address the privacy implications of these practices. While, increasingly, large communications companies like Google and Vodaphone were releasing annual transparency reports about the number of times they had been approached to share personal information, the government was not following suit and releasing similar reports.[26] According to documents leaked by Snowden, in the US an internal audit found that the NSA broke privacy rules thousands of times.[27] To all intents and purposes, national security has trumped informational privacy laws.

In addition to seeking legal protections through ensuring the enactment of data protection laws, privacy advocates have mounted legal challenges to enforce privacy rights, initially through complaints-receiving bodies on surveillance matters and, if these did not succeed, through the courts. This strategy has yielded mixed results, with the most positive being achieved in Europe, through the European Court of Human Rights. In the UK, several legal challenges have succeeded, and many of these have been brought by NGOs such as Privacy International and Liberty. Much of their work has focused on lodging complaints with the IPT, and then appealing against unsatisfactory decisions. As a result of the Snowden revelations and of sustained advocacy by NGOs, the number of complaints received by the IPT has grown by over 250 per cent, and increasing public scrutiny of this formerly little-known body has placed it under pressure to hold more hearings in public and communicate its findings more widely.[28]

Overall, though, the IPT has been unwilling to reconsider the intelligence agencies' arguments for mass surveillance powers. Privacy International, joined by several internet companies, has brought a complaint about GCHQ's use of bulk hacking outside the country, but this was not successful as the IPT refused to rule on the matter, leading to its being referred to the European Court. However, during the case GCHQ did admit that it undertook hacking to obtain information, modify target devices and carry out intrusive activities, which it had previously refused to confirm or deny.[29] Privacy International, the National Council of Civil Liberties and other organisations have also filed separate complaints about mass surveillance and intelligence-sharing with the UK government. The IPT ruled that intelligence-sharing between the US and the UK – where the UK accessed information from the PRISM and UPSTREAM programmes – was illegal because the rules governing these activities had not been made available publicly, but that once some of them were, the sharing was rendered legal, making this case the first in which the IPT had ruled against the UK intelligence agencies.[30]

This victory showed that with persistence, gains can be won even from institutions that appear to be captured by the very agencies they were meant to oversee. However, the organisations disputed the IPT's argument that the release of some of the relevant rules automatically rendered such intelligence-sharing lawful, especially given the fact that during the case GCHQ itself admitted to requesting and receiving bulk data without a warrant.[31] The IPT's unwillingness to rule on the GCHQ's current activities meant that the agency continued to enjoy massive powers to collect the personal data of large numbers of people without even a reasonable suspicion of their having been involved in a crime, and in secret. Another victory was when the IPT found that GCHQ and MI5 had secretly and illegally harvested massive amounts of personal information from various databases between 1998 and 2015, as these activities were not subject to sufficient supervision, but again stopped short of saying that the surveillance itself was unlawful, thereby confirming a trend in the tribunal's judgments to shy away from this all-important question.[32] The UK government has also been very canny in responding to IPT judgments: if a power is not authorised sufficiently in law, then the government merely changes the law to give the power a legal backdrop, without addressing the substantive issues about whether that power is appropriate in the first place.[33]

More substantive rulings have been forthcoming from the European Court of Human Rights, which rules on cases relating to the member states of the European Council according to the European Convention on Human Rights. The difficulty with taking mass surveillance cases to court, though, is that courts do not like considering cases in the abstract; as a result, there need to be specific complainants. But given the high levels of secrecy surrounding surveillance, communications users may not know if they are the targets of surveillance. On the other hand, investigatory tribunals such as the IPT require lower burdens of proof, as they both investigate and determine complaints. The court has addressed this problem by deciding to rule on complaints from people or organisations that are potentially at risk of being subjected to surveillance. It has also found Russia and Hungary guilty of contravening the European Convention on Human Rights through their surveillance practices, expressing concern in the case of Russia about insufficient oversight, and the potential for abuses when security services have direct, warrantless access to communications networks.[34] In the Russian case, brought by the editor Roman Zakharov, the court made a strong statement against mass surveillance, stating that it 'considers that a system, such as the Russian one, which enables the secret services and the police to intercept directly the communications of each and every citizen without requiring them to show an interception authorisation to the communications service provider, or to anyone else, is particularly prone to abuse. The need for safeguards against arbitrariness and abuse appears therefore to be particularly great.'[35]

In the case of Hungary, the European Court expressed concern about the overbroad powers wielded by the security services in conducting anti-terrorism surveillance, subjecting nearly all citizens to surveillance with no proper oversight, especially judicial oversight.[36] The court also recognised the right of users to be informed that their communications had been subjected to surveillance. However, unlike the ruling in the Russian case, this one took an ambiguous approach towards whether mass surveillance in principle should be considered unlawful, leaving the door open to its accepting the necessity of mass processing of data in future, provided certain safeguards were put in place.[37]

These rulings followed in the wake of two landmark rulings by the European Court of Justice (which rules on cases relating to EU members – the UK will no longer be subject to it once it leaves the EU). The first case found that the EU legislature had exceeded the legal requirement of proportionality when a data retention directive mandated the indiscriminate storage of metadata by public electronic communications companies for a period of between six and twenty-four months. It found that the very act of storage impacted on the right to privacy, even if the data had not been processed; however, the court remained silent on the appropriateness of data retention for law enforcement purposes.[38] The second case (involving an Austrian lawyer called Maximillian Schrems based in Ireland) found that the transfer of data to a country that did not have adequate privacy protections could not be condoned legally, even if the destination country claimed that it provided a 'safe harbour' for received data. In possibly the strongest legal statement yet against mass surveillance, as well as a slap on the wrist for the Irish Data Protection Commissioner, the court argued the following: 'In particular, legislation permitting the public authorities to have access on a generalised basis to the content of electronic communications must be regarded as compromising the essence of the fundamental right to respect for private life, as guaranteed by Article 7 of the [EU] Charter [of Fundamental Rights].'[39] While this judgment related to communications content, it was silent on the mass surveillance of metadata.

Legal precedents are still emerging from the US. A negative precedent was set shortly before the Snowden revelations in the *Clapper* judgment, in a major setback to civil society attempts to litigate around mass surveillance programmes. The US Supreme Court rejected a challenge to the FISA Amendment Act, which broadened the grounds for the surveillance of international phone calls and emails, although the judges were split along ideological lines.[40] The applicants included Amnesty International, the ACLU and a range of other civil society and journalism organisations. The majority opinion of the court argued that the applicants could not prove that they had suffered particularised, imminent harm from surveillance, and they were reminded that as the plaintiffs, they were under an obligation to provide concrete evidence of surveillance. As a result, they lacked standing to litigate on these matters, and the case was dismissed.[41] This setback underscored the more conservative approach of US judges to judicial oversight of executive surveillance powers, and put civil society organisations in an impossible position. Without clear and demonstrable 'victims', these organisations could not turn to the courts for relief; yet excessive secrecy prevents such information from coming into the public domain on national security matters.

After the Snowden leaks began, divisions opened up in the judiciary about mass surveillance, and consequently the legal position has remained unsettled. Immediately after the leaks revealed the existence of a top secret court order requiring the US company Verizon Wireless to collect the telephone records of millions of US customers, some of these customers (including the ACLU) brought a lawsuit against President Barack Obama, the NSA and others, alleging that the bulk collection of their phone and internet metadata was illegal. Federal Judge Richard J. Leon upheld their case, delivering a stinging rebuke of the NSA's bulk collection programme as being most likely unconstitutional, describing it as 'almost Orwellian', and ruling that in this case the plaintiffs did have standing as they could demonstrate a clear interest. However, the judgment was reversed and remanded back to the district court. In 2015, the US Court of Appeals for the Federal Circuit rejected this ruling and found that the bulk collection of metadata was illegal on the grounds that innocent people were targeted.[42] This was the most significant court victory in the US to date, and suggested that the courts had been revitalised by the Snowden revelations. In response, the House of Representatives passed the US Freedom Act, which limited bulk collection, and restricted law enforcement agencies to more targeted surveillance, although other provisions have arguably broadened their surveillance powers.[43] The year before, the Obama administration also issued a presidential policy directive announcing policy reforms aimed at limiting the circumstances under which signals intelligence could be collected to genuine national security situations, and not for purposes of curtailing dissent; however, this directive has been criticised as weak and easy to revoke by another President.[44] At the time of writing, other legal challenges to the US government's surveillance powers were still unfolding. While it remains to be seen what the election of Donald Trump as the new US President, and the shift from a Democratic to a Republican administration, will mean for the fight for accountable surveillance, it could well entail a reversion to more conservative judgments that are more deferential to the executive.

With respect to the US FISC, privacy advocates have attempted to address its bias towards the very spy agencies it is meant to preside over, by arguing that FISC should include a special public advocate. This person would have the powers to interrogate cases before the courts, engage in discovery of relevant evidence, brief the court on matters relevant to current cases (including technically complex matters), and appeal against adverse rulings. Such an advocate would make sure that court decisions were debated vigorously even if the court processes took place behind closed doors.[45] Privacy advocates have noted that the European Commission for Democracy through Law has argued that an internal privacy advocate in a secret court process could raise arguments on behalf of people who have nothing to do with the investigations at hand, but whose metadata was nevertheless being intercepted. In the case of content, the agencies might use selectors that could be attributed to an individual, and in those cases the advocate could ensure that the court strengthened its justification requirements.[46] As surveillance issues have become highly technical, a public advocate could also introduce expert technical evidence into court to inform proceedings on matters with which the judges might not be conversant.[47] Furthermore, in its standards for democratic oversight of intelligence agencies, a team linked to the University of Amsterdam's Institute for Information Law have argued that oversight needs to incorporate the adversary principle, which they point out is a basic rule of law principle. The introduction of a public advocate into the system could be one way of incorporating this principle into strategic surveillance oversight, without necessarily compromising the need for secrecy in the process.[48] While the Freedom Act has provided for an amicus curiae role, this differs from the public advocate role in that these individuals do not have the right of consistent representation, as the court can rule an amicus inadmissible or inappropriate, particularly if the legal issue is not one the court considers novel or significant. The amicus will only enjoy restricted access to information relating to current cases, which could limit his ability to participate fully and even counter the state's legal arguments, and the amicus also does not play a meaningful role in deciding whether the FISC's decisions should be taken on legal review.[49]

Another strategy adopted by privacy advocates has been to lobby various UN bodies to adopt positions on various aspects of surveillance. On this level, the advocates have met with considerable success. In the wake of the Snowden revelations, the Special Rapporteur on the rights to freedom of assembly and expression emphasised the importance of privacy for freedom of expression and, within this, the essential role of encryption and anonymity for the privacy of communications.[50] The UN General Assembly also adopted a resolution entitled 'the Right to Privacy in the Digital Age'. While the resolution stopped short of condemning surveillance practices, it expressed concern about the impact that surveillance, especially mass surveillance, may have on the enjoyment of human rights. It also reaffirmed the right to privacy, and the right of people to enjoy the same rights online as they do offline, and recognised the open nature of the internet. It called on states to respect privacy and to review their surveillance procedures, and requested the High Commissioner to submit a report to the UN Human Rights Council and, ultimately, the General Assembly on privacy and surveillance. The report's authors expressed concern about countries engaging in surveillance, but not providing adequate legislative safeguards, as weak safeguards and poor accountability increased the potential for abuse. They noted that while the report was an important first step, they acknowledged that much more work needed to be done to develop mechanisms to ensure that surveillance practices complied with international human rights law.[51] The Human Rights Council also appointed its first Special Rapporteur on the right to privacy, Joseph Cannataci, who began the process of elaborating on these mechanisms in a preliminary report to the council, which referred rather optimistically to the Schrems and the Zakharov cases (mentioned above) as 'the beginning of the judicial end for mass surveillance'.[52] He argued that the UK Investigatory Powers Bill failed the judicial tests set by these two cases and expressed concern that the government would be setting a bad precedent for the rest of the world.[53] These efforts at the UN level are clearly bearing fruit in that a set of legal principles is in the process of being developed, and is bound to have great utility in the years to come as different countries review their legal protections (or lack of them) for privacy in the face of widespread surveillance.

At the international level, civil society has also focused on placing pressure on governments to impose export controls on surveillance equipment that qualifies as dual-use technology. The 2013 revision to the Wassenaar Arrangement (on export controls for arms and dual-use goods and technologies) to include IP-based surveillance equipment has greatly increased its utility for privacy advocates. The fact that 86 per cent of surveillance companies are located in countries that subscribe to the Wassenaar Arrangement makes this agreement even more important to the fight to control the spread of surveillance technologies.[54] Moreover, the 2013 additions to the Wassenaar Arrangement have been added to EU dual-use regulations, creating a further layer of compliance for European-based companies. At the same time, the surveillance industry has continued to grow by an estimated 20 per cent a year.[55] A specific coalition has been established to focus on campaigning against sales of mass surveillance technologies that do not have sufficient legal controls to prevent human rights abuses. Called the Coalition Against Unlawful Surveillance Exports, it seeks to encourage governments to regulate exports of mass surveillance technologies, and private sector companies to exercise responsibility in deciding to whom they sell such equipment, to prevent them from empowering authoritarian governments. However, the question does arise why the mass surveillance industry is booming if it is subject to unprecedented export controls. One of the problems is that the agreement does not have the status of a legally binding treaty, which means that countries can choose whether to, and how to, codify the Wassenaar Arrangement into domestic law. The EU has already implemented the Wassenaar Arrangement, and the US is in the process of doing so. An increasingly important surveillance player, Israel, has not subscribed to the Wassenaar Arrangement, although it has implemented its key features in exports, while not subscribing fully to all of them.

Companies like HackingTeam have argued that their surveillance software does not qualify as a weapon, and is therefore not regulated by the arrangement.[56] In fact, the application of the Wassenaar Arrangement has been controversial as it could also cover IP-based monitoring systems that have a more general application and that could be used to improve network security. In such situations, the arrangement may well work against one of the very objectives it is attempting to realise, namely greater online security, which is an important precondition for privacy. However, these arguments have been debunked on the basis that the definitions of the types of products that are covered are narrow enough to prevent products that have more benign or even positive uses from being caught in the net.[57] Some efforts on the export control front are bearing fruit, but it remains to be seen how the US responds, and whether this arrangement can be elevated to treaty level and how many countries domesticate the arrangement into law.

THE ROLE OF MULTILATERAL PLATFORMS ON SURVEILLANCE AND INTERNET GOVERNANCE

The Wassenaar Arrangement is not the only multilateral platform that has been used to respond to surveillance in the wake of the Snowden revelations. Other forums took place, focusing on the broader principles that should guide the development of the internet in the wake of these revelations, including NETmundial and the Stockholm Internet Forum (which preceded the Snowden revelations). The United Nations Educational, Scientific and Cultural Organisation (UNESCO) also launched a research project to identify internet first principles, revolving around the concept of 'internet universality'. The Internet Governance Forum, established in the wake of the 2006 World Summit on the Information Society, continues to meet and debate the future of internet governance.

Traditional communications surveillance was confined to plain old telephones and, more recently, mobile phones (or cellphones). As its use became more widespread, state spy agencies began to recognise the internet as a surveillance tool that would allow them access to unprecedented amounts of information. Initially invented as a communications tool for the US military, the internet became popularised as the first truly global medium of communication in the 1990s. At the time, its founders insisted on some important first principles to ensure that the internet was maintained as a global public resource. These included ensuring that its architects used freely available standards that everyone could build on, and ensuring that the various components of the internet were interoperable. All data was supposed to be treated equally, irrespective of its contents, so that the internet could remain a level playing field for all its users (the 'net neutrality' principle). To all intents and purposes, the internet was meant to be a self-managed network of users, designed for communication and collaboration, and its publicness was meant to be central to its nature as a communications medium.[58]

However, since those heady days, governments and corporations have enclosed the internet in various ways, in the process compromising these foundational principles: governments by controlling internet content through filtering and censorship, and at the same time conducting surveillance of internet users on a worldwide scale – thereby threatening other countries' sovereignty – while corporations have commodified internet traffic by selling users' data to advertisers. Several powerful governments, notably the US, continue to champion internet freedom, subscribing to a free market ideology that does not problematise sufficiently the question of who controls the internet. In fact, Snowden exposed the hypocrisy of the US and other Five Eyes countries in supporting internet freedom rhetorically, while in practice promoting mass surveillance that went far beyond what was needed to fight international terrorism. The Snowden documents also revealed the extent to which internet companies were willing to collaborate in surveillance programmes uncritically.

One of the thorniest issues about internet control concerns the body that manages the domain name system for internet. Currently managed by the Internet Corporation for Assigned Names and Numbers (ICANN), this institution was established by the US Department of Commerce in 1998, and has become extremely powerful as it controls the reach of the internet as a global commons.[59] ICANN has remained controversial in that, while it operates at arm's length from the US government, the department still maintains crucial oversight and control functions, particularly through the Internet Assigned Numbers Authority (IANA) functions contract.

Several governments in the global South, especially some of the so-called BRICS countries (Brazil, Russia, India, China and South Africa), have complained that, while the US gave birth to the internet, its status as a truly global medium makes even indirect US control inappropriate; consequently, they have argued that a new governance model needs to be explored that reflects the global nature of the medium. These complaints have intensified in the wake of the Snowden revelations as more countries become concerned about the US's control over the internet being abused by the country to expand its global influence. This it could do by pressuring ICANN to create or remove online property. To its credit, though, the US did not use its influence to demand the removal of WikiLeaks's domain name, presumably because it feared a backlash from countries that were already concerned about US control of the internet. While some of the BRICS countries have called for greater state involvement in internet governance issues and multilateral decision-making, others have even argued for greater UN involvement as an antidote to US and corporate control.

In an attempt to prevent attempts to control the internet by other governments, the US has committed itself to establishing ICANN as an independent entity, run according to the principle of 'multi-stakeholder governance'. The race to establish such a model is on, as the US Department of Commerce indicated that it did not intend to renew its contract with ICANN for the management of the domain name system, in the wake of controversies about this institution. On the surface of things, this principle looks attractive, as it appears to offer a 'touchy-feely' form of democratic control, in which a global entity is established which uses open, transparent and consensus-building decision-making, and where internet stakeholders meet one another as equals. However, the multi-stakeholder approach is unlikely to deliver truly democratic control of the internet. While this model remains relatively vague, the ground rules set by the US government for relinquishing control will ensure that it adopts operating procedures and principles acceptable to it. The model will limit government involvement, and, where it does become involved, it will operate on an equal footing with other stakeholders, such as business and civil society. However, the US can afford to relinquish control as it will have approved the new body's rules of engagement. Furthermore, the danger of a consensus-based model is that groups that have diametrically opposed interests (corporations and consumers, for instance) could block decision-making simply by refusing to agree, which may paralyse this aspect of internet governance. In any event, the de facto control of the US through its control over other internet governance organisations, as well as the world's major internet companies, is almost certainly assured even if a new multi-stakeholder body is established.[60] And if this happens, then the worldwide struggle against surveillance will become even harder.

CONCLUSION

In the dying days of 2016, the UK Parliament passed the Investigatory Powers Bill into law, despite significant opposition from digital rights and privacy groups. According to research conducted by academics at Cardiff University, in the campaign against the Bill too much attention was paid to specialist lobbying and advocacy work, and not enough to broader public awareness-raising and mobilisation. Organised formations and social movements that focused on a range of social justice issues were not engaged in the campaign, and consequently felt alienated from it. In spite of the fact that many activists expected to be subjected to surveillance, organised responses to surveillance were left to expert communities rather than being integrated into broader activist concerns.[61] The mainstream press tended to be pro-surveillance, as they were dominated by the voices of politicians, and the public became resigned to security discourses as an inevitable feature of a landscape where terrorist threats were real and present. As a result, there was no significant mass opposition.[62] This analysis suggests that anti-surveillance campaigns that are driven by specialists, and that eschew, or do not pay sufficient attention to building effective mass opposition, will be doomed to fail. According to Gus Hosein, the campaign against the Investigatory Powers Bill was inadequate for a number of reasons. In spite of the fact that the UK has a strong tradition of grassroots activism, and highly successful activism at that, privacy advocates did not reach out to parliamentarians and lobby them, and failed to engage the more conservative media in the UK. While *The Guardian* became the paper of record of the Snowden revelations, the issue was mostly marginalised in the media discourse. The narrowness of the media discourse was in contrast to the earlier campaign against the smart ID card, in which Hosein had been involved. This campaign engaged the spread of media across the political spectrum, leading to widespread cynicism about ID cards. According to Hosein:

> We have to own some of the failure [around the Investigatory Powers Act], which is we made this entirely about intelligence agencies, we made this all about mass surveillance, we didn't articulate a positive framing of the issue, we didn't get into *The Telegraph* or *The Times* or the *Daily Mail*. This is in spite of the fact that the [Investigatory Powers] Bill contained similar powers, if not the exact same powers that two years before had been stymied by the lib-dems [the Liberal Democrats], and ... yet the same media and the parties that admonished the government for these exact same powers in 2013, came out in support of it. When it was post-Snowden, and *The Guardian* took to owning the story, and with the chaos in the Labour party, there was no similar dissension on it.
>
> It's not easy to frame it [the Bill] positively. There were powers in there that you wouldn't want any government having, apart from your own. For example we can frame the struggle as being one for secure devices, not just that government is trying to stop bad people. [We needed to say], you are going to be affected by this in the following ways. [In the campaign] we didn't relate to the British lived experience. Privacy advocates and technology rights advocates in the old days were accustomed to not having any friends, so we worked really hard to get the message across. But now tech issues have become cool, we have our own media for crying out loud, we have our circuits, and we intermingle with each other. There isn't the same sense of need to reach out. There's a comfort in our worldview, a liberal NGO club that doesn't attempt to get into the right wing media.[63]

For Hosein, a narrow approach towards the advocacy around the bill, where advocates focused on their own circles of influence, meant that they were unable to have a significant impact on the public discourse, which largely accepted the need for expansive counter-terrorism measures. Ironically enough, in spite of the increased resources that flowed to privacy work, especially in the wake of the Snowden revelations, their public traction did not necessarily increase. Advocates failed to create doubt in the public debate about the necessity of these measures. All the same, the approach of limiting surveillance largely to a specialist community did have its own logic, in that it was difficult for broader movements to focus on a wide spread of issues, as well as surveillance.

It should be noted that some real gains are being made in the European courts, but with the UK having decided to exit from the EU, it is unclear how much attention will be paid to European Court rulings in future. It is possible that the UK will want to embrace the court's rulings in future to argue that it still remains part of the vanguard of international human rights law.[64] According to the Privacy International legal officer, Scarlet Kim, there have been notable gains, but key issues relating to the lawfulness of mass surveillance still remain to be decided in a key European Court of Human Rights case. According to Kim:

> What progress has been made post-Snowden? The most positive developments are around transparency and data and retention. These came from a lot of different places, and came about through court cases. The IPT started requiring additional transparency about the type of surveillance being undertaken. Of course, this had its limits as the agencies don't have to give over information to the IPT. But they have released information in response to a number of our claims. They have also released a draft code of practice [on equipment interference]. We've also got some transparency about their [GCHQ's] policies and procedures [on bulk personal datasets].
>
> In the context of Zakharov and Schrems, the court started articulating some basic principles around bulk surveillance, namely individualised reasonable suspicion, prior authorisation and notification of individuals that have been subjected to surveillance. So, if you have to review the positive developments that have come out of our cases, they have ensured the enforcement of the safeguards. Those are really blockbuster judgments, but there is a question about how do you judge a country like the UK, so it'll be really interesting to see what the court has to say about the necessity of the safeguards.[65]

The UK's experiences with the Investigatory Powers Act bring to the fore the need to take movement-building seriously as part of anti-surveillance work, and the precondition of such work is public awareness-raising. Furthermore, a precondition for public awareness-raising is using empowering concepts that can make a seemingly unassailable problem challengeable. Relying on privacy articulated as a 'me, me, me' right is unlikely to provide a compelling enough basis for collective action, and, after all, collective action is what is needed to give campaign positions social force. Powerful social actors, especially those in government, are unlikely to be persuaded to adopt different positions purely on the basis of good arguments; this is especially so if their material interests are threatened by those arguments.

It is clear that the surveillance industry has become extremely powerful, as it provides an alternative outlet for the profits soaked up by the conventional arms industry, which is now in decline. These challenges suggest that a theory of agency in relation to surveillance needs to be developed. It needs to ask and answer the question, What collective behaviour is needed to rein in unaccountable surveillance? In order to reach this point, it is necessary to identify the social forces that are most likely to bring about this change. While the capitalist state incorporated elements of surveillance in earlier periods in history, technological developments have since allowed an unprecedented expansion of the surveillance capacities of the state. Government uses of these capacities have moved far beyond their stated purposes of fighting crime and terrorism. As neoliberalism has intensified inequality, so there has been an increase in the number of the unemployed and those in insecure work, youths (especially urban youths), black people, Muslims, and lesbian, gay and transgender people. In the earlier phase of industrial capitalism, it was fairly easy to identify the social force that had the most to gain and the least to lose from challenging exploitation and oppression, and that therefore constituted the main motor for progressive social change: the organised working class and their allies. The post-industrial era saw new social movement theorists make claims for a broader range of actors as drivers of progressive change, including cross-class identity-based movements. However, while the shift towards more cross-class social movements may have been more apparent in the global North, class-based movements remained active in many parts of the global South, and class never really lost its salience in analyses of social processes.

In conditions of neoliberal precarity, where the industrial working class has declined in power and, with it, their organised formations, it is less easy (but not impossible) to identify the most likely motors of potentially emancipatory social change, including anti-surveillance work. These must surely be the very 'problem populations' that are the targets of surveillance, as they have a compelling interest in resisting unaccountable surveillance. With the advent of the 2008 global recession, anti-austerity movements have developed in different parts of the world, and these movements, too, have an immediate interest in anti-surveillance work.

But in order to make the work relevant to these movements, it is necessary to find ways of 'mainstreaming' this work in the everyday campaigns that bring ordinary people into organised social and political actions. Of necessity, working-class communities are often highly organised; so, with some creative campaigning, it should not be difficult to relate surveillance and its dangers to mobilisations in defence of public services, for jobs and free education for young people. The important part of campaigning is to take people where the campaign finds them and to relate the work to existing struggles on the ground. In doing so, the role of surveillance in the creation and reproduction of inequality would need to be emphasised, which is what the critical perspective implies. The conflict inherent in social inequality should drive social change, as it is this conflict that is behind the massive expansion of the global security apparatuses, industries and discourses. If resistance to this expansion is going to be effective, it needs to provide a political voice to the otherwise voiceless, and this involves articulating an understanding of privacy that makes most sense to these social groups. This means that privacy as an organising concept is likely to focus less on privacy as an individual right, and more on its content as an enabler of collective rights. So, if privacy is denied these actors, this will prevent collective discussion and organisation.

The forces of reaction are growing stronger by the day in the very countries that lie at the heart of the surveillance industry, and if they are going to be challenged effectively, then anti-surveillance and pro-privacy campaigners clearly need to 'do' their work differently. This needs to start with mapping those social forces and their organisations that are making progressive socio-economic and democratic claims, and placing them at the centre of anti-surveillance work. In this regard, there seems to be much to gain from drawing links between social movement studies, political economy and surveillance studies – fields of study that tend to operate in silos. Some possible synergies in this regard will be explored in the next chapter, which focuses on the context of surveillance and social control in South Africa.

3

The context of surveillance and social control in South Africa

Since the Marikana massacre in 2012 – when scores of mine workers were shot by the police after a protracted strike – several journalists, academics and media commentators have argued that South Africa is reverting to a repressive state. They have interpreted violence at the hands of the police generally, and Marikana specifically, as signs that the post-apartheid social order can no longer be held in check through consent alone. They argue that the ruling African National Congress (ANC) and other powerful actors have concluded that naked violence is now needed to stabilise increasingly fractious social relations.[1] Some have even used the term 'police state' to describe post-Marikana South Africa.[2]

As a police state is one in which the police act as a political force to contain social dissent using arbitrary force, it is an important manifestation of a more repressive state; another is a society ruled by its military. In the past, the apartheid state used its intelligence services – especially those in the police and military – to identify and target political activists, and this chapter sketches some of this history. How likely is South Africa to descend into a state of full-blown repression, in which intelligence is misused once again to repress dissent violently? How likely is it that there will be more Marikanas? This chapter engages with these broader questions.

THE INTELLIGENCE SERVICES IN APARTHEID SOUTH AFRICA

South Africa's intelligence services date back to its establishment as a Republic in 1961, although the South African police had developed intelligence capabilities before then, under the watchful eye of the UK. The declaration of the armed struggle by the major liberation movements in the wake of the 1960 Sharpeville massacre also added impetus to the apartheid government's decision, as it felt that this new threat could only be countered effectively through intelligence. The South African Defence Force (SADF) established its own intelligence arm, in the form of the Directorate of Military Intelligence (DMI), the year after the declaration of the Republic, but infighting between the police and military agencies led the government to form an entirely separate civilian intelligence agency devoted to national intelligence, Republican Intelligence (RI). This agency was expanded and transformed into the Bureau of State Security (BOSS) in 1969, and its mandate included the collection and analysis of intelligence, although it developed operational elements, too.[3]

The growth of BOSS fuelled resentment in the police and the military, and increased inter-agency competition, to the point where the agencies started to spy on one another. As a result, in the 1970s the government clarified that BOSS was the prime intelligence agency in South Africa, responsible for strategic intelligence, and it also established the State Security Council (SSC) to co-ordinate the work of the feuding intelligence agencies. The SSC was meant to be subordinate to cabinet and advise it on intelligence matters. Strategic intelligence is distinct from tactical and operational intelligence, in that governments can use it to formulate high-level policy and strategy, while the agencies generally use tactical intelligence to formulate plans to implement strategy. Strategic intelligence is the visionary component of the intelligence cycle. Consequently, it should be developed by civilian agencies that are not operational, as agencies that both develop and act on intelligence experience intolerable conflicts of interest. Yet the various intelligence agencies in South Africa were all highly operational, engaging in counter-insurgency attacks against the liberation movements and their supporters in the regional states.

When P.W. Botha became President of South Africa, he elevated the SSC above cabinet as the strategic decision-maker on policy. He also promoted the DMI to the level of lead intelligence agency, responsible for the strategic intelligence function, in spite of the fact that he had restructured the civilian intelligence function by replacing BOSS with the National Intelligence Service (NIS) – based on academic principles of passive intelligence-gathering – in the wake of a politically damaging scandal involving BOSS. This pro-military restructuring led to the widespread militarisation of society from the late 1970s onwards, and prevented the emergence of political (as opposed to military) solutions to South Africa's crisis, at least until the late 1980s. This was because the military 'securocrats' – or senior officials in the security establishment (especially in the military), who exercised undue influence over national policy – saw the struggle against apartheid and capitalism in South

Africa through a counter-revolutionary lens requiring overwhelmingly military responses, with some concessions being granted to ensure limited incorporation of what were considered to be moderate black figures into the political system. The P.W. Botha regime also promoted the development of special operations units in the various intelligence agencies, to deal with the perceived revolutionary threat. These units conducted many covert operations against the liberation movements both inside and outside the country. They engaged in the full repertoire of dirty tricks against their enemies, including spreading disinformation about them, and engaging in kidnapping, arrest, torture, poisoning and assassination. As these units were meant to operate 'off the books', in that their operations were not meant to be traced back to the government, the most violent units were expected to raise their own funds as well. As a result, a unit like the notorious Civil Cooperation Bureau (CCB) morphed into a criminal outfit involved in trafficking drugs, diamonds and weapons, prostitution and extortion, in addition to engaging in extra-legal assassination of political activists.

As in many other countries, South Africa's signals intelligence capabilities were located in the military, as government considered cryptography to be a military function primarily. The SADF established a Signals Intelligence Unit as part of its tactical intelligence function.[4] Until 1975, GCHQ had a direct presence in South Africa, through the naval base in Simonstown, but it abrogated this role after the North Atlantic Treaty Organisation (NATO) imposed an arms boycott on the country. Reportedly, at the time both GCHQ and the NSA were accommodated at the South African Navy's listening post in Silvermine, Cape Town, which was located strategically between the Indian and Atlantic Ocean trade routes, and which monitored the movements of Russian and Chinese shipping around the Cape. This signals intelligence facility was built and paid for by NATO countries in 1973 in spite of mounting international pressure on them to cut ties with South Africa.[5] However, in terms of the UK–US agreement (the forerunner of the Five Eyes agreement), GCHQ retained responsibility for monitoring sub-Saharan Africa. As a result, it resorted to using its listening posts in British High Commissions in front-line states such as Swaziland, Zambia and Malawi, intercepting intelligence on South Africa after the Simonstown Agreements and collecting intelligence on the activities of the various liberation movements in the region, including the ANC, as well as South Africa's counter-insurgency activities in the front-line states. On balance, GCHQ's interventions supported apartheid and disadvantaged the front-line states, as the British feared that the Soviet and Cuban presence in the region might increase if South Africa's liberation movements became stronger. The UK and Germany also provided communications surveillance equipment to apartheid

South Africa, in spite of a 1977 UN arms embargo on the country, with Germany supplying most of the equipment. GCHQ and the apartheid government resumed a more explicit partnership in the 1980s, sharing intelligence about the activities of the ANC, including intelligence gathered from GCHQ's listening post in Zambia, where the ANC was headquartered for much of the time it was in exile. GCHQ had superior signals intelligence-gathering capabilities, and thus shared its intelligence on the ANC with South Africa, in return for information on Cuban and Soviet activities in the region.[6]

ANC INTELLIGENCE IN EXILE

The ANC also established its own intelligence capabilities in exile. According to the Truth and Reconciliation Commission (TRC), there was no evidence presented to it that the ANC's main rival in exile, the Pan Africanist Congress (PAC), had a security division responsible for dealing with suspected dissidents or infiltrators.[7] The ANC established defensive intelligence capabilities in 1969, called the Department of National Intelligence and Security, or 'NAT' (apparently shorthand for National Security), under the leadership of Moses Mabhida, after the organisation had suffered significant military losses.[8] At the time of its establishment and into the 1970s, NAT was small, with no formal structures, and focused mainly on providing security services to the office of the ANC president. But as the apartheid offensive intensified and new recruits flocked to join the ANC in wake of the Soweto uprisings and subsequent crackdowns, the ANC began to recognise that it needed more intelligence capacity. As a result, it established collaborative relationships with Soviet bloc countries – largely the USSR and East Germany – for military and intelligence training. These countries had a vested interest in seeing the collapse of apartheid and colonial domination around the world, given their commitment to proletarian internationalism. The liberation movements, in turn, were extremely grateful for these displays of solidarity, and forged close ties with countries in the Soviet bloc and with the non-aligned movement, which opposed the apartheid regime.

The USSR provided the most training to liberation movements, including the ANC, followed by the East German secret police (or Stasi, as they were known), which offered instruction from 1976 onwards in personal and building security, secret service methods and handling explosives, as well as counter-intelligence training, which emphasised the superiority of the Soviet system of communism over capitalism. By that stage, training courses also incorporated critiques of

Stalinism. Yet, the separation of the ANC cadres who were undergoing training from the broader society in the USSR prevented them from confronting many of the contradictions of the Soviet system, making them less critical of its basic claims of egalitarianism and fairness.[9] While the Stasi were not as well known for brutal forms of repression as their Russian counterparts, they specialised in 'spy on your neighbour' tactics to maintain social control, and consequently established one of the most extensive surveillance bureaucracies in the world, which included spying on ordinary citizens. Their network of informants allowed them to track down and persecute those who committed 'ideological subversion', or engaged in acts or expressions of dissent against the Soviet bloc.[10] There can be little doubt that these counter-intelligence tactics – which equated expressions of dissent with subversion – rubbed off on their trainees, but the human rights abuses that were to emerge in the ANC in exile cannot be attributed solely and simplistically to this training. According to the TRC, members of Umkhonto we Sizwe (MK) selected for intelligence work were sent to the USSR and East Germany in the late 1970s. The first camp commander of Quatro, Gabriel Mthembu, testified about the counter-intelligence training he underwent, and described the standard as high. Mthembu stated that the training 'emphasised that the use of force was counter-productive, and stressed the use of the intellect'.[11]

While the massive influx of new recruits from the 1976 uprisings was a huge boost to the military capacity of the ANC in exile, it also increased the risks of infiltration. According to the MK Chief of Staff, Chris Hani, when the apartheid state's assault on the movement intensified – including through infiltration and assassination – the ANC in exile began to suffer from what he described as hysteria and paranoia.[12] As a result, the ANC enhanced the institutional status of NAT by re-establishing it as a committee of a Revolutionary Council, responsible for directing the armed struggle in South Africa. However, in spite of these dire threats, it was only in the 1980s that NAT was restructured into a directorate of the ANC's National Executive Council with more formal and professional structures focusing on intelligence, security and the processing of information. The department also became responsible for strategic intelligence, analysing the direction of the apartheid government and developing a longer-term vision for the country's future based on its threat assessments.[13] The revamped department included intelligence and counter-intelligence units, as well as a security unit (which became known as Mbokodo, or the 'grinding stone'), a central evaluation unit and VIP protection. In undertaking this restructuring, the ANC aimed to separate its security from its military functions, turning the former into an intelligence-gathering outfit for the latter and for the ANC more generally. In reality, though, and controversially, MK developed a dual command structure, and eventually became subordinate to NAT operationally.[14]

According to Stephen Ellis, cadres began to allege that the NAT wielded enormous power, even to the point of beatings and killings:[15] an allegation that was echoed by several commissions of inquiry. NAT, and especially Mbokodo, developed a terrible reputation in the 1980s for moving beyond identifying and rooting out apartheid spies, to persecuting ANC dissenters and enforcing ideological conformity. Throughout the 1980s, Mbokodo was accused of human rights abuses in ANC camps in the front-line states, the most notorious of which was Quatro in Angola. A mutiny by MK members in 1984 led to NAT being accused of suppressing democracy by its own members who had participated in the mutiny; they pointed fingers at the ANC leadership for whipping up what has been called an 'internal-enemy-danger-psychosis'.[16] A subsequent internal commission of inquiry chaired by James Stuart made damning findings against NAT. It noted accusations that NAT had morphed into an army within an army, as it resorted to using force much too easily. In the process, the commission found that NAT had strayed from its original purpose of being the eyes and ears of the movement, and recommended that it be brought under more effective political control, with those responsible for the most serious human rights abuses being redeployed.[17] Corruption was a persistent blight on the ANC in exile, with some ANC members engaging in smuggling cars and drugs.[18]

In the wake of these controversies, and as prospects for secret negotiations with the apartheid government loomed, in 1987 NAT was restructured once again into the Department of Intelligence and Security (DIS), accounting to the National Executive Committee. Joe Nhlanhla became its head, and Jacob Zuma its deputy head and subsequently its head of intelligence. However, tensions between NAT and MK continued to bubble and eventually boiled over once again with the death by poisoning of a prominent MK member, Thami Zulu. Key ANC members attributed his death to the apartheid security forces, but there remained lingering suspicions that the movement itself was responsible.[19] The TRC was unable to make a finding either way.[20] According to Ellis, from 1987 onwards, intelligence became Zuma's main institutional base.[21] After the ANC returned from exile, another commission was established to inquire into NAT's excesses in exile. Chaired by a senior official in the ANC's legal department, Zola Skweyiya, the commission was set up after thirty-two people whom the ANC considered to be suspected spies and agents provocateurs were released by the movement. On their return to South Africa, some alleged ill-treatment at the hands of the ANC. The commission set up in the wake of their allegations concluded that the limited evidence provided to it pointed to shocking violations of the ANC's own code of conduct by the security department, and noted that there was deep unease in other ANC structures about this department's activities. They hoped that the problem would be remedied by the 1987 restructuring, and indeed it did improve somewhat, but the ANC's Officer for Justice, Zola Skweyiya, still expressed frustration with security officials who resisted being made accountable to the organisation's code of conduct. According to the commission, 'We were left with an overall impression that for the better part of the 80s, there existed a situation of extraordinary abuse of power and lack of accountability. Nobody was beyond the reach of the security apparatus.'[22] The commission compiled a list of those directly responsible for abuses in exile (which has not been made public), but it also argued that the leadership of NAT should be held politically responsible for failing to prevent abuses and creating a climate of impunity in the movement.[23] Another report into human rights abuses in exile, this time by Amnesty International, criticised the Skweyiya report for lacking independence and for its narrow terms of reference, and, while it praised the ANC for taking full responsibility for these abuses, it felt that the party lacked the will to bring those responsible to book. Nevertheless, the ANC endorsed the recommendation that no one who was implicated in these abuses should be allowed to hold positions of authority, including public office.[24] Jacob Zuma, who was head of counter-intelligence in exile from 1987 to 1993, played a key (and shadowy) role in all the events and processes investigated by the several commissions. In fact, the Motsuenyane Commission directly implicated Zuma in human rights abuses in exile committed by Mbokodo.[25]

There can be no comparison between the apartheid and ANC intelligence structures, as there is no moral equivalence. Nevertheless, some parallels present themselves. Both apartheid and ANC intelligence structures were operational, and resorted to violence readily. Both struggled to keep their intelligence structures accountable – with operatives engaging in underworld criminal activities – and both assumed great power over organisational policy. The apartheid government was defence intelligence-led, while the ANC's military arm and its intelligence arm were actually in tension and even in conflict. However, the centrality of the armed struggle for the ANC, rather than mass mobilisation, led to it adopting a substitutionist approach to liberation in which it de-emphasised democratic self-organisation, and this mistrust of democracy was reflected in the way its intelligence structure operated. As heroic as it was, the ANC's armed struggle was largely unsuccessful. On the other hand, the mass struggles led by workers and the youth inside South Africa did far more to challenge the apartheid regime than armed insurgency, as they made it impossible for the regime to maintain an ideological hold on the broader society.

But at the same time, continued widespread repression threatened to destroy South Africa, and even the regime could not afford the economic, political and social costs of complete collapse.

STATE SECURITY IN A DEMOCRATIC SOUTH AFRICA

In the late 1980s, the old bipolar order crumbled. The Soviet Union collapsed and, with it, Soviet bloc support for the armed struggles of liberation movements around the world. This development forced these movements to consider political solutions to their struggles. In the South African case, the apartheid state's own economic crises, precipitated in part by sanctions, meant that the government faced the prospect of entering into political discussions with the liberation movements, and especially the dominant ANC. However, such was the power of the intelligence community in P.W. Botha's South Africa that it was only once cabinet reasserted authority over the SSC, and the civilian NIS – the apartheid predecessor of the National Intelligence Agency (NIA) and, ultimately, the SSA – assumed greater control over strategic intelligence, that political solutions became imaginable. Given the shift in the balance of forces globally, P.W. Botha's 'securocrats' began to lose influence to reform-minded politicians and officials in the government, many of whom were located in the NIS and were at the forefront of secret exploratory talks with the ANC on the possibilities of a negotiated settlement. However, the ANC intelligence function was to become controversial during negotiations, for besides playing a leading role in talks, the organisation at the same time actively recruited moles inside the apartheid state and established underground structures inside South Africa. As a result of these actions, the apartheid government accused the ANC of bad faith, though it seems that the ANC was motivated by concerns that negotiations might fail and that it needed a 'Plan B' if they did, including a reversion to armed struggle.

The liberation movements and the apartheid government entered into negotiations on a range of transitional issues, including a new intelligence architecture for a democratic South Africa. The interim constitution, negotiated by a Transitional Executive Council (TEC), remained silent on the future shape of the civilian intelligence service. However, the TEC did engage in discussions about this issue with all the main intelligence structures, and established a Joint Coordinating Intelligence Committee (which in time to come became the National Intelligence Coordinating Committee). The committee's work gave rise to the 1994 White

Paper on Intelligence, which set out the policy framework for the democracy-era intelligence services, and informed the thinking of those who drafted the 1996 final Constitution.[26]

The White Paper advanced a new 'national security doctrine', informed by the human security definition of national security. The school of thought that underpins this definition became ascendant after the Cold War and made the argument that, given the cessation of Cold War hostilities, the most likely causes of insecurity were problems internal to a country, and came from non-conventional sources, such as poverty, unemployment, disease (including the HIV/AIDS pandemic) and environmental degradation. It argued for all issues that threaten human advancement to be considered possible threats to national security, and consequently for the individual citizen and his or her protection to become the main referent for national security policy, rather than the state and its protection. The authors of the White Paper embraced these arguments, aware as they were that, given South Africa's own apartheid history, the narrow, state-centric definition of national security could lead to the government abusing the security apparatus to protect itself or its ruling party from criticism, while failing to address the underlying factors that make society vulnerable.

The White Paper also proposed certain measures to lessen the potential for abuse of the intelligence apparatus and to ensure democratic accountability. Intelligence agencies were required not to accept any changes to the doctrines, structures and procedures of the national security framework unless approved of by a democratic process (namely through Parliament). Two security agencies – one focusing on domestic intelligence and the other on foreign intelligence – rather than a single one, were considered necessary to allow them to focus on their respective mandates and operate according to different line-function responsibilities. However, they were expected to share the same operational services, to avoid duplication. The domestic intelligence agency became the NIA and the foreign agency the South African Secret Service (SASS). The White Paper proposed parliamentary oversight of the services, through the Joint Standing Committee on Intelligence (JSCI). It also insisted on political neutrality, disallowing the services to be used to undermine, promote or influence any South African political party or organisation at the expense of another, and forbade intelligence interference in the normal political processes of other countries and the lawful political activities of individuals inside the country.[27] The White Paper emphasised as well the importance of transparency, arguing that a more open intelligence community could help to build trust in the services, after decades of abuse. Acceptable limits for secrecy should also be publicly debated, to build consensus on this tricky issue.[28]

The final Constitution, adopted in 1996, was largely in line with these key proposals. It included the human security definition of national security, which was captured thus: 'national security must reflect the resolve of South Africans … to live as equals, to live in peace and harmony, to be free from fear and want and to seek a better life'.[29] The Constitution also set out a framework for a democratic security dispensation, including transparency, civilian (and, more specifically, parliamentary) accountability of the intelligence services, respect for the Constitution and the principle of legality, and rejection of political partisanship. Its drafters required that national legislation establish a national co-ordinating structure for all intelligence services (which became the National Intelligence Coordinating Committee, or NICOC) and that these services be monitored by an Inspector General of Intelligence approved by Parliament.[30] This system of checks and balances was meant to ensure that the intelligence abuses that had taken place under apartheid would become impossible.

As a result of these changes, democratic South Africa has a very different intelligence architecture from the one that existed under apartheid. The NIA, and subsequently the SSA, became the lead agency on strategic intelligence matters through NICOC, which was made subordinate to cabinet. According to a document containing an organogram of the SSA, leaked to Al Jazeera news network, the SSA was based at the apex of civilian intelligence, with the foreign and domestic branches accounting directly to the SSA's Director General. The foreign branch includes intelligence management and foreign collection sub-branches, which suggests a particularly strong emphasis on the collection of foreign intelligence on African countries. The domestic branch includes intelligence and counter-intelligence sub-branches, with domestic intelligence incorporating economic intelligence as well as intelligence about South Africa's borders. The counter-intelligence sub-branch includes protective security (presumably VIP protection), intelligence clearance vetting, intelligence around special events, counter-terrorism and special operations. The communications surveillance functions of the SSA fall into a separate entity called National Communications (NC), which incorporates information and communications technology security (Communications Security, or COMSEC, previously a private entity, but incorporated into the SSA when it was established in 2009), signals intelligence collection and production, the Office for Interception Centres (OIC), and management services. The OIC undertakes targeted interceptions in terms of RICA. Presumably, the signals intelligence collection and production unit incorporates the NCC, COMSEC and OIC and renders services to other government departments (in the case of the OIC, to the South African National Defence

Force (SANDF), the SSA, the SAPS and the Financial Intelligence Centre), while the NCC is focused on providing signals intelligence to the SSA.[31]

The overall intelligence function is governed in terms of a triad of Acts passed in 1994: the Intelligence Services Act (which provided for the establishment of the NIA and SASS), the National Strategic Intelligence Act (which provided for the establishment of NICOC), and the Intelligence Services Oversight Act (which provided for the establishment of the JSCI, the parliamentary committee responsible for overseeing the intelligence services, as well as the Inspector General of Intelligence).

SUBVERSION EVERYWHERE: THE BALLOONING DOMESTIC INTELLIGENCE-GATHERING MANDATE

Given that national security has been defined so broadly in democratic South Africa – as freedom from fear and want – there was always a danger that the definition would be used to securitise more and more issues. This danger has come to pass, as the definition has provided justification for a massive expansion of the intelligence mandate and services, including political intelligence-gathering. In 2003, the Thabo Mbeki presidency required an expansion of the NIA's mandate, resulting in a directive that included political and economic intelligence. In the case of political intelligence, the NIA was to focus on 'the strengths and the weaknesses of political formations, their constitutions and plans, political figures and their roles in governance, etc.'.[32] By 2004, the intelligence services had ballooned in size, and personnel accounted for an unsustainable 74 per cent of the total domestic intelligence budget.[33] A year later, signs emerged that intelligence operatives were becoming embroiled in internal factional battles in the ANC: a problem that was proved to exist by a commission of inquiry, which partly blamed the culture of secrecy in the intelligence services as a source of the problem.[34] In the early 2000s, evidence also began to emerge of agents gathering intelligence on political activists. The heightened activities of these agents coincided with the establishment of social movements struggling for land and against the commodification of basic services, as well as with the expansion of the NIA's mandate. A social movement established to resist electricity and water cut-offs, the Soweto Electricity Crisis Committee (SECC), launched 'Operation Khanyisa', which involved illegally reconnecting residents to the electricity supply. The SECC also opposed the installation of pre-paid water meters by removing and destroying them. In 2005, members from the Vaal and Thembelihle branches informed the Anti-Privatisation Forum (APF) leadership that they had been approached by NIA operatives and offered money to become NIA informants about APF meetings and activities. They were asked not to report these approaches.[35]

Shortly after Zuma took office, the NIA and SASS were centralised into the SSA, in spite of the fact that the 1996 White Paper on Intelligence cautioned against such centralisation.[36] The SSA also justified its own establishment by referring to international intelligence failures. It argued that US intelligence agencies had failed to uncover the plot that led to the 9/11 terrorist attacks, because inter-agency competition for status and resources prevented them from co-operating with one another.[37] In order to court the favours of powerful politicians, US intelligence operatives stovepiped raw intelligence directly to them. In doing so, these operatives undermined their own professional intelligence analysts. The SSA maintained that it wanted to prevent catastrophic failures like these in South Africa, by consolidating all the services into one entity. The SSA also argued that its establishment amounted to consolidation, not centralisation, and fought tooth and nail for political intelligence-gathering to remain part of its mandate. This was in spite of the fact that the Matthews Commission of Inquiry into abuses of the intelligence services, established in 2006 by Minister of Intelligence Ronnie Kasrils, had argued that this mandate was almost always going to be abused to harass political critics. Kasrils set up the commission to provide him with recommendations about any policy or legislative changes that needed to be made to prevent such abuses from taking place again, and the commission finalised its report in 2008. Its contents are known because it was leaked to the media.[38] The SSA insisted that national security threats had to be dealt with, wherever they came from. Parliament mitigated the dangers of the political intelligence-gathering mandate being misused by forbidding the SSA to spy on individuals and organisations engaged in legitimate, lawful advocacy.[39]

Yet evidence of surveillance emerged again in the context of workers' struggles for higher wages in the platinum belt of South Africa, and there were also signs of collusion between intelligence operatives and private security firms linked to the mining industry. In October 2013, the Democratic Socialist Movement (DSM), affiliated to the Committee for a Workers' International, received a leaked risk assessment report originating from the private security firm Fidelity Security Services, which stated that a political party they had helped to establish ahead of the national elections, the Workers and Socialist Party (WASP), was active among the workforce of the Mogalakwena mine of Anglo American Platinum in Limpopo, and that they were planning a WASP meeting and labour action in the area. Most of the report was taken from news reports and press releases, but it also included information provided by 'a contact in WASP (DSM) in Rustenburg', as well as the names and telephone numbers of key WASP/ DSM organisers, including leading DSM activist Mametlwe Sebei. All this strongly suggested that the organisations had been infiltrated.[40] According to Sebei, he received several calls after the assessment was released, including one from the Crime Intelligence Division (CID) of the SAPS to find out if they had permission to organise a rally in the area. According to Sebei, these interactions made it clear that the security intelligence of the mining company was sharing information with the CID.[41]

Eight years down the line, has the establishment of the SSA led to a more effective intelligence product? It would appear not. Significant intelligence failures are not episodic; they are systemic. Granted, there have been intelligence successes, too. The fact that the services are making gains in the war against rhino poaching and other aspects of the illicit economy is an indication of this. But when rhino poaching is compared to the failures around the systematic capture of the state by corrupt elements, then the successes pale in the face of the failures.

The political intelligence-gathering mandate has also allowed the government to normalise spying on domestic political groupings on the most tenuous of grounds.[42] A document leaked to the media in 2016, apparently summarising the SSA's classified National Intelligence Priorities for 2014 – which are developed every year to guide the use of the state's surveillance capacities – stated that the SSA should investigate and engage in counter-planning for a 'so-called "Arab Spring" uprising prior to [the 2014 national] elections'.[43] The SSA claimed it would resort to the 'maximum use of covert human and technical means' to counter these threats.[44] The document's reference to the Arab Spring – a legitimate struggle against authoritarianism – is significant, as it implied that this protest wave in the Arab region was essentially illegitimate. In the South African context, the risk of such a priority straying from the covert surveillance of illegal political activity into legitimate activities should be self-evident: a risk that is compounded by the SSA's overly broad mandate, excessive secrecy, recent history of abuse of this mandate, and inadequate reforms to increase public accountability.

The doctrines that justify the expansion of domestic political intelligence-gathering need to be understood – surveillance decisions are not necessarily irrational, but draw on coherent bodies of thought. One of these is the 'colour revolution', which has been invoked by the ANC and State Security Minister David Mahlobo, and which has been developed into a full-blown intelligence doctrine. It is being used to construct new national security threats including NGOs and social movements, even if they are engaged in lawful advocacy, as well as journalists.

This term has its origins in the former Soviet Union and the Balkans, and refers to pro-democracy protests that took place in these regions from the early 2000s onwards, with the significant involvement of students and NGOs. The protests adopted particular colours or flowers to represent their struggles. The doctrine was developed by governments targeted by the protests to explain them and why they spread. It posits that protests have spread because Northern countries with imperialist agendas have sponsored them, and not because of the 'demonstration effect' (a well-recognised phenomenon in social movement theory, whereby protest in one locality organically inspires protests in another).

Regimes that were targeted by the protests adopted similar repertoires of colour revolution prevention strategies (or 'anti-colour insurance' strategies), after a process of authoritarian learning. Authoritarian leaders were almost certain to survive if three conditions existed: a highly cohesive ruling party bound together by a non-material ideology, such as a revolutionary tradition; an extensive, well-funded and cohesive repressive apparatus; and extensive state control over the economy.[45] These regimes could respond by using at least one of five strategies: isolation (where the regime insulates itself from the protest movement), marginalisation (where the regime pushes the movement out of the political mainstream), distribution (where the regime distributes rents unevenly to benefit some movements and disadvantage others), repression (where the regime contains the movement by using force or threats of force) or persuasion (where the regime attempts to reason with the movement to persuade it to change its course of action). For instance, the Russian administration of Vladimir Putin attempted to insulate itself from these protests by delegitimising them as being proxies for US domination. The doctrine has had enormous utility for authoritarian governments, as they have been able to demobilise pro-democracy movements without having to resort to full-scale repression. The colour revolution was used by regimes to engage in what Vitali Silitski has called pre-emptive authoritarianism, adopting strategies to prevent collective actions from arising, rather than acting against them once they had. The fact that the Arab Spring protests were less successful in achieving social change than the earlier pro-democracy protests showed that authoritarian governments had learned how to contain the protests.[46]

More recently, the ANC and the SSA have claimed that imperialist interests have subverted pro-democracy protests: these include the Arab Spring, the 'Orange Revolution' in the Ukraine, and the uprisings in Yemen and Syria. The colour revolution's intelligence doctrine states that powerful Northern countries are using NGOs and social movements that claim to be progressive to gain control over natural resources in the global South. This they do by supporting these organisations to spread their ideologies in society, capitalising on state weaknesses to encourage others to engage in 'regime change', and using these weaknesses to promote alternative 'celebrity' leaders. Hence, these struggles are not legitimate struggles against authoritarianism, waged through the self-activity of oppressed and exploited communities, but are instead steered by a hidden hand to ensure that Northern countries such as the UK and US continue dominating the global South, to the former's benefit. According to former State Security Minister David Mahlobo:

> In Africa we have, as intelligence and security services, observed the importance of non-governmental organisations (NGOs) in Africa's development and poverty alleviation programmes. We however remain concerned that the nefarious activities of rogue NGOs contribute to Africa's persistent insecurity. We note that rogue NGOs are not only a threat to the national security of our respective states but they also threaten our collective security as a continent and have the potential to derail the African Union vision of a conflict-free Africa.
>
> It is for this reason that South Africa, as a member of both BRICS and Africa's multilaterals, stands firm against external interference or imposing one's will on others, opposes external forces in seeking regime change or colour revolution. We are, therefore, supportive of BRICS' initiatives geared towards opposing and countering external interference, even if it is indirectly carried out through rogue NGOs. In this regard, we concur with the need to strengthen cooperation on NGO management, including improving laws and regulations, upgrading the management level and improving the oversight mechanisms.[47]

In the case of the protests and broader movements for social change in South Africa, painting these struggles as being motivated by illegitimate 'regime change' allows the ANC to portray them as subversive; in other words, they have an express or implied intention of committing crimes against a democratically elected state. It is not difficult to understand the attractiveness of the 'colour revolution' doctrine for the ANC, as the party can blame internal instability on imperialist manipulation, rather than on the unequal social relations that were forged under apartheid and that the ANC – as the main party of government – has perpetuated in the democracy. It also allows the ANC to construct mass struggles, such as the struggle in the platinum belt against exploitation, or the struggles against the capture of the South African state, as national security threats. Doing so then permits state agencies to conduct surveillance of lawful advocacy – despite the narrowed definition of national security in the General Intelligence Laws Amendment Act (GILAA) – once an aura of illegitimacy has been created around these struggles. As the ANC has portrayed the media as a key tool of agitation, it too can be considered a legitimate target for surveillance.[48] By invoking the colour revolution to characterise the protest in South Africa, and by using authoritarian imitation and replication techniques developed elsewhere, the ANC has deepened its pre-emptive strategies against emerging protest movements, which presumably it hopes will make overt repression on the scale seen in Marikana less necessary. More specifically, the ANC has chosen marginalisation as a preferred strategy over repression.

In 2016, the JSCI called in its report for the SSA to prioritise economic intelligence and cybercrime.[49] However, a recent Privacy International investigation has exposed a revolving door between the intelligence agencies, the mining industry, and private security companies in the communications surveillance sector. In other words, spies leave the employ of the intelligence agencies and set up private security companies that ply their trade in the private sector, especially in the mining industry, where some of these players also have business interests. This collusion appears to have intensified in the wake of the Marikana massacre.[50] In fact, the evidence that has surfaced in the public domain suggests that the SSA's economic intelligence focus is being used to legitimise government spying on perceived political critics, and to protect the exploitative business practices of mining companies. It also suggests that there is growing public–private collusion in cracking down on such dissent, made possible by insufficient controls on conflicts of interest. When the position of the Inspector General of Intelligence, the executive oversight body of intelligence services, was vacant for close to two years, before being filled towards the end of 2016, the intelligence agencies enjoyed practically a free pass.[51]

Comments made by Minister of State Security David Mahlobo in his 2017/18 budget vote speech strongly suggested that South Africa's National Intelligence Priorities were being skewed inappropriately towards focusing on legitimate political activities, in spite of the narrowed definition of national security in GILAA. Mahlobo argued that the pre-eminent threats to national security were domestic and political in nature. He flagged violent industrial, student and community protests as looming threats. However, consistent with a securitised approach to social problems, he failed to reflect on the reasons why protests have turned violent, such as the general closure of democratic space and police violence. He also identified another threat, namely of foreign powers collaborating with 'negative domestic forces' to 'drive a wedge amongst the public' and effect unconstitutional regime change. This is a very serious allegation, as those responsible could be charged with subversion and even treason. According to Mahlobo,

> [Their] general strategy they use a range of role players to promote their agenda and these include, but are not limited to certain mainstream media; non-governmental organisations and community-based organisations; foreign and multinational companies; funding of opposition activities; infiltration and recruitment in key government departments; religious bodies, prominent influential persons; and punning [*sic*] of covert intelligence networks and covert action on our soil.[52]

The special operations function of the SSA has proved to be particularly controversial. In 2014, the *City Press* newspaper exposed the Special Operations Unit as a rogue unit engaged in intelligence activities that benefited the President and discredited public figures critical of him and his supporters. These included setting up a rival union to the Association of Mineworkers and Construction Union (AMCU) to destabilise its influence in the platinum belt, the Workers' Association Union (WAU). One of its founding members, Thebe Maswabi, filed a civil suit against Zuma and three ministers, claiming that he had reneged on an agreement to pay him for forming the WAU as a bogus shell union. He also claimed that he was tasked to spy on AMCU by the SSA, and that the SSA said they would continue 'using' him even after the settlement agreement.[53] At the time of writing, the case was still to be decided, but the claims pointed to the SSA having moved from passive intelligence-gathering to becoming an operational entity that intervened actively in political developments to change the course of events to the benefit of the ruling party. It has also emerged that a husband and wife team, both apparently on the payroll of the SSA, turned up as platinum mining company Lonmin's head of human resources and the South African Revenue Service's (SARS) head of risk management division respectively.[54] The *City Press* also alleged that this unit had its own communications surveillance capabilities, including a device for intercepting mobile phone calls, and suggested it was operating as a parallel intelligence-gathering unit to the existing ones.[55]

The intelligence agencies in the police and military have had controversies of their own, too. Military intelligence has declined in importance, to the point where it failed significantly when put to the test. In March 2013, thirteen members of the SANDF were killed in conflict with rebel insurgents seeking to topple the highly unpopular President François Bozizé of the Central African Republic. According to Helmoed Heitman, their deaths could be attributed, at least in part, to a defence intelligence failure. For Heitman, the intelligence that the troops relied on when combat started was out of date and did not make use of local intelligence sources sufficiently, leaving the troops vulnerable to attack without sufficient prior warning.[56] SAPS claims to be intelligence-led. Yet, the CID has been racked by internal divisions, rendering it ineffective. An acting head of Crime Intelligence, Lesetja Mothiba, stated in Parliament that the division was in such a poor state that its officers weren't getting the information they needed to fight crime, while 'you can go into any carwash in any township and get information there for free'.[57] At the time of writing Crime Intelligence had been without a permanent head since 2011, and its previous head, Richard Mdluli, was, without doubt, a political appointee who wreaked havoc in the division. Yet, six years after his suspension, disciplinary proceedings against him had not been concluded,[58] strongly suggesting that he was being protected politically.

At the same time, there have been significant intelligence failures in relation to undisputed threats to national security. For instance, in 2008 South Africa experienced a massive wave of xenophobic attacks, which the NIA did not anticipate. Non-South African Africans were attacked on account of their status as non-nationals, and the attacks spiked again in 2015. In spite of the fact that the government had several years' warning about the possibility of such attacks recurring, it claimed to have been caught unawares.[59] The problem pointed to a significant failure by the government's intelligence services, and while it could be argued that the attacks could not have been anticipated, the argument is weak. There is more than enough evidence to show that the problem of xenophobia in South Africa is systemic, not episodic. This places an obligation on the government to develop early warning systems to anticipate flashpoints of conflict.

In any event, given that the government claims to embrace a human security definition of national security, it should be committed to addressing the totality of factors that cause human insecurity. This mandate obliges it to develop strategies that address the root causes of xenophobia; yet in spite of this commitment, the SSA maintained the discredited government position that the attacks were purely criminal, not xenophobic.[60] In making this argument, the SSA also contradicted its own intelligence. In September 2014, the police revealed that the 'stability committee' of the National Joint Operational and Intelligence Structure (NATJOINTS) had identified 'anti-foreigner sentiment' as an 'immediate security threat', along with 'labour issues, especially [the] mining section' and 'service-delivery protests'. NATJOINTS highlighted these threats on the basis of priorities developed by NICOC.[61] Rightfully, the government should have revealed whether it had developed a national intelligence assessment of xenophobia. Unless the SSA accounts transparently for such a failure, it risks creating the impression that its considerable resources are not being used in the universal interest, but in the service of the elite and the political class they represent, or even a section of the political elite.

Perhaps the most significant intelligence failure of all has been the agencies' inability to stem the rising tide of organised crime in South Africa, including corruption. According to the Institute for Security Studies, organised crime syndicates are expanding their reach: syndicates that could be tackled by an effective CID.[62] Several public media, the Public Protector and academic investigators have pointed to state corruption on a massive scale, involving the Gupta family capturing elements in the state to extract rents from them, including possibly even the President. Furthermore, leaked emails between the Guptas, their business partners and various state officials (the 'Guptaleaks') point to classified documents having been stovepiped to the Guptas, in spite of the fact that the SSA was tasked with maintaining their secrecy.[63] They show that Atul Gupta knew of allegations that former Public Protector Thuli Madonsela was a CIA spy days before State Security Minister David Mahlobo announced an investigation into the allegations.[64] According to the investigative journalist Pieter-Louis Myburgh, in 2009 UK and US intelligence agencies expressed concern that the Guptas were acquiring one of the largest uranium mines in the country, given the potential for uranium to be misused for manufacturing nuclear weapons. In 2010, the SSA apparently identified the Guptas formally as an intelligence target, but the investigation was stymied by Intelligence Minister Siyabonga Cwele. The determination of senior officials in the SSA to continue the investigation led to massive ructions in the agency and ultimately the expulsion of these officials.[65] These events pointed to the intelligence services having themselves become captured by the very individuals they should have been investigating.

Significant intelligence failures are more likely to occur in excessively secretive intelligence environments. In this regard, there is a constitutionally indefensible information blackout on the intelligence services, which is dangerous, as it creates space for abuse of this most sensitive area of government. Clearly, secrecy in relation to operational methods is justifiable, with the caveat that if it is in the public interest for operational methods to be revealed (in cases of abuse, for instance), then the public interest must trump secrecy. But there is no justification for excessive secrecy about policy, as policy determines the ground rules according to which the intelligence services operate. Unjustifiable secrecy can lead to the intelligence community becoming its own echo chamber, where its own assumptions are never tested by contrary views. In such situations, intelligence work can quickly become driven by incestuous groupthink, where analysts gradually lose touch with the very reality they are meant to be assessing. Far from strengthening intelligence work, such secrecy can, in fact, cripple it.[66]

Cabinet's National Intelligence Priorities, which are based on NICOC's estimates, should be released and publicly debated: in fact, they should be finalised in an open sitting of Parliament. This will allow the public to assess whether the priorities the government has set itself should in fact be the priorities. Furthermore, estimates should be declassified and released on a regular basis. In closed, secretive systems, faulty assessments may never come to light. In contrast, the release in the UK of the national intelligence estimate on Iraq's manufacture of weapons of mass destruction confirmed what had been long suspected, namely that the intelligence justifying the invasion of Iraq was manipulated to tell the administrations of Tony Blair and George W. Bush what they wanted to hear.[67] As estimates are evaluative documents, they can be tailored to support the worldviews of those in power. This is why it is in the public interest for such documents to be declassified and released.

On the whole, there can be little argument with the statement that South Africa's democratic government under its fourth President, Jacob Zuma, strengthened the coercive capacities of the state, consisting of the police, the intelligence and the military, which are located in the Justice, Crime Prevention and Security Cluster. In fact, it would appear that this cluster became the praetorian guards of an increasingly embattled presidency.[68] The well-reported growth in the levels of police violence against ordinary civilians and protesters, and police militarisation, are the most visible manifestation of this shift, as was the normalisation of the military in domestic policing functions, which suggested a growing militarisation of society.[69] However, the huge public controversies over police violence and police militarisation mask the fact that there are fundamental shifts in the coercive capacities of the state, away from overt repression and towards less visible, more pre-emptive and surveillant forms of repression. What are the indicators of this shift, and why is it significant?

FROM HUMAN INTELLIGENCE TO SIGNALS INTELLIGENCE

The first indicator is that intelligence work has become increasingly important to stabilising social relations. Surveillance provides the state with a politically low-cost form of social control, as abuses are very difficult to detect. Political surveillance is part of an arsenal of tools available to the state to profile problem subjects, and to use this knowledge to stymie protests it may consider problematic. The state can use such surveillance, or the threat of surveillance, to create fear that organised violence will be employed against perceived opponents. At the same time, the fear of being watched may force people to self-police their own behaviour, as Foucault theorised in his appropriation of Jeremy Bentham's panopticon.[70] The risk associated with human intelligence is that the identities of intelligence operatives deployed to spy on organisations can always be uncovered, leading to politically costly scandals about intelligence abuses. As a result, the intelligence community has taken advantage of the digital 'revolution' to shift away from using human intelligence (intelligence gathered through physical means) to signals intelligence (intelligence gathered from communications surveillance). It is difficult to tell whether South Africa has embraced this global shift, but it would be unsurprising if it has, given the under-regulated nature of the state's mass surveillance capacities.

FROM MILITARISED POLICING TO INTELLIGENCE-LED POLICING

The second indicator, closely related to the first, is the shift from militarised policing to intelligence-led policing. As its name suggests, this policing model uses risk assessment as its main tool to direct policing decisions about where and how to intervene. It has been made possible by a shift in computing to anticipatory analytics, now that data can be analysed in real time, which allows the authorities to make predictions about how someone is likely to act. The model is more recent than paramilitary policing, as it was conceptualised in the UK and the US in the 1990s, but it really gained currency after the 9/11 attacks on New York and Washington. Intelligence-led policing relies heavily on covert techniques for crime detection, including paying informants, spying on individuals and organisations, using CCTV cameras, communications surveillance, and intercepting voice and data traffic.[71] At a broader level, the mandates and functions of the police and intelligence services are becoming increasingly blurred, and as a result innocent citizens are being treated as potential suspects and being subjected to surveillance.[72]

Intelligence-led policing does not necessarily make human rights violations go away; it merely makes them less visible. This form of policing encourages problematic profiling of individuals or social groups that may resort to crime, which can lead to stereotyping of particular social groups as being predisposed to crime. Activists who are considered to be politically threatening to existing ruling groups may be placed under surveillance to gain more information about their activities and to intimidate them; this risks chilling political activity. The US police used intelligence-driven policing to infiltrate organisations linked to the anti-globalisation movement, to identify and isolate 'troublemakers'.[73] But like overt forms of violence, generalised surveillance techniques also erode public trust in the state. In fact, the latter can do so more readily than the former, as surveillance proceeds from the premise that states do not trust their citizens from the outset.[74]

In South Africa, the CID of SAPS holds the key to this new policing strategy. It is therefore unsurprising that the CID has become so powerful (and controversial) in recent years, as this policing model makes it the lynchpin of policing strategies.[75] Heightened power without heightened accountability is a recipe for disaster. Yet, in spite of its increasing importance to policing work, there are signs of Crime Intelligence having lost its effectiveness, leading to a resurgence of organised crime.[76] The SAPS has embraced intelligence-led policing for several reasons. Police violence is eroding trust between the police and communities, making it more difficult to revert to community policing.[77] Yet at the same time, SAPS cannot risk many more high-profile shoot-outs with protesters, as the long-term political costs will simply be too great. So, it stands to reason that the SAPS would search for a policing model that still allowed it to contain dissent by using a less politically risky approach, and intelligence-led policing provides just such a model.

FROM POST HOC TO PRE-EMPTIVE REPRESSION OF PROTESTS

The third indicator is an increasing use of pre-emptive methods of containing protests through manipulation of the Regulation of Gatherings Act (RGA), to stop more protests from spilling out onto the streets in the first place. A research study on the right to protest in eleven municipalities[78] – which involved the physical collection and logging of municipal data about gatherings and protests over a five-year period (2008–13) – found that none of the municipalities studied received a clean bill of health.[79] A research team collected all notifications for protests and gatherings sent to municipalities in terms of the RGA: they yielded incredibly rich data about how many protests were taking place relative to gatherings, the reasons for the protests, the protest actors, and municipal responses to the protests.

The municipal and the police statistics suggest that the majority of protests take place peacefully and uneventfully, which is not the dominant image of protests either in the media or in the public imagination. In fact, from SAPS's incident registration information system (IRIS) database for the areas with the most unrest-related incidents between 2009 and 2012,[80] it became clear that despite being labelled unrest-related, most of the incidents (which included protests) did not escalate beyond barricade-building and tyre-burning into violence, and in fact were recorded as being fairly incident-free.[81] The protests itemised in the municipal records constitute a humdrum sequence of events, taking place day in, day out throughout the country with little incident. Given the media and police hype about 'violent service delivery protests', it is this wider picture of peaceful protests that is so often missed, and unsurprisingly so. The security cluster can use images of marauding mobs, apparently predisposed to violence, to create moral panics in the public about protests, to turn the public against protesters (even those whose demands are legitimate), and to justify heightened security measures against them.

Yet in spite of protests remaining largely peaceful, all the municipalities surveyed instituted unreasonable restrictions on the right to protest, and these have curtailed this right to varying degrees. While the misapplication of the RGA has been a problem at least since the early 2000s,[82] a particularly significant shift became apparent from 2012 onwards. In the wake of the local government elections, the Department of Cooperative Governance sent out a circular to local governments outlining proactive measures that municipalities needed to take to deal with protests. These measures included '[working] with the office of the speaker [and] public participation units to ensure ongoing engagement between councillors and communities and residents'.[83] Several municipalities used this memo as a pretext to change the way they administered the RGA.

This shift increased the already onerous bureaucratic obstacles that municipalities put on protests, many of which already shared an assumption that the notification process in terms of the RGA was actually a permission-seeking exercise, and that they had the right to grant or deny 'permission' to convenors to engage in a gathering or protest. This municipal misapprehension of the process set the tone for how notifications were dealt with, both by the municipalities and by the police. Practices that limited the right unduly included a requirement on the part of convenors to seek a letter from the institution or person they were marching against, guaranteeing that they would be willing to accept the protesters' memorandum. The rationale for seeking such an assurance appears to be to prevent frustration on the part of protesters, which could boil over into violence. However, it has also become a censorship device: those who are being marched against can quash the protest simply by refusing to accept the memorandum.

The City of Johannesburg requires protest convenors to seek permission from a ward councillor to protest. After the 2012 Cooperative Governance memo, they and the Mbombela municipality instituted a filtering system to reduce the number of service delivery protests, requiring convenors to show that a meeting had taken place between the mayor's office, the community and the ward councillor involved in that community, or at the very least that an attempt was made to bring all parties to the table to resolve the issues at hand.[84] But this prescription is not lawful, as the RGA does not prescribe what process people should follow before they take to the streets. The number of 'approved' protests increased in Mbombela once the filtering process was introduced, suggesting that the potentially 'troublesome' protests did not even enter into the system. But the municipality did admit that the condition had led to an increase in the number of 'unrest-related' protests taking place outside the framework of the RGA, and that the police were more likely to be heavy-handed against such protests, as they were not involved in facilitating them in the first place. These were led mainly by individuals or organisations that were in dispute with the structures they were meant to negotiate with. This suggests that an increasingly restrictive approach towards protests on the part of the municipality was changing the character of the protests, forcing them to become what the authorities would consider 'unlawful' and driving up the potential for the protests to become disruptive.

While the municipalities studied gradually closed spaces for the right to protest, this closure was highly uneven and met with considerable contestation. Spaces were much more closed where the political and economic elites were united in their intention to stifle protests and prevent criticism and alternative forms of mobilisation (the Rustenburg municipality being a case in point), but this unity was not found uniformly across the municipalities. As Pamela Oliver and Daniel Myers have argued, erratic government repression arises not because the government has chosen to be erratic, but because of inconsistencies among political actors.[85] Furthermore, non-conventional actors are more likely to be repressed than conventional ones (such as unions or well-known political parties), as the security apparatus considers the former to be less predictable than the latter.[86] The evidence supports the view of the state put forward by Gramsci that it is not monolithic but is rather a site where ruling-class alliances take place or even shift.[87] In times of significant political de-alignment, elements of the state can even work against one another. Erratic repression is likely to occur when divisions have opened up within the political elite, or between the political elite and the bureaucratic layer: in such circumstances, spaces for alternative voices remain open, albeit constrained and subject to reversal.

Internationally, the academic literature has recognised that ruling elites have expanded their repertoires of social control beyond outright repression. As a result, the literature has shifted away from focusing on the concept of repression to that of pacification. According to Markus Kienscherf, pacification includes measures that produce undisruptive and unthreatening forms of collective action.[88] However, this is not to say that repression, as it is commonly understood, and pacification are mutually exclusive: in fact, they can be complementary strategies. For instance, the intelligence services can be used to separate out 'good' protesters from 'bad' ones, and the resulting protest policing may be either facilitative or militarised depending on the type of risk management strategies that the police identify through the intelligence gleaned.[89] But the fact that the elites have found it necessary to shift from more visible to less visible forms of social containment at all is not a sign of their strength; rather, it is a sign of their weakness, as they recognise that they lack the capacity to repress openly. Why is this so? The next section will attempt to answer this question.

ORGANIC CRISIS: GROWING POPULAR CAPACITY FOR INDEPENDENT ACTION

It seems fair to say that South Africa is manifesting more elements of a classic Gramscian organic crisis. For Gramsci, crises become organic when they are thrown up directly by contradictions in the way the capitalist system functions; when they are dynamic, in that they are not confined to particular actors, events, issues or moments in time or place; and consequently when they are a process rather than a momentary eruption. The demands being raised may be diverse, and at times even incompatible. Such crises usually arise when a particular regime of capitalist accumulation becomes unsustainable because of its own internal contradictions. In such circumstances, the ruling bloc (or the coalition of interests that underpins a particular ruling group) loses its legitimacy on a mass scale. An organic crisis develops when the following conditions obtain:

- popular capacity for action increases;
- more people can be detached from the previous hegemonic bloc and persuaded to side with the subaltern classes;
- there is a decline in the capacity of the elite to offer significant concessions; but
- there is also a decline in the capacity of the hegemonic bloc to mobilise effective repression.

When these conditions obtain, the hegemonic bloc cannot offer concessions easily, nor can it repress easily.[90]

With regard to the first condition, while the number of crowd management incidents in South Africa increased year on year from 1996, too little can be deduced from this upward swing, as the police database that logs these incidents (the IRIS system) records both protests and gatherings. However, from the municipal data referred to earlier, it is apparent that protests peaked in 2011 (the year of the local government elections) in municipalities such as eThekwini, Johannesburg and Lukhanji (Queenstown), which is when crowd management incidents recorded by SAPS peaked too. So it is not unreasonable to assume that the peaking of incidents in 2011 can be attributed at least in part to an uptick in protest action, suggesting an increase in popular capacity for action as expressed through protests.

There was little evidence of co-ordination across protest sites, though. Such co-ordination as did occur took place when a trade union movement organised a national action, or when there was a strike in different parts of the country, for instance a public sector strike. While there was little evidence of these protests coalescing into more generalised political demands, they have the potential to do so if a national political movement comes into being that links these different struggles together. The municipal data pointed to high levels of organisation, and of new formations or even organisations emerging all the time, suggesting that Patrick Bond's term 'popcorn protests'[91] – used to describe seemingly sporadic, spontaneous protests – ignores the extent of organisation that actually exists. There was no evidence of unions and community organisations uniting around shared grievances.

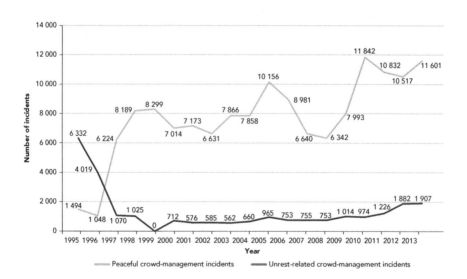

Source: Author's graph, based on SAPS IRIS information, released in response to a SAHA information request.

Figure 3.1: Peaceful and unrest-related crowd management incidents between 1995 and 2013

However, it was apparent from the municipal data that struggles at the point of consumption are becoming as important to the political life of direct action politics as struggles at the point of production, and in some cases (in the Makana municipality in the Eastern Cape, for instance) the former are overtaking the latter as flashpoints of struggle.

When South African protests are viewed in the global context, it becomes apparent that popular capacity for action is not only increasing, but these increases are being sustained. The protests could easily be described as a cycle in the sense used by Sydney Tarrow.[92] However, is the protest cycle in South Africa of even greater historical significance? For instance, could it be part of a broader regional or even global protest wave? The question whether the protests, including those in South Africa, are part of a wave, rather than being isolated, single-country protest cycles, is an important one, as it speaks to whether the protests will fizzle out in time or escalate into fundamental and transformative challenges to the system on a worldwide scale. According to Colin Beck,[93] the difference between a protest cycle and a protest wave is that the latter is present in at least two or more societies within a decade of each other, and these protests are tantamount to revolutionary situations. In other words, the protests affect more parts of the world over a longer period, and are not concentrated in a fixed period in time or driven by a small, well-defined set of actors. These features suggest that the unfolding struggles are responses to broader crises in the world economy and, in spite of their heterogeneity, are capable of being sustained and even escalated into an insurrection, precipitating an organic crisis.

The mobilisations in Chiapas, the Occupy movement in the United States, the 'pink tide' in Latin America, the 'Arab Spring', Palestinian struggles against Israeli occupation, and anti-austerity protests in different parts of the world, are all examples of challenges to the system in different regions of the world (some more successful than others). Less well-known and studied are the wave of protests that engulfed sub-Saharan Africa in the wake of the Tunisian and Egyptian political revolutions, with the most pronounced ones erupting in Swaziland, Mozambique, Zimbabwe and Malawi.

For Cox,[94] if protest cycles are sustained in more than one region of the world over a period of at least fifteen years, this is a further indication that the crisis is organic, rather than episodic. Accordingly, the multiple resistances that have been mounted against the system could be credibly described as a revolutionary wave. Sustained regional disruptions usually happen at least once every twenty years. The fact that some have not led to regimes falling, or, where political revolutions have been achieved, they have not necessarily deepened into social revolutions, becomes less significant if revolutionary waves are understood as a process rather than an event. If these protests have brought new political actors onto the streets, resulting in new forms of organisation, and extracted significant concessions from ruling elites, shaking the state in the process, then they could be described as moving in an anti-systemic direction. This is because the protests build confidence in the power of collective action, and consequently have the potential to extract even more significant concessions in future.[95] When viewed in this global context, it becomes apparent that South Africa's protests are of world-historical significance, and part of a broader global wave of heightened popular action. They are also likely to place popular limits on the state's ability to use organised violence, as doing so may well intensify popular action rather than dampen it.

With respect to more people detaching themselves from the hegemonic bloc, the municipal data before 2011 pointed to the ANC alliance dominating the protest space – especially in smaller towns and rural areas – but that its dominance declined after 2011. The ANC alliance has proved to be a combustible one, with political alignments coming under considerable pressure. At community levels, the municipal data suggested that the South African National Civic Organisation (SANCO) – often considered to be a fourth member of the ANC alliance – is largely a spent force, and is being overtaken by a host of independent community organisations or civics. In fact, while the protests cannot be said to have a distinct ideological character, the data points to the hegemony of the ANC diminishing. This does not support arguments advanced by Susan Booysen[96] and Ebrahim Fakir[97] that the protests are merely about holding the ANC to account. Rather, there is growing evidence of more communities becoming subjectively available for a politics alternative to that offered by the ANC alliance.

ORGANIC CRISIS: CONCESSIONS OR REPRESSION

With respect to Gramsci's two other conditions for an organic crisis, namely that the elite cannot offer concessions very easily, nor can they repress very easily, the neoliberal phase of capitalism has entered a period of organic crisis in several regions of the world. This phase is characterised by the financialisation of the economy, the rise of permanent mass unemployment and declining rates of profit. These features make this phase particularly unstable in that it creates conditions for mass revolt, as fewer concessions can be offered than in earlier expansionary periods (such as under social democracy), while the system cannot generate enough profit to prevent itself from contracting and even collapsing, worsening the socio-economic conditions even more. In the case of South Africa, while the Zuma administration promised a more redistributive state, and undoubtedly many of its more principled office-bearers remain subjectively committed to a more just and equal society, the objective conditions in which they came to office did not favour radical redistribution.

Yet at the same time, managers of the neoliberal system – governments, financiers and other big capitalists – need to maintain consent in order to continue ruling, and this they find increasingly difficult to obtain. If they resort to coercion to stabilise the system, they risk losing legitimacy, and state violence is used most effectively when consent remains for its use.[98] Their inability to resolve these crises lies at the heart of the current period's organic crisis. For instance, there are limits on the extent to which paramilitary policing can be used to contain growing dissent. While many police are clearly 'getting away with murder', public antipathy is building against the police and the political order they seem to be propping up. There have not been nearly the same levels of protest against police violence in South Africa as there have been in US cities such as Ferguson, in the wake of Michael Brown's fatal shooting by the police. But Marikana has hastened political shifts that have been under way for some time now, and has not dampened protest levels: to that extent, it has not been a particularly successful massacre for the ruling elite. The massacre was a precipitating factor in the formation of new opposition movements such as the Economic Freedom Fighters (EFF), a political party, and the Congress of South African Trade Unions' (COSATU) largest affiliate, the National Union of Metalworkers of South Africa (NUMSA), has been expelled from the federation, spurring it on to form a United Front in collaboration with community organisations and social movements. Large numbers of workers defected from COSATU affiliate the National Union of Mineworkers (NUM) to a competitor union, AMCU. The state cannot risk going even further down this path. Violence against dissenters on a mass scale is likely to eat into the ANC's still considerable legitimacy, and hasten its slow but steady demise at the polls. This is especially so if a national movement comes into being that generalises protesters' demands, and relates them to the neoliberal system of governance. Workers and the poor, who face the brunt of the system, are increasingly unlikely to consent to supporting and funding their own oppression.

Another factor that makes full-scale repression unlikely is that the government's security cluster appears to be an increasingly divided house, and not insignificant cracks are beginning to show. The police commissioner at the time of the Marikana massacre, Riah Phiyega, was suspended and ended her contract while on suspension.[99] A spate of top management resignations in the SSA in 2011 was linked to refusals to use the surveillance capacities of the state to spy on Zuma's detractors ahead of the ANC's elective conference in Mangaung.[100] Furthermore, in order to repress openly, the police would probably need the assistance of the SANDF. But the military is industrialised and unionised. In spite of arguments that unionisation can compromise combat-readiness, in 1999 the Constitutional Court legalised the formation of military unions.[101] There is evidence that a significant number of soldiers have a consciousness of themselves, not just as soldiers, but as workers, who are exploited like other workers. Frustrations with poor working conditions boiled over during the ill-fated march on the seat of political office, the Union Buildings, in August 2009. This very public confrontation – the dynamics of which were misreported by many media organisations[102] – led to the Chief of the Army, Solly Shoke, accusing the soldiers involved of mutiny, and warning them that some other countries would have shot them for their actions.[103]

In view of these fractious relations, the political elite face a gamble: if the current administration put soldiers in front of exploited, protesting workers and told them to shoot, what would they do? What if they refused? Can they risk a rebellion in the military, which really would amount to mutiny? The political consequences could be too great for the elite to gamble on the military.

The more historically aware security officials are also likely to make political calculations about how long they will last if they intensify open repression. As the embarrassingly weak presidency of Jacob Zuma splutters to a close, the ignominious fates suffered by the likes of Saddam Hussein and Muammar Gaddafi could well be top of mind when they attempt to weigh up the long-term political costs of engaging in an all-out defence of their positions. Regimes that rely on repression to maintain power have never lasted.[104] It is not coincidental that since 2009 – the year that Zuma came to office – evidence has mounted of some even resorting to political assassinations to silence their critics, especially in Mpumalanga and KwaZulu-Natal.[105] The 2014 murder of Abahlali baseMjondolo activist Thuli Ndlovu by two ANC councillors is a case in point.[106] But resorting to informal repression is itself an indication that more violent sections of the political elite recognise that they cannot engage in open repression. Furthermore, the three conditions for the continued existence of semi-authoritarian revolutions targeted by 'colour revolution' protests do not necessarily exist in South Africa. While the ANC remains bound together by a non-material ideology dating from the liberation struggle, it is not a cohesive party any longer, and in fact it is racked by internal divisions. While sections of the repressive apparatus appear to be well funded, it is not as cohesive as it needs to be to ensure successful repression. Furthermore, it cannot be argued that the ANC exercises extensive state control over the economy. The party has attempted to do so through black economic empowerment and state steering of parastatals, but the reality is that the bulk of the economy remains outside ANC control – perhaps the starkest legacy of apartheid.

CONCLUSION

The current government's ability to offer meaningful concessions is limited, but so too is its ability to repress easily. This means that the South African political landscape bears all the hallmarks of having entered an organic crisis. Crises of this nature are not necessarily negative; they can allow fundamental societal contradictions to surface in ways that force society to confront them, grow from them, and move forward. In spite of the fact that the current political moment seems so dark, we need to recognise that the political space is wide open, and is actually pregnant with great promise. Does the state have the capacity to repress on a broader scale? It appears not. There are unlikely to be more Marikanas in the sense of an organised, armed assault on protesters, although the possibility cannot be ruled out that state violence could occur as an unplanned reaction to particular events. While there are clear and well-acknowledged legal limits on its ability to use violence, the political limits, and more specifically the limits imposed by popular agency, are less well acknowledged.[107] This is because repression is often studied as a static structural factor constraining movement activities, but not as a factor that is changed dynamically through interactions between state structures and popular agency. Arguably, the social and political conditions that would allow the state to use ongoing (as opposed to sporadic) violence do not exist in this current conjuncture, as the balance of power is shifting gradually towards popular movements outside the hegemonic bloc. No matter how powerful the men and women with guns seem, there are important signs that they are actually quite vulnerable, and the shifting modes of repression point to that. While overstatements about the power of the coercive capacities of the state are understandable in the wake of Marikana, they are not helpful, as they can lead to fear, and even political paralysis. What Cox[108] has referred to as 'repression horror' can cause movements to see the state as omniscient and omnipotent, even when this is, in fact, not the case. Repression horror becomes less paralysing if the precise nature of the state's repressive capacities is understood. To this end, the next chapters will seek to understand the nature of South Africa's surveillance capacities, the uses to which they are put, and the way these capacities and uses change over time in view of the broader social and political shifts discussed in this chapter.

4

Lawful interception in South Africa

South Africa had direct experiences of damaging surveillance under apartheid. The potential for abuse is thus still fresh in many people's minds, yet it is unclear how concerned South Africans are today about their privacy. One survey conducted by Ipsos for the Centre for International Governance Innovation came to the unsurprising conclusion that most people believe law enforcement agencies should have a right to access the communications of citizens, especially if someone is suspected of having committed a crime. However, indicative of a greater concern for privacy than in other countries surveyed on the continent, the survey found that South Africans were less likely to agree to this right than people in most of the major world regions surveyed.[1] When asked a different and more pointed set of questions in another survey, about whether the US government should have the right to conduct mass communications surveillance, and whether technology companies such as Google and Yahoo should protect communications privacy from unwarranted access, 66 per cent of South Africans felt that the US should not have this right. Although this score was the third lowest of a total of thirteen countries, it was still high. These surveys suggest that the South Africans surveyed were relatively open to recognising the right of the state to conduct targeted interception as distinct from mass surveillance. The relatively low score in the second survey also suggests that South Africans felt less touched by the Snowden revelations than other countries. In contrast, the countries that felt the most strongly had direct experience of the NSA's excesses, such as Germany and Brazil.[2]

While there is evidence of a growth in the coercive capacities of the South African state, the forms of coercion have changed, and the state has come to place particular emphasis on intelligence work relying, in part, on communications surveillance. This chapter will examine the growth of communications surveillance in South Africa, and will seek to answer the question, how concerned should South Africans be?

LAWFUL INTERCEPTION IN SOUTH AFRICA

Lawful interception is governed by RICA. This replaced the Interception and Monitoring Prohibition Act of 1992, which was passed during the transition to democracy, and which itself replaced the apartheid-era law on interception of communications. South Africa emerged from a long and sorry history of abuses of the intelligence capacities of the state. The apartheid regime used overt and covert forms of repression, such as communications surveillance, to track and repress the activities of the anti-apartheid movement.[3]

Since the 9/11 attacks on the US, South Africans have been lulled into believing that drastic limitations on their rights to privacy and freedom of expression – through laws like RICA – are necessary to contribute to the 'wars' on crime and terrorism. The Act regulates the interception of certain communications, and makes it illegal for communications to be intercepted except according to the framework set out in the Act. This provides for a designated judge to issue interception directions when requested by law enforcement officers on crime-related or national security grounds. The judge is selected from the pool of retired judges, and is appointed for a period of a year, with the possibility of renewal.[4] A small, clearly defined basket of security agencies can apply to the judge for interception directions. They must provide an application in writing, and the information contained therein must be supported by a sworn affidavit. The applicant must set out the reasons for requesting the direction, the individuals whose communications are to be intercepted, and the nature of the crime they are suspected of having committed. There is provision for urgent applications, but these must be made only in exceptional circumstances.

In considering these applications, the judge is required to meet strict standards in deciding whether to grant an interception direction. These are whether the applicants have shown that all other investigative methods have failed; there are serious grounds to believe that an offence has been, is being, or probably will be committed; the application concerns a serious threat to public safety or national security; the information needed for the investigation will most likely lead to the solving or prevention of the alleged crime; and there is a clear link between the information needed and the individuals whose devices are going to be intercepted.[5]

Apart from setting out the grounds for the issuing of interception directions, RICA also makes it illegal to establish communications networks that are not capable of surveillance. It places obligations on communications service providers, including internet service providers (ISPs), to assist the state in the interception of communications. It also makes provision for employers to monitor the communications of their employees lawfully for legitimate purposes, provided they have given consent to this monitoring. Telecommunications operators and ISPs are required by law to facilitate the interception and monitoring of communications and to store communications-related information at their own expense for not less than three and not more than five years. Furthermore, all cellphone users are required to register their SIM cards, and provide proof of residential address and identity numbers. RICA was part of a basket of laws passed in the early 2000s to assist in the global fight against terror, which included the Protection of Constitutional Democracy against Terrorist and Related Activities Act (POCDATARA) and the Financial Intelligence Centre Act (FICA). All these Acts were contested during deliberation in Parliament, because they threatened the rights to privacy and freedom of expression, and while many controversial clauses were amended, they were not completely cured of deficiencies; as a result, they still continue to evoke controversy. At the time they suggested that South Africa was following the global trend of promulgating new anti-terrorism legislation in a rush.

RICA-related interceptions are undertaken by the OIC on behalf of the applicants. The head of the OIC must report on its activities on a quarterly basis to the SSA.[6] The OIC houses the fibre optic cables from the communications service providers, which use them to hand over the communications of interception targets after the judge has granted an interception direction. While metadata can be collected by the OIC, it can also be made available through other routes. For instance, network providers can hand metadata over to law enforcement officials provided they have a warrant from a high court, regional court or magistrate's court. Officials can (and do) also use section 205 of the Criminal Procedures Act to obtain metadata. Sources inside the law enforcement agencies have admitted, though, that it is fairly easy to obtain metadata without a warrant, in violation of the law, to expedite investigations. What is more, trading in metadata is rife, according to other sources who spoke to the journalist Heidi Swart.[7]

As we have noted, RICA requires communications service providers to retain all metadata (or what it calls communications-related information) for between three and five years. Blanket retention of metadata has become a hugely controversial issue. In spite of the fact that in 2014 the European Court of Justice struck down the European Union Data Retention Directive as being disproportionate to the aim it sought to achieve, South Africa remains out of step with this important development.

The blanket retention of metadata should be of concern because RICA is also weak on metadata protections. The law sets a lower standard for approving access to archived metadata, in that ordinary judges who do not necessarily have the specialist knowledge of the designated judge can approve a request. However, section 205 of the Criminal Procedures Act provides law enforcement officials with an even less cumbersome route for obtaining metadata. This section allows a judge at the request of a prosecutor or an attorney-general to request the presence of an individual who is likely to give information or evidence about an alleged offence. If he or she does so to the satisfaction of the attorney-general or the prosecutor, that person does not have to appear in court. The police find this route less cumbersome, as any court can grant the request, and the service providers find it less cumbersome, as they do not have to appear in court to testify about the data they have provided. Hence, the vast majority of metadata requests take place in terms of the Criminal Procedures Act, and not RICA.[8] This is a positive development in that it does not overburden the RICA judge with vast numbers of metadata applications, but it is a negative development in that other courts do not have the specialist knowledge to assess the appropriateness of such requests, especially their likely impact on privacy. Furthermore, the grounds for access to archive-related communications in terms of RICA are more stringent than those set out in s.205. The fact that there is only one RICA judge is a serious problem, as he or she is burdened unduly with a vast number of applications, which increases the risk of poorly considered decisions. Furthermore, applicants can wait up to five days for a response from the judge, which creates bottlenecks in the system. As a result, it is hardly surprising that law enforcement agencies prefer to use the s.205 route. A more feasible approach would be to require that the more stringent RICA standards apply to s.205 metadata requests.[9]

RICA has major strengths as it prevents arbitrary communications interceptions. The Act sets in place procedures for deciding whether interceptions should be granted or not, and it gives the decision-making powers in this regard to a judicial authority. However, the Act also contains systemic weaknesses. One of the most serious is that people are not informed that their communications have been intercepted, even after the investigation is complete. This means that the authorities in South Africa are given a power that is, to all intents and purposes, hidden from the public eye. While other countries such as the US, Japan, Austria and Chile do have user notification, its absence in South Africa violates the requirement in the Necessary and Proportionate Principles that individuals should be notified of a decision authorising communications surveillance and given enough time and information to enable them to appeal against the decision, and should also have access to the materials presented in support of the application for authorisation.[10] Needless to say, this principle should apply only if there is no risk to the purpose of surveillance, in which case post facto notification is appropriate. In the US criminal justice system, in order to protect the rights of people under surveillance in criminal matters, within ninety days of the termination of the court order the judge must ensure that the person whose communications were intercepted is informed about the order.[11] The fact that a similar provision does not exist in RICA lays it open to abuse, as the authorities can rest assured that their abuses will most probably never come to light. The SSA has argued that user notification would defeat the purpose of the intended surveillance, but this appears to assume that the proposal is for notification before the fact (which it is not).[12]

Another problem in RICA is the speculative nature of the grounds for the issuing of interception directions. Privacy International has argued that the grounds are too vague, and that the higher standard of 'probable cause' or a similar level of finding is generally required for a judge to issue an interception direction.[13] Directions can also be issued in relation to serious offences that may be committed in future: this may not be constitutional as it allows law enforcement officers to speculate on future acts that have not yet occurred.[14] Furthermore, the granting of directions is an inherently one-sided process, as the judge has to take the information given to him or her on trust. No public advocate is present to represent users' interests, and, as a result, the process lacks an adversarial component, which also predisposes it to abuse. The SSA has expressed concern that introducing a public advocate would slow the process down, thereby neutralising the ability of the services to conduct investigations speedily. The public advocate would need time to familiarise himself or herself with the facts of a case, and including the advocate in the specifics of cases could increase the potential for security risks.[15] However, these problems could be addressed by including several public advocates, so that they work at speed. One possibility is to convert the office of the designated judge into a full-blown court, with the capacity to handle matters quickly.

While the level of information provided by the designated judge that is eventually released has improved significantly, it is still inadequate. The annual report provides bare details about the number of applications for interception directions, the state agency that made the applications, and the number that were granted or refused. The judge may also include some general comments on trends. No information is available in these reports on the number of interceptions that actually result in arrests and convictions. In contrast, in the US the publicly available annual reports on what they call wiretaps include information on the number of arrests and convictions resulting from intercepts. If made available, this information could be used to assess whether surveillance is actually bringing down crime levels, or whether the authorities are merely engaged in fishing expeditions. Aggregate information on the nature of the crimes for which directions were granted would also be important to provide.

Given the growing concerns in the intelligence and law enforcement communities about encryption, and the extent to which it is placing more communications beyond their reach, the judge's report should provide details about the number of interceptions where encryption is encountered. When combined with information about arrests and convictions, this information will allow basic questions about effectiveness to be answered and act as a brake on the tendency of intelligence agencies to request even more powers if the ones they currently enjoy are not being used to full effect. In the US, for instance, intelligence agencies have vastly overstated the threat of encryption to their investigations, to justify more expansive powers. Hopefully, in South Africa, in the absence of hard empirical evidence about the extent of the problem, encryption will not be used as an excuse to legalise more intrusive forms of surveillance. As discussed earlier, in 2016 the UK Parliament legalised bulk hacking through its controversial Investigatory Powers Act, to address the encryption challenge. Yet David Anderson's investigation into the operational case for mass surveillance found that when the UK government made its case for the surveillance powers it sought, that for bulk hacking was the weakest of all.

If the US can provide information about encryption and lawful interception, then there is no apparent reason why South Africa cannot, too. This is especially so given that RICA recognises that information gained from the interception of communications may be admissible into evidence: in other words, intercept information is used not only for intelligence-gathering purposes, but for evidentiary purposes as well. This feature of RICA strengthens the abilities of the judges presiding over those cases to assess the importance of intercept information to these cases. Not all countries admit intercept information into evidence: the UK, for instance, has had a long tradition of avoiding the admission of intercept information into evidence, as it may lead to operational secrets being disclosed, although this interpretation of the law has been disputed. New York law ties the admissibility of evidence to user notification; so, if a user has been notified about the fact of interception, and does not file a successful motion to suppress the intercept information, the information is admissible. To this extent, user notification and admissibility of evidence are two sides of the same coin.[16] The fact that South Africa allows intercept information to be accepted into evidence, but does not recognise the need for user notification, already tilts court proceedings towards the authorities and away from the accused.

Furthermore, other democracies have established independent commissions to oversee all monitoring and interception activities. Such commissions undertake full and public reporting processes, while removing the most sensitive areas. Yet in South Africa, the parliamentary reports are written by the very judge who took the decisions. This is not healthy, as the judge is unlikely to reflect adequately on the weaknesses of his or her own decisions.

Another feature of RICA that enables communication surveillance, and with which ordinary South Africans are perhaps the most familiar, is the requirement for all cellphone users to register their SIM cards with communication service providers. This provision allows state agencies that have access to the RICA database to link a particular SIM card to an individual, making it impossible for cellphone users to communicate anonymously: a prerequisite for privacy of communications. The government has argued that SIM card registration is necessary to allow SIM cards to be traced back to their owners if they are used in criminal acts. However, many countries frown on this practice as a de facto violation of privacy, and the evidence that it actually contributes to crime-fighting is disputed.[17] Furthermore, an investigation into the mechanics of SIM card registration in South Africa has shown that the process was flawed, which defeated the whole point. Network operators outsource the registration process to distributors, who appoint agents to undertake it, and these agents then enter the required information into the network operator's SIM card registration database. Customers are then expected to provide proof of identity and address in order to register a SIM card in their name, but the agents have no way of verifying the information that is given to them, and they do not keep copies. While they could be given access to the Department of Home Affairs's National Population Register (NPR), which contains the biographic information of South Africans, strict access rules means that the department cannot risk doing so, as there are too many agents. Agents can also sell pre-RICA'd SIM cards for vastly more than non-registered ones, which creates a perverse incentive to do just that. Furthermore, while access to the RICA databases is strictly controlled, the agents can use personal information for identity theft as their activities are not strictly controlled. There is also no clear evidence of its adding any significant value to investigatory processes, and in fact they can derail such processes through inaccurate information. Instead, alternative sources of information, such as call-related or location-related metadata, have proved to be much more valuable to investigations. As a result, several countries have not pursued SIM card registration, or have abandoned it.[18]

JOURNALISTS AND RICA

Nowhere have the systemic weaknesses of RICA been more visible than in relation to journalists. Hard evidence of journalists having been spied on by the intelligence agencies has emerged into the public domain. Spy agencies like the NSA and GCHQ have recognised journalists as potential threats to national security and therefore legitimate targets of government surveillance.[19] So what happened to Stephan Hofstatter and Mzilikazi wa Afrika, who were part of the investigative journalism team at the *Sunday Times*, should come as no surprise.

Hofstatter and wa Afrika were responsible for a story that saw South Africa's most senior police officer, National Police Commissioner Bheki Cele, being fired by President Jacob Zuma in 2012 for dishonesty, unlawfulness and mismanagement in concluding a lease deal for offices for the SAPS in Pretoria and Durban. The deal was concluded with businessman Roux Shabangu, who was close to the President. The journalists' stories exposed how Cele had broken Treasury rules to advantage an associate of Zuma's financially. The team also investigated allegations of corruption against Cele when he was a Member of the Executive Council (MEC) for Transport, Safety and Security in KwaZulu-Natal. They also published stories about the serious and violent crimes unit of the SAPS in Cato Manor, which they claimed had turned rogue by operating a 'death squad' and killing suspects – stories that have since been discredited.[20] Hofstatter and wa Afrika went to extreme measures to protect their sources, including those located inside the police. In an attempt to do so, they carried two phones: one with a SIM card that had been registered in terms of RICA and one with a card that had been registered by someone other than themselves. Pre-RICA'd SIM cards can be bought fairly easily in South Africa, and cannot be tracked back to their users, as they are not registered in their names. The journalists used the first for non-sensitive and the second for sensitive communications with confidential sources, whom they did not wish to be traced.

Wa Afrika had a sinister run-in with the authorities in 2010, when his communications were intercepted by the police on the pretext that he was gun-running. The journalist had travelled in and out of the country several times on stories, and the police used this as 'evidence' that he might well have been involved in crime. The existence of the interception direction was confirmed by the Inspector General of Intelligence, who also confirmed that the direction was lawful.[21] The use of vague and speculative grounds for the issuing of interception directions worked to the police's advantage, and they resorted to this to pursue an investigation of a non-existent crime.

However, according to Hofstatter and wa Afrika, later in 2010 the police managed to obtain their non-RICA'd cellphone numbers, and slipped them into a larger application for an interception direction for approval by the designated judge, Joshua Khumalo. The police claimed that the numbers – those of the journalists were included under fictitious names – belonged to suspected members of a criminal syndicate. Oddly enough, the police commissioner's number was also included in the application, although it was subsequently cancelled. Apparently the police obtained these numbers from one of their sources, who had decided to betray the journalists in return for a promotion.[22] Two officers were subsequently charged for having violated RICA. The penalties for having done so are stiff: any person intercepting communications unlawfully could be imprisoned for up to ten years or fined up to R2 million. The journalists claim that they have not been involved in any crimes, and as a result there is no valid reason for the police to investigate them.[23]

Presumably, the police wanted to uncover their sources so that they could plug the leaks. In fact, in an affidavit for the case, one of the police officers in the trial, Brian Padayachee, stated that he was given instructions by a higher-ranking officer to undertake a covert investigation into the activities of certain journalists who, it was claimed, posed a threat to the organisation; this included the interception and monitoring of their calls.[24] Apparently, the ultimate instruction came from Cele, who was concerned that the journalists were attempting to infiltrate the police with the intention of tarnishing the image of SAPS. However, in a bizarre twist, this very direction for which he had given the instruction was used against him to place him under surveillance.

These incidents show just how easy it is to intercept journalists' communications or, indeed, the communications of any citizen who asks inconvenient questions about those in authority. Unless the state's surveillance capacities are regulated properly, they can be abused for political reasons. As Hofstatter noted, 'There is a complete free for all for the intelligence services to intercept whatever they want. They just come up with spurious grounds. There is a time-honoured practice to circumvent RICA, and all they do is just slip the numbers in.'[25] The Act also does not recognise the right of journalists to protect their sources of information, either in the form of express provisions in the Act or in the form of a protocol to which law enforcement or intelligence officials are required to adhere in investigating journalists. The *Sunday Times* achieved a significant victory in the state's case against the CID of SAPS, in that one of the officers, Bongani Cele, was found guilty of spying on the journalists illegally, and sentenced to three years' imprisonment. However, this victory was limited in that the sentence was suspended for four years, did not identify the officers responsible for giving the orders to spy on the journalists, and did not challenge the constitutional foundations of RICA. Commenting on the judgment, Hofstatter said:

> Spying on journalists and activists has become almost routine for South African security services and the private firms subcontracted by corrupt politicians, policemen and government officials facing exposure. What makes this case significant is that we were able to find proof that the police were spying on us because of our work as journalists, and that at least one official was brought to book for doing so. Hopefully this will make lowly intelligence agents think twice when they are given patently illegal orders to spy on journalists. Now they know there can be real consequences if they are caught, including a criminal conviction. However, it's disappointing that the police generals who gave the orders got off scot free. This only serves to reinforce perceptions that senior officials in the security services can abuse their power with impunity. If the prosecution really wanted to send a strong message that illegal surveillance won't be tolerated, they should have gone after the real perpetrators with more vigour. But perhaps that was never really their intention.[26]

The amaBhungane Centre for Investigative Journalism, a journalism unit formerly based in the *Mail & Guardian* newspaper (it is now independent), has experienced similar problems. The journalist and managing partner of amaBhungane, Sam Sole, had his communications intercepted while he was investigating a story about alleged corrupt practices in a highly controversial arms procurement package of the late 1990s. While he was working on a story related to this deal in 2008, a police informant tipped off Sole that his communications were being intercepted. A complaint laid with the Inspector General's office evoked the response that there was no evidence of wrongdoing on the part of the NIA. In 2015, it emerged that Sole's communications had, in fact, been intercepted in 2008. Transcripts of an intercepted conversation between an advocate in the National Prosecuting Authority, Billy Downer, and Sole, were produced in a legal case brought by the main opposition party, the Democratic Alliance (DA), contending that the withdrawal of corruption charges against President Zuma was irrational. The President's legal representatives in turn contended that Downer had purposely leaked information to prejudice the President's chances of assuming the highest office in the land. At the time, Downer was investigating Zuma's role in the arms deal, and whether he was involved in corrupt activities. The SSA subsequently confirmed that the interceptions took place in the context of investigations concerned with the detection, prevention, suppression or curtailment of subversive or hostile activities.[27] This response made it clear that for the SSA, journalistic communications with a state official amounted to subversion, which, in terms of the National Strategic Intelligence Act, is defined as 'any activity intended to destroy or undermine the constitutionally established system of government in the Republic of South Africa'.[28]

With such a hostile attitude to investigative journalism, it is perhaps inevitable that the SSA and other state security organs have come to see investigative journalists as legitimate targets for surveillance. The amaBhungane journalism unit has alleged that it was undertaking its constitutionally protected journalistic duties in interviewing Downer, and used this disclosure to launch a constitutional challenge to sections of RICA. At the time of writing, the challenge still had to be heard in court. AmaBhungane alleged in the founding papers that there were five constitutional deficiencies in RICA:

- Firstly, that the subject of an interception is never informed of the existence of the direction.
- Secondly, there is no provision in RICA for how intercepted communications are meant to be stored and examined.
- Thirdly, mandatory data retention violated the right to privacy.
- Fourthly, RICA failed to protect the process of the designated judge, in that there is no fixed term for the judge, which undermines his or her independence; the minister appoints the judge at his or her discretion; and there is no adversarial process before the designated judge.
- Fifthly, there are inadequate protections for journalists and their sources.[29]

AmaBhungane also argued that the bulk surveillance capacities of the state were under-regulated, which was a serious problem as there had been evidence of abuse in the past. Moreover, the Matthews Commission had found bulk surveillance to be illegal and yet the activities of the NCC, responsible for bulk electronic surveillance, still continued in spite of an inadequate regulatory framework, which predisposed it to abuse in future. On the other hand, the spy agencies contended that journalists should not be exempt from RICA. While the agency that applies for an interception direction should make the judge aware that the subject is a journalist, no special privileges or interception regime should apply to journalists' communications if they are suspected of criminal conduct.[30] As was the case with wa Afrika, the Inspector General confirmed the lawfulness of the interception direction. According to the Inspector General's report, the NIA had applied for the interception direction in the context of an investigation into information peddlers. The Inspector General was persuaded to make this finding on the basis of two applications to the RICA judge and of interviews, and concluded that the time frames for interceptions had been adhered to. He noted that the target of the interception directions was 'Sam Sole, amongst others', but gave no information about who the others were. The RICA judge at that time was made aware of the fact that the target was a journalist. The purpose of the investigation, it was claimed, was not to establish Sole's sources, but rather to establish whether there was any link between Sole and the alleged information peddlers.[31] In his 2010/11 annual report as RICA judge, Khumalo claimed: 'I am personally not aware of any unlawful secret surveillance carried out by the state agencies. If such is the case the Departments concerned should investigate as a matter of urgency.'[32] Yet, as has become clear (and, so far, one court case has confirmed), even the lawful interception process is capable of being subverted for unlawful ends. In commenting on the significance of their constitutional challenge, the amaBhungane Centre stated the following:

> We are going to court to strengthen the protection of journalists and the public against the abuse of this arguably necessary, but intrusive surveillance law, RICA. RICA serves as the basis for the lawful interception of citizens' communications, but we contend that there are fundamental flaws in RICA and that various sections are inconsistent with the Constitution.
>
> Interception remains a potentially powerful tool in the fight against crime and corruption. But when conversations between journalists and their sources are intercepted, it chills access to information as sources become unwilling to talk. It also appears that it is too easy to abuse interception to manage 'political' threats in a way that does not meet the intelligence services' legitimate mandate. Our court application, among other things, asks that interception is subject to proper constitutional checks and balances.[33]

TRENDS IN THE USES OF LAWFUL INTERCEPTION

Trends in the uses of RICA, gleaned from the designated judge's report, are also useful to assess as they point to how RICA is employed on a day-to-day basis. In the early years of reporting on RICA, the NIA was the leading source of requests for interception directions, followed by SAPS, the Secret Service and the Directorate of Special Operations, or the 'Scorpions' (an investigatory arm of the National Prosecuting Authority, which was subsequently closed down in controversial circumstances). Then in 2008/09, SAPS Crime Intelligence overtook the NIA as the leading requester for interception directions, and the majority of directions were granted to assist the investigation of drug-dealing and drug-trafficking, vehicle theft and car hijacks, armed robberies, corruption and fraud, assassinations, murder and terrorism. The designated judge would not provide more information on the NIA interceptions on the grounds of secrecy.[34] There was also a huge 232 per cent increase in the number of interception directions granted by the designated judge between 2009 and 2010, with SAPS being most responsible for this increase. Furthermore, while 826 interception orders were granted between 2006 and 2010, in a report to the Joint Standing Committee on Intelligence the director of the OIC noted that approximately three million interceptions were undertaken in those years. This figure implies that each interception direction involved many intercepts, and suggests that the scope of many of these interception orders was very broad indeed. After this, there were decreases in the application and approval rates for 2012/13, accompanied by an increase in the number of emergency directions, about which the designated judge also expressed concern at the time. The numbers rose once again in 2013/14, although the increases were unremarkable. For 2014/15, though, the number of applications by SSA and Crime Intelligence rose massively, with the SSA registering a particularly large increase. Two new state agencies were also added as applicants: the Financial Intelligence Centre (FIC) and the SANDF.

The judges' reports also showed a tendency to refuse only a small fraction of the applications. This indicated that the judges were willing to give the applicants

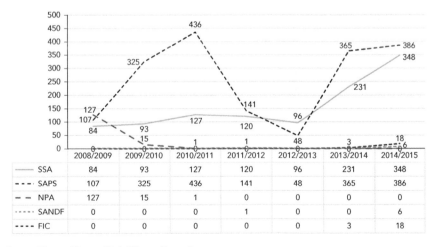

	2008/2009	2009/2010	2010/2011	2011/2012	2012/2013	2013/2014	2014/2015
SSA	84	93	127	120	96	231	348
SAPS	107	325	436	141	48	365	386
NPA	127	15	1	0	0	0	0
SANDF	0	0	0	1	0	0	6
FIC	0	0	0	0	0	3	18

Source: Murray Hunter, Right2Know Campaign.

Figure 4.1: Total number of interception direction applications and reapplications in terms of RICA

the benefit of the doubt, and pointed to biases in the system towards the applicants. In fact, SAPS Crime Intelligence recorded the largest percentage of refusals overall, but even then the refusals never exceeded 18 per cent of their total
applications.

Judge Mokgoro attributed the Crime Intelligence refusals to incomplete or
sloppy applications. However, the SSA applications presented a different species
of problem, as the agency often provided too little information on which to make
decisions: it assumed that using the grounds of national security would be sufficient to convince the RICA judge of the need for the interception direction.
However, she turned down several SSA applications because they did not meet
the evidentiary standard of RICA. She also expressed concern about the tendency
for the SSA to seek directions to conduct surveillance on protests, even in circumstances where she felt it inappropriate, as there was no discernible threat to
public safety and, in any event, people had a right to protest. In fact, it appeared to
her that protests per se were considered to be national security threats. Mokgoro
explained:

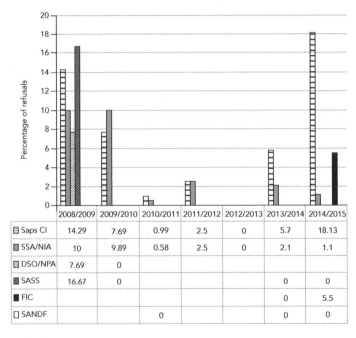

	2008/2009	2009/2010	2010/2011	2011/2012	2012/2013	2013/2014	2014/2015
⊟ Saps CI	14.29	7.69	0.99	2.5	0	5.7	18.13
▦ SSA/NIA	10	9.89	0.58	2.5	0	2.1	1.1
▨ DSO/NPA	7.69	0					
▩ SASS	16.67	0				0	0
▪ FIC						0	5.5
▢ SANDF			0			0	0

Source: Own calculations.

Figure 4.2: Percentage of refusals of applications for interception directions

Note: The 2010/11 statistics were for an 18-month period.

The idea that the State Security can apply for an interception direction simply on the basis of the protection of security of the State is never sufficient. I would always insist as the Act requires, on the need to justify the application on a firm factual basis i.e. showing what facts point to an existing threat to public safety or state security. A mere public protest outside court or a service delivery protest to which people have a right I always emphasised, cannot be viewed as a threat to public safety if it is peaceful. If journalists professionally cooperate with each other supplying local public interest information for purposes of more effective international dissemination, it cannot be regarded as a threat to state security in an application for an interception direction unless it is factually shown in a sworn affidavit how state security is at stake. Besides, even for the National Intelligence an interception direction cannot be a matter of first resort. It must be shown why the same information cannot be secured by conventional means.[35]

It may be argued that the efficacy of an interception direction could be interrogated once an investigation reaches the trial stage and is subjected to an adversarial process. At that stage, if a defendant's legal representative has concerns about a direction, then he or she could file a motion to suppress the evidence. However, on national security matters, this opportunity is unlikely to present itself as the SSA is unlikely to allow its uses of interception to come to light. According to the former co-ordinator of government intelligence and head of the National Intelligence Coordinating Committee, Dennis Dlomo:

[Our] interceptions are not meant for court processes, but for understanding modus operandi, so that you can begin a process of collecting information. Remember that we're talking intelligence here. They can only use these for non-evidence related purposes, because we do not drive the criminal justice system. We can make the case for why cases should be opened, but then the NDPP [National Director of Public Prosecutions] decides whether to open cases or not. Intelligence cannot make the arrests.[36]

As a result, if the RICA process was misused on national security matters, these abuses would almost certainly not come to light at the trial stage. In spite of the sharp rise in the number of applications, the NC as a whole, including the OIC, complained about under-resourcing, and consequently they struggled to undertake the interceptions. In fact, the OIC claimed that most of its equipment dated back to its establishment in 2002, and consequently it was unable to keep up with technological advances.[37] The OIC had argued repeatedly that its equipment needed to be modernised, but with little success.[38] This complaint was, in fact, an old one: the JSCI noted in its 2013 annual report that the NC was under-resourced, and recommended that this problem be addressed with urgency. 'The outdated technology and equipment used by the NC (OIC, NCC and COMSEC) must be replaced and sufficient funds must be allotted to the division. The capabilities of the intelligence entities have been adversely affected by the outdated technology and equipment in use.'[39] According to the chairperson of the JSCI, Charles Nqakula, by the end of 2017 this matter still had not been addressed, and the NC's budget still remained of concern to the committee. In an interview, Nqakula linked this problem to broader crises in government budgets:

> It is one of the problems that the intelligence community has. And of course, it talks to the matter of a budget that is in crisis, and therefore no huge amounts of money have been allocated to the various entities in government, especially within the intelligence community, which is quite a big problem. This time around, obviously, it would be better if people sat down and did a proper assessment of what is required and how this matter of ailing budget can therefore be sidestepped by way of ensuring that it is one of those things in a given financial year that it's necessary to adapt. But this matter of technological advancement is very, very important, given the fact that now, most crimes, serious crimes, are defined as cybercrimes. In order for you to find them you need personnel that is adequately trained ... Secondly you need to have the necessary budget in order for you to train the personnel and to purchase the instruments that you require to deal with cybercrime. This is still a matter that is under discussion.[40]

In addition to these resourcing problems, the internet aspects of RICA have not been implemented. According to the special adviser to the ISPA, Ant Brooks, but speaking in his personal capacity, ISPs do collect information about their clients to verify their identities and, to that extent, they comply with RICA, although this provision was difficult to apply in the case of internet cafés and hotspots. In the decade following the promulgation of RICA, the internet service provider community also spent a great deal of time drafting directives to ensure compliance with the law, which included storage of internet headers. However, the definition of what constituted an ISP was so broad in the Act – it included any person who provides access to, or any other service related to, the internet to another person – that it proved impossible to draft a directive capable of being implemented. According to Brooks,

[The definition] is so delightfully broad that it became clear that it wasn't possible to draft an email-header-retention directive that would only apply to ISPs. Any such directive would also require every university, school, or private company providing access to their staff to also keep five years of email headers. And that would likely have been an impossible thing to sell to the public.[41]

The worldwide trend in communications (South Africa included) is away from voice and towards internet-based and data-driven forms of communications. Yet the wildly unrealistic internet provisions in RICA, coupled with under-resourcing, meant that the OIC was confined to a form of communications surveillance that was rapidly becoming outdated, and was being outstripped by more modern methods (to be discussed in the next chapter). This disclosure suggested that the NC was being run down: a serious concern, given the spiralling crime levels in South Africa, but undoubtedly a gift to the agents of organised crime and corruption.

Another cause for concern was that the office of the designated judge remained under-resourced, in spite of the sharp increase in the number of interception directions. This problem placed tremendous strain on the designated judge, who was required to exercise considerable care in making decisions, but was under pressure to respond to more and more requests. The fact that the RICA process lacked an adversarial component meant that mistakes could creep in: the judge had to make decisions on a one-sided basis with only the benefit of the applicants' arguments. According to Judge Mokgoro, the need for applicants to provide a sworn affidavit that the facts they presented in the application were true provided a safeguard. But she also argued that most judges were averse to taking on the role of designated judge, because the way the system operated violated the legal principle of hearing the other side before deciding. The fact that the system was so under-resourced increased the risk of making mistakes, and a diligent judge who insisted on strong evidence to justify privacy violations would most likely find the role extremely stressful.[42] In this regard, the experiences of Joshua Khumalo – who was duped into granting directions against the *Sunday Times* journalists and Bheki Cele – cast a dark shadow on the office of the RICA judge. According to Mokgoro, these lapses created great stress and anxiety for the judges that followed. She noted:

There was the question whether there is a need to have two designated judges appointed at a time. SAPS thought it was necessary considering what they saw as an increased number of applications, sometimes 40 per week, which they would sometimes submit, making it quite tricky for one judge to handle. My approach was to insist on going through the applications with a fine comb, comparing the sworn affidavit in the application with the previous one to assess the progress made in applications for an extension direction. And there would be times when applicants would have to wait for over a week for directions. I would communicate with the applicant, writing notes in the inner flap of the file, indicating why the direction has not been granted. At times this meticulous method would require working overnight to expedite matters.

If there is insufficient capacity we certainly run the risk of overlooking transgressions. And one cannot take lightly people's right to privacy. Besides it can also mean delaying the timeous acquisition of critical information and thus frustrating the investigative process. I would always remind applicants that this is a difficult role for judges who come from an environment where they rely on the *audi alteram partem* principle which means we always hear the other side of the case before we make judicial decisions. Here you rely only on the evidence provided by the applicant to make inroads into the rights of a person. It is for that reason you require the evidence to be provided in a sworn affidavit before the interception direction is granted, making the applicant liable for criminal action in the case of misrepresentation. If there is indeed a growing trend towards an increasing number of applications for interception directions, then the appointment of an additional designated judge to manage the workload would be justified.[43]

Mokgoro's reflections on her own experience as designated judge point to some of the pitfalls in the existing process and her own deep discomfort at being the only person scrutinising the applications. In an interview, she supported the idea of appointing a public advocate, to assist the judge to consider issues that had escaped his or her attention, and while it could slow the process down, more public advocates and even more judges could address this problem. Yet, at the same time, the parliamentary oversight body on intelligence matters, the JSCI, was reliant on the designated judge's report, as well as those of the Inspector General of Intelligence, to raise the alarm if the RICA process was being misused. Nqakula explained in an interview:

We have to rely on the interception judge that what is being done is legal all the time. The interception judge will know if a particular interception is done legally, and we assume in terms of the law that they check because they are the people who give the permission for those interceptions. Now if there are interceptions that have not gone through that process, then it means that they are illegal. Of course we don't know which ones are done without the authorisation of the interceptions judge, and I would assume that there are interceptions that intelligence agencies throughout the world do without the authorisation of the relevant authority.

... [That's] one of the problems that we have. That's one of the things about oversight. You have to rely on people to give you information because you don't have capacity for investigation as the committee. But available to the committee of course is the Inspector General of Intelligence; that is the office that is responsible for the investigations. And usually we refer matters to them for investigation.[44]

So, based on Nqakula's statements, it is clear that the oversight bodies are reliant on the designated judge to interrogate the applications; yet the designated judge's office lacks the capacity to scrutinise the applications thoroughly, and is in turn reliant on the affidavit which the applicants provide. In other words, the affidavit is the lynchpin around which the entire system turns. As the number of applications and applicants grow, the pressure on this office is increasing. If the affidavit contains incorrect information, then it almost certainly will not come to light, as there is no user notification and hence no after-the-fact scrutiny of the applications. In the case of the *Sunday Times* journalists, that they became aware of incorrect information included in an affidavit was an extraordinary and exceptional case, even a happenstance, rather than the outcome of any investigations by the designated judge or the Inspector General. In fact, the Inspector General's handling of the *Sunday Times* and amaBhungane cases suggests that the investigation into the legality of these interceptions amounted to checking whether the RICA process had been followed or not. As the Inspector General's office refused an interview, it is impossible to verify the exact process that they follow. But the upshot of the process is that if an applicant puts incorrect information into an affidavit, it is more than likely that it will not be detected. As a result, the checks and balances to prevent abuses of RICA are inadequate, as the system is predicated almost completely on the correctness of the affidavit.

In spite of inappropriate levels of secrecy surrounding the RICA process, the amount of publicly available information about RICA and its application increased considerably when Yvonne Mokgoro took over the position of RICA judge. During her term, she raised the bar in reporting on her work, providing an unprecedented amount of information about her activities and the challenges she faced. In 2013, for instance, she expressed concern about the intelligence agencies' lax approach towards RICA applications, as they cut too many corners and made her work more difficult. Mokgoro was also emphatic about the need for capacity-building in state institutions about RICA and its requirements; this undoubtedly has improved compliance. However, Mokgoro has argued that it is not possible to assess the effectiveness of RICA in bringing down crime as such an assessment is of necessity 'highly subjective'.[45] Other factors impact on the success of an investigation, she claimed, including information obtained by other means. Yet if such information can be provided in the US system, then it is difficult to see why South Africa cannot follow suit.

Mokgoro did recognise the need for reforms to RICA, but the reforms she listed were biased towards the intelligence agencies. These included the need to ensure that state surveillance kept pace with technological developments and addressed deficiencies, such as the ease with which criminals can bypass SIM card registration requirements. However, Mokgoro's report remained silent on the legislative reforms needed to address the privacy-violating weaknesses in the Act. Furthermore, her assumption seemed to be that SIM card registration requirements need to be tightened to prevent criminals from obtaining pre-registered SIM cards, but she did not engage with the argument that SIM card registration per se is ineffective for crime-fighting and in fact creates other categories of crime (such as identity theft). Also, according to Mokgoro, the devices utilised by the agencies under RICA did not require judicial authorisation. In fact, once they have obtained an interception direction, they can exercise their discretion as to the interception devices they use.[46] This argument is problematic, as it ignores the international push for judges to regulate particularly intrusive surveillance devices like international mobile subscriber identity (IMSI) catchers (or 'Grabbers', as they have become known in South Africa). This is because Grabbers inevitably collect more information than is needed to target specific individuals. In fact, the judge's report should provide aggregate information about the methods of interception. Hacking alters the device that is hacked, and so the integrity of the information that is exfiltrated from the device is tainted; at the very least, intercept information obtained through hacking should not be admissible as evidence in court. Preferably, more invasive forms of surveillance, like hacking and IMSI catchers, should be subject to higher legal standards than less invasive ones, as not all surveillance equipment is equal when it comes to privacy impacts.

To her credit, though, Mokgoro tacitly acknowledged the dangers of the state's surveillance powers being misused for nefarious ends. In her 2013/14 report, she stated: 'There is a continued general public perception that some law enforcement and other institutions and/or officers use these intrusive interception methods to advance their own interests with no regard to the rights and values the RICA aims to protect in the context of the Constitution.'[47] She also noted media reports containing 'allegations and comments of manipulation and abuse of the interception system by officials and even individuals', for example, where intelligence agencies bypass the judge to intercept communications, or where they do not provide strong enough justifications for their applications. Mokgoro argued that these problems could not be fixed by legislative reforms only. Instead, they required a shift in the culture and practices of intelligence agencies that may be tempted to resort to communications surveillance as an investigative method in the first instance. While undoubtedly there is merit to her argument, it fails to take into account that the problem is not just one of institutional culture, but of law, too. However, the Ministry of Justice and Correctional Services has argued that the safeguards provided in RICA are sufficient to prevent abuse, namely that communications interceptions are investigative methods of last resort; they may only be used in investigating specific, serious crimes; judicial decision-making ensures that the decisions are independent of government; and the Inspector General and the JSCI provide sufficient oversight.[48] However, as should be clear from the discussion above, the system contains inherent weaknesses which point to RICA being a flawed Act, in spite of its very good points.

CONCLUSION

That South Africa has a lawful, targeted interception 'regime' that forbids arbitrary interception, and requires judicial authorisation for interceptions, is a major advance on the situation under apartheid. It is also ahead of other countries where the granting of interception directions are political decisions taken by the executive arm of government. However, there are clearly major flaws in the system. The targeted surveillance capacities of the state, and the law that underpins them, have become dated. It would also seem that despite these problems, they are also increasingly heavy users of the RICA system, suggesting that the need for interception capabilities is growing. Intercept information has been used in the successful prosecution of a number of cases, especially where criminals had committed basic mistakes by using their cellphones. In 2011, for instance, university student Mutshutshu Milton Muvhango was convicted for the murder of his girlfriend after the police obtained their cellphone records; these played a key role in the investigation.[49] In a ringing success for RICA's utility as a crime-fighting tool, in 2012 members of an abalone smuggling gang were convicted after their calls were recorded by the Scorpions following an application to the designated judge.[50] In a 2014 case, Ivan Jacobs was convicted for the murder of his wife after his cellphone records contradicted a statement he made about his whereabouts at the time of her death.[51] In another case where judgment was delivered in 2015, SIM card registration information proved useful in tracing the associates of a suspect, who was subsequently convicted, as the communications records eventually linked the suspect to the murder through a massive trail of circumstantial evidence.[52]

On the other hand, there have also been cases where the intercept information introduced into court proceedings has proved controversial. In a 2008 case that spanned three years, involving the theft of a large consignment of cigarettes from British American Tobacco, some intercept information which was obtained through the Criminal Procedures Act was ruled inadmissible as the magistrate failed to appreciate the test that he was required to apply in considering the application for a procedure. The case provided interesting insights into the type of information service providers give to law enforcement officials on receipt of a subpoena. This includes the IMSI number associated with the particular SIM card, the handset's IMEI number, call dates and types, whether the call was made or received and its duration, the number dialled or received, outgoing SMSs, the base stations to which the phone connected, and the originating base station. The police used that information to determine not only the movements of the suspect, but linkages to his number as well, using a method of mapping geographic movements called 'geo-infomatics'. As this technique allows calls and cellphone locations to be linked by using call tower identification, it was possible to generate maps that provided damning evidence of the planning and execution of the robbery.[53]

However, there is insufficient evidence that the state's seemingly insatiable thirst for intercept information is resulting in increased arrests and convictions, and the specific examples of the successes mentioned above do not help to answer this broader question. On the contrary, the infamous trial of Glenn Agliotti pointed to holes in the system. Agliotti is a controversial businessman who was accused of murdering mining magnate Brett Kebble, but was subsequently acquitted. Part of the reason why Agliotti was found not guilty was that his cellphone records were obtained illegally during the investigation. In his judgment, Judge Kgomo had this to say about the cavalier approach of the police to their acquisition of cellphone records, drawing attention to the fact that interceptions were not as targeted as they should be:

> Abuse of the system by the police was demonstrated by Hodes SC during cross-examination of these cellphone 'experts'. For example, he elicited evidence to the effect that cellphone records of the accused's attorney; himself,

Hodes SC, accused's counsel herein; his (Hodes') father's, also an advocate who has nothing to do with this case; other clients of accused's counsel, Hodes SC, like one Peter Skeet; phones of private attorneys' firms and private investigator Warren Goldblatt, among many others, were subpoenaed and obtained by the police from the cellphone companies.

This elicited a question from me at one stage to the effect whether if and when this country's State President's phone records were subpoenaed, whether they (the cellphone companies) would issue them out without much ado. The answer was that those records would be extracted and handed over without asking another question. It is my considered view that if this state of affairs did occur or does occur and is allowed to persist, WE SHOULD ALL BE AFRAID, VERY AFRAID!!![54]

Heidi Swart's investigations have also pointed to the fact of police adding numbers to existing surveillance projects without permission from a judge.[55] In any event, it is more than likely that the judge will approve applications for interception directions even if they come before him or her: by 2014, the judge was handling approximately three applications per day. With limited capacity to scrutinise these applications, it is hardly surprising that serious failures have crept in. The RICA process and institutions have been run down, and the public safety and security risks of doing so are huge. In spite of spiralling crime levels, there is scant evidence that the government considers the proper resourcing of the RICA process to be a priority. Some of the weaknesses of RICA may well be addressed by an upcoming Cybercrime and Cybersecurity Bill; however, if the Bill is going to make the RICA judge responsible for s.205 metadata requests, without attending to the lack of resourcing of the judge's office, then disaster looms. Furthermore, the Bill seeks to compel communications service providers to store internet browsing information, in addition to call-related metadata; this will compound the privacy violations, without necessarily addressing the very real practical problems that made this provision in RICA unworkable in the first place.[56] Even more worrying, though, are the uses to which the mass surveillance capacities of the state are being put. These will be addressed in the next chapter.

5

State mass surveillance, tactical surveillance and hacking in South Africa

This chapter focuses on mass surveillance, tactical surveillance and hacking in South Africa. It seeks to answer the following questions: Are the kinds of abuses that were revealed by Edward Snowden possible in South Africa, and what in fact is the relevance of Snowden's revelations (if any) for the country? To what extent is South Africa subjected to these forms of surveillance by other countries, especially the Five Eyes, and to what extent does South Africa itself engage in them, too? Needless to say, answering these questions is extremely difficult, given the high levels of secrecy, but it is not impossible to build up some sort of picture, drawing on existing sources.

SOUTH AFRICA AND THE GLOBAL MASS SURVEILLANCE DRAGNET

South Africa's position in the global mass surveillance picture needs to be considered on two levels: as a target of mass surveillance and as a user and producer of mass surveillance equipment. In relation to South Africa as a target, according to documents leaked by Snowden about the NSA's Boundless Informant programme (the programme that initially triggered Snowden's concerns about surveillance of US nationals), southern Africa as a whole is of little interest to the NSA, though South Africa is of slightly more interest than other countries in the region. Predictably, the NSA's attention was focused much more on North and East Africa, especially Egypt, Kenya, Somalia and Libya.[1]

Furthermore, South Africa is not listed as being part of the worldwide signals intelligence operation spearheaded by the NSA in co-operation with its Five Eyes partners, involving the sharing of intelligence, not even as a regional partner. Rather, their main focus areas were countries that could provide intelligence on the activities of Russia and China. Given the sheer scale of the signals intelligence operations, the NSA was concerned about entering into partnerships with other countries to expand its intelligence-gathering capabilities. Several African countries struck up third-party agreements with the NSA to assist it in signals intelligence-gathering, among them Algeria, Ethiopia and Tunisia.[2] South Africa was not included in the names of those disclosed.

However, it would seem from the Snowden revelations that South Africa has not slipped under the NSA's radar completely. The agency intended to build a real-time map of global internet traffic, called the Treasuremap project. This incredibly ambitious project relied in part on thirteen 'unwitting data centres' – including one in South Africa – which gather data on internet-enabled devices and which are linked to the NSA's global data-gathering arm called 'Packaged Goods'. The purpose of the project was to anticipate possible cyber attacks or to lodge a cyber attack of its own.[3] Access to the data centres is not obtained through hacking, according to the *New York Times*, but through front companies set up by intelligence agencies and leasing space on the servers.[4] While the leak does not show that South Africa's networks are included in the NSA's SIGINT collection points, a Pakistani peering partner of South African company Internet Solutions is included.[5] This revelation did not point to South Africa actively facilitating intelligence-gathering for the NSA, although it would seem that the data of South Africans is most likely being scooped up by the NSA dragnet, at the very least for the purposes of network monitoring.[6]

Another programme revealed by Snowden, XKeyscore, also did not feature South Africa. XKeyscore, which searched and analysed global internet traffic using search terms (or 'fingerprints'), was shared with other countries' spy agencies, especially those in the Five Eyes network. It could harvest information from over 150 sites around the world, and looked at browsing histories, emails and calls.[7] In fact, of the 150 sites worldwide, the only one in southern Africa appears to be located in Zambia, GCHQ's well-established listening post on the continent.[8] The documents released so far from Snowden's leaks appear to confirm that South Africa is of very little geostrategic interest to the US and its Five Eyes partners, whose sights are trained on more obvious theatres of actual or potential global tension and conflict. This is in spite of the fact that in August 2010 the US Foreign Intelligence Surveillance Court granted the NSA legal authority to spy on 192 countries, including South Africa.[9]

South Africa has featured slightly more on the UK's radar. According to a 2010 GCHQ document leaked by Snowden, South Africa became a target of dragnet surveillance when the GCHQ stole network keys from the world's biggest provider of SIM cards, Gemalto, which has an office in South Africa,[10] and which also produces South Africa's smart identity (ID) cards. These keys would allow GCHQ to harvest cellphone data. According to a secret wiki leaked by Snowden, Gemalto South Africa was being targeted, too.[11] Moreover, GCHQ was responsible for intercepting the communications of the South African public interest law clinic, the Legal Resources Centre (LRC). In a judgment handed down by the IPT, it found that the LRC's communications were retained and examined in terms of the Regulation of Investigatory Powers Act, and that while the interception was lawful and proportionate, GCHQ did not follow its own internal procedure for the selection of communications to be examined. However, because GCHQ did not make use of the communications, and did not store them either, the LRC did not suffer any material detriment and, consequently, the IPT made no compensation order.[12] At the time of writing, no information had come to light as to why this surveillance was conducted. Significantly, even though the IPT implied that the interception of the LRC's communications was incidental, it failed to consider the negative implications of interception, even if incidental, in potentially threatening attorney–client privilege. This determination underlined the dangers of mass surveillance programmes: privileged communications can easily be scooped up in the spy agencies' dragnet.

SOUTH AFRICA AS PRODUCER AND USER OF MASS SURVEILLANCE

Apart from the traditional arms manufacturers, some companies have carved out niches as major surveillance actors. Little is known about surveillance companies based in countries outside the US and Europe, like China and Russia, but what has become clear is that some countries are responding by becoming producers and exporters of specific products, especially countries that have not dominated the arms industry, but whose production capacities could expand if markets were found for their products, such as Israel and even South Africa. Security experts in mid-sized military powers like Israel are attempting to position themselves by monetising skills gained in warfare against opponents.[13] In fact, Israel has the highest number of surveillance companies per capita. Israel's lack of controls over the transfer of security knowledge from the public to private sectors makes the commercialisation of military knowledge possible, and its own military-industrial complex has become an incubator for surveillance start-ups.[14]

South Africa does not appear to be as prominent as Israel in developing its surveillance industry, but there are indications that local firm Vastech is attempting to expand its role in 'developing country' contexts where markets for social control technologies are not as saturated by the established players. The company has boasted that it offers cutting-edge passive surveillance technologies that rival those of the most advanced government agencies, although it claims that it does not sell its products to countries that are subject to any sanctions.[15] The company was incubated in the Innovation Hub, a science technology park in the capital city of Tshwane, established by the Gauteng provincial government in 2001. According to the Innovation Hub, Vastech was not provided with funding, but as a start-up company was offered space to operate and provided with business mentorship.[16] Yet the company received start-up government funding from an innovation fund in the Department of Trade and Industry. This suggests a close relationship with the South African government although Vastech has claimed it is a private company independent of the state.[17] In fact, Sam Vaknin, an Israeli author with knowledge of global intelligence matters, told journalist Heidi Swart that 'they are considered government in global intelligence circles. People talk about them as if they are the long arm of the South African government. No one will regard them as private sector.'[18] Yet, there is little evidence of due diligence having been conducted on the likely impact on human rights of Vastech's funded mass surveillance products.[19] Vastech refused requests for an interview on these issues, but produced a statement stating that it provides products for lawful interception by law enforcement agencies, for use only by governmental agencies, and only those that are internationally recognised by the UN and not subject to any sanctions. If the status of any country changed for the worse, Vastech said it would review its commercial relationship with that country.[20]

While all these companies provide different surveillance technologies targeting different forms and stages of the communication process, governments are increasingly seeking 'one-stop-shop' surveillance solutions that allow them to conduct surveillance from centralised points. More surveillance companies are responding to this demand by marketing monitoring centres, allowing governments to access communications content over voice networks, as well as any IP-based traffic, and store this traffic to permit retroactive searches to be made. The integration of various forms of communication, combined with their searchability, turns them into far more powerful surveillance tools than those focusing on specific networks or surveillance functions, as communications are pooled in one point, making analysis easier. As they offer panoptic central surveillance points, monitoring centres can be particularly dangerous if they fall into the hands of authoritarian governments.[21]

For instance, Vastech's Zebra monitoring centre – which boasts the ability to 'reach back in time and discover new targets and networks of collaborators'[22] – was sold to Libya while Muammar Gaddafi was President, and was reportedly used to monitor the communications of thousands of citizens, including activists, vastly increasing the ability of the government to crack down on pro-democracy protests.[23] With such capabilities, it is small wonder that governments have become ready markets for such technologies, and more and more companies are lining up to oblige. Yet, at the same time, many monitoring centres are also being subjected to the export controls of the Wassenaar Arrangement, including Vastech's Zebra.

South Africa has its own mass surveillance capabilities. In fact, evidence has emerged of the country having established its own mass surveillance centre (the NCC), as well as manufacturing, exporting and importing mass surveillance technologies. In the days of voice only, foreign signals intelligence-gathering was relatively simple as it merely needed to concentrate on telephone networks. Now, there are multiple communications platforms, including some that operate on a cross-country basis, making it difficult to distinguish between foreign and local signals. These technological advances present spy agencies with enormous challenges. With some of the longest-running internet exchanges in the region, South Africa has a highly developed internet infrastructure. A great deal of internet traffic stays in South Africa, as it is passed between various local internet service providers and exchange points. The South African internet is connected to the rest of the world via five undersea cables. Their combined capacity is in the region of 42 terabits. By way of contrast, the UK has capacity to tap 21 petabytes per day, through probes it has installed in 200 cables.[24]

Given the high levels of secrecy around the trade in surveillance tools, it is very difficult to map the sales of surveillance technologies to South Africa. What have been confirmed are sales from two European countries to South Africa since the Wassenaar Arrangement was amended in 2013. These were uncovered when a network of European media outlets launched a series of information requests in EU countries.[25] In terms of the first transaction, the Danish subsidiary of BAE Systems, BAE Systems Applied Intelligence (formerly ETI) sold large-scale mass surveillance software, in the form of an IP Network Communications Surveillance software suite, to South Africa for serious crime and national security purposes. This will allow the agency to undertake network communications interception and analysis. Sources in this investigation into the sale have stated that the equipment sold was either the Evident or the Vigilant system. The systems are apparently the same product, the difference being that the former is meant for law enforcement purposes, while the latter is for intelligence purposes. These products were sold by the

BAE Systems subsidiary in the 5a001.j category of the Wassenaar Arrangement.[26] This category is extremely narrow, covering network surveillance equipment that is capable of processing large volumes of internet traffic, undertaking application-layer content inspection, and extracting and indexing metadata and content. The equipment should also be capable of searching the indexed data for individual identifiers, as well as of mapping the relationships between individuals based on the collected data. The category also covers software capable of operating these systems, as well as technical data or assistance to operate them.[27]

While typically the sellers' identities are kept confidential in surveillance technology sales, the Danish authority responsible for approving sales did not redact the released documents very well, which made it possible to identify the seller. Furthermore, the authority failed to redact the name on an end-user certificate, which indicated that the purchaser was the SSA. The sale also included servicing, testing, maintenance and support for the system.[28] The system was delivered to South Africa before 31 December 2014, and an additional licence was sought in 2016 for upgrades.[29] There were four components of the sale, listed under separate categories. The first was 5A0001.j, referring to IP network communications surveillance systems or equipment, which is capable of conducting analysis at the application layer of the internet, extracting data or metadata and analysing it, executing searches based on hard selectors, and mapping the relational networks of an individual or group of people. The second was 5A002.a.1, referring to cryptographic equipment for information security purposes. The third and fourth were 5D001.c and 5D002.c.1, covering software specially designed or modified to provide characteristics, functions or features of IP network communications surveillance systems.[30] So invasive are the tools sold under these categories (particularly 5D002.c.1) that they can threaten other countries' national security.[31]

ETI, which developed the Evident/Vigilant systems, was taken over by BAE Systems when demand for internet surveillance equipment increased in the wake of the Arab Spring, creating a lucrative marketing opportunity for the UK company.[32] While the system was designed to assist in targeted, lawful interception – and in that regard was both ETSI and CALEA compliant – it had powerful mass surveillance capabilities. The system could either be used with the co-operation of communications service providers or provide the agencies with direct access. The Evident system was designed to address the challenges of communications across multiple platforms in that it could provide interception, storage and analysis solutions across a range of circuit-switched and packet-switched (or IP) networks, although its main speciality was in relation to IP networks. Its automatic speaker identification or voice recognition capabilities could exclude the voices of people other than the device's owner (such as a person who borrows the target's cellphone to use it). This feature also included gender and language recognition, and could even distinguish whether a language was spoken by a foreign language speaker. It could handle large amounts of IP data, and offer passive and active monitoring solutions, either through collecting data from a probe in the network or having the data captured by network elements and then forwarded to its interception units.

A standard version of the Evident system offered a thousand selection criteria, including Voice over the Internet Protocol (VoIP) phone numbers, chat names, email addresses and phone numbers. It could also store network traffic for twenty-four hours.[33] Apparently, an add-on allowed the system to monitor the internet communications of an entire country, and could also be used to follow people around, as it had a Geographic Information System (GIS) viewer. This viewer allowed an agency to identify the location of a target from cellphone intercepts, follow a target's movements and travel patterns, and identify when the target used an irregular route, thereby enabling the agency to link a particular incident to a target.[34] Another add-on allowed an agency to use metadata to generate relationship charts, showing when the target communicated, with whom and how often, so that the agency could build up a picture of those with whom the target was associating, and enable it to expand its surveillance to those individuals, too. In order to access the metadata, all the user needed to do was to click on a link between people or communications to obtain direct access to the data.[35] However, while Evident could intercept, decode and render data from standard email packages, VoIP, chat packages and unencrypted internet protocols such as Hypertext Transfer Protocol (HTTP), until 2011 the system was unable to decrypt encrypted forms of communication such as Skype and Hypertext Transfer Protocol Secure (HTTPS). In such cases, all it could do was detect and intercept the raw encrypted data, and store it for further cryptoanalysis, or use it as a basis to implant intrusion tools in the target's laptop.[36] Apparently a later version does have decryption capabilities, but how strong those capabilities are is not known. Confirmation of the Evident system sale means that South Africa has access to an extremely powerful mass surveillance tool across multiple communications platforms.[37]

The Evident system has been sold to several countries with terrible human rights records, such as Saudi Arabia, Qatar, Oman, Morocco and Algeria, and it is highly likely that the technology was used to crack down on Arab Spring-style protests and movements.[38] The equipment is also very similar to that sold to the United Arab Emirates, which includes capabilities to map a target's social networks and extract personal information from communications devices.[39] The Tunisian government under the authoritarian leader Zine el-Abidine Ben Ali used it to track down his opponents. According to a source speaking to the British Broadcasting Corporation (BBC), the system was operated to provide intelligence about dissidents to Ben Ali directly, leading to their being targeted by the regime. As the case of Evident shows, Denmark has become an important exporter of surveillance equipment, and consequently offers considerable expertise in the area.[40]

As regards the South African purchase of Evident, it does not appear from the export document that the SSA acquired the location tracking or decryption add-on during the licence period, although this did not preclude it from doing so at a later date. Given that the chairperson of the JSCI, Charles Nqakula, confirmed in an interview that by the end of 2017 the under-resourcing of National Communications still remained a concern, the question arises why this extremely large and significant purchase had not ameliorated the problem. It also raises questions of where in the SSA this piece of equipment has gone and what uses it is being put to, given the spiralling levels of organised crime in the country. As Nqakula argued, state surveillance has to present the country with a 'value-for-money' proposition, otherwise the whole state communications surveillance system is called into question:

> For starters, when you use the RICA Act in order for you to deal with crime, there must be reasonable return on investment. One of the things about the secret account [of the SSA and Crime Intelligence] is that if you are given a particular amount of money, let's say R500 million, over a given financial year, that R500 million has to be commensurate with your product ... and it has to be visible. It becomes visible when you look at the crime statistics that are there in that year, released by the Minister of Police. You only apply to the interception judge to use interceptions when you want to break a big criminal syndicate. Now if you are unable to do that, then the question arises, why did you need the RICA Act? If you don't arrest the people who are planning, then what was the purpose? We must check if these translated into arrests.[41]

Yet, in spite of the need for this 'value-for-money' proposition, the surveillance equipment and the interceptions undertaken appear to be disappearing into a black hole.

A less significant sale than that of Evident involved the purchase, by an unknown South African entity, of telecommunications interception equipment in the mobile surveillance category, which includes IMSI catchers. The UK government approved this purchase, so it must have been made from a UK-based company. The listed device was a Searchlight Plus GSM/UMTS Detection and Location System, which is manufactured by the London-based International Procurement Services. This is a form of IMSI catcher that allows the operator to detect and locate the exact position of a mobile device. According to the manufacturer, it sells this product only to government end-users or accredited technical surveillance countermeasures companies.[42] It is unclear to which government agencies these pieces of equipment were sold, but given the reference to national security in relation to the Danish sale, it is not unreasonable to assume that the sale was for the SSA's NCC. It seems that the sales were not for the OIC.

Since the revision of the Wassenaar Arrangement, there has been more evidence of South Africa importing and exporting dual-use software, although too little information is provided by the NCACC to be able to determine the exact nature of the technologies, and whether they would qualify as communications surveillance tools. In 2012 and 2013, there was no evidence of software being listed either for import or for export.[43] However, in 2014 the NCACC approved the significant sale of command and control software to Angola, and a much less significant sale to Sweden.[44] In 2015, the NCACC approved a sale of software for spectrum surveillance to Saudi Arabia and simulation software to China.[45] In 2016, India and Saudi Arabia were recipients of South African unspecified 'software'. The NCACC also approved the importation of software from France, Germany and Sweden for insignificant amounts. In the same year, it also approved signal jammers sold to Kenya and Serbia.[46] These can be used to jam a range of electromagnetic signals, including signals emitted from communication devices, as happened during the South African President's 2015 State of the Nation address in Parliament. Significantly, there was no evidence of the importation of the Evident system from Denmark or the IMSI catcher from the UK.

Attempts have been made to bring the NCC under greater legal controls. In 2008, a bill setting out the mandate and function of the NCC was introduced in Parliament, but was subsequently withdrawn. Consequently, the NCC operates without a statutory basis, which is highly problematic as, according to the Constitution, rights can be limited only through laws of general application. It would appear, though, that the NCC does fall under the Intelligence Services Oversight Act, as well as the National Strategic Intelligence Act, but there is no law setting out the NCC's powers and functions explicitly. According to the JSCI, the NCC has the following responsibilities: to analyse the electromagnetic spectrum and programme the acquired signals to extract usable information; to install and maintain SIGINT collection platforms; and to conduct feasibility studies to identify new geographic signal collection sites. This description means that not only is the NCC continuing to undertake mass surveillance for intelligence purposes, but it is actively expanding its capacity to do so.

In justifying its bulk surveillance activities, the SSA has resorted to well-rehearsed arguments that spy agencies have made elsewhere. It has argued that bulk surveillance is an internationally accepted method of monitoring transnational signals to screen them for certain key phrases and to ensure that the country is protected from transnational threats from individuals or organisations outside South Africa's borders; the information may be intercepted from transnational signals – including electromagnetic, acoustic and other signals – and undersea fibre optic cables. For the SSA, bulk surveillance is an automated process, with no real human intervention. So the selection of traffic for further analysis is carried out by machines, not humans, and the rest is discarded without anyone having looked at it. The SSA has also argued that it has a vested interest in retaining only that data that is of interest to the agency, as it would be too expensive to store too much.[47] It has also set out its understanding of what constitutes foreign signals intelligence, which 'includes any information that emanates from outside the borders of the Republic (in this case, South Africa) and passes through or ends in the Republic'.[48] Conceivably, this definition could also include the communications of locals, as some of their internet traffic is likely to be routed through foreign-based servers (particularly in the US), and could qualify as a foreign signal if a South African is pulling data from a foreign server. The GCHQ has recognised this complexity, but has muddied the waters even further by arguing that a social media network like Facebook is a 'platform' as opposed to a service. In practical terms, for GCHQ, communications such as commenting on a friend's post would qualify as an external signal, even if all the friends are in the UK. This assertion is based on the misapprehension that friends communicate, not with one another in the first instance, but with the platform. While this may not be the correct legal interpretation of foreign signals, it is possible that the SSA follows the same definition for operational purposes. In the case of GCHQ, this operational definition, coupled with the practical realities of how the internet works, meant that up to 85 per cent of foreign signals intercepted consisted of the internet traffic of UK residents.[49]

In making these arguments, the SSA assumes that the privacy impacts of bulk surveillance are minimal or non-existent, as human beings are not intervening in the process. Furthermore, the agency argues that surveillance is not arbitrary: it is informed by the cabinet's National Intelligence Priorities, and includes 'classical' national security concerns (such as terrorism and organised crime), as well as national security concerns informed by South Africa's human security mandate (such as food and water security, and illicit financial flows). The SSA also has a vested economic interest in not storing too much data, as the costs of doing so would be prohibitive; so it is forced to be discerning in what it stores.[50] There are other controls that the SSA claims exist, such as the oversight provided by the JSCI in terms of the 1994 Acts, as well as the Inspector General of Intelligence. Furthermore, the SSA has argued that its bulk surveillance capacities are covered by RICA. Lastly, the SSA is reluctant to provide any more information about the NCC and its activities as this could expose operational methods and would be detrimental to national security. According to the former co-ordinator of the National Intelligence Coordinating Committee, Dennis Dlomo:

> RICA and the National Strategic Intelligence Act provides for regulation, what should and shouldn't be done. The mandate is foreign signals intelligence collection, the method is … if you say you want to put into the public domain, you are informing people about how you do your business. At an academic level, you may be able to say this is an operational policy and this is an operational method. From where we sit, RICA provides for foreign signals … it's not how you do it, it's what it is. Foreign signals is not the what, it's the how. The broad principles in RICA are applicable to foreign signals, but the interception direction is for domestic interception. There is a possibility of a secret court for foreign signals. In 2005–2008 there was a big debate that National Communications Centre should be closed down, but in 2009 government decided to keep it.[51]

The SSA's arguments do not, however, meet a six-part test laid down for strategic intelligence-gathering recognised by the European Court of Human Rights – a test that any mass surveillance law should meet. While the ruling predated the kinds of internet-based mass surveillance being discussed here, the case did concern strategic surveillance of telecommunications networks to avert national security threats. The test includes a clear statement on the nature of the offences giving rise to the surveillance; clearly defined categories of people liable to have their communications intercepted; limits on the duration of interception; adequate procedures for the examination, analysis and storage of the data obtained; adequate precautions when disseminating data to other parties; and clear statements about when the data obtained may be erased or the records destroyed.[52] While the government has the discretion to decide when to engage in strategic surveillance, this cannot be an unfettered discretion, and the public needs to know the circumstances that will trigger such surveillance. Compounding the problem is the fact that there is no provision for reasonable suspicion that interception subjects have committed crimes; there is no prior independent authorisation of mass surveillance by a judge, even through bulk warrants, and there is no requirement for subsequent notification made to interception subjects of the interception measures taken against them.[53]

As mentioned already, the selection of data of interest requires human intervention in the communications flow. This human intervention happens when the SSA decides on the selectors to be used to sift the data of interest. So privacy is affected at that very point. In fact, privacy violations begin when there is an interference with the ordinary flow of data, and it is diverted from its intended paths into the country. Selectors are applied only once the traffic has been extracted, which is where the initial intrusion occurs. Furthermore, the SSA's argument that it lacks the resources to store large amounts of data is cold comfort and does not address the issues of principle. If the resources available to the SSA increased, or its technical ability to store more data improved, then the inference of the agency's argument is that it would collect and store more data. As a result, the resources argument cannot be considered a safeguard.

Deciding on selectors is a subjective process, and analysts' assumptions and even prejudices can be brought to bear on the sifting process. The broader the selectors, the more subjective the process is likely to be. The SSA has made it clear that its grounds for monitoring the electromagnetic spectrum are broad, which may not be supported by the narrowed definition of national security in the GILAA. Also, the broad grounds for monitoring the spectrum imply soft as opposed to hard selectors: the softer a selector, the greater the potential for privacy violations, as these selectors will intercept more traffic than hard selectors. As South Africa does not have a foreign signals intelligence-gathering court, the selectors used are not approved by a court process, which implies that their approval is undertaken internally, thereby increasing the potential for abuse. Even if it is accepted that mass surveillance is a legitimate agency practice, as soon as agencies decide that they want to look at intercepted communications, they should seek a warrant. There is no indication that the SSA follows this procedure.

Furthermore, the SSA has not provided a clear statement about the offences that trigger bulk surveillance. The application of the human security definition of national security to this process makes this requirement even more necessary. As there is also no requirement for individualised reasonable suspicion, the communications of innocent people are thus being diverted and stored, with no known limits placed on the duration of the surveillance or the categories of people to be surveilled. Whether or not the use of mass surveillance is proportional to the level of external threat the country faces is an important consideration in South Africa, as the SSA has insisted repeatedly that it faces no major external threat to national security. As Ben Emmerson has argued about dragnet surveillance:

In the end, in order to justify these programmes as proportionate on that macro level, because there is after all no individual specific proportionality analysis to be conducted, where you're drag netting vast amounts of data from an unidentified number of people, the only way to really justify this proportionate is if states are in a position to persuade their electorates that the total abrogation of the right to privacy is justified on counterterrorism grounds, so as to make it proportionate to have the capacity to survey, read, monitor the communications of a potentially infinite number of innocent people anywhere in the world.[54]

If bulk surveillance in South Africa is focused on foreign signals, despite the country facing no major foreign threat, then it is difficult to understand how the SSA justifies the inevitable invasions of privacy. The SSA's mass surveillance regime is also premised on the problematic assumption that foreigners are somehow less deserving of rights than locals, which makes the regime discriminatory on the grounds of national origin. In effect, the SSA is using the fear of foreign threats to national security to engage in speculative fishing expeditions to check the behaviour of entire populations, whether innocent or guilty. As has been shown in the US, such mass surveillance is inherently susceptible to abuse.[55] The South African government could argue (like the UK government) that when it comes to foreigners, it lacks the domestic instruments to investigate possible or actual crimes. Therefore, intercepting foreign communications traffic in bulk is the only way it has to obtain external communications for national security purposes, and it needs the 'haystack' in order to find the 'needle'. The government could also argue that the very nature of internet traffic – which is broken up into packets when it travels – requires it to intercept large amounts of traffic to obtain all the packets needed to reassemble suspect communications.[56] However, if it is collecting and analysing more data than it actually needs, then there are no publicly available rules compelling it to discard unwanted communications, and not store and analyse collateral data. In other words, the technical nature of data traffic should not be used to justify fishing expeditions.[57]

The public could be forgiven for being suspicious about possible abuses of the NCC, as there has been evidence of abuses in the past. These make the lack of legislative clarity about the NCC unforgivable. In 2005, the state's mass surveillance capacity was misused to spy on perceived opponents of Jacob Zuma, then a contender for the presidency. This was in spite of the fact that the NCC was meant to confine itself to collecting foreign signals intelligence, and was not allowed to collect domestic intelligence. In the investigation by the then Inspector General of

Intelligence, Zokile Ngcakani, into these incidents, he found that the bulk scanning or mass surveillance facilities at the NCC had been used to keep at least thirteen South African politicians, businessmen and officials in the public service under surveillance, including businessman Saki Macozoma, former head of the Scorpions Leonard McCarthy, former Director of National Public Prosecutions Bulelani Ngcuka, and journalism professor Anton Harber.[58] A subsequent report into these incidents, commissioned by the Minister of Intelligence, argued that the activities of the NCC were unconstitutional because they involved spying without permission from a judge, and recommended that the NCC should fall under RICA.[59] The Inspector General also argued that the powers of the NCC were under-regulated, and that a law needed to be developed to give it a statutory backdrop.

After the commission completed its work, and in response to its damning findings about the NCC, Minister of Intelligence Ronnie Kasrils introduced two bills, the Intelligence Services Amendment Bill and the National Strategic Intelligence Amendment Bill. The first provided for the establishment of the NCC and the second for its functions, including the collection and analysis of foreign signals intelligence. Both bills were withdrawn in the same year that they were introduced, as the parliamentary committee apparently felt that they required more work, and recommended that they be reintroduced when the new Parliament was established, as a national election was pending. However, it was only in 2011 that the Ministry of State Security (formerly the Ministry of Intelligence) tabled a General Intelligence Laws Amendment Bill in Parliament. The main purpose of the bill was to bring all several existing intelligence agencies under one roof, and establish the SSA, as the number of agencies had proliferated down the years, leading to potential incoherence. Yet, at the same time, centralisation carried new dangers with it, in that it increased the potential for political control for nefarious reasons: this was why the 1995 White Paper on Intelligence argued for the establishment of two security agencies – one focusing on domestic intelligence and the other on foreign intelligence – rather than a single body, as this was considered necessary to allow them to focus on their respective mandates and operate according to different line function responsibilities, and to avoid the dangers of undue political control.[60]

During deliberations in Parliament, the initial idea of establishing the NCC as a separate body was scrapped, as it would fall under the SSA in line with the bill's intention of consolidating existing intelligence entities. However, all references to the NCC and foreign signals intelligence were withdrawn, and so the NCC no longer fell under the bill and remained without an underpinning of primary legislation. While its existence could be provided for in regulations, this would be an entirely unsatisfactory arrangement as, in terms of the Constitution, rights such as privacy should only be limited by primary laws of general application, and, in any event, intelligence regulations are generally developed in secret.[61] According to a minute of the ad hoc committee's deliberations on this issue:

> The Chairperson advised that the omission of any reference to the NCC and NICOC was a matter of policy. The proposed new White Paper on Intelligence would be a more suitable forum for introducing policy changes relevant to the NCC and NICOC. The intention of the Bill was to establish the SSA as a legal entity so that proper managerial and financial controls could be implemented.[62]

Consequently, the NCC was centralised into the SSA without the most controversial aspects of its existence being addressed through a public process. During the deliberations, the ANC argued that the regulation or non-regulation of foreign signals intelligence, which fell within the mandate of the NCC, was a policy matter, not a technical matter. It maintained that as the bill was advanced as a technical bill to give the newly established SSA a legislative mandate, the NCC had to be stripped out. The SSA also argued that, in any event, the NCC is 'regulated' by the Constitution and that the JSCI and the Inspector General perform oversight. However, as the Inspector General's office itself and the Matthews Commission highlighted, this form of 'regulation' is completely inadequate as it does not address the specificities of the NCC, its powers and functions, and consequently the NCC could not be held under constant review. The JSCI and Inspector General operate largely in secret, making transparent oversight of the NCC impossible. These legislative lacunae predispose the NCC's mass surveillance capacities to abuse. The fact that in its 2013 report the JSCI expressed concern that the NCC's Operations Audit Committee was not carrying out all its operational audits did not provide much comfort, either. Such audit trails are essential for establishing which interceptions have taken place, and who has accessed the interceptions.

South Africa mirrors the global shift in communications networks from voice to data.[63] This means that the information which the law enforcement and intelligence agencies need is not flowing through South African telecommunications companies only, which are regulated by RICA, but through US companies like Google, Facebook and Skype. Increasingly, these companies are using encrypted communications, and as a result countries like South Africa risk 'going dark', or losing the ability to intercept communications. As consumers become more privacy-sensitive, they are more likely to entrust their communications to companies that take security seriously and that have rolled out secure sockets layer (SSL) encryption – which allows a website to make an encrypted link with a server – as a matter of course. End-to end-encryption, where communications between sender and recipient are encrypted and the encryption keys are installed at the end points rather than being retained by the service provider, is eroding the effectiveness of dragnet surveillance. This is most likely where the future surveillance battles lie.[64]

Law enforcement and intelligence agencies are responding by compelling communications service providers to retain data and decrypt data pursuant to a decryption order. South Africa also has a provision in RICA compelling decryption keys to be handed over after a decryption direction has been issued by the designated judge. However, these agencies may well be overestimating the problem of encryption. Encryption is unlikely to be adopted on a very widespread basis for practical reasons, and in any event, even if it is, there are many more sources of online information available to the agencies. Metadata, which has grown in importance as an investigative tool, is not currently encrypted, for instance, and it cannot provide the clarity available from content, as it can also present a great deal of investigative 'noise'. Patrick Ball of the Human Rights Data Analysis Group has even referred to official claims of 'going dark' as a fallacy in an era of information abundance. In fact, while some sources of information are 'going dark', others have become 'brilliantly bright'. What is more, the agencies will face even more dangers from an investigative point of view if people abandon their devices altogether.[65] The agencies need to weigh up how many people can be helped by exceptional government access to encrypted data with how many people will be harmed by it. To that extent, the fight against surveillance should not necessarily become a stark fight between individual liberties and the collective national security interest, as this is a false binary.[66]

ENCRYPTION AND HACKING IN SOUTH AFRICA

Countries can respond to the encryption challenge (if they respond at all) by raising the technical capabilities of their agencies or diminishing the protections for everyone.[67] Several governments, including the US, UK and China, have sought to compel communications companies to build backdoors into their equipment, but so far these attempts have been unsuccessful. As a relatively insignificant player in the global communications picture, South Africa is unlikely to exert much influence in this debate, and attempts to insist on national legislation are likely to result in US-based companies pulling out of the country or providing significantly weaker products from a security perspective. Unless the major players agree to do so, especially the US, it will be practically impossible for South Africa to consider this possibility, and, in any event, the US administration has taken the proposal of leg-islating for backdoors off the table, at least for the moment. The only other option a country like South Africa has is to increase its use of spyware and hacking tools, and to become an importer of off-the-shelf equipment acquired from specialist multi-national companies. Hacking also assists agencies to circumvent the often lengthy process of seeking the co-operation of communication companies outside their borders and, therefore, outside the jurisdiction of their courts. Spyware like that offered by the Gamma Group and HackingTeam may be considered 'poor person's surveillance tools', as richer and more powerful governments like US can afford to build their own custom spyware and buy and stockpile zero-day vulnerabilities (that is, vulnerabilities in computer software that hackers take advantage of on the same day that they are discovered).[68]

Confirming sales of exports is not the only way of tracking export flows to South Africa: tests can also be conducted to detect the presence of surveillance tools on communications networks. The University of Toronto's Citizen Lab, which special-ises in detecting communications surveillance tools on networks, has identified controversial deep packet inspection (DPI) equipment manufactured by the US surveillance technology company Bluecoat on the servers of many major internet companies in South Africa. Citizen Lab is a multidisciplinary, university-based research entity that examines the use of internet equipment for political purposes, and analyses its human rights implications.[69] It detected a specific product called PacketShaper in South Africa. This software can be used to maintain network traffic and filter malware such as viruses; however, these uses do not require inspections to penetrate to the content layer of the internet, which it is capable of doing.[70] It is generally recognised that there are seven layers of the internet, with the applica-tion or content layer being the deepest. DPI can penetrate this deepest of layers. Such software can also be used for surveillance purposes as well, as it allows intel-ligence agencies to inspect network traffic; however, given PacketShaper's broader network management uses, it would not necessarily be defined as a dual-use tech-nology in terms of the Wassenaar Arrangement. It is unclear what the exact uses of PacketShaper are in South Africa.[71]

Citizen Lab also identified FinFisher on two IP addresses belonging to commu-nications parastatal Telkom in South Africa. FinFisher is a weapons-grade intru-sive spyware suite sold exclusively to governments, and has been implicated in sev-eral surveillance abuses in authoritarian countries such as Bahrain and Ethiopia. FinFisher is particularly useful for monitoring security-conscious and mobile tar-gets who make extensive use of encryption, as it can be used to take control of a target's computer as soon as it is connected to the internet, and it can even turn on web cameras and microphones for surveillance purposes. It is much more targeted than other mass surveillance tools, as it is used to track the online habits of a known target, rather than for indiscriminate, dragnet surveillance.[72]

The existence of FinFisher in South Africa was confirmed after the Gamma Group's servers were hacked and information leaked about its clients, although it is difficult to authenticate the leaked documents with any certainty. According to the documents leaked from the group's systems and subsequently published by WikiLeaks, by 2014 FinSpy was the most popular product in the suite. It is a Trojan (or a malicious computer program designed to hack into a device) which can intercept and record a wide variety of information from an infected device, including Skype chats and calls, instant messaging, emails, audio from the microphone, and video from the webcam.[73] FinSpy is particularly useful for hacking cellphone- and laptop-using mobile targets who are security aware and hence make use of encryption, and who travel internationally, as the product can allow the operator to take control of a mobile device anywhere in the world.[74] Other products in the suite, such as FinFisher Relay and FinFisher Proxy, relay the intercepted communications to the operator in ways that disguise the operator's identity, and the data is ultimately stored in a FinFisher master server, which is installed on the operator's premises. South Africa was the third largest named user of FinFisher after Slovakia and Estonia, with a total of 23 licences, while the largest unnamed user held 47 licences: in other words, the WikiLeaks evidence suggests that South Africa is indeed a significant FinFisher user.[75]

According to the WikiLeaks documents, South Africa has purchased three base licences for FinSpy: one in 2009, which expired in 2011; one in 2009, which expired in 2013; and one in 2009, which expired in 2014. No information is available about licences from 2015 onwards. Each base licence allowed the operator to target up to a hundred devices, and also included three agents. Other licences were for other FinFisher products, such as FinIntrusion, which allowed the operator to hack into a wireless network, capture the user names and passwords of the targets, and take control of their accounts;[76] FinFly LAN for local area networks; and FinFly USB for when the operator has physical access to the target's computer. Citizen Lab detected FinFisher command-and-control servers on the Telkom network in 2013. More seriously, it detected a master server in South Africa, which meant that not only was FinFisher present in South Africa, but that it was most likely being operated by a government department, given that the manufacturers sell only to governments. Citizen Lab's discovery strongly suggested that the South African government continued to be a FinFisher user beyond the expiry of the last recorded base licence in

2014, and that it could well have renewed a licence. However, Citizen Lab could not confirm which government department was using FinFisher.

Furthermore, three sources with links to the South African security establishment confirmed to journalist Heidi Swart that the government was using FinFisher, with one stating that the NCC was the holder of a base licence, and another stating the same for the SSA.[77] The former source also claimed that South Africa had a strong reputation for using malware to spy on people, with journalists, politicians and activists being key targets.[78] The Department of Justice and the Ministry of State Security maintained that RICA provided sufficient regulatory guarantees to prevent privacy violations if hacking software was used, but given that the activities of NCC are not covered, and that the RICA judge does not consider the types of technology used when granting interception directions, it is evident that this most invasive form of surveillance is grossly under-regulated.

It is also not wise to adopt a technologically neutral approach to surveillance, as hacking alters the devices that are hacked, affecting the integrity of the information that is collected and thereby rendering it useless for evidentiary purposes. As hacking can circumvent encryption, it is a particularly invasive form of surveillance, and it also threatens cybersecurity. Therefore, hacking needs to be regulated as a discrete form of surveillance conduct, and with even more stringent controls than other forms. The standard legal principles should apply to hacking, such as the need to prescribe these powers explicitly in law, and seek a court warrant before using this power. The potential risks and damages to the security of the targeted device, and how these risks can be mitigated, should also be assessed and this assessment should be included in applications for warrants. The grounds for issuing a warrant for hacking should be even more stringent than those applying to more passive forms of surveillance, and the judge should be empowered to consult with a technical expert to assess the application before granting it. There should also be provisions in the law to prevent agencies from altering, deleting or adding data to the targeted device, and in addition to notifying the surveillance subject as soon as possible, the hardware and software manufacturers should be informed too.[79] Former RICA judge Yvonne Mokgoro could recall processing only two applications for hacking interceptions: these were from the FIC. In those cases, she conceded that she was required to apply the usual RICA standards in deciding whether to grant the directions, in spite of the evidentiary problems to which hacking can lead, and the lack of special procedures for hacking in the law. However, she argued that the fall-back position would always be whether the approval of the interception direction could be constitutionally justified.[80] Given that the FinFisher licences were in operation at least partly during her term of office as RICA judge, her disclosures suggested that much more state hacking was taking place on an extra-legal basis.[81]

The company that is widely considered to be FinFisher's competitor in the intrusion software market is the HackingTeam, whose footprint appears to be larger than that of FinFisher, particularly because it has established footholds in the massive Middle East, North African and Russian markets. The HackingTeam sells only to governments, and markets a spyware product called Remote Control System (RCS), which can capture data on a person's computer even if it is never sent over the internet. It can also capture encrypted information. The spyware is geared towards defeating encryption, and is installed on unsuspecting users' devices when they open an executable file, or authorise the installation of an application; alternatively, the spyware can make use of exploits or 'bugs' in the computer's software.[82] Leaks of internal correspondence suffered by the company in 2015 suggested widespread contact between this company and various state entities in South Africa, including the SAPS and SARS. Leaked documents and correspondence from the HackingTeam indicated that it was quite aggressive in seeking new markets, including in South Africa,[83] although the company's correspondence with a SAPS official suggested that instability in state agencies rendered them unable to take full advantage of the most invasive surveillance technologies. However, in spite of extensive contact between HackingTeam and several South African state agencies, South Africa does not feature on Citizen Lab's list of suspected government users of RCS.[84] Furthermore, it does not appear that HackingTeam has managed to establish a foothold in South Africa.[85]

IMSI CATCHERS AND TACTICAL SURVEILLANCE IN SOUTH AFRICA

Another increasingly important form of surveillance is tactical surveillance: that is, surveillance that does not require physical installation of surveillance tools in a network. Surveillance undertaken on physical networks, on the other hand, is likely to involve the modification of network equipment to pass network traffic from communications service providers to intelligence or law enforcement agencies, although traffic can also be delivered directly to them, thereby bypassing the service providers. Tactical surveillance has the advantage of being unencumbered by these considerations as it does not have to involve the co-operation of the service providers. One of the most controversial tactical surveillance tools, which has become more visible in the past few years, is the IMSI catcher, otherwise known in

South Africa as the 'Grabber'. In South Africa recently, the police caught criminals in the act of trying to buy one, and apparently a second Grabber is still at large.

State law enforcement or intelligence agencies typically use these devices to identify a suspect's location, provided they know the person's cellphone number, or, if they do not, to identify a suspect's number for tracking purposes. IMSI catchers can also track data-only devices. If they fall into the hands of criminals, they can be used for a range of purposes, including espionage. The problem is that in order to identify a targeted individual these devices have to suck up the information of all other cellphone users in the vicinity, even if they are not suspects. This means that the information of thousands of cellphone users could land up in the hands of the state, for no good reason, or of criminals. These devices allow the state to identify whether people are at home, and even where they are in their homes: in other words, this constitutes a search, and no search of a private space should be conducted without a warrant. According to Christopher Soghoian of the ACLU, 'If the government shows up in your neighbourhood [with an IMSI catcher], essentially every phone is going to check in with the government … The government is sending signals through people's walls and clothes and capturing information about innocent people. That's not much different than using invasive technology to search every house on a block.'[86]

Location data is part of metadata, yet many state agencies in other parts of the world have resisted proper regulation of these devices, basing their arguments on the outdated assumption that metadata should receive lower privacy protections than communications content. Many agencies also refuse to confirm or deny the use of these devices, arguing that the disclosure of operational methods could jeopardise their investigations. Yet, secrecy may have a grubbier motive, which is to force state agencies to keep information from the public to prevent a backlash against their usage. Some agencies have signed non-disclosure agreements with manufacturers, and have even attempted to hide their usage from judges, prompting a judicial backlash.[87]

The devices can be extremely valuable for law enforcement. In one case, for example, they were used to track a rape victim's cellphone to the rapist's home. But governments can also abuse these devices to spy on legitimate political dissenters, not just on criminals. Activist organisations have claimed that the police are using them to monitor legitimate protests, a recent example being during anti-police violence protests in Chicago in 2014. Governments need to start accounting properly for their use of these devices, which can be done without jeopardising specific investigations.[88]

The ACLU released recommendations for federal uses of the devices. Not only should policies require a search warrant based on probable cause, but these warrants should also contain information about the number of people that stand to be affected. They should also spell out measures the agencies have taken to minimise invasions of privacy. The ACLU argued that law enforcement agencies should purge all non-target information immediately, and disallow its dissemination or use. Agencies should stop attempting to conceal their use during court proceedings, and they should be prevented from signing non-disclosure agreements with manufacturers. Information about the number of times the devices have been used should be disclosed publicly, as should all operational policies relating to their use. These proposals provide a useful starting point for privacy advocates. After years of judicial criticism and civil society pressure, the tide began to turn in the US. In 2015 the US Justice Department released a policy requiring its agencies to seek warrants for use of the device, although the policy does not apply to state and local agencies. Divisions using the device need to provide annual reports on their use.[89] In fact, in 2016 a federal judge suppressed evidence gathered by the US Drug Enforcement Administration using a 'Stingray' without a warrant, on the basis that its use constituted an unreasonable search.[90]

What is the position in South Africa? RICA prohibits the manufacture, assembly, possession, sale, purchase or advertising of interception equipment without a certificate of exemption issued by the relevant minister. Furthermore, a regulation issued in 2005 in terms of RICA forbids the manufacture, assembly, sale or purchase of surveillance equipment, including cellular telephone interception devices. However, while the law is silent on IMSI catchers specifically, the device could be considered to fall under the forbidden equipment listed in the regulation.[91] Apparently, the device can be bought only with presidential authority.[92] Heidi Swart has reported that several sources told her that IMSI catchers had been used by South African law enforcement agents to effect renditions of at least two foreign nationals suspected of being involved in terrorism, one of which was subsequently declared illegal (the rendition of Pakistani national Khalid Rashid in 2005).[93] The UK sale of an IMSI catcher to South Africa has made it clear that the equipment is present in the country, and two criminal cases that were under way at the time of writing also pointed in a similar direction.

The first case involved Paul Scheepers, a SAPS Crime Intelligence official who also operated as a private investigator, and who was arrested and accused of trafficking in metadata and other charges, including selling an IMSI catcher to a cash-in-transit company illegally. The state claimed that his company acted as an agent for a UK company called Forensic Telecommunications Services which manufactured an IMSI catcher called FTS Seeker.[94] This device can allow its operator to detect the identity of a cellphone in a specific area, by recovering the IMEI number and SIM card number of the device, which then can be used to check against the billing records of network operators.[95] The second case involved four people, including an employee of the Department of Public Service and Administration, who were accused of conspiring to sell an IMSI catcher illegally after they had bought it from the Israeli company Verint. The IMSI catcher sold by Verint, the Engage PI2 Tactical Location System, was more powerful than the ones reportedly imported from the UK, in that it had a variety of 'smart' functions. Not only could it intercept cellphone traffic over a wide area, including voice and metadata, but it could also identify suspicious communication patterns using voice recognition, location and text matching, decrypt encrypted communications, and analyse calls for multiple users at the same time.[96] The company was reportedly under the impression that the sale was an official sale to the South African government, and that it obtained official verification. At the time of writing, it was unclear whether the official verification provided to Verint was bona fide.[97]

When asked about whether they were using the devices in their work, and, if so, whether they had applied for an interception direction from the designated judge in terms of RICA, SAPS did not respond to the questions.[98] Yet a newspaper article quoted Hawks spokesperson Hangwani Mulaudzi as confirming that government security organisations do have access to the devices, and use them for national security purposes.[99] The Ministry of State Security's spokesperson Brian Dube neither confirmed nor denied their use. According to Dube, 'Well, it becomes difficult for us to reveal the make and details of the equipment we use for the very simple reason that it has the potential to compromise the very work we are doing. With the technological race that is out there between states and organised crime syndicates, it's not advisable to disclose such details.' When he was asked whether the SSA would apply for an interception direction if it did use them, Dube responded, 'On the matter of procedure, the interceptions protocol applies whenever an individual's communications are to be intercepted. Such a protocol doesn't provide for "mass interception" as the interception judge must hear each case on its merit.'[100] This statement speaks volumes about the ministry's attitude towards the devices: it sees them as being about mass surveillance in the main, and, according to the ministry, mass surveillance would not be regulated by RICA. The inference is that even if the SSA used them, there would be no judicial oversight of their use.[101] In fact, former RICA judge Yvonne Mokgoro confirmed that during her term of office, she did not process any applications for the use of IMSI catchers, though she recalled the OIC expressing a great deal of interest in obtaining one, as it was clearly a powerful crime-fighting tool.[102] Furthermore, the JSCI was aware of certain Grabbers having found their way into private hands, in spite of the fact that intelligence-gathering was restricted to the designated state entities. According to its chair, Charles Nqakula:

> The problem that we have is that the JSCI basically has responsibility for oversight over government entities. But let me tell you, there are a number of people who have brought in Grabbers, and there are many people who are into hacking, and it's causing big problems. The rule that talks to intelligence is clear in the Constitution, that only entities that can collect intelligence information are those that resort under government, these three entities that we are responsible for, the SSA, defence intelligence and crime intelligence. But there are many people who are collecting intelligence out there, and are using very advanced intelligence instruments for this purpose including the grabbers, the hacking tools. But we've not been able as a country to prosecute anyone. For instance it is known that there are about eight grabbers that are not under the control of government. There are so many people who are involved in hacking. It's one of the biggest problems, hacking especially, in the world.[103]

Yet at the same time, the JSCI has made it clear that RICA does not require specific surveillance devices to be authorised. Once clients have been authorised, they are free to use any device they see fit: an unsatisfactory position for a device that is as invasive as an IMSI catcher.[104] In fact, arguably, the judicial regulation of IMSI catchers in South Africa is even more urgent than in the US. This is because South Africa has SIM card registration, while the US does not. The device allows for the tracking of unknown phones, which in countries that do not have SIM card registration is less of a problem. The devices will merely generate a series of numbers, and the state will not be able to track these back to specific individuals without considerable effort. But in countries with SIM card registration, such as South Africa, the state could, at the touch of a button, print out the names and addresses of every single cellphone-carrying participant in a rally or protest, for instance.[105] Furthermore, unlike forms of mass surveillance that involve network probes, IMSI catchers leave practically no trace of their surveillance activities, which means that they can be used practically undetected.

SOUTH AFRICA, PRIVACY, SURVEILLANCE AND MULTILATERAL INSTITUTIONS

Systemic problems with South Africa's communications surveillance policies and practices have not gone unnoticed in international forums. In 2016, the UN Human Rights Committee released a report on South Africa's compliance with the International Covenant on Civil and Political Rights (ICCPR).[106] The ICCPR is an international agreement that protects a range of human rights, including privacy. South Africa ratified it four years after the transition to democracy, in 1998. While the report focused on South Africa's general performance in relation to the ICCPR, there were specific findings on the country's regulation of communications surveillance in terms of RICA. In fact, the report included a blistering attack on the government for failing to respect the privacy of communications users. The committee's findings repudiated the government's claims that RICA was justifiable, given the country's extremely high crime rate and the global terrorist threat. It criticised South Africa for inadequate privacy safeguards in RICA, and expressed concern about 'the relatively low threshold for conducting surveillance in the State party and the relatively weak safeguards, oversight and remedies against unlawful interference with the right to privacy [in RICA]'.[107]

The UN committee raised a number of specific concerns about communications surveillance in South Africa, including the fact that the NCC did not appear to fall under RICA, and that the grounds for issuing interception directions in RICA are vague and speculative. The committee also expressed concern about the lack of independent oversight of the designated judge's work, which increased the scope for abuses. Disappointingly, though, it did not pronounce on SIM card registration. It also did not pronounce on the fact that RICA does not make provision for user notification, despite the growing international lobby supporting notification as a general rule.[108] In spite of these silences, the committee's report was a major advance for the struggle for privacy of communications in South Africa, and it remains to be seen if the government reforms RICA to take these criticisms into account.

If the government's responses to other UN initiatives on privacy are anything to go by, it is very possible that it will merely laugh off the committee's findings. South Africa voted against a UN resolution on the 'promotion, protection and enjoyment of human rights on the internet', along with a number of other countries such as Kenya, China, India, Cuba and Venezuela. In this case, China and Russia voted for amendments to the resolution that would weaken online freedom of expression and strengthen governments' abilities to shut down the internet in times of social conflict.[109] According to South Africa's Deputy Permanent Representative to the UN, Ncumisa Notutela, while South Africa supported the right to freedom of expression, this right is not absolute and cannot extend to incitement to hatred. Online users must exercise both rights and responsibilities in this regard, she argued.[110] This decision came as no surprise to UN watchers. A year earlier, South Africa failed to support a resolution calling for the establishment of the Special Rapporteur on Privacy, on the grounds that it was not a priority for the country. According to the UN report, 'The draft resolution on the right to privacy in the digital age raised pertinent issues of priority for South Africa … While recognising the importance of this thematic issue, the creation of a new mandate to deal with the right of privacy was not the appropriate way. It would have been appropriate to incorporate it with the mandate of the Special Rapporteur on Freedom of Expression.'[111] However, this approach would have overburdened this Special Rapporteur, and the novel nature of the issues required a dedicated focus, necessitating the establishment of a separate Special Rapporteur. Ironically, the move for a Special Rapporteur was spearheaded by Germany and Brazil, one of South Africa's partners in BRICS. Patterns in South Africa's voting suggest that it promotes an anti-colonial stance at the UN, not voting against countries that have been the victims of colonial rule, while not voting for motions favoured by former colonial countries, although the fact that the resolution on the Special Rapporteur on Privacy was supported by Brazil problematised this position.[112]

CONCLUSION

The available evidence suggests that South Africa is not a serious target for mass surveillance by the US and other Five Eyes countries, although perhaps because of the relatively more important geostrategic role of South Africa for the UK, slightly more interest has been shown by GCHQ. On the whole, however, it does not appear that South Africa is an ongoing focus of interest, which confirms the longstanding view of intelligence agencies that it is not considered a terrorism hub. Yet, in spite of there being no major threats to the country's national security, there are signs that South Africa's own intelligence agency has developed potent tools of passive and active surveillance; in doing so, it has participated in the global surveillance technology race, rather than challenging it and its underlying logics. In fact, it has sought to become a global player itself in this very race, by attempting to become self-reliant and developing its own industrial capacity to produce and export mass surveillance tools.

So it is hardly surprising that the South African government has been neutral, at worst, and downright obstructive, at best, when it comes to global multilateral attempts to develop appropriate human rights standards in the wake of the Snowden disclosures. It would be against the country's military-industrial interests to see tighter regulation of surveillance technologies, as it would reduce its access to markets. Its membership of the Wassenaar Arrangement is encouraging, but the arrangement is proving to be a weak framework for regulating the global trade in surveillance, as it does not prevent sales of these tools to countries that violate human rights on a regular basis. In any event, confining the regulation of the trade to rights-violating countries only is not an adequate response to their global proliferation, as these tools are under-regulated even in countries that are widely considered to be 'mature democracies'. Certainly, in South Africa they are under-regulated. At the same time, there may not be compelling enough political reasons for South Africa to invest too heavily in mass surveillance. As the Israeli author Samuel Vaknin has argued:

> It would be journalists, liberal activists, academics, enemies of intelligence services. This equipment (like the Zebra) is truly all-pervasive. It's for countries who want to monitor literally every single phone call, every single sms, every single email and IP, and Voice Over IP conversation. With minimal investment – a tiny room, toilet size – you can have equipment that could listen in on twenty million people. South Africa is not this kind of country – whatever you may think of the government. South African authorities and intelligence services are definitely widely tipped to be abusing surveillance for their own ends. But they are far more likely to use malware injectors, and software like FinFisher or FinSpy.[113]

It is only a matter of time before the crypto-wars around encryption and hacking, which are unfolding in other countries like the US and the UK, begin to play themselves out publicly in South Africa. That they have not done so yet is because there has not been a proper public debate about the use of hacking tools by the South African government; as a result, it has not felt the need to justify its acquisition of invasive hacking software like FinFisher. While there has been slightly more debate about the regulation of tactical surveillance tools like IMSI catchers, this debate, too, is in its formative stages. The fact that former RICA judge Yvonne Mokgoro has argued that RICA does not regulate specific surveillance technologies has not helped matters. However, South Africa appears to lack the capacity to produce next-generation hacking tools, and so it is still dependent on the some of the larger multinational surveillance technology companies. As things stand, it appears to be unable to exercise full sovereignty in surveillance matters. As a result, South Africa could be said to play a sub-imperial role in relation to surveillance. While it has taken a critical stance on the US's prosecution of the war against terror on several occasions, and to that extent has appeared to play an anti-imperialist role, when its role in the global surveillance networks is examined, it becomes apparent that it is acting as a collaborator with imperialist forces. This it is doing by acting as a middle power in the surveillance industry, and even potentially playing a 'deputy sheriff' role (to use Patrick Bond's term) by positioning itself as an exporter of surveillance technologies to other countries in the global South. It is also reproducing the very surveillant relationships that have come to characterise countries in the global North. To that extent, it is collaborating with, rather than challenging, imperialism.[114]

6

Privacy, surveillance and public spaces in South Africa

Communications networks are not the only sites of data-driven surveillance; increasingly, public spaces are being placed under surveillance, too. This chapter assesses the extent to which this is the case in South Africa by looking at the growth in the use of CCTV cameras, drones and other forms of locational tracking for surveillance purposes. Before the advent of computers, street-level surveillance was mainly physical; people would be followed and suspicious vehicles or individuals would be stopped in roadblocks. More recently, computerisation has greatly enhanced the ability of the authorities to track people in public spaces. Unlike the kinds of communications surveillance that Snowden exposed, CCTV cameras represent more visible forms of surveillance. Although, theoretically, this makes it more likely that publics will debate the pros and cons of such technologies, public debate has largely been muted, with most of the critical debates taking place in academia and rarely finding their way into popular discourse.

Increasingly, these street-level (or, in the case of drones, above street-level) forms of surveillance are going 'smart': that is, they are incorporating features that allow them to collect and transmit data for further analysis by computers, thereby becoming powerful policing tools. This information can allow law enforcement or intelligence agencies to identify individuals and track their movements. In some cases, locational tracking systems set up for commercial or public safety purposes – such as to monitor traffic flow or to bill people for premium road usage – may begin to be used for policing purposes as well: a form of function creep that can raise serious data protection concerns. This chapter explores the extent to which these challenging issues are emerging in South Africa, by examining the concept of locational privacy and its relevance to three street-level or public surveillance projects:

CCTV roll-out in major cities, surveillance and automated e-tolling, and emerging regulations around drone usage in public.

CCTV, STREET-LEVEL SURVEILLANCE AND LOCATIONAL PRIVACY IN SOUTH AFRICA

Locational privacy refers to the right of people to move about freely, without having their movements tracked. A person's movements constitute personal information, which he or she has a right to exercise control over. This right is becoming increasingly important, as information about people's movements can reveal a great deal about their personal, social and political activities. Governments of a more authoritarian bent can, for instance, misuse this information to establish a person's political involvement and associations. Locational privacy is a fairly new and novel aspect of privacy rights. Some jurisdictions do not even recognise it as a justiciable issue yet, arguing that people cannot have a reasonable expectation of privacy in public spaces. But these arguments miss the point that location-related devices are becoming cheaper and more widespread, which means that the potential for them to be used for anti-democratic surveillance purposes has increased. These devices may be mobile, such as mobile phones, which can pinpoint a person's location through their Global Positioning System (GPS). Location data can also be inferred from the base stations to which a mobile phone connects, although it may not allow for a person's precise location to be pinpointed.[1] Law enforcement or intelligence agencies can obtain such information in real time from a communications network service provider, or as metadata archived by these providers. Location-based services are the perfect mass surveillance tools, as they collect and store vast quantities of locational information for further analysis.

CCTV cameras are becoming more widespread in public spaces, to assist in a range of public functions such as crime-fighting; as a result, it is becoming more difficult for people to protect their locational privacy in public spaces. CCTV cameras are linked to a display monitor, used for the purposes of monitoring human movement in particular spaces, like streets and shopping centres. A video recorder can also be added to record activities, but the problem with CCTV is always the human capacity to process the information gleaned. CCTV cameras can only film fixed areas; unless they are ubiquitous they cannot be used to track movements. The need for human monitoring places a natural limit on the analysis of camera footage, but with digital tools of analysis this is changing. When linked to a computer with algorithmic software, huge amounts of footage can be analysed. These camera-based surveillance systems can capture information about a person's physical location, although some may provide only real-time information, while others may record information for further analysis. Privacy-enhancing technologies, such as software to blur people's faces, are also available and should be used, unless this defeats the purpose of using the cameras in the first place. It is important that measures should be put in place to limit the amount of personal information collected, and there should be controls on who has access to it and the basis on which it is disclosed.[2] Increasingly, however, CCTV cameras are becoming a 'normal' feature of public life, with cameras tracking people's movements as a matter of course. Video analysis tools also allow for more sophisticated analyses of footage: facial recognition technology, for instance, can be used to identify a particular person from a facial database. As these could be used to identify people engaging in politically sensitive activities, such as protests, the concern arises that governments may be tempted to use them for anti-democratic purposes. Computer analysis enables CCTV to be turned into dataveillance devices (that is, devices that conduct surveillance through the collection and computerised analysis of data), which make individuals and their movements more visible to the state.

CCTV cameras also impact on another form of privacy, namely physical privacy – the right of people to protect the personal space around them and restrict access to their bodies, relationships or other personal spaces. Physical privacy is less well regulated than informational privacy, especially physical privacy in public spaces. While it is often assumed that people do not have a right to privacy in public spaces, invasive activities that erode a person's right to privacy – such as photographing a person in public without consent or making permanent video recordings of a person's movements – can be considered to be covered under privacy rights, as constant surveillance in public spaces can violate a person's right to autonomy and anonymity.[3]

Once CCTV cameras contain personal information, the footage can fall under data protection laws. In the UK, the Data Protection Act requires people who are under camera surveillance to be informed that this is being done, and by whom, and people can also request images recorded of themselves. When CCTV cameras are installed, the authority should also erect signs stating that the area is being subjected to CCTV camera surveillance, and listing the responsible authority and its contact details. Because of the privacy-invasive nature of CCTV, some privacy commissioners have issued guidance notes on how cameras should be installed, and the rights of those who traverse an area monitored by CCTV. These include the right to be informed of the existence of the cameras, the right to know who is operating the cameras, the right to request personal information recorded by those cameras, and the right to request deletion of that information. Policies and procedures governing these cameras should be made publicly available and should be developed through a public consultation process. The number of staff collecting the information should be limited to those who are absolutely necessary to perform the stated function; extraneous information should be deleted and the information should not be used for purposes other than those for which it was intended, without the consent of the person whose information it is, unless it is covered under a law enforcement or national security exemption.[4] And therein lies the problem: the criminal justice and national security exclusions create huge scope for abuses on the grounds of fighting crime or protecting national security.

There are widely celebrated examples of major successes with street-level surveillance. For instance, CCTV was central to police operations after the '7/7' bombing attacks on London's Underground in 2005, in that the arrival of the bombers at King's Cross station was captured on CCTV footage. After scouring thousands of hours of footage, the police were able to release the identities of three of them.[5] After the London attacks, surveillance cameras proliferated throughout the UK, as officials feared similar incidents happening again, and needed to demonstrate to scared publics that they were doing their utmost to prevent attacks. While there was wide public support for their roll-out, the UK authorities began to introduce more invasive technologies linked to CCTV, yet with little public debate about the implications. It has proved to be very difficult to use CCTV footage in police cases, as the footage is often of not very good quality, and the cost of running extensive networks of CCTV cameras and analysing the footage can outweigh the benefits. As a result, regulation of these technologies has not kept up with technological advances.

Automatic number-plate recognition (ANPR) software, a UK invention (it was developed at Cambridge University as an anti-terror tool),[6] is particularly under-regulated, and involves CCTV cameras taking photographs of vehicle licence plates, identifying the plates using optical character recognition (OCR) software, and then transmitting the information to a reader that compares a vehicle's licence plate to databases so as to allow the owner's identity to be established. As this data can be transmitted off-site through the internet, it means that CCTV cameras that are loaded with it are not, strictly speaking, acting as CCTV cameras anymore, in the sense of being non-broadcast closed circuit devices.[7] Typically, ANPR software locates the date, time and location of the vehicle and even photographs of the driver and front-seat passengers. In the UK, this information can be stored for up to two years.[8] Official reasons for ANPR have shifted from tracking stolen vehicles to documenting unregistered vehicles to a more generalised 'vehicle intelligence'.

The shift towards intelligence-led policing as the dominant policing model has provided policy grounds for the growing use of locational information as a form of intelligence. The police have also relied on the growing prominence of property crimes in overall crime statistics, rather than contact crimes: a growth that was driven by increases in the number of such crimes being reported to insurance companies (although these increases could well have been driven by insurance-related fraud, rather than actual property crimes).[9] As a result, more UK cities have developed 'rings of steel' around their perimeters.

Media reports of investigative successes from CCTV surveillance may give a misleading picture of the effectiveness of this form of crime-fighting. Academic studies that focus on the broader context, and not just isolated incidents, have questioned the success of CCTV cameras in fighting crime. CCTV is more effective at countering property offences than violent offences. Some research points to their being most effective in specific contexts, such as parking lots, and least effective in open spaces. Needless to say, other kinds of crime are not recorded by street cameras, for example, white-collar crime and domestic crime, and this feeds the perception of crime as being mostly street crime perpetrated by strangers.[10] Critics have also accused CCTV systems of displacing crime rather than deterring it. Where reductions in crime levels have taken place as a result of CCTV, they were localised and often not statistically significant. In the case of London, CCTV did not contribute significantly to prosecutions – and this reduced its usefulness as an investigatory tool. In fact, in 2016 the Westminster Council announced its intention to scrap its CCTV cameras, in order to save costs.[11] In justifying this decision, the council pointed out there was limited evidence that CCTV cameras prevented crime and disorder.[12] On balance, CCTV cameras are not very effective in preventing crime, and do not necessarily make people feel any safer.[13] In fact, Clive Norris has described the continued spread of CCTV, in spite of limited evidence to the contrary of its crime-fighting value, as 'the success of failure'.[14] What is attractive about CCTV, though, is that it is part of a broader ideological construct in which the authorities are seen to be doing something about crime: this sits comfortably with the shift in neoliberalism from rehabilitation to retribution as the main model of criminal justice.[15] Experiences with CCTV also demonstrate a technologically determinist faith in the superiority of technology to solve social problems: a faith which in the case of CCTV has proved to be largely misplaced.

It is surprising that ANPR has not been more controversial, as it is premised on a shift in policing away from suspicion as a basis for conducting a vehicle check to random checks: in other words, no longer is the citizenry considered innocent. Rather, every car and its driver become potential suspects until computer analysis determines that they are not. Tracking the movements of vehicles 'just in case' is indisputably a form of mass surveillance, similar in scope to that exposed by Snowden. Presumably, the lack of controversy about the system stems in part from the fact that, to their credit, the software developers used a 'privacy by design' approach, whereby information about a particular driver will become visible to a law enforcement official only if the driver is on a 'hot list'. This feature has made concerns about privacy easily dismissible;[16] instead it focuses attention on how members of the public get to be on hot lists and whether they should, in fact, be there in the first place.

The roll-out of ANPR in the UK has been much more panoptic in nature than in the US, as in the former the system is nationally controlled, whereas in the latter local police agencies have established their own ANPR capabilities.[17] The accuracy of ANPR has also been the subject of controversy, leading to the possibility of vehicles being misidentified: these problems relate to the accuracy of the OCR software, inappropriate camera installation and the sharpness of the images.[18] However, ANPR captures can be extremely accurate.[19] Furthermore, ANPR does not have to be used on a mass surveillance basis for it to be effective, as the data generated by these systems does not have to be stored for it to be used to track suspicious vehicles, as these can be stopped once they are flagged. In other words, the surveillance uses of ANPR are in excess of what is needed to meet the stated purpose of bringing down vehicle-related crimes.[20] While there have been notable detection successes, the excessive nature of ANPR can lead to its being ineffective in crime-fighting situations.

However, as with conventional CCTV, when viewed on a broader scale ANPR has not been particularly successful at achieving its stated purposes. In fact, it is at its most effective when used as an adjunct to other, more traditional and targeted investigative tools. For instance, in 2009 ANPR was used to identify a sex offender who murdered a teenager, yet the police failed to stop his car. Following this incident, the official police watchdog body, the Independent Police Complaints Commission (IPCC), found that the police units involved either failed to monitor their CCTV news feeds consistently or, when they did, they missed crucial information. Furthermore, the IPCC expressed concern about the police involving themselves with minor offences, leading to their becoming distracted and missing information crucial to major offences.[21] A case has also been reported in the UK of ANPR being used to identify a vehicle at a peaceful protest; as a result its occupants were profiled as domestic extremists and stopped by police.[22] While the different functions of ANPR have largely been kept separate – especially the traffic management functions on the one hand and the policing and national security functions on the other – there is a possibility that in future the two will be merged and traffic surveillance systems will become available for law enforcement and anti-terror purposes as well.[23] In other words, the nature of the ANPR system lends itself to function creep.

More CCTV cameras are also loaded with facial recognition software, which matches faces seen on camera to individuals listed on various watchlists, such as lists of criminals or terrorists. CCTV cameras have played a role in tracking the movements of those they put under surveillance, but they have been unable to identify the individuals caught on camera: facial recognition allows them to do just that. In the past, it was extremely difficult to recognise individuals from CCTV footage, as so much of it was blurred, but improvements in camera technology, involving the use of ultra-high definition lenses, allow for easier recognition of faces. However, these technologies are making it more and more difficult for people to participate in public life anonymously, as they create the possibility of their being identified remotely against their wishes. It is estimated that the FBI has approximately 14 million faces in its image databank, and in the UK the police are estimated to have a databank of 18 million faces. Many of these will be the faces of innocent people; but they are likely to remain on file for life, even if no crimes have been committed.[24]

Facial recognition has become controversial in that it has used personal data gathered for one purpose, for another, and not necessarily with the data subject's consent. For instance, in 2011 the British Columbia Privacy Commissioner criticised the Insurance Corporation of British Columbia and the police for using the corporation's driver's licence database to identify people involved in a riot at a hockey match.[25] Indeed, this is one of the most criticised features of facial recognition: if it is confined to matches using criminal 'mugshot' databases, then fewer privacy issues may arise, but the fact that databases of ordinary, innocent civilians may be searched raises serious questions about their privacy rights. In effect, innocent citizens are being subjected to what has been described as a virtual, perpetual line-up.[26] Facial recognition carries with it the risks of false positives or false negatives; police studies have also suggested that the technology may have an in-built racial and age bias, in that it has more difficulty identifying black and younger people accurately, increasing the potential for falsely accusing people of a crime based on race or age, and hence leading to racial or age profiling.[27] Most controversially, some police departments are exploring the use of facial recognition in CCTV cameras in public spaces to scan and identify ordinary passers-by in real time: a truly frightening prospect, as it means that pedestrians can have no expectation of privacy in public spaces whatsoever.[28]

CCTV IN SOUTH AFRICA

South Africa is no stranger to CCTV, given the high levels of paranoia about crime in public and private spaces. While the state has lacked the funding to roll out a national CCTV network, most major cities have CCTV cameras in their inner-city areas, and cameras have also been installed in universities, schools, shopping centres and residential areas.[29] Many of these cameras are privately owned and funded, and their operations have been largely unregulated owing to non-existent privacy and data protection measures: a lacuna that will hopefully be addressed when South Africa's information regulator is established. CCTV initiatives have been confined mainly to the bigger cities in South Africa, where public–private partnerships have made them viable. Furthermore, CCTV systems have not been integrated with other databases, such as the SAPS criminal record system or the stolen vehicle registry system.[30] This means that CCTV cannot be said to be part of an overall panoptic system of state surveillance. Reported successes with CCTV surveillance in central business district (CBD) areas, leading to successful prosecutions of street-level crimes, have ensured public buy-in for increasingly ubiquitous CCTV coverage.[31] However, when the evidence moves beyond anecdotal cases, and the more widespread effects are examined, the findings become less certain. The difficulty of assessing the impacts of CCTV on crime is made harder by the fact that no independent impact assessments have been undertaken,[32] and the public is consequently forced to rely on the state's version of events, which for public relations purposes emphasises the positive impacts. When police research is undertaken away from the glare of the media, a more troubling picture emerges. For instance, a study of CCTV use in the Gauteng town of Benoni suggested that crime was being displaced to parts of the city that were not under surveillance. Furthermore, the admissibility into evidence of CCTV footage remains unclear.[33]

Notwithstanding these unclear outcomes, various state actors are increasing the sophistication of the cameras and are beginning to roll out smart CCTV cameras. In 2016, the City of Johannesburg (CoJ) announced that it was introducing smart CCTV cameras complete with ANPR and facial recognition technology, as part of its 'Safe City' initiative. In a statement that had echoes of pre-crime policing, former Mayor Parks Tau said about this initiative, 'These cameras have face recognition technologies, number plate recognition technologies and are able to detect or anticipate when a group of people are planning a smash and grab.'[34] CCTV has been in existence in Johannesburg for over fifteen years, with a network of cameras being run in co-operation with the local police force (the JMPD), the national police (SAPS) and a number of other law enforcement agencies.[35] Publicly, the city has boasted a huge reduction in crime in the inner city as a result of the CCTV cameras,[36] although a 2012 Johannesburg City Safety programme report was rather less sanguine about the successes. Confirming international experiences with CCTV, the report noted successes with property crime, but found that the cameras were an insufficient deterrent against violent crime. It also noted that the city lacked the capacity and skills to analyse the camera feed. The report concluded by stating that 'the CoJ CCTV System was not entirely effective in the reduction of contact crime rates, in making people feel safer in the Inner City, and in the decrease of disorder/urban management issues in the CCTV area of coverage'.[37]

By 2017, the city was operating 242 CCTV cameras, with most of these located in the CBD and the surrounding suburbs of Braamfontein, Fordsburg, Hillbrow, Joubert Park, Doornfontein and Newtown. The city also operated CCTV cameras along its cycle lanes.[38] However, it was unable to provide any plans for the roll-out of smart CCTV cameras, as well as any evaluation reports concluded prior to, during or after the roll-out plan, claiming that such documents did not exist because no budget had been allocated to the plan. Rather, CCTV cameras that were installed by the city were requested and financed by the city's entities and private sector companies such as ABSA and the Johannesburg Property Company. The JMPD, which falls under the control of the city, only monitors and provides maintenance for the cameras.[39] This suggests that there is a lack of policy guiding the roll-out of cameras, and points to a lack of transparency in how decisions are taken about the CCTV camera system, including how the city mitigates its privacy impacts.

According to the JMPD's Wayne Minnaar, the city's CCTV project was part of a broader 'smart city' initiative, designed to use data tools to better the lives of Johannesburg residents.[40] The JMPD had concentrated on rolling out CCTV at various crime hotspots in Johannesburg, and claimed it had a high success rate in catching criminals here on the strength of CCTV footage. In 2017, it relocated and upgraded its CCTV control room and was actively involved in expanding its surveillance capabilities. The city's network was linked together by a powerful fibre network operated by a municipal entity called the Metropolitan Trade Company (MTC), set up to provide the city with broadband connectivity. MTC's activities were under investigation by the city for the huge cost of construction relative to the scant delivery on its initial promises.[41] For the JMPD, though, the MTC network provided it with reliable links, including backup links, to operate its CCTV network.[42]

ANPR has been in use for several years in Johannesburg. As the CCTV system is linked to the Electronic National Administration Traffic Information System (eNATIS), which falls under the Road Traffic Management Corporation, the link was used to identify suspects from its vehicle registration information. In addition to ANPR, the JMPD was in the process of considering a proposal from a foreign multinational for the addition of facial recognition to its CCTV network. The JMPD will develop its own local facial database for the city from public and private entities in the city that register visitors. Furthermore, the system is likely to be linked to the SAPS facial database, as well as the Department of Home Affairs. The JMPD also has a relationship with the commercial banks, which have cameras outside their premises, and the plan is to use this footage to source faces for its facial database as well.[43] What is not clear from these plans is the criteria for determining how faces land up in the database, and the procedure for their removal if those of people other than convicted criminals are stored. This issue should be of concern as the city is expanding its capabilities to store and process data from its CCTV network. Currently, the JMPD stores all footage for a period of sixty days, but it is exploring the possibility of at least doubling the period of time for storage while expanding the storage capacities of its databank. If possible criminal incidents are caught on camera, that footage is archived for an indefinite period.[44]

Currently, the city's CCTV control room is manned by staff working in shifts. Their manual monitoring of the footage is complemented by software that detects suspicious incidents, such as if a suitcase is left in an area for a long period of time. The system then flags this footage for further analysis. The city has enacted no requirement for signage at the entrance to areas under CCTV surveillance: in fact, according to Minnaar, pedestrians in the city centre were unaware that they were being monitored by the control room. Several areas operated private CCTV networks in different parts of the city, and the JMPD had a working relationship with many of the private security companies that operated them; in fact, there were discussions under way about some of the companies bringing their footage to the JMPD's control room.[45] Several of these relationships were so good that the private operators provided patrol and response vehicles that were then manned by JMPD officers. However, apart from this working relationship, there was no formal requirement on the part of private CCTV providers to comply with specific regulations. The city was in the process of finalising a policy on CCTV roll-out, coupled with a master plan, but these were still at draft stage – a sure sign that the technology had run ahead of the policy.[46]

The City of Cape Town has a much more extensive network of CCTV cameras, whose establishment was guided by a master plan, which placed particular emphasis on readying the city for the 2010 FIFA World Cup. Noting the well-recognised problem of CCTV systems displacing crime, the plan argued for a crime containment strategy, in which policing encompassed the city in full rather than only part of it. The plan noted the importance of CCTV in bringing down crime, especially in the CBD, but also that the city was unable to bear the responsibility on its own, and argued for public–private partnerships. In fact, the containment strategy of the plan could not be realised without the integration of public and independently run CCTV systems in areas like shopping malls; but such a partnership would require giving private sector companies representation on relevant decision-making structures. According to the plan, 'In terms of this master plan, an attempt should be made to harness the independent systems through protocols of engagement and information sharing. This is a key element of a crime containment strategy. Many international countries have embraced this philosophy and in exchange for a voice on a strategic surveillance committee, they make their systems and expertise available to the policing agencies.'[47]

By 2014, there were 886 CCTV cameras in the city, with 360 being under the control of the city's Metropolitan Police, and the rest being related to transport and highway management, particularly the city's integrated rapid transport system.[48] By 2017, this had expanded to more than 1,300 cameras, with 886 being owned and managed by the municipality.[49] This network allowed it to undertake freeway management and monitor crime hotspots. There were also a host of privately owned CCTV cameras in operation, mostly fitted with ANPR, but they were not cross-matched with official police databases or with eNATIS, which records all motor vehicle registrations in the country. After a string of mall robberies, the city announced its intention to change this, using the CCTV network to roll out a 'ring of steel' around the city, by retrofitting all the city's CCTV cameras with ANPR technology. All these cameras would be linked together and their information pooled into a common-data island, similar to London's model. The fixed network of cameras would be bolstered by mobile units.[50] The city does have a policy on private and state-owned CCTV cameras on city property, requiring private CCTV owners to register their cameras, while promoting the uses of CCTV in overall crime-combating. However, the policy is completely silent on privacy and data protection issues, implying that the city does not think it necessary to bind CCTV operators to privacy and data protection principles, such as limits on data retention as a requirement for registration.[51] Given the potential for abuse by private operators, this silence is of concern. The city itself had demonstrated a great capacity for storing mounds of CCTV footage: when the draft policy was being debated, the city disclosed that it had already stored 750 terabytes of surveillance footage culled from its CCTV cameras.[52]

Yet at the same time, in a township of Cape Town that has one of the highest crime rates in the country, Khayelitsha, a commission of inquiry into policing found that CCTV cameras were used ineffectively, and rarely did the footage appear as evidence in criminal cases. In fact, the police made use of CCTV evidence a mere five times over a ten-year period.[53] The following year (2015), the police were criticised again for making only 107 arrests after 2,640 criminal incidents had been caught on camera in the broader Cape Town area, which shows that the problem was not confined to Khayelitsha only.[54] The commission of inquiry threw a spotlight on disparities in the distribution of CCTV cameras, with over a quarter of all cameras being based in the CBD, but this was so because the cameras were funded through a public–private partnership. On the other hand, cameras in townships like Khayelitsha were state-funded, and, as a result, some areas with even higher crime rates did not have CCTV cameras at all; where they did exist, they were underutilised by the police. Undoubtedly, the cameras in the CBD had contributed to a reduction in particular categories of street crime – such as muggings – and to the gentrification of the area,[55] but they also reproduced special inequalities in the way policing resources were allocated across the city. In other words, CCTV roll-out followed the money: it was prioritised, and appeared to work well, in upper-middle-class areas where attracting and retaining investments was a priority, but in working-class areas that were at the periphery of Cape Town's wealth divide, CCTV coverage was minimal and consequently played a negligible role in bringing down crime. Furthermore, it appeared that the city was underutilising the CCTV footage it had collected.[56] This raised questions why the city was being allowed to store such huge amounts of footage 'just in case', if the likelihood of its being used was minimal.

Subsequent to the Khayelitsa Commission, the city expressed a commitment to addressing the disparities in CCTV roll-out and, to that end, increased its budget for areas that fell within a mayoral regeneration programme, which included Khayelitsha.[57] The city was also integrating its CCTV roll-out into a more ambitious data-driven safety and security strategy, called EPIC (the Emergency Policing and Incident Control Programme), which was a key feature of its efforts to turn Cape Town into a smart city, using data-driven technologies to enhance service delivery and improve the overall quality of life. The programme provides an integrated response platform for police and emergency responses in the city, and allows them to analyse the data to identify crime hotspots. It has also been extended to include information provided by the city's CCTV network. Already the police use ANPR technology to track down drivers with outstanding warrants or who are driving stolen vehicles or vehicles with false number plates, as part of a 'Smart Cop' programme. This initiative was meant to be folded into the EPIC programme, which would also be extended to include police officers wearing body cameras. The city has assured the public that it does not intend to become overly reliant on these technologies, suggesting that it recognised the dangers of algorithmic surveillance, which should not be allowed to replace human judgement. If this happened, then machines could engage in discriminatory practices that profiled particular communities as being predisposed towards crime.[58] However, given the fact that the city has already experienced problems with optimising the use of CCTV footage in crime-fighting, it is possible that its reliance on automated analysis could grow. Yet there was no indication of the city having conducted a privacy impact assessment of its data-driven initiatives – a necessity given the increasingly data-driven nature of its safety and security strategy.[59]

SURVEILLANCE AND AUTOMATED TOLLING IN SOUTH AFRICA

Apart from crime-fighting, CCTV cameras are also used in automated toll systems, where drivers are charged by an automated method for using a road. As the vehicle drives under a CCTV camera, it records the vehicle registration plate using ANPR, and the driver is then billed. Automated toll systems trigger particular privacy concerns because they involve the observation of specific vehicles through licence plates or e-tags, in a way that allows the identity of the vehicle's owner to be revealed. If these practices are left unregulated, the authorities can misuse this information in much the same way that they can misuse communications metadata to profile people. When locational information is collected for administrative purposes, fewer privacy concerns arise. But if it is used for law enforcement purposes too, the privacy concerns increase. For instance, in the UK location-related information has been streamed in real time to the police on a warrantless basis. The erosion of judicial oversight erodes state accountability, and increases the potential for abuse. CCTV cameras may also be integrated into intelligent transport systems (ITSs). ITSs use digital technologies to monitor and analyse traffic flow, reduce congestion and respond to crises such as road accidents. But they have been controversial for threatening privacy, and South Africa has not escaped these controversies,[60] although they have been muted compared with elsewhere.

As a basic principle, people should have a right to travel without being coerced into revealing their location information. Payment options for electronic tolling should be available to allow people to maintain their privacy. In view of the dangers for locational privacy, the state should collect the minimum amount of information to achieve its intended public policy purposes. Locational data should be stored and processed according to a person's privacy preference, with a narrowly defined exception for law enforcement. According to the Electronic Frontier Foundation (EFF), 'We need to ensure that systems aren't being built right at the zero-privacy, everything-is-recorded end of that spectrum, simply because that's the path of easiest implementation.'[61] They have argued that the best way to protect locational privacy is to build systems that do not collect location-based information in the first place.[62]

South Africa introduced an e-tolling system on its major freeways in 2013 in the richest province in the country, Gauteng, after years of public opposition, largely on the grounds of cost. A parastatal organisation, the South African National Roads Agency (SANRAL), tracks a vehicle's locational information on tolled freeways, by taking photographs of the registration plates as the vehicle drives under the gantries. Vehicles with e-tag transponders will communicate with the gantries. The system is linked to the Department of Transport's eNATIS system, which provides information for billing purposes. Automated toll systems such as the one run by SANRAL in Gauteng trigger particular privacy concerns because they involve the observation of specific vehicles in ways that allow the identity of the vehicle's owner to be revealed. Although conceivably someone other than the owner could be driving the vehicle, ultimately the vehicle can be traced back to its owner. The government introduced the system to fund improvements made to the major freeways around the province, under the auspices of the Gauteng Freeway Improvement Project. Although the plan evoked mass opposition on the grounds that it would overburden already financially stretched vehicle-driving commuters, the government decided to continue with it in Gauteng.

The government's decision followed an advisory panel report on the issue, which made a case for the Gauteng Freeway Improvement Project to continue being funded by e-tolls, although it recommended reduced tariffs.[63] Commendably, the panel claimed to adopt a human rights approach to its assessment, as it argued that the impact of e-tolls should be assessed in terms of 'actual human experiences and relations'. However, its mandate was confined to the socio-economic impact of e-tolls. One human rights issue that remained unaddressed in the panel's report was the impact of e-tolls on people's right to locational privacy. SANRAL also installed cameras, electronic noticeboards and other traffic management features along national routes, and included these features on Gauteng's e-toll routes, too. Furthermore, the panel recommended that all vehicle owners be issued with an e-tag at the time of motor vehicle licence renewal to facilitate full realisation of the ITS capability.[64] This proposal was in line with SANRAL's ultimate objective of a centralised system of real-time traffic management. Gauteng's e-tolling was meant to be a state-of-the-art system, but its privacy settings are anything but that. In fact, SANRAL rolled out the most privacy-insensitive e-toll system possible, mainly because the threats e-tolls posed to locational privacy were not made into an issue by the public and public controversies focused instead almost exclusively on cost. This meant that SANRAL failed to embrace the principle of privacy by design, where privacy is embedded at all stages of a technology's design and implementation.

Privacy-enhancing alternatives to the current system were in fact possible. Academics elsewhere have proposed alternative systems designed with privacy in mind.[65] These systems make use of cryptography to allow electronic tolling companies to collect cash, but without knowing where a person is. One option involves the use of electronic cash, where a driver uses a digital signature to guarantee payment of tolls. This electronic cash would be loaded onto the transponder, which would pay the service provider anonymously. Alternatively, a pre-paid transponder can be purchased for cash. Another option involves a vehicle carrying an on-board unit that computes the cost of a trip once it has been made, and sends it on to the service provider for billing at the end of each tax year.[66] This option preserves privacy by ensuring that no location-related information leaves the unit. Yet another option is for a driver to buy a wad of dynamic licence plates, or cryptographic numbers, on a pre-paid basis.[67] When the driver drives under a gantry, the transponder sends the number to the service provider, but because the numbers are dynamic, they cannot be traced back to the driver. The driver then pays the total amount owed using an anonymising payment method that cannot reveal how the amount was arrived at. These alternatives are only an option in systems that enjoy public legitimacy, and when people consent to paying. In some other countries, drivers have embraced e-tolls as a time-saving innovation.

Ideally, people should consent to their personal information being collected; in other words, the default position should be an opt-out one, and they should opt in after having given informed consent. SANRAL and the government can always argue that people do not have to use the tolled roads, and that, if they do, they are giving implied consent to having their personal information collected. In any event, they could argue that there are compelling public interest reasons why consent should be implied, such as preventing traffic congestion. But this ignores the argument made by, among others, the Opposition to Urban Tolling Alliance (OUTA), that there are few real alternative routes to Gauteng's highway grid. It also ignores the fact that people cannot opt out of the system and refuse to have their personal information collected. The inability to opt out is unfair. An added concern is that road users' personal information has proved not to be secure, in that the e-toll system contained a security flaw on the company's website, whereby a user's identity number, vehicle licence registration plate, postal address and payment method could easily be obtained by a hacker: this exposed its users to potential data theft.[68]

SANRAL was not the only transport-related state agency to suffer security flaws. The eNATIS, on which SANRAL was dependent for billing, was reportedly hacked several times between 2007 and 2012. The database, in any event, had many historical problems with incorrect information.[69] The number of private sector providers in the e-toll system also increases the risk of data breaches, with one company acting as the e-toll vendor and another providing the software.[70] Furthermore, SANRAL's e-tolling information proved to be useless for evidentiary purposes in one court case. The son of President Jacob Zuma, Duduzane Zuma, was accused of culpable homicide after having been involved in an accident on a major national road falling under the e-toll system. When camera footage of Zuma's trip was sought from SANRAL about the speed he was travelling at, the information proved to be unusable because it showed Zuma's car on the road well after the accident took place; in fact, the e-toll gantries recorded a trip that he could not have made. All this raised serious questions about the system's speed measurement and the accuracy of its data overall.[71] In other words, if the security services were looking to SANRAL to provide locational information for surveillance purposes, they would most probably be very disappointed indeed.

EYES IN THE SKY: DRONES AND AERIAL SURVEILLANCE

Drones are often associated in the public imagination with their most lethal variety. The Barack Obama administration developed a drone programme that killed many Pakistanis, Afghanis and Yemenis in 'targeted' strikes against suspected terrorists. Yet in reality, there was also significant civilian 'collateral' in these countries, especially Afghanistan.[72] Even if actual terrorists were targeted, Obama's drone strikes were summary, extra-judicial executions, as the victims never had a chance to defend themselves against the accusations made against them. Yet, the controversies around Obama's drone strikes obscure the positive benefits of drones, which can also be used to detect crop diseases early and assess disaster areas. Next-generation drones may even be able to rescue people. Journalists have been experimenting with them for news-gathering purposes. Drones have been tested in South Africa too, in spite of the fact that the state entity responsible for regulating civil aviation safety and security, the CAA, declared their use illegal until it had finalised regulations on their use (which it did in 2015, following consultations).

Drone manufacturers and operators prefer to see minimal regulation of the industry in order to encourage innovation, yet civil society organisations elsewhere have been warning about the dangers of under-regulation. What are the issues, and how concerned should South Africans be? Drones have an unprecedented potential to violate privacy, because they lower the cost of aerial surveillance, which has always been extremely expensive. This is why drones need to be regulated, not just for their safety and security aspects, but their privacy aspects too. They can pose a safety risk to manned aircraft. Drones can also malfunction and fall out of the sky, potentially injuring or even killing people. As a result, more countries are regulating drones to ensure public safety, but the concerns do not stop with safety only. Many drones are being equipped with highly sophisticated video equipment, night vision and zoom lenses. More sophisticated drones have the technological capabilities to identify human targets or intercept communications, and are barely audible. Their unprecedented capacity for undetected, pervasive mass surveillance of people – including of actions that may not usually be discernible to the naked eye – makes it easier for governments to collect information on their citizens.

Drones can also contribute to a routinisation of surveillance in public life, which can alter people's behaviour in undesirable ways, becoming more fearful and timid when they suspect the government may be watching them (even if it is not). Drones can become yet another building block in the ever-expanding surveillance state and make people feel dehumanised. People have a right to know the circumstances under which they will be watched by the government, and there need to be specific, articulable reasons for drone uses. Drones can play a hugely important role in disaster management situations, where public safety is more important than the right to privacy, and in other functions where reasonable expectations of privacy do not arise. But governments enter into dangerous territory if they start to use them for dragnet policing practices, law enforcement fishing expeditions and even speculative, pre-crime-type law enforcement, over private property, or to monitor protests. As the ACLU has argued, drones are notoriously susceptible to mission creep, where having been acquired for one set of stated purposes, they are then used for another.[73] So, a drone that is acquired for utility management, for instance, could be used to keep tabs on public utility workers. Drones with 'hover and stare' capabilities can violate physical privacy – by, for instance, filming people without their consent and even knowledge – and also informational privacy, in that this data may be used to expose things about people against their will. That drones operate well above eye level gives them massively intrusive potential. In 2014, a Seattle woman was surprised – and felt violated – by a peeping drone hovering outside her apartment window when she had no clothes on. Its operator claimed that the drone was filming property.[74]

In this regard, the ACLU has developed a set of core principles that should govern drone use, especially in the context of law enforcement and intelligence-gathering, where their use is likely to be the most invasive. They argue that states should impose usage restrictions on drones, so that they do not intrude on privacy unduly. They should not be allowed at all for indiscriminate mass surveillance, especially of constitutionally protected activities such as engaging in public assemblies. When it comes to law enforcement purposes, they should be deployed only for clear purposes, in a targeted fashion against a person where a reasonable suspicion of wrongdoing exists and where the law enforcement officers have obtained a warrant, or where there is a time-limited emergency or where privacy will not be substantially affected, such as for geological or environmental purposes. The state should also limit the retention of data unless there is a reasonable suspicion that the images show wrongdoing and may be used as evidence in criminal proceedings. The policies and procedures that guide the overall use of drones should be written and explicit, and subject to public consultation. These decisions should be democratically controlled and information should be made openly available, with narrowly tailored exceptions to protect ongoing investigations. Drones acquired by the state for law enforcement purposes should be subject to independent audits, so that the public can assess whether they are being used for the stated purposes, and whether their acquisition and operation represent 'value for money' for the taxpayer. In particular, the public should be in a position to assess if 'function creep' is apparent. Drones should also not be fitted with weapons.[75]

The US-based Electronic Frontier Foundation (EFF) has also suggested some baseline principles for the use of drones for law enforcement purposes. These include limiting data collection to the minimum necessary to achieve the stated purpose, defining clear rules on the legal process required for data collection, and limiting the amount and type of data stored without legal process unless clearly defined exceptions apply. The EFF also argued that drone operators should put in place measures to minimise the over-collection of data, such as scrubbing out the faces of people who may be caught on the footage. Drone operators should also not be allowed to combine the data collected for one purpose with that collected for another, thereby allowing them to engage in tracking and surveillance. Data retention should be limited only to the most necessary periods; and people who suspect that their images have been caught on camera should have a right to request that the footage is expunged. Data should not be shared automatically with other state agencies without a warrant being obtained. Drone operators should also practise strong measures to protect the data that has been collected, to prevent potentially damaging data breaches. If data is transmitted, then it should be encrypted. If drones are going to be used to collect information on people, they should be notified, and the notice should state how long the data will be kept and what needs to be done to have it expunged. An audit trail should audit all transactions involving personal data, from collection to retention and transmission, and should be independently assessed. Finally, all drone use that involves human subjects should be subject to independent oversight, and people who feel aggrieved by the collection of their data should have recourse to this oversight body.[76]

Even before the CAA's regulations were finalised, in 2014 at least one local government – the City of Cape Town – was already testing drones for safety and security purposes. The city expressed interest in acquiring a drone and conducted a test of a multi-rotor quadcopter manufactured by the multinational Skycap. According to the company, the quadcopter was designed to address the unique challenges of monitoring rhino poaching, and it is capable of 'hover and state' aerial surveillance stints of up to an hour.[77] Compared with its brethren elsewhere, this drone has limited capabilities. However, once the precedent is set in Cape Town, then many other public and private entities may want drones too, and they are likely to grow in sophistication. The City of Cape Town stated that it intended the drone to be used for a variety of functions, such as preventing crime, including metal theft and land invasions, aerial mapping, surveying disaster areas, and checking the condition of various public utilities.[78] This open list of intentions was worryingly broad. The city dismissed privacy concerns, arguing that communities do not need to be informed about the purposes of drone flights, just as they are not informed about the purposes of helicopter missions, but this misses the essential difference between helicopter surveillance and drone surveillance. Yet, as a study undertaken for the European Commission argued, something as well intentioned as infrastructure inspections can lead to the recording of personal data of people living in the vicinity, which is why public explanations of their use are so important. This risk is increased in urban areas such as Cape Town.

The constitutional right to privacy demands that restrictions be placed on the use of drones, but in the case of South Africa the technology has moved faster than the law: hence the decision by the CAA to forbid drone usage until after it had developed its regulations. But the CAA was also under tremendous pressure to expedite the regulations, as many potential operators were eager to take to the skies. The Civil Aviation Act, which established the CAA, confines its role to airspace safety and security: it was not set up to consider privacy issues, although it could read the security aspect of its mandate broadly to include such issues. In this regard, it is instructive to look at what happened when US civil society petitioned the Federal Aviation Administration (FAA) to conduct a public rule-making process on drones and their implications for privacy and other civil liberties.[79] The FAA refused, claiming that doing so did not fall within its mandate. In South Africa, the POPI Act of 2013 could prevent the misuse of personal data recorded by drones, but its remit is confined to informational privacy, which raises the very real risk that the physical privacy aspects of drone usage could be unregulated.

In this regard, the CAA draft regulations, released in December 2014 for public comment, were completely silent on privacy questions.[80] The regulations also made no mention of the POPI Act. The final regulations, developed by the CAA and promulgated by the Department of Transport (the government department under which it falls), did not address these lacunae either.[81] The regulations provided for four categories of drone use: commercial, non-profit (which included state agencies like the police), private and corporate. Private operators were restricted to using drones over properties that they controlled, and so had very limited rights of use. The other categories of users had to comply with a series of requirements. They cannot operate drones without a licence, and each drone needs to be registered. Drones that are imported and used for military purposes have to be cleared by the NCACC first. Anyone operating a drone (unless for private use) needs to have a remote pilot's licence, and should receive training from an accredited training organisation beforehand. When pilots apply for a licence, they need to submit an operations manual, the basic contents of which are set out in the regulations, and they also need to develop a safety management system. There are in addition numerous prohibitions on places where drones can be operated. For instance, they cannot be operated above 400 feet above ground level, within a radius of ten kilometres of an aerodrome, within restricted or prohibited airspace, or adjacent to strategic installations or national key points, such as nuclear facilities, courts, police stations, prisons or crime scenes. No drone should be operated over people's heads, or within a lateral distance of 50 metres from any structure or building that does not fall under the control of the pilot. However, all of these prohibitions do not apply if the pilot has a licence to operate the drone, and has been approved by the director.[82] The circumstances under which the director may exercise this discretion are not spelt out, which gives him very wide discretion indeed.

While aviation authorities the world over are reluctant to move beyond their traditional roles of maintaining airspace safety and security, clearly the CAA had chosen to focus on this mandate narrowly, which risked leaving the privacy aspects of drone activity under-regulated. The CAA failed to set baseline standards for privacy, incorporating basic principles, and as a result drone operators will most likely not be privacy-sensitive, as there is no requirement on them to be so. By the time the regulations were finalised, the information regulator, envisaged by the POPI Act, was still in the process of being set up, which made it all the more important for the CAA to take the initiative and set privacy standards. It would appear that the CAA has chosen to deal with privacy concerns on a case-by-case basis as they arise, rather than setting privacy-enhancing standards in advance.[83] This is problematic, as it is not sensitising the drone industry to these considerations at the point of licensing, which increases the potential for privacy violations. Most concerning is the lack of controls over using drones for surveillance purposes, with wide discretion given to the CAA's director to authorise drone use for surveillance purposes, although by October 2016 the CAA had yet to receive applications from law enforcement or intelligence agencies.[84]

The CAA regulations were particularly weak on the responsibilities of drone operators to respect privacy. Rightfully, the CAA should have specified minimum privacy requirements, and required each operator to comply with them. The CAA should also have ensured that all drone operators were familiar with the requirements of the POPI Act, and required explicitly that all data gathered from drones should be handled in terms of the Act. In addition, the CAA should have made sure that the contents of the Act and its data protection and fair data processing principles were included in the theoretical knowledge examinations and the flight training. Another gap was that drone operators were not required to have written plans for the use and retention of data collected by the drone, including a data minimisation statement. Rightfully, the regulations should have spelt out these requirements when it came to operations in the vicinity of people, or in the vicinity of property, structures and buildings, or public roads. In fact, the duties of a pilot should have explicitly included minimising unwarranted invasions of privacy. In order to make certain that this duty is adhered to, drone operators should ensure that their system of record-keeping covers privacy aspects, and, to the extent that they contain personal information, people should have a right to request the information or request that it be deleted.

Furthermore, the CAA should have committed itself to an annual review of operators to verify compliance with the stated privacy policies, and to sharing these outcomes publicly and inviting public feedback on its findings. Drone operators should also be required to log the privacy impacts of their flights in their pilot logbook. When they report to the CAA, they must be specific about the actual drone being deployed; they need to record the capabilities of that model of drone and they need to provide information on the data the payload is capable of collecting, for instance, which type of camera, its accuracy, and how much footage it can store or transmit back to the operation site. The CAA should also have required drone operators to specify exactly what payload data the drone operator should provide. The regulations were silent on all these duties.

Rightfully, if drones are going to be deployed for the purposes of law enforcement or national security surveillance, then even more stringent principles should apply. Such surveillance should require a warrant, and be deployed to address only a real, pressing and substantial need; in fact, it should be viewed as an exceptional step, only to be taken when less privacy-invasive means of addressing the problem have failed. The privacy impacts of the surveillance should be assessed before the operation and should be consistent with applicable laws. Unless there are pressing public interest reasons not to do so, the public should be informed about the surveillance missions and they should also be able to give inputs on the circumstances in which public surveillance is acceptable or not. No drone operator should release data acquired through a drone mission to a law enforcement agency unless a warrant is present, or if the operator believes in good faith that the data pertains to an imminent or ongoing emergency involving danger, death or serious bodily injury to a person and the release of the data would result in remedying the emergency. With regard to drone sales or resale labelling, the label should state explicitly that use must comply with the POPI Act. The regulations were silent on all these issues, too.

Another gap in the CAA's regulations was that they did not ban weaponised drones entirely: while they did forbid drones to carry dangerous objects or substances, the CAA director can give permission for them to do so. Such drones are dangerous as they can potentially cause great injury, with little threat to the actual operators, thus increasing the risk of their being used recklessly. That the drone operators function at some distance from their targets can create a moral vacuum, in which engaging in violent incidents becomes easier. This point is not germane only to the US and its drone strike programme; a South African company has manufactured weaponised drones to control strikes in the wake of the Marikana massacre.[85] This 'risk-free' method of policing strikes could well propel the drone operators to use excessive force, even where there is no compelling need to do so.

South Africa has a burgeoning drone industry, in much the same way that it has a burgeoning communications surveillance industry. It is in the best interests of this industry to remain under-regulated, as this will allow it to grow relatively unhindered by government constraints. The industry has already expressed concerns that the regulations are overly bureaucratic, and that they may stifle innovation. But, in terms of their ability to collect information about people, they are very weak indeed, and in fact bear all the hallmarks of regulations that favour the industry rather than citizens and their rights. By June 2017, the CAA had issued 494 certificates of registration for drone operators and 471 remote pilot licences. It has also issued 60 letters of approval for the operation of drones for commercial, non-profit and corporate purposes (although it declined to provide a further breakdown by category of licence), 7 approvals for training organisations and 13 operator certificates for drones. Only one approval was issued for operations beyond visual line of sight and two for operations in controlled airspace, suggesting that the majority of approvals were for operations that were not considered to be particularly intrusive.[86]

CONCLUSION

Street-level surveillance is becoming increasingly commonplace and can lead to the normalisation of mass surveillance systems in public life. The consequence of this is that people may withdraw from public life, and become more timid about their public actions, thereby eroding one of the fundamental positive features of active citizenship, namely to protect and promote public spaces as places for common associational and expressive activities. In an era when increasingly powerful public dataveillance tools are becoming commonplace, old arguments about people not having a reasonable expectation of privacy in public spaces ring hollow. Such surveillance is reversing the onus of proof in criminal investigations, and people are increasingly being subjected to remotely controlled street-level searches, often without their knowledge. South Africa has followed international trends in street-level surveillance and embraced technologies whose impacts on crime-fighting and intelligence work are, at best, unclear and contested. Invasive forms of data analysis such as ANPR and facial recognition are being introduced with practically no public debate about the implications for privacy in public spaces, or for the ability of South Africans to practise a range of rights in these spaces, such as the right to assemble. Given the extremely high levels of crime, it could be surmised that South Africans would be willing to give up at least some of these rights in order to increase their safety in public spaces. However, the evidence that street-level surveillance deters serious contact crimes is very far from clear. CCTV roll-out tends to follow patterns of wealth in major metropolitan cities, thereby contributing to the enclosure of city spaces by private capital, and consequently to the privatisation of public spaces and the reproduction of spatial inequalities. Furthermore, greater private sector involvement in street-level surveillance, as compared with a country like the UK, may actually frustrate rather than enable ambitions to integrate such systems into a larger panopticon, as the various systems are proprietary and consequently are difficult to integrate with one another.

As things stand, it is not at all clear that the growing capacity of local governments to collect street-level data on people's movements is making a substantial contribution to policing, because the police are not making use of this data on a routine basis. Technology is being used as a silver bullet for the policing of public spaces when more basic interventions may be more appropriate (such as improving investigative techniques), yet at the same time the regulation of CCTV for privacy impacts is lagging behind the actual roll-out of technology. When it comes to e-tolling, South Africa has introduced a privacy-insensitive system, which increases the potential for it to be used for purposes other than those for which it was intended. However, this potential is minimised by the fact that the integrity of some of the transport-related data that has been collected is in question. This suggests that it may have limited value to a state that wants to build up a picture of people's movements as part of more wide-ranging surveillance efforts.

It is too early to tell whether drones will make a contribution to official efforts to establish a surveillance state, but the fact that the CAA has failed to regulate drones for privacy increases this risk. The CAA's decision to interpret its mandate narrowly by focusing on the safety aspects only, and not the privacy aspects, was particularly inappropriate in view of efforts in other parts of the world to include privacy as an important dimension of drone regulation. But the fact that existing street-level surveillance systems, or existing administrative systems that could be harnessed for these purposes, were fragmented, and there was little evidence of integration being possible, suggested that their potential to contribute to the construction of a larger surveillance state was not going to be realised for some time to come, if at all.

7

Privacy, surveillance and population management: the turn to biometrics

This chapter examines the use of biometrics as an enabler of state surveillance in various state-run population management functions in South Africa. Biometrics involves the measurement and analysis of unique physical characteristics for the purposes of identification, the most commonly used being irises, fingerprints, voice or DNA. State agencies that use biometric identifiers assume that this form of identification is much more reliable than barcodes or personal identification numbers (PINs), as they relate to a person's unalterable features. Facial recognition technologies used in the context of CCTV surveillance (discussed in the previous chapter) are a form of biometrics, as they use people's facial features to identify them. However, that physical characteristics are used for identity management at all triggers privacy concerns in that some of the most personal features of an individual – namely body parts – are collected and stored by the state for identification purposes, thereby interfering with a person's bodily autonomy and hence privacy. Biometrics enables state surveillance in very powerful ways, as it provides the state with some of the most intimate details about a person to monitor them and track their movements.

It is thus small wonder that biometric information is so heavily sought after by spy agencies. In 2010, for instance, it emerged that the US government had run an intelligence campaign to collect the biometric information of the most senior UN officials, including Secretary General Ban Ki-moon and certain UN Security Council members. While it was unclear why this information was needed, it could potentially have been used to hack into the UN officials' communications, to the extent that they were protected using biometric identifiers.[1] Snowden's leaks revealed that the NSA was collecting millions of faces from web images as part of its mass surveillance programmes, with the intention of running them through facial recognition software and increasing the agency's ability to find intelligence targets around the world. While traditional communications were still a major source of intelligence, for the NSA it was important to exploit a broader range of data sources to enable it to undertake a 'full arsenal' approach to surveillance, in which the agency could develop more comprehensive profiles of individuals.[2] Given the extreme sensitivity of such personal information, it is hardly surprising that citizens in many countries have resisted attempts by states to collect and use their biometric information, and state attempts to do so have become fraught with controversy. This chapter will examine how this contentious form of identification has been implemented by the South African state, with a particular focus on the social security system and the 'smart' ID card system.

BIOMETRICS AND PRIVACY: THE ISSUES

Biometrics can be used to check that people are who they say they are when their identity is known (verification), or at least claimed, and to identify a person by matching these characteristics against those of others when their identity is not known (identification). The term has evolved a new meaning in the computer age, as it has become tied up with the storage of information in digital formats and analysis by computers, but states used biometrics to track their 'subjects' even before computers were invented.[3] Biometric forms of identification have existed for many years; for instance, fingerprints have been used in policing for many years. What has changed is the application of computers to biometric enrolment and processing, which has expanded the ability of administrations to process huge amounts of biometric data, and to link to one another's biometric databases. Biometrics are being used increasingly for an array of public administration purposes: fingerprints most commonly, and facial or voice recognition as well. Governments that have implemented, or attempted to implement, biometrically based identity schemes give similar reasons for these schemes: they are secure, they argue, as the personal information can be used to incontestably identify a person, and this information can be stored securely in contactless microchips that are difficult to tamper with. They argue that these security measures will stamp out identity fraud and theft. As a result, biometrics have been used in the registration of citizens for a variety of services, as well as border control to prevent illegal entry into a country. Biometrics are also being used in the global fight against terrorism: the biometric identifiers of individuals flagged as terrorism suspects (if they are available) are put on international databases so that their movements can be tracked as they enter and exit different countries.

Civil society organisations have argued that if citizens give such information to the state, this will allow the government to build up a profile of individuals that could be used against them in future if they are considered to be threats to government interests. These organisations have opposed the collection of biometric information as yet another form of dataveillance, in which electronic databases make possible lifelong surveillance by enabling governments to build up a clear picture of people's ongoing movements, habits and preferences. The amassing of this information can allow governments to profile those regarded as political threats to ruling interests. In fact, centralised biometric databases are the perfect police state tool. Since the 9/11 attacks on the US, governments are turning themselves increasingly into one-way mirrors: they can see into more aspects of people's lives, while their own actions are becoming more opaque owing to excessive secrecy. These databases can act as powerful mechanisms of social control: fear that the state is watching may make citizens more subservient.

Why is biometric surveillance so very controversial? Contrary to what many biometric proponents argue, biometrically based identity verification is susceptible to error, as it offers only a probability of a match based on the likeness of stored physical characteristics; it cannot verify identities with certainty. Some people, such as miners and others who work with their hands, have difficulty enrolling as they may not have well-defined fingerprints. Biometrics also suffers from controversial margins of error, including false matches ('false positives') and lack of recognition ('false negatives'). Fingerprints have the highest rate of error. In extreme situations, a person could even become a criminal suspect based on false information; US attorney Brandon Mayfield's experience, as discussed in the introduction, is a case in point. Criminals can also synthesise (or 'spoof') fingerprints and create fictional identities. Electronic databases are also vulnerable to hacking, which can lead to biometric information being stolen, altered or even destroyed. If this happens, the consequences could be much more serious than breaches involving databases that are not biometrically based. People's identities are compromised permanently when their biometrics are compromised, as they cannot replace their fingers, eyes or voices. Such breaches create the risk of someone becoming an 'unperson', unable to prove that they are who they say they are.

Identity theft is more common in biometrically based single reference systems such as centralised national population registers, as these create a single point of failure. Centralisation increases rather than reduces the potential for fraud. Doppelgänger matches also become more likely in large-scale databases, when someone's biometrics match well with someone else's, leading to misidentification. In view of these uncertainties, there needs to be a record to refer back to, such as physical fingerprints. Yet too many governments are failing to build these safeguards into these systems, in their overzealous bid to 'modernise' and transform themselves into paperless societies. The dangers became apparent in Israel in 2006, when the personal information of nearly every Israeli citizen was stolen from the country's national population register, sent to the criminal underworld and then dumped on the open internet.[4] In other words, one of the most 'national security obsessed' states in the world has been unable to ensure the security of its citizens' personal data once these had been centralised. Biometric information may also be used for purposes for which it was never intended when the person enrolled. This 'function creep' risks violating a person's right to data sovereignty in the process, which is the right to determine how your personal data is used. Fingerprinting is also inherently associated with criminality. Sorting individuals according to their physical characteristics is dehumanising, and can become a dangerous tool in the hands of authoritarian governments bent on social sorting according to particular characteristics such as race, gender or age.

Given the dangers, the tide has begun to turn against centralised biometric databases in the North, and an increasing number of countries have lost the political will to establish them or have had to dismantle them if they have already been set up. For instance, the Mauritian government decided to compel its citizens, on pain of imprisonment, to enrol in a biometrically based national identity system. However, after massive public opposition, the Mauritians were forced to dismantle their centralised one-to-many database, leaving only one-to-one verification intact.[5] Nevertheless, countries in the South have jumped on the biometric bandwagon, including South Africa, in spite of the many red flags about the technology. INTERPOL, the World Bank and private security multinationals have worked tirelessly to promote biometrics in the South, to manage what they perceive to be problem populations and to keep them out of an increasingly fortified North. Some Northern countries that have refused to subject their own populations to biometrics have nevertheless implemented the technology in border control. Yet opposition is growing in the South, too. India is an important experiment for biometric enthusiasts, as the Unique Identification Authority of India is in the process of compiling the world's largest demographic and biometric database, which involves issuing unique identity numbers to Indian residents. In 2013, in an interim order, the Indian Supreme Court directed the government to withdraw orders making the ID card mandatory for providing any public service, and disallowing it from sharing any ID information without the prior permission of the card holder. In spite of the controversies around the privacy implications of the database, the majority of Indians have enrolled. While the government has requested the court to relinquish its order, claiming that the identity system will be used for a range of services, the court has insisted that the system is not a mandatory requirement for accessing welfare benefits.[6]

BIOMETRICS AND SOCIAL SECURITY IN SOUTH AFRICA

In South Africa, the post-apartheid government has provided a social safety net that protects millions of South Africans from outright destitution. This is administered by the Department of Social Development. The expansion of this social safety net is one of the country's most important post-apartheid achievements. Yet, controversially, the grant system is not universalised, in spite of there being strong arguments in favour. When social grants were introduced on a massive scale in the early 2000s, they were administered through the provinces. This proved to be disastrous, as the provinces lacked the capacity to undertake this responsibility. As a result, the department established the South African Social Security Agency (SASSA), and centralised the grant-making system in SASSA from 2006 onwards. However, it outsourced the payment system a year later in a form of privatisation that made payment the responsibility of a private service provider, rather than of SASSA itself.

Many grant beneficiaries assumed that their payment problems would be solved. Yet this was not to be. In 2014, the Constitutional Court ordered the reversal of a massive tender, worth R10 billion, that had been irregularly awarded to a service provider to pay social grants on SASSA's behalf. This tender required the use of biometric means of identifying recipients. Fingerprints were needed to register recipients, as were voiceprints and photographs, to prevent the sorts of fraudulent payouts to which token-based systems using pin numbers apparently lend themselves. This information would be stored in a national database of recipients, thereby eliminating duplications. Government officials employed various approving discourses to legitimise their turn to biometrics, arguing for the need for the national standardisation of identification systems to make recipients more legible to the state, thereby finding 'objective' ways of identifying grant recipients so as to stamp out illicit access to grants and bureaucratic inefficiencies. They maintained that if they shifted identity processes away from paper-based systems and humans to computer-based automation, they would remove the margins of error that are always possible in a process involving human judgement (not to mention the wiggle-room for local-level corrupt practices). As Kevin Donovan has argued, the perception of efficiency and objectivity is not necessarily borne out in actual everyday practices, which are invariably much more complex. Nevertheless, the continued existence of this perception is important for biometric enthusiasts, as it creates new markets for their products and sustains existing ones.[7]

However, SASSA changed the requirements of the tender process at a very late stage of the process, requiring biometric solutions not only at the point of registration, but at the point of payment too. This change led to Cash Paymaster Services winning the tender, and a competitor, AllPay Consolidated Investment Holdings, fell out of the running, as its security solution for payment was pin-based. As a result of this and other irregularities, the Constitutional Court declared the award of the tender to Cash Paymaster constitutionally invalid, and instructed SASSA to issue a new tender.[8] By that stage, the amaBhungane Centre for Investigative Journalism had reported that Advocate Norman Arendse, a member of the bid adjudication committee, had been offered a bribe by someone claiming to represent Cash Paymaster.[9] Furthermore, President Jacob Zuma's lawyer, Michael Hulley, played a major behind-the-scenes role in the awarding of the tender to Cash Paymaster, strongly suggesting political interference in the decision, although corruption has not been proved. As a result of these revelations, the non-governmental watchdog Corruption Watch called for the tender to be investigated by the Hawks, a special investigative unit linked to the police. Cash Paymaster was also implicated in dubious deductions from grant beneficiaries for airtime bundles, actions for which the Social Development Minister Bathabile Dlamini condemned the company.

While these controversies were unfolding, no real debate took place about SASSA's decision to shift to biometric forms of identity verification, saved in a national database, and its implications for users' rights to privacy. The problem with centralised biometric databases is that their data security must be foolproof. Identity theft of a biometric identifier can have devastating consequences for the victims, as – unlike PIN numbers – they cannot replace their fingerprints or voices. Yet, identity theft is as possible in biometric systems as it is in token-based systems, as both information sets are stored digitally. These dangers have led information security consultant George Tillman to argue that biometrically based security measures may leave organisations in worse places than they were. According to Tillman, '[The] reality is that biometrics are a feel-good measure designed to give people the false impression that they are more secure than they were before, when in fact they are more at risk.'[10] In view of these risks, the company that has access to such databases must be beyond reproach. If users have any concerns about the possibility of their information being leaked or misused, they must be able to leave the system and have their biometric data expunged. Should the option of voluntary enrolment not be available to South Africa's grant recipients, as it is in India, then their right to privacy will be automatically violated.

In a bid to improve efficiency in the social grants system, the government made several deeply flawed assumptions. It assumed that centralisation, automation and privatisation of the payment system would lead to greater efficiency; instead, these changes did not necessarily remove the potential for abuse, but merely centralised it. South Africa's social security-dependent poor are a massive captive market for profit-seeking companies. In the name of efficiency, SASSA entrusted the administration of millions of South Africans' livelihoods to a private company that appeared to see the social grant system as a massive source of profit-making.

For those beneficiaries of the social grants system who were unable to travel to payment points, voice recognition as a means of authentication seemed like a magic bullet. However, the system required beneficiaries to buy new SIM cards from the major cellphone networks and 'RICA' them for voice recognition purposes. In response, critics argued that grant beneficiaries should be allowed to choose their own network provider and not be burdened with having to buy an extra SIM card which they were not going to use again.[11] The Black Sash in the Western Cape (an NGO providing advice and support on social assistance matters) has reported on a woman who was denied a grant because she did not have an identity document, which apparently had been stolen two days beforehand: and this in spite of the fact that SASSA's service provider had her voice and fingerprints recorded on its system. If biometrics are meant to replace paper-based systems, then it makes no sense to deny payment of the grant because the applicant could not produce a paper-based form of identification.[12] In fact, when Natasha Vally examined the real-world implementation of the new system ethnographically, she found that far from increasing efficiency and, ultimately, social security, the biometrically based payment system introduced new forms of insecurity that profoundly disadvantaged social grant recipients. Not only did it turn the system into a vast treasure trove for private companies seeking to profit from the recipients, but it failed to resolve the problems. The queues in which recipients had to wait to receive their grants did not get shorter and the technology was by no means foolproof, as it on occasion failed to recognise the fingerprints of elderly workers or developed other faults.[13]

After attempting to find a new contractor, SASSA decided that the payment system would be brought back into SASSA, but SASSA fell behind in meeting its obligations.[14] The agency claimed that it needed to build internal systems to handle aspects of this responsibility, including biometric verification and authentication, and also indicated that it intended to interact with the Department of Home Affairs for biometric authentication of staff and system users. But it needed at least a year to insource the biometric functions, indicating that it faced problems in developing the capacity to undertake these particular functions in-house.[15]

While the government asserts that biometrics makes the grant system 'easy and fraud-free',[16] it is apparent that this claim is not matched by the reality. Not only has the system introduced new layers of complexity and inefficiency, but it has been plagued by mismanagement, which is the kindest interpretation that can be placed on the turn of events. It has opened up grant recipients to rapacious actions by private companies, leading to SASSA itself laying charges against Cash Paymaster and the bank that administered the grants on its behalf, Grindrod Bank, for failing to put a stop to illegal deductions from grant recipients' accounts.[17] There can be little doubt that the biometric system embraced by SASSA has reduced the number of fraudulent claims by recipients.[18] However, the shift towards a centralised, privatised and biometrically based system does not appear to have stamped out illegal practices so much as displaced them to higher levels in the system. Indeed, the outsourcing of this function has increased the scope for such practices. This is because the government has chosen a technical rather than a social and political approach to these illegal practices, which assumed that technology would provide a silver bullet for addressing them[19] – an assumption which must be questioned.

BIOMETRICS AND NATIONAL IDENTIFICATION IN SOUTH AFRICA

Governments have given many reasons for adopting centralised identity registration systems, such as needing to protect national security or improve efficiencies in service delivery. However, as these systems are digitised and database-dependent, they can present substantial opportunities for the surveillance of citizens and threaten the integrity of people's most sensitive personal data.[20] Such is the case in South Africa, too, which has had a centralised biographical national population register for many years. In the dying days of the twentieth century, as it prepared for the new millennium, the government announced its intention to establish a centralised biometrically based database integrated with the existing register. Called the Home Affairs National Identification System (HANIS), the database was meant to ensure access to social benefits for all South Africans. Nevertheless, the underlying logic of needing to register all citizens using their biometrics (more specifically their fingerprints) remained unexamined.

As the old green barcoded identity document proved to be insecure, leading to widespread identity fraud, the government went on the search for a more secure form of identification. A biometrically based identity card, which stored a user's fingerprint information on a chip, appeared to offer just that.[21] The government decision to use smart cards meant they could be used for a range of other government functions, and become a record of the citizen's interactions with the state. The intention early in the project was to ensure tight integration with the social security system, and to provide businesses (especially the banking system) with a fail-safe means of identifying people. However, the government's plans were thwarted by the fact that an interoperable biometric standard, which of necessity would have to be an open standard, had not been developed. Moreover, biometric surveillance on a widespread basis was difficult to achieve as so much biometric information was sunk into proprietary systems, leading to the inevitable development of incompatible system architectures.[22] This technical challenge was a blessing in disguise from a privacy point of view. When all data is accessed by all parts of the administrative system, there may well be benefits for citizens as they become more visible to the state, but this heightened visibility also creates the dangers of an administrative panopticon.[23]

Yet the concerns do not stop there. Identity management functions can become securitised, and if connections are established between the different databases, state intelligence institutions can have full access to the population register for surveillance purposes. Certainly, the security dimension of HANIS was always important for the department, with its four critical purposes being identified as 'improved and heightened security, administration, and governance improvement, service delivery and economic development in line with the NDP [National Development Plan]'.[24] Equal attention to these four purposes would be made possible by integrating the department's various record management functions into one integrated, digitised National Identity System (NIS). This planned modernisation would allow a range of government departments to have a 'single view' of both the citizens of the country and visitors to it.

South Africa does not compel its citizens to enrol and carry identity cards, as countries like Mauritius attempted to do (to massive public opposition),[25] but there is compulsion by stealth, as people will be gradually unable to undertake basic civil functions without a card. Why have biometric databases not become as controversial in South Africa as they have elsewhere? According to Keith Breckenridge, opposition usually begins when engineers and scientists, who understand the technical issues, team up with journalists, civil society and grassroots movements to publicise the dangers.[26] In South Africa, low levels of public awareness of the dangers allowed biometrics to be introduced to the social security system, and then extended to the national identity register. The technology press has tended to publish articles extolling the virtues of biometrics, while the investigative press has focused on corruption and mismanagement in Home Affairs. The fact that the reportage has been confined to a fairly narrow range of issues has left the broader issues around privacy and surveillance largely unaired. With one or two notable exceptions, the technical part of society has not spoken out.

The department appeared to idealise biometric technology, arguing that not only will the system prevent identity theft, but it will also become a gateway to service delivery and a lynchpin of all citizen engagements with government. In fact, the department has said that, in future, South Africans may use just one card for all their official documentation requirements, including identity, driving licence, national health insurance and social grants. As several other departments had expressed interest in becoming involved in the project, the department would look into how it could upscale the chip on the cards in order to accommodate them. The department's statements suggested that data-sharing across departments was envisaged, and that function creep was considered to be unproblematic. Officials are also vague about the future shape of the system and have, for instance, floated the possibility of extending the system into electronic purses. In response to a parliamentary question on this very issue, the department said that the card 'will include, amongst others, demographic information which is in the current green bar-coded identity book, a picture, fingerprint biometric security features and other security information which cannot be disclosed for security reasons'.[27] This reply implied that the number of registerable facts was likely to increase in time. To its credit, though, the department instituted an elaborate audit trail to deter officials from misusing the database to commit fraud, but such an audit trail was unlikely to deter hackers.

By April 2016, the Department of Home Affairs claimed to have issued over four million smart ID cards, and increasingly passports were biometrically based as well, although over 30 million people still needed to convert their green bar-coded identity cards.[28] By the end of that year, most banks were able to access the HANIS system to verify customer identities. But the system also developed problems, leading to accusations by the DA that the department had rushed through the system without having the necessary capacity to implement it.[29] The department recruited a number of banks to assist with the roll-out of the smart cards to alleviate the problem,[30] although, needless to say, the more actors involved in the enrolment process, the more likely that data breaches occur. While the department itself has not suffered any data breaches,[31] other state entities have. Some of these have been attributed to Anonymous – a hacktivist organisation that in the case of South Africa sought to highlight issues relating to corruption and child labour – and included hacking into a SAPS database and databases of the Government Communication and Information System and the Department of Home Affairs, and leaking personal employee data onto the internet.[32] In the case of the SAPS breach, which a hacker claiming to be linked to Anonymous said was in retaliation for the Marikana massacre, the personal information of those who had reported crimes through the SAPS website, including serious crimes like rape, were leaked onto the internet as well, which placed those who had complained at very real risk of retribution.[33] Furthermore, late in 2017, it was discovered that the personal information of most South Africans had been leaked onto the open internet, including their identity numbers, addresses, tax numbers and cellphone numbers.[34] This breach showed how vulnerable data-bases of personal information are to disclosure. However, according to the department, the information was leaked as a result of carelessness, not because it was hacked; furthermore, the smart ID card system was designed to prevent such data leaks, as the centralisation of personal information in one government data-base would reduce the reliance on private companies for personal information.[35]

As discussed in a previous chapter, the producer of the smart ID card, Dutch multinational Gemalto, had its own data breached when GCHQ stole SIM card network keys from it. As a company that rose to prominence in the ePassport mar-ket, it has become one of the most important global providers of smart ID cards, along with Thales and Unisys.[36] However, in spite of the reputational damage it suffered after the GCHQ hacking, Gemalto maintained that its smart ID cards were secure, but government systems needed to retain their integrity, as fraud was still possible if these systems were weak.[37] This concern was not misplaced. Corruption has been an endemic problem in the Department of Home Affairs, especially in the immigration section, where some desperate foreign nationals have been willing to pay bribes to settle their immigration status, according to Corruption Watch.[38] Access to HANIS information is governed by the Identification Act, which requires the department's Director General to grant access to the register.[39] However, he or she may furnish information from the register to certain public or private institu-tions, provided it is required for the exercise of other rights (with the exception of institutions whose business is banking or insurance, which do not have to meet this requirement). In other words, the bar for the release of information by the depart-ment is set very low indeed, and it does not appear to recognise basic data protec-tion principles (such as not passing on personal information for another purpose without the consent of the data subject concerned). A further reason why fraudu-lent documents continued to be issued by corrupt officials was that the HANIS sys-tem, the SAPS Automated Fingerprint Information System (AFIS) and the eNATIS system did not 'talk' to one another, with the result that cross-referencing of these systems to weed out fraudulent transactions could not occur.[40] Yet technical challenges remained a barrier to interoperability and, ultimately, full integration of these systems.

Furthermore, the system did not meet SAPS requirements; this could not be addressed if the two systems did not 'talk' to each other.[41] Consequently, the department's grand ambitions to turn the HANIS project into a biometric panopticon proved impossible. In any event, biometric projects targeted at a single service work better while the global search for an open standard continues. As things stood, experiments with using an open standard for biometric identification delivered vastly more false positives and false negatives than proprietary systems.[42] In any event, in 2016 the department maintained that it was not its intention to give other departments full, unmediated access to the national population register.[43] However, by 2017 the department confirmed that SAPS had full, unmediated access to the database in real time.[44] Apparently, other departments had as well, but Home Affairs would not disclose which departments these were. The Deputy Director General for Institutional Planning and Support, Thulani Mavuso, stated in an interview that the department's plans to integrate existing Home Affairs databases into one NIS were in motion, and that the intention was also to include more biometric datasets such as iris scans and photographs of faces for facial recognition purposes. The purpose behind including at least three biometric datasets was to ensure that if one form of identification threw up false positives or false negatives, a person's identity could be verified by using the other biometric identifiers. Mavuso argued that while the department's activities could not in any way be considered surveillance, he did acknowledge that such a database could be used for surveillance purposes in time to come. Commenting on the police's direct access to the database, he said:

> But, obviously when police are investigating, you remember that they only keep the fingerprints of people who are criminals, but when they get to a crime scene, they need to be able to identify people from the fingerprints they gather, so they'll have to come to us in order for them to verify that particular individual. When someone talks of surveillance, in my own understanding, it's regular monitoring, you know movements of people and all those things, so in our case I think it's not about that, it's about how do you resolve complex crime, how do we service people quickly.
>
> Remember that the police have continuous investigations, there are people who don't want to give their identity documents, they give wrong names, the police should be able to say, no, no, no, you are not Thulani, you are Joe,

you know, check who you are because some people lie. So we also want a situation where the state does not create multiple databases. So, as Home Affairs we want to be able to offer this service government to government, government to business.[45]

While there are clear benefits if the police can identify suspects whose fingerprints are not on the AFIS database, unchecked police access has dangers of its own as it could allow the police to conduct dragnet searches of the entire population. These dangers will intensify as Home Affairs expands the range of biometric data it collects. The police need to ensure that they institute meaningful measures to prevent the misuse of these biometric data, which includes a standard operating procedure setting out grounds for accessing the HANIS database, procedures for doing so, and levels of access according to police rank. For instance, policy should forbid the police to use biometric identifiers such as facial recognition to track individuals engaging in political, religious or other forms of protected free expression. As facial recognition tends to be less accurate than fingerprinting, the purchase of technology should include accuracy tests and thresholds.[46] Furthermore, police should not be allowed to access the database willy-nilly, but only in circumstances where there is a reasonable suspicion of criminality, and the circumstances of access should be subjected to public reporting and internal audits, including audits for abuses of the system and algorithmic bias.[47]

Identity cards are tied up with surveillant practices, such as social sorting, where the cards are used to classify different population groups so that some may be treated differently from others. Already, it has become apparent during the smart identity card enrolment process that South Africans with foreign links have been profiled as potential security risks, and blocked from enrolling.[48] According to Mavuso, all those people who have received citizenship through naturalisation, as well as permanent residents, are being scrutinised, as processes around their acquisition of citizenship had been somewhat lax in the past; citizens who were so affected could continue to use their green barcoded ID documents.[49] However, an increasing number of people were having their identity numbers blocked: a problem which Lawyers for Human Rights said would be compounded by the smart ID card conversion, and which risked leaving people stateless, in the process violating their right to nationality. According to Lawyers for Human Rights, identity cards were playing a role in turning the country into 'fortress South Africa', where the state constructs national identity in more exclusive terms.[50]

BIOMETRICS AT THE BORDER: SECURITISING AND MILITARISING BORDER CONTROL

Borders are integral to the practice of surveillance. Borders help to define a 'them' and an 'us', where 'they' are subjected to surveillance to prevent contamination with 'us'. To that extent, surveillance is central to national identity management. Historically, governments have treated foreign nationals as appropriate targets for more intrusive forms of surveillance than local nationals, whose rights (including those to privacy) receive higher levels of protection as part of broader citizenship rights. Countries that have been extremely reluctant to implement biometric forms of identity management domestically have not hesitated to use biometrics in border control, especially at airports. For instance, while the UK government was forced to abandon the idea of a biometrically based identity card system for its citizens, it requires foreign nationals to obtain a biometric residence permit, issues biometric passports, and uses biometrics in border control. In fact, some of the heaviest forms of surveillance in the world take place at airports, ostensibly for security reasons. Borders have become increasingly securitised, and many countries consider the maintenance of border controls to be integral to national security concerns. A considerable amount of social sorting takes place at borders. Border control agencies experience no qualms in engaging in social sorting, profiling travellers as potential national security threats, at times in the basest, most stereotypical, even racist ways. It is the one zone where people must be made visible to the state, ostensibly to ensure the safety of fellow passengers and countries of entry, but these measures also serve a broader political function of keeping what that state may consider as problem populations from entering the country. Identification is central to making travellers visible, including biometric forms of identification. Biometric checks at borders do not just focus on verification of a person's identity – in other words, confirming that a person is who he or she says he or she is – but on identification, too, in that a person's identifiers are checked against a host of other databases to provide a bigger picture of travellers and their desirability as potential visitors.[51]

South Africa is no exception to these general rules of border control, although it was a relative latecomer to using biometrics in border control. In 2015, it began to pilot biometric registration of non-nationals at ports of entry. Minister of Home Affairs Malusi Gigaba explained this measure as necessary for protecting national security. According to Gigaba, 'To protect our national security, South Africa is in the process of enhancing its capacity to uniquely identify individuals and confirm the identity of travellers with the highest possible degree of certainty, security and efficiency. To this end, the Department has identified the capturing of biometrics as a key element in securing movements of persons in and out of South Africa. The purpose of taking biometric data at ports of entry is to accurately identify people and determine whether they pose a risk to South Africa.'[52] The department announced its intention to collect the fingerprint and facial data of all people passing through South Africa's borders. Frequent travellers who had no criminal records would be able to pass through border control more quickly, as the biometric system would be able to expedite their entry, and visitors travelling through South Africa to another country would no longer require transit visas. When the system was piloted at major airports in the country, it applied to all travellers – national and non-national alike – but after extreme delays at airports, the department backtracked and required biometric enrolment of non-nationals only.[53] In any event, it was inefficient for the department to subject South Africans to the process, as they had already provided biometric information for HANIS. Yet, well into the pilot phase, it was discovered that the department's Movement Control System, which logged visitors' biometric data, was not linked to the national population register, with the result that the department could not cross-reference South Africans' travel information with HANIS.[54] This meant that, surprisingly, the department's own biometric databases were operating on separate and parallel tracks and that, incredibly, the databases had not been merged before the biometric system was piloted.

It is surprising that South Africa has taken so long to implement biometric forms of border control, as the country is not exactly known for its welcoming stance towards non-nationals, especially those of African origin. Not only has the country been securitising its borders: it has been militarising them too. South Africa's border management has been described by security commentators as 'chaotic', resulting in failure to prevent cross-border crime as well as illegal immigration.[55] This chaotic approach led to an announcement by the Ministry of State Security in 2009 that a Border Management Agency would be established, accounting to the Justice, Crime Prevention and Security Cluster, and tasked with '[ensuring] border post security and borderline integrity'.[56] The military was also deployed for border control from 2009 onwards when it was instructed by cabinet to take back this function from the police – a role it occupied under apartheid.[57] South Africa displayed particular reluctance to allow visitors from Zimbabwe, or those transiting through the country, into South Africa, with the Beit Bridge border post accounting for the most number of refusals of entry, followed by the Lebombo border post between South Africa and Mozambique and the Ficksburg border post on the border of Lesotho. Refusals of entry at South Africa's main airport, OR Tambo International, accounted for the most number of refusals after these ports of entry. This suggests that people travelling from Africa to South Africa by road were disproportionately represented among those refused entry.[58] South Africa has used the global fight against terrorism and the need to protect national security as the reasons for the introduction of the biometric system. It has noted the global perception that South Africa has relatively porous borders, which can allow the country to become a transit point for terrorists and even the target of a terrorist attack. While biometric identification has been constructed as being absolutely necessary to thwart threats to national security emanating from outside South Africa's borders, in its daily reality border control has been far more about keeping non-South African Africans out of the country.

Migration is a reality of the globalising world. Everyone has a right to seek a better life for themselves and to travel in search of that life. This is especially so in countries racked by poverty, inequality and internal instability, many of which are in Africa. South Africa is emerging from the most severe spate of xenophobic attacks since 2008, although the attacks have never really stopped. A key problem is political leaders' ongoing ambivalence towards foreigners, which can lead to political leaders and citizens lapsing into the temptation to scapegoat foreigners for a range of social ills, to deflect attention from their own performance. For instance, in the wake of the Marikana massacre the ANC secretary-general, Gwede Mantashe, blamed foreign-born left activists for fomenting unrest in the platinum belt of South Africa, and he also argued for refugee camps to make it easier to document foreigners.[59] Such public utterances by a senior official of the ruling party set the tone of the discourse in the broader society.

Mantashe has not been the only political leader to raise the need for tighter controls of foreigners. King Goodwill Zwelithini issued an elaborate set of instructions to traditional Zulu leaders to increase surveillance of foreigners in areas falling under their authority.[60] Underpinning these statements appeared to be an exclusive 'us-and-them' nationalism, premised on sealing South African identity from influences from the rest of the region. Yet the lessons of nation formation throughout Africa show that these identities are not frozen in time; in fact, people juggle identities continuously. Given the potential for South Africa to descend into ethnic conflict, it is of the utmost importance that political leaders do not lapse into national chauvinism, but rather promote an inclusive approach to nation-building that is capable of evolving and incorporating regional influences.

The rights to freedom of movement, and to seek a better life elsewhere, are fundamental human rights. They stand above narrow national boundaries; that is why they are universal. Yet the South African government's attempts to tighten border controls cut across this basic human right. But its actions do not happen in a vacuum, as South Africa is not the only country seeking to tighten border controls. The richer North is adopting tougher controls to stem the migration of people from the more impoverished, conflict-ridden South. Thousands of Africans and Arabs continue to risk (and lose) their lives in desperate boat trips across the Mediterranean. The UK has voted to leave the European Union largely in order to regain the right to control its borders, and US President Donald Trump has also promised to strengthen border controls. These political shifts in the North suggest that an aggressive form of deglobalisation is taking place, in which political leaders resort to narrow, exclusivist nationalism to dissuade foreigners from entering their countries.

The South African government has officially condemned xenophobia, on the one hand (although it has also denied the xenophobic nature of attacks against non-South African Africans), while promoting discourses of exclusion, on the other. This it does by framing migration as a problem to be controlled, rather than as a basic human right and a resource capable of enriching a country's socio-economic life. Rather than addressing the underlying factors driving migration into South Africa, the government has turned migration into a national security threat, requiring the intervention of the security cluster. It has been pursuing a more securitised response to the immigration question by deploying more troops to the border, and expediting plans to establish the Border Management Agency to strengthen South Africa's border security.[61] Policing interventions in the wake of the 2015 attacks reinforced in the public mind the xenophobic relationship between foreign nationals and crime. The army has also been deployed to various hotspots, ostensibly to assist the police in stemming the xenophobic violence and to root out crime through the controversial Operation Fiela, a joint police–military operation to address general criminality in various communities. Touted initially as an anti-xenophobia initiative, it morphed into a general policing operation against crime in general. During this operation, signs emerged that the army was using xenophobia as a cloak behind which to harass the very foreign nationals it was meant to be protecting, and suppress dissent in areas beset by protests, like Thembelihle informal settlement, in this way suggesting that the policing operation was not politically neutral.[62] At the same time, the criminal justice system has a dismal record of bringing the perpetrators of xenophobic violence to book. It seems there are systemic biases against those the state has branded problem populations: in this case, immigrants.

Arguably, violence against foreign nationals serves a broader political purpose, as do the threats of greater surveillance. It keeps them insecure, and makes their presence in the country more precarious and more exploitable. Furthermore, the expanded role for the military in controlling South Africa's borders and responding to xenophobia strengthens the Ministry of Defence's bid for two per cent of GDP.[63]

an argument that has been difficult to justify in a country that is at peace with its neighbours, and that has other pressing socio-economic needs.

As a concept, xenophobia is being made to perform particular kinds of work in South Africa. Xenophobia is not an irrational set of beliefs; it plays a regulatory role in that it creates the conditions for continued unequal exchange in southern Africa, to the benefit of South Africa. The government is securitising and militarising its borders to prevent labour from southern Africa from entering the country; yet South African capital is allowed to roam freely in the region. So there is a pan-Africanism for capital, but not for labour. The official argument for limiting the freedom of movement of foreigners is really an argument to maintain, and intensify, unequal exchange between South Africa and the region. South Africa's wealth is built, in part, on the extraction of surplus value from the region. Yet the government wants to prevent those who contributed to making what South Africa is today from benefiting from the country's relative prosperity. Although anti-xenophobia messages play an important role in reducing social conflict, xenophobia cannot be eradicated simply by calling on people to change their attitudes to foreigners. These attitudes are underpinned by an exploitative system that benefits from prejudice and violence.

One of the most unexamined contributors to the xenophobic violence is the official obsession with borders. The need for countries to have borders has become so self-evident that their necessity has reached the level of common sense. Yet many African nations have emerged from colonial boundaries, which imposed irrational divisions on previously united communities. These boundaries do not serve the interests of the region's most oppressed and exploited – including people in South Africa – whose destiny must be a shared one that lies in unity rather than division. The most sustainable, socially just response to xenophobia is to open the region's borders to migrants, rather than to seal them up even more. But regional integration needs to take place on terms set by labour, rather than capital. The counter-argument will inevitably be that integration is unworkable, as South Africa does not have the resources to support such a decision. However, arguments that foreign nationals are stealing South African jobs and dominating the informal sector are not supported by recent research.[64] The size of the migrant community in the country is relatively small, and South Africa's capital-intensive growth path is the biggest contributor, by far, to local job losses. Politically, it is important to recognise that the ANC is divided on the integration question, but in the wake of the most recent attacks, the more securocratically minded leaders seem to be winning the battle against the democrats in the party and in the state more broadly.[65] This balance of forces informs the way the state is deploying biometrics for border control.

However, the roll-out of biometrics in border control has been thwarted by budgetary constraints, and it remains to be seen how quickly it will be extended to road-based ports of entry that working-class people in the main use. Despite the government's commitment to using biometrics at ports of entry, the implementation of the pilot project has been fraught with problems.[66] These showed that while South Africa may have the political will to tighten its borders, and to use biometrics to do so, Treasury stymied that will by refusing to provide the resources necessary to make this most intrusive form of surveillance a viable prospect for South African border control, at least in the short term.

CONCLUSION

According to Kevin Donovan, biometric technologies in South Africa have been harnessed mainly for redistributive welfare purposes rather than social control.[67] However, in reality, the boundaries between the two have become increasingly porous, especially when it comes to separating out nationals and non-nationals. The surveillant dimensions of biometrics have become more apparent in relation to border controls, as South Africa appears intent on following the examples of wealthier countries in the global North to exert even more control over the free movement of people, while continuing to promote the free movement of capital. Biometrics enables the registration and tracking of bodies for this purpose. South Africans have not objected to the increasingly widespread uses of biometrics for an array of public functions, perhaps because their uses and possible abuses have not been politicised as they have been in some other countries.

In the case of the social security system, the introduction of a biometrically based identity system has certainly contributed to bringing down the number of fraudulent claims, but it has also introduced new problems and frustrations for grant holders. It has also made the state dependent on private entities whose interests appear to be driven primarily by profit, potentially threatening the integrity of the most sensitive personal information of some of the most vulnerable members of South African society. In fact, the government has not really interrogated its own assumptions about biometric forms of identification, assuming their inherent technical superiority without considering their vulnerabilities. This is problematic as the dangers are real, especially given the recent data breaches in other parts of government. South Africa suffers from a legacy of lack of respect for privacy, and it still lacks public policy around key privacy issues. Furthermore, the specific uses of biometrics are not covered by legislation. In countries where basic administrative infrastructures are weak, the dangers of opting for biometrics as a form of identification increase. Rightfully, before opting for biometrics, state institutions should ask whether they are going to strengthen infrastructures or weaken them, but there is no evidence of these questions having been answered in South Africa, or even asked for that matter. However, the full surveillant potential of biometric forms of identification is unlikely to be realised in the short to medium term, as the state's reliance on private service providers means that biometric information has been sunk into proprietary systems that cannot be accessed easily by different state institutions. These realities raise questions about whether it is possible to talk about the South African state assuming a new state form, as a biometric state.[68] The available evidence suggests, however, that it is premature to make any such assessment.

8

Stopping the spies: resisting unaccountable surveillance in South Africa

State spying has always been a secretive business. However, digitisation has changed many areas of life, including the work of the intelligence agencies, a lot of which are shifting from relying on human intelligence to signals intelligence. As the latter is even less visible than the former, using it potentially carries fewer political risks, as spying is less likely to be uncovered. In the analogue era, activist movements could always uncover spies in their midst (and often did). Some even learnt to recognise when their phones were being tapped. When it is 'well' conducted, modern communications surveillance is much more difficult to detect than the phone-tapping of old. This means that activists face enormous difficulties in mobilising around this less visible but more ubiquitous and insidious form of surveillance.

This chapter assesses the impact of state communications surveillance, or the threat of it, on professions and constituencies that are particularly vulnerable to surveillance in South Africa, as the privacy of communications is central to their work, rather than incidental to it. It focuses on the phenomenon of political surveillance, that is, surveillance of professionals and activists who work in politically sensitive areas, in particular academics, journalists, political activists and lawyers. Through semi-structured interviews, it analyses personal accounts of all these actors to understand their experiences of surveillance generally and communications surveillance specifically, and how they are resisting surveillance or the threat of surveillance. The interviewees – four academics, three lawyers, three journalists and thirteen activists – are not named to protect their confidentiality.

Drawing on the experiential knowledge of these actors, I outline a framework for effective resistance to surveillance. Contrary to the views of those who have (wrongly) characterised it as an elitist issue that is of little relevance to workers, the unemployed and the global South more generally, I explore how activists and information professionals are crafting resistance strategies that could, potentially, address the bigger political and economic context in which surveillance practices are expanding. Such a context, arguably, requires an organised political response that links resistance to surveillance to resistance to the broader political economy. In this respect, South Africa could be considered something of a 'laboratory' for resistance strategies.

Academics need to have the privacy of their communications guaranteed as a precondition for academic freedom, as these can be very sensitive.[1] Academics may, for instance, offer confidentiality to interviewees in the course of research, and may be unable to maintain this ethical duty in the absence of such privacy. Sources of information are the lifeblood of journalism, too; without them, reporting on sensitive topics would become difficult or impossible. Like academics, journalists have an ethical obligation to protect sources once they offer them confidentiality, and surveillance erodes their ability to do so. Lawyers also need to maintain attorney–client privilege to ensure that interactions between them and their clients are as open and robust as possible. Their work, too, is potentially compromised by state surveillance.

While human rights defenders have paid less attention to the position of academics in public debates about state surveillance and communications privacy, they have recognised journalism and the legal profession as being sensitive professions in need of special protections from surveillance. In fact, the state has a positive duty to shield these professions from unwarranted intrusions into the privacy of their communications.[2] On the other hand, as there are no legally recognised special protections for political activists against state surveillance, they are particularly vulnerable to privacy violations. This is especially so when their advocacy threatens ruling interests, even if such advocacy is legitimate. The UK government has recognised that members of Parliament need privacy protections to communicate in confidence with their constituents,[3] but it does not extend this protection to political work more generally. As a consequence, activists remain vulnerable to surveillance.

As was noted in Chapter 1, much of the organised resistance has been led by NGOs rather than mass movements, in spite of the fact that mass movements have, historically, often been subjected to surveillance, even in countries that consider themselves democracies. This means that these movements are not central to shaping a political response to such practices. As important as they are, anti-surveillance struggles led by NGOs risk depoliticising the problem, by reducing it to a rights-based struggle for civil rights. In doing so, they risk missing the bigger point that surveillance has become a central organising principle of contemporary society, which is likely to make the problem more intractable than they realise.[4]

Although there have been revelations about the South African state's (mis)use of its surveillance capacities, these have not been on nearly the same scale as those made by Snowden. In fact, it seems fair to say that South Africa still has to have its own 'Snowden moment', when leaked documents reveal the full extent of the state's surveillance capacities and the uses to which they are being put. This makes it all the more difficult for activists to mobilise around surveillance, as the full extent of the problem is not well understood. Nevertheless, professions and constituencies that recognise their vulnerability to surveillance are concerned, and are taking steps to protect themselves to different extents.

JOURNALISTS AND SURVEILLANCE

Journalists' resistance practices to communications surveillance are probably the most developed of all the constituencies surveyed, as they are under an ethical obligation to protect confidential sources of information and have taken the threats posed by surveillance very seriously. This could be attributed to the fact that some have direct experience of being surveilled by the state on the flimsiest of grounds, to uncover their sources of information and punish them for speaking out.

Investigative journalists go to great pains to protect the privacy of their communications, as their work often attracts the ire of the authorities. One of the most common strategies is to obtain pre-RICA'd SIM cards (SIM cards that have already been registered in the name of another person, who may not actually exist or whose identity may have been stolen), so that their true identities can be disguised. This anonymity allows journalists to speak to sources confidentially. In fact, it has become standard practice for many journalists to carry two cellphones: one with a SIM card that they themselves have registered, and one with a pre-registered SIM, for discussions with confidential sources. However, this practice failed to protect the two *Sunday Times* journalists whose cases were discussed in Chapter 4, as the police routinely used illegal surveillance practices against them. According to the one *Sunday Times* journalist:

> We used pre-registered SIM cards which are not registered in our names, we buy cheap phones with pre-registered SIM cards. Basically, so this IMEI [international mobile equipment identity] and this SIM card numbers will not have any link to us. The main advantage is that when people try and

sniff who our sources are, they don't go to the RICA judge, but just ask for a printout from their sources at telecomm companies. They don't go to a judge or anything like that. There is a particular official in each cellphone company who deals with that sort of thing. They will know that person. So if you are talking with a person with a registered SIM card they can easily track who your sources are and who you are. This means there will be an immediate record of your conversations. They can often just ask them. If you are dealing with government sources, then you can endanger them. They can be fired. So that they don't have a physical record of us, although they know we are talking to those people. They can't prove it, they can't use it against them. The problem was that we gave the numbers to a source [who became a snitch]. What then happened was that we gave the numbers of those pre-registered source who then became compromised. He gave those numbers to a crime intelligence chief in KwaZulu-Natal (KZN).

The police chief instructed his subordinates to insert our numbers in the surveillance court order which was approved by a judge. The result was that for several months, all SMS [short message service], MMS [medium message service] conversations and GPRS [general packet radio service] were recorded. They inserted those pre-registered phone numbers in a court order which was sent to the RICA judge. All GPRS positioning or conversations were being recorded. We were told that there were piles of CDs of our conversations, which is amazing because we didn't use those phones that much. We ended up with proof that they inserted our numbers in that court order. They did active surveillance on those phones. The reason why this case is important is that we managed to obtain the copy of that court order. That court order laid bare the facts that you wouldn't ordinarily get from anyone. It showed that our numbers were inserted in the surveillance court order. They lied that these numbers were those people's phones. They gave us false names and lied to the judge that we were part of a criminal syndicate.[5]

The fact that a police officer had been found guilty of violating RICA, could deter other police members from misusing the RICA system. However, investigative journalists are never free from surveillance or the threat of surveillance. These harsh experiences meant that in order to say ahead of the police in protecting their sources, the journalists had to change tactics and resort to meeting sources in person, which slowed down their work considerably. In a climate of cost-cutting in newsrooms, such constraints make investigative journalism even less appealing to news organisations, which are likely to steer clear of time- and resource-consuming investigations, even if they are of considerable public importance. The journalists avoid storing information in the cloud as they consider cloud-based services to be insecure, but revert to external hard drives. They also resort to communications that are end-to-end encrypted, but these forms are not suitable for lengthy exchanges, and this increases the risk of miscommunication. According to the same journalist:

> There is constant surveillance. We end up doing a lot of travelling to meet sources. This is expensive because sometimes you have to go to Cape Town. You can't be telling your boss that I want to go every now and then to Cape Town just to meet a source. It's very expensive. But without that, you can't get people to talk to you at all. It slows you down incredibly. There are complex issues you are following up and you need constant communication, we end up using end-to-end encryption like Telegram. We use a lot of them depending on which the source is comfortable with.[6]

It is important that journalists should not allow the fear of surveillance to deter them from their work. Intelligence and law enforcement agencies are not omniscient and omnipotent; they lack the capacity to analyse huge amounts of data, and persistent surveillance is extremely expensive. One interviewee cautioned against assuming a 'myth of competence' on the part of intelligence operatives, as they may not be nearly as skilled and well organised as is assumed. After all, intelligence work is a human activity and, like other human activities, is subject to human error. Apart from meeting face to face, the journalists have found that the most effective way of guarding against surveillance is to keep on making the task of surveillance more difficult for those undertaking it, by placing inconveniences in their way:

> You should always assume that your electronic telephonic communication can be surveilled. Go for face-to-face communications as a rule. If you are going to use a telephone call, use, then add extra hurdles. If you are going to use phones, then use feature phones not smartphones. If you are going to go with your phone to a meeting, then carry with you a Faraday bag [a bag made of conductive mesh that prevents a device from emitting signals]. Use double passwords. This is enough as a hurdle. Just keep adding more hurdles. Most of the government departments do not have the capacity to break sophisticated hurdles. But let's face it, when they feel that they would like to surveil you, they can do it. All intelligence agencies have knowledge of these measures, but you need to keep adding extra barriers.

The weakest factor is the human factor. You should not just stick in any flashstick into your laptops. Sophisticated surveillance costs a lot of money, it costs a lot, it means reams and reams of data, of which 99 per cent of journalists are not that interesting to intelligence organisations. Never open attachments unless you know the person you are dealing with. The point is that you have to work, you have to continue. Face-to-face communication is the best. Leave your phones and laptops. The only other saving grace is human beings' incompetence.[7]

Investigative journalists operate in a poisonous environment, where there is a real possibility of their sources being disciplined, attacked or even killed. This is especially so in provinces where assassinations of political figures and whistleblowers have been rife, such as Mpumalanga and KZN. In these politically volatile contexts, political leaders are emboldened and may not even attempt to disguise the fact that they are surveilling journalists. According to one journalist based at a community newspaper in Mpumalanga, the Premier of the province had even confronted him about stories he had written that were critical of the provincial government, and that relied on a confidential source inside the government.

Communications surveillance is tapping my telephone calls and listening to my conversations. In my case, the Premier of Mpumalanga province, David Mabuza, confronted me and accused me of having spoken to a source. The only way he could have known about my telephone discussion could only have been through listening to my telephone conversations.[8]

Like the others, this journalist used end-to-end encryption for his communications, as well as different SIM cards to throw the spies off track, and also disabled location-based services when working on stories, so that his movements could not be tracked. He was particularly suspicious of cellphones, as he considered them to be insecure. He preferred to meet sources on a face-to-face basis, which was easier for him to achieve than for the *Sunday Times* journalists, as his paper was locally focused, not national. He had also begun to practice 'sousveillance' – resistance practice involving inverse surveillance of those who had put him under surveillance – to make them aware that he was tracking their spying activities. On one occasion, he noticed that there was a person stationed in front of his newspaper's offices, and he took photographs of what he described as the 'suspect'.

Another investigative journalist used a risk-based approach towards securing his communications: the greater the level of sensitivity of the story, the less likely he was to use electronic communications, reverting instead to face-to-face encounters. He had every reason to be concerned. When he was covering one story about former police commissioner Jackie Selebi – who was subsequently convicted of corruption – he was told by reliable sources inside the police that they intended to plant drugs on him to discredit him. However, he does not allow the reality, or even the threat, of surveillance to deter him from being transparent in his own activities, as he believes that journalists should lead by example. In other words, being transparent in one's own work strikes a blow against the general culture of secrecy in society. However, he was not willing to be transparent to the point where confidential sources might be threatened, as reckless acts could derail the transparency project in the longer term. According to the journalist:

> I believe in transparency, to the point where I would generally not mind outsiders listening to me interviewing people for stories. But there is one serious caveat: if whistleblowers and other confidential sources speak to journalists off the record, they have an absolute right to privacy. Not granting them that will discourage them and cut off the flows of essential information. This undermines the constitutional rights of freedom of speech and the media, and of the public to be informed.[9]

These journalists were in a unique position of having contacts inside the security services, which made verifying the fact that they were being surveilled easier. One challenge that the profession faces, though, is that journalists' responses to surveillance are often the result of their individual initiative, although some institutions do play a supportive role. While the individual media organisations most heavily affected by surveillance are pursuing various legal and advocacy options, no national organisation of journalists has taken up a campaign against surveillance abuses. This is a significant gap that has left less well-resourced and less knowledgeable journalists exposed.

ACADEMICS AND SURVEILLANCE

Academics are not as well organised when it comes to resisting surveillance practices as journalists, which is hardly surprising, as there has been little evidence of the intelligence services taking an interest in their activities. However, some incidents have given rise to alarm in the sector. The University of Johannesburg's Centre for Social Change – which is associated with the South African Research Chair in Social Change, and has been researching protests in South Africa – has experienced mysterious burglaries and data theft. The chair's work shot to prominence in 2012, when the research team associated with the chair undertook research in the immediate aftermath of the Marikana massacre, and uncovered evidence indicating that the police killings of mine workers were much more extensive and premeditated than had been reported initially. This groundbreaking work laid the basis for a commission of inquiry into the massacre, which found that the police had used excessive and inappropriate force against the mine workers.

Researchers working on the project suspected that their Marikana work had earned the ire of the authorities, which was a reasonable suspicion as many in the police stood to lose their jobs, and even face criminal prosecutions, because of the investigations which their research had precipitated. In 2014, the centre also held a press conference on its research on protests in South Africa, which was followed by a string of burglaries and data theft.[10] According to two interviewees:

> I think we have been targeted because of our research on service delivery protests and the Marikana issue. For me, it's even worse because I am a foreigner working in South Africa focusing on the ills of the post-apartheid democracy. Our research focuses on things that put the current regime on the spot, and goes against the grain in the sense that it disputes the notion that Marikana was caused by the third force. Instead our study shows that protesters were not part of some third-force agenda aimed at destabilising the government. There was very little correlation between the elections and the number of protests, and the protests were for the most part not politically orientated. We found that miners' grievances included housing, water and sanitation, political representation and electricity (Respondent 1).[11]
>
> I would like to add that it has everything to do with the kind of research we do here. We focus on service delivery protests, which the present government is not comfortable with. They would rather blame someone for instigating these protests rather than owning up (Respondent 2).[12]

In the academic context, while academics who are working on socially sensitive topics are scared about the possibility of intelligence surveillance, such unwelcome attention reinforces their resolve to continue focusing on their work, as it makes them realise how important such work is. To that extent, surveillance has the opposite of the intended effect, namely to ensure quiescent subjects. As one researcher noted:

Yes, I am afraid, but all of a sudden I have realised how important the work we doing is. Because if the NIA are interested in our work, it means we are doing something in the public interest (Respondent 2).[13]

Another researcher made a similar point:

Through this incident I have gotten to realise how important the kind of work we are doing is. When I joined this centre I thought I was just doing any other job, but now I have realised it is very important. Because the state is interested in what we do, it means we are doing something important (Respondent 3).[14]

After a particularly nasty experience when researchers lost access to their Dropbox account, containing some of their protest data, they decided to avoid cloud services and stop communicating over cellphones. They have also shifted from conducting individual interviews to focus groups, where the anonymity of participants is easier to guarantee. According to one interviewee:

We are no longer using mobile phones to keep in touch with the field unless it's extremely necessary. We have other ways of safeguarding the confidentiality of our research respondents. The lesson we've learnt is that researchers need to be less naive and more vigilant. But I have realised the importance of using focus group discussions in the South African context, which allow participants to hold their fellow comrades to account. Participants are not comfortable with individual face-to-face interviews (UJ respondent 1).[15]

While these researchers had found value in running focus groups, the same groups can limit in-depth exploration of issue, as individuals felt they could not say whatever they wanted in the presence of their comrades. Ideally, both qualitative methods should be available to researchers, but in this case their ability to use them has been limited by the realities of conducting sensitive research. Apart from implementing data protection measures, the researchers were also clear about the need for institutional and political responses to surveillance, otherwise they may not take the problem further. As the academy lacks a culture of protest against surveillance, individual academics do not know where to take their problems, and end up preferring to stay silent. According to one researcher:

In our case we received a lot of support from our university administration. Other academics told us that they have experienced similar state harassment, but have done nothing about it. The problem is that people don't protest after being surveilled. They complain behind closed doors and also put in place individual coping mechanisms to deal with surveillance. There is need for a broad-based coalition which puts anti-surveillance politics at the centre of national discourse.[16]

As we have seen in Chapters 3 and 4, the political intelligence-gathering mandate of the SSA has also allowed it to normalise spying on domestic political groupings on the most tenuous of grounds. This has had a knock-on effect on academics researching socio-political dynamics. In view of the SSA's overbroad National Intelligence Priorities, it is hardly surprising if the intelligence services should take an interest in the UJ centre's work, as it would provide them with a useful pool of information about the protests and organisers.

However, apart from the UJ experiences, there were no other examples of intelligence surveillance of activists that came to light during the interviews. Another academic had been told by police informants that he was under surveillance, but it appeared that this was linked to his activist rather than his academic work. According to him, he had experienced no interference with his academic work or received any sign that it had triggered surveillance. In any event, like one of the journalist interviewees, he felt that openness and transparency were the best answer to surveillance as, in his experience, spies were present in mass organisations in any event. However, when it came to security measures for movement activists, he resorted to face-to-face discussions. Discussions about political activity are generally undertaken in the open, but when it comes to plans to counter state repression, these take place in direct discussions so as not to alert the authorities. According to the academic:

I have nothing to hide and so I generally speak and write freely. Given that there are also paid informants in political organisations, secrecy is not helpful. I write, communicate and engage freely and openly but in the knowledge that one cannot ever assume that communication is not being monitored. The only exception to this is when I have been involved in responding to serious repression, particularly when it has involved death threats, and there are discussions with activists about arranging safe houses, getting people out of Durban for a bit, etc. Then I don't use email, cellphones, etc. We use face-to-face communication (with no live phones present), payphones, etc. We also would not use our own cars to travel to safe houses. However, discussions with academic colleagues are always open.[17]

For this academic, struggles against surveillance need to be mass-based, and led by oppressed people, not by NGOs. According to him, the main organisational response in the country, co-ordinated by the R2K Campaign,[18] was deeply flawed:

> What is required, ultimately, is political pressure against state repression. This is the most important thing. It needs to be rooted in mass-based struggle under the direction of oppressed people. I don't find the NGO networks to be helpful. For instance, in Durban, R2K [the Right2Know Campaign] is experienced as seriously patronising by many black grassroots activists. They say that they feel that they are not included in decision-making but are just expected to be bussed in to make up the numbers at protests. There is a clear elitism in how things work, and it is also plainly raced.[19]

ACTIVISTS AND SURVEILLANCE

The SSA's political intelligence-gathering mandate means that political activists are at severe risk of surveillance, and they are aware of this. When political fissures emerged in the ruling ANC alliance – leading to NUMSA breaking away from COSATU – evidence of political surveillance increased. NUMSA documented several cases of surveillance of their activists, made these cases public and threatened to lay a complaint with the Inspector General of Intelligence. NUMSA had facilitated the establishment of a United Front, a coalition of trade unions and community organisations committed to campaigning for social justice outside the ANC alliance, and also entertained the idea of forming a workers' party, although at the time of writing no such decision had been taken. In one case, an activist was contacted by a woman identifying herself as an SSA employee, demanding more information about a march they were planning in the Ekurhuleni region of Gauteng. Apparently the woman asked the activist, 'Who are these people who want to march all the time, to disrupt this work of the government?'[20] Other incidents also emerged that pointed to intelligence surveillance, not only of NUMSA members, but of United Front activists too.

NUMSA is not the only union that has complained of intelligence harassment. AMCU assumed prominence in the mine workers' struggles in the platinum belt that culminated in the Marikana massacre, and many workers disaffected with COSATU affiliate the National Union of Mineworkers defected to it. In view of these developments, it seems fair to say that the ANC alliance viewed AMCU as a significant threat to its interests. The SSA confirmed that it was investigating AMCU's leader, Joseph Mathunjwa, as well as an unsubstantiated allegation made on a website that he and other prominent individuals were engaged in espionage activities. This investigation fuelled paranoia in the organisation, leading to a climate of mistrust and a fear that allegations of spies in their midst could be used to discourage internal debates that the leadership might find uncomfortable. As Mathunjwa has been the most prominent AMCU leader by far, this risks creating a cult of personality that could undermine internal democracy, and allegations of spies in the organisation can only make matters worse. According to an AMCU shop steward: 'If I go against my leadership in a meeting and afterwards they tell people "that man is a spy for the government", I won't be safe walking home.'[21]

Potentially, surveillance can sow division and create confusion in organisations, paralysing internal discussion. It can make activists and unionists suspect one another when discussing complex and potentially divisive organisational questions. But it can also have a galvanising effect, causing an organisation to unite around a common problem, confront its causes transparently, and openly disclose approaches by intelligence operatives or other suspicious occurrences.[22] What is instructive is that NUMSA responded to evidence of state surveillance very differently from AMCU, by opening up a discussion democratically in its ranks, identifying those worst affected and offering them support, then turning the issue outwards and making their experiences public, and finally demonstrating a willingness to lodge an official complaint that could then be investigated. NUMSA has also not been shy about politicising the problem, linking the issue of surveillance to broader challenges to the status quo. As for AMCU, there is no evidence of its having taken the matter up. NUMSA was not surprised by state surveillance against it and the United Front, as a pattern had emerged in which the surveillance capacities of the state were being used to monitor perceived dissidents. According to the union:

> It happens to activists in social movements involved in 'service delivery protests'. It happens to investigative journalists digging up all the rot on corruption. It happens to all those who are critical of the status quo. There is a pattern where intelligence forces are used to deal with legitimate and lawful struggles and campaigns. It is a sign of creeping authoritarianism.[23]

This threat could lead to activists self-censoring out of fear that the authorities might act on the intelligence they gather. In this regard, one respondent noted the following:

> I am scared. Just to know that the NIA are interested in your whereabouts is reason to fear. Those people mean business when they follow up on you. You never know when they can knock on your door.[24]

The activists, many of whom were highly experienced and had clashed repeatedly with the authorities, were clear that surveillance was not about detecting criminals, but about tracking their activities so as to give the state and its political controllers advance warnings about protests. In fact, the state saw activist work as essentially criminal in nature, and did not see the value in activists exercising their right to protest. In this regard, two activists noted the following:

> I think it's because the government is afraid that people can end up rising against them. So activists are an easy target because most of the protests here are co-ordinated by us. They want to know our friends, our thoughts and our plans (Thembelihle Crisis Committee activist).
>
> They want to get into our heads. They think we are planning evil against them so they surveil our phones, social networks and emails. They are always building a case against us. Instead of seeing us as concerned citizens who want the best for our people, they think negatively about us. I think that's why we are on the firing line (R2K Western Cape activist).[25]

The R2K Western Cape activist's comments about intelligence operatives wishing to 'get into our heads' is telling, as it points to a shift on the part of the SAPS towards intelligence-led policing (which was touched on in Chapter 3). In the case of this activist, intelligence operatives made no attempt whatsoever to disguise the fact that they had her under surveillance. They also used personal information about her life circumstances to try to intimidate her into withdrawing from her activism, implying that her work in relation to gangs in the Western Cape made her a suspect by association. She explained:

> They took me to a secluded place and told me that they had tons of information about me and my activities in various social movements in the Western Cape. They asked me why I hang out with gang leaders in the Cape Flats and participate in so many social movements yet I am a single mother (R2K Western Cape activist).[26]

Activists are clear that the state is using intelligence-gathering to put the police at an advantage in dealing with those perceived to be threatening to ruling interests:

> My view is that it's just the government which is interested in knowing more about our activities as activists. They want to be on top of the situation when it comes to dealing with marches and demonstrations.

Information is power, so I think by conducting surveillance on what we do, they would like to be able to predict and plan ahead of us. Before we are burning tyres in the streets, they want to be able to deploy police details and minimise the impact of our protests.

I am not sure why activists are being targeted, but my gut feeling is that the state fear being caught unawares and unprepared to deal with protests. For them activists can make their governance difficult, hence the need to ensure they snoop on our operations.

It's part of their political intelligence-gathering exercise. It's only that activists are viewed with suspicion. That's why their activities are vigorously monitored especially in South Africa where protests are so widespread.[27]

Knowing that they are vulnerable, activists had begun to protect themselves against surveillance by encrypting their communications, favouring face-to-face encounters, switching phones off during public meetings, and pre-screening Facebook friends and Twitter followers. Others update their anti-virus software constantly and avoid opening attachments unless they are absolutely sure that they are bona fide. However, these threats had eroded trust inside organisations, and bred a climate of suspicion. As one activist noted, 'The rule is: trust no one.' Yet at the same time, activists were making extra efforts to use tried and tested methods of mobilisation, rather than relying on social media, which lessened the chance of their descending into 'slacktivism'. So, ironically, the lack of internet penetration in South Africa's poorer communities has been something of a boon for activists, as it has made their work more difficult to track, which is probably why physical surveillance techniques are still so prevalent. According to one activist:

We use the word of mouth to spread the information in informal settlements. This is much better than using new media, which can be monitored, plus most of our members cannot afford them. We call for community meetings where we plan for demonstrations and marches (Respondent 13, Thembelihle Crisis Committee).[28]

LAWYERS AND SURVEILLANCE

South Africa's spy agencies are not the only culprits when it comes to surveillance of communications on questionable grounds. As mentioned in Chapter 5, communications of the LRC have been intercepted by GCHQ. The LRC has four regional offices and employs over sixty-five lawyers in South Africa, all undertaking human rights-based public interest litigation. The LRC had been shocked by the GCHQ revelations, and had changed their communications practices to protect the confidentiality of communications with their clients. According to one respondent:

> We are certainly now cautious. Going forward we are putting in place a number of mechanisms to protect ourselves. It is difficult to communicate with emails anyway with our clients because of low internet penetration amongst the poor and marginalised communities in South Africa. Although we rely on telephonic interviews because the mobile phone is generally accessible by most people, we are careful not to put our clients at risk. Communications surveillance also complicates our efforts to receive whistleblowing information from our clients. People will be scared, so they hold back what they know and have.
>
> Another strategy has been to start digital security education with our LRC offices so that people are aware of the risks and opportunities involved. This relates to information around password protection and how to avoid phishing of emails. An in-house team has been set up to assist us with digital technology security capacity.[29]

However, the interviewees also noted that responses at the level of individual practice were inadequate, and that they needed to contribute towards a more organised response, which also included participating in advocacy efforts and engaging in strategic litigation against GCHQ. But they recognised that the lack of an organised response hampered these efforts. As lawyers, they were, needless to say, also considering the option of strategic litigation.

> We support the R2K Campaign because it brings together various organisations and activists who share similar difficulties in relation to communications surveillance. We support their efforts because, like other organisations, we are facing similar challenges. The problem, however, is lack of co-ordination amongst various stakeholders. There is need for co-operation so that we can fight this issue as a collective rather than as individuals.
>
> We are also a member of the International Network of Civil Liberties Organizations[30] (INCLO), they are able to institute strategic litigation cases against the GCHQ at the European Human Rights Court. They are also lobbying for the respect of the right to privacy at the international level ... As a member of INCLO organisations, we have benefited immensely from advice we have received from the American Civil Liberties Union and Liberty, which has experience handling cases involving communications surveillance. They

are assisting with building up the case against the British intelligence agency. There are chances that we can take the matter to the European Human Rights Court in future. We are looking at a number of options.[31]

CONCLUSION: TOWARDS AN ANALYTICAL FRAMEWORK FOR CHALLENGING SURVEILLANCE

As omnipotent and omniscient as it may seem, state surveillance can be challenged. But what should effective mass resistance to seemingly invisible but all-pervasive surveillance practices look like? Not enough has been said about the power of mass movements, and the necessity of mass struggle more broadly, to transform the social relations that are so dependent for their continued existence on surveillance. Activists who are serious about challenging surveillance state powers need to place both the politics and the economics of surveillance at the forefront of these struggles. When surveillance becomes part of the programmes of mass movements, various questions beg to be answered. Under what circumstances does surveillance have a demobilising effect on activism? What kinds of resistance are being practised against surveillance, and under what conditions does resistance become possible? Why do some people fight and others cave in? What demands enable effective resistance to these practices (and, given its visibility, how can this even be measured)?

Perhaps the primary challenge in crafting effective resistance to surveillance is to see the problem in an empowering way, in order to do something about it and not feel overwhelmed. Achievable programmes of action that also politicise the problem allow activists to plan, and serve as a guide to action. However, much of the theorisation of surveillance – which often uses Jeremy Bentham's 'panopticon' as a touchstone concept – tends to have a paralysing effect, in that it sees surveillance as being everywhere and nowhere. As discussed in Chapter 1, some surveillance studies scholars claim to have moved beyond Foucault and the panopticon as a metaphor for surveillance in modern societies, noting that surveillance takes place on a much more distributed basis than was originally thought, as a variety of actors (state and non-state) engage in surveillance. This approach has been associated with the Deleuzian turn in surveillance studies, according to which surveillance can be likened more to a rhizome than a panopticon.[32] But that description does even less to assist activists to identify the people and interests behind surveillance.

In order to move beyond the faceless, nameless and potentially disempowering effects of the panopticon and the surveillant assemblage, it is necessary to bring both the state and agency back into the picture, while not reducing surveillance to a simple phenomenon. In this regard, Laurence Cox and Alf Nilsen[33] have provided a useful conceptualisation of the state as a movement from above, consisting of individuals who can be challenged, rather than a faceless structure that cannot be changed through activist agency. This allows activists to recognise that states, and the governments they are beholden to and the interests they represent, are social constructs, in much the same way as movements from below, and this makes them appear less unassailable. They are constructed by individuals, and hence can be challenged by individuals. As discussed in Chapter 1, Henry Giroux has also provided some useful pointers for resistance strategies, through a critique of current strategies. The value of Giroux's critique is that it lays the ground for a totalising theory that links surveillance to the broader functioning of capitalism, but not in a way that makes the problem look so huge that it frightens activists off.

David Lyon has also suggested some useful elements of a framework for resistance. According to Lyon, Snowden's release of documents about the US's mass surveillance programmes was a sign of resistance, and a successful one at that, as it obliged governments to rethink their policies. For Lyon, resistance to surveillance needs to take place on three levels: at the level of the material and technological, where the bases and conduits for surveillance are addressed; at the level of the cultures of surveillance; and at the level of the institutions that support mass surveillance. Resistance on all these levels must be set in its proper political context – where those who are responsible for unjustifiable surveillance practices are held to account – and must lead to cultural critique and policy renewal.[34]

Building on the theoretical advances of Giroux, Lyon, Cox and Nilsen, and drawing on the experiential, historically grounded knowledge of a range of social movements in South Africa – as well as the lawyers who defend them, the academics who research them, and the journalists who write about them – we can propose the beginnings of a framework for effective mass-based resistance against these practices. Many older activists still carry memories of apartheid-era spying that pointed clearly to the political functions of surveillance, and their memories continue to inform democracy-era movements. As a result, there is an already highly developed mass consciousness of the inherently political nature of surveillance, which is an essential subjective condition for effective mobilisation beyond the confines of elite civil society and limiting rights-based discourse. We should therefore draw on the learning of those that have been subjected to state surveillance, and the way they have translated this learning into action. The interviews recorded in this book make it possible to propose a typology of factors that impact on resistance to surveillance. These factors can then be used to predict how successful or unsuccessful resistance is likely to be, depending on whether these factors exist or not.

Table 8.1: Factors affecting resistance to surveillance

Factors affecting resistance to surveillance	Effective resistance to surveillance	Ineffective resistance to surveillance
Material/technological level		
Technical knowledge	Knowledge of how to protect sensitive information through encryption, avoiding insecure communications, etc.	Lack of knowledge of how to protect sensitive information through encryption, avoiding insecure communications, etc.
Access to technical expertise and support	Individuals can receive support and learn about surveillance and how to protect themselves	Individuals lack learning opportunities about surveillance and how to protect themselves
Cultural level		
Access to information	Adequate information is available to expose abuses	Inadequate information is available to expose abuses
Historical memories of repression	Individuals are aware that surveillance is possible because it has happened in the past	Individuals have no historical memories to draw on
Supportive organisations	Organisations provide support to victims of surveillance	Organisations leave individuals to deal with the problem of surveillance
International networks	International networks are available to provide support	No international networks are available to provide support
Suspicion of authority	Suspicion of authority ensures that government arguments about the need for surveillance are not taken for granted	Trust in authority ensures that government arguments about the need for surveillance are taken for granted
Legal knowledge	Communications users know their legal rights and the state's legal obligations	Communications users don't know their legal rights and the state's legal obligations
Political knowledge	Communications users understand the political uses of surveillance	Communications users don't understand the political uses of surveillance
Ethical knowledge	Communications users have ethical knowledge that favours openness	Communications users lack ethical knowledge that favours openness
Media access	Victims of surveillance can publicise their cases, raising public awareness of the problem	Victims of surveillance cannot publicise their cases, leading to low public awareness of the problem
Current experiences of repression	Communications users can link surveillance to broader cases of state repression	Communications users experience surveillance as isolated cases of state repression, rather than symptoms of a broader systemic problem
Culture of activism	Victims have experience of activist work, and how it can be used to challenge state abuses	Victims have limited to no experience of activist work, and how it can be used to challenge state abuses
Culture of internal democracy in mass organisations	Mass organisations can overcome fear and internal suspicion of spies in their midst and expose intelligence abuses	Mass organisations cannot overcome internal paranoia and elevate surveillance into a campaign

Factors affecting resistance to surveillance	Effective resistance to surveillance	Ineffective resistance to surveillance
Awareness of importance of work that triggered surveillance	Victim is aware of importance of work that triggered surveillance, and is subjectively committed to it	Victim is not aware of importance of work that triggered surveillance, and is not subjectively committed to it
Institutional level		
Availability of allies inside the state	Sources with insider knowledge provide information about surveillance	No insider information about surveillance is available
State authoritarianism/ democracy	States that act in unjust ways are more likely to provoke opposition	States that act in just ways are more likely to garner support
Politicisation of state bureaucracy	State takes administrative decisions about who to surveil	State takes political decisions about who to surveil
Political level		
Divisions in the political elite	Elite divided about use of surveillance	Elite united about use of surveillance
Availability of allies outside the state	Affected individuals can build alliances to campaign against surveillance, thereby ensuring a collective response	Affected individuals do not have access to alliances and respond in an individualised fashion
Legal and policy framework	Legal and policy framework supports accountable uses of surveillance	Legal and policy framework is too weak to support accountable uses of surveillance
Availability of mass organisations with progressive politics	Mass organisations are willing to take up surveillance as part of broader campaigns for social change	No mass organisations available to take up surveillance as part of mass campaigns for social change
Rupture in mass politics	Surveillance becomes more likely, but so do new organisations and alliances to counter it	Surveillance remains likely, but new organisations and alliances do not come into being
Economic level		
Knowledge of economic actors	Knowledge of the surveillance providers, their economic interests and links to the state	Limited to no knowledge of the surveillance providers, their economic interests and links to the state
Campaigns against the unchecked manufacture and export of surveillance equipment	Well-targeted campaigns that raise the political costs of a country allowing the manufacture and export of surveillance equipment	No campaigns targeting the manufacture and export of surveillance equipment

Source: Author, drawing on David Lyon's keynote presentation to the International Association for Media and Communications Research, 14 July 2015, https://www.youtube.com/watch?v=Vzgok3kUl0o (accessed 7 June 2016).

In other words, effective resistance to surveillance needs to take place on the following levels: the material/technological, the cultural, the institutional, the political and the economic. In relation to the material/technological level, if activists have knowledge of how to protect sensitive information and have access to technical expertise and support, their resistance is more likely to be effective. In relation to the cultural level, activists are more likely to be effective if they have historical memories and current experiences of surveillance abuses, if they have adequate information to expose abuses, if their experiences are taken up as part of a mass-based organised response rather than as individuals and these organisations handle the problem openly, if they understand the political and economic functions of surveillance, have access to international networks knowledgeable about surveillance and provide the necessary levels of support to victims. The victim is also more likely to disclose surveillance practices if he or she is given the necessary levels of support by an organisation, and is aware of the importance of the work that triggered the surveillance. Organisations are more likely to take up surveillance cases if they share a suspicion of authority, understand the political uses of surveillance and the broader environment of repression, if their members are experienced activists and are aware of their legal rights and ethical obligations to society, and have access to the media to publicise surveillance abuses.

On the political level, resistance to surveillance is likely to succeed if there is a broad rupture in a country's politics and, consequently, political elites are divided about the use of repression generally and surveillance specifically; if victims are in a position to build alliances against surveillance abuses, thereby ensuring a collective response; if the legal and policy frameworks support the exposure of such abuses and discourage them from arising again; and if mass organisations are willing to take up surveillance as part of broader campaign strategies for progressive social change. On the economic level, campaigns are most likely to succeed if movements have knowledge of the surveillance providers, their economic interests and links to the state, and are able turn this knowledge into well-targeted campaigns that raise the political costs to a country that allows the manufacture and export of surveillance equipment (especially mass surveillance, as the argument for mass surveillance is much flimsier than the argument for targeted interception). If resistance can take place at all these levels, then it is more likely to be effective.

9

Conclusion

I started out this book with a series of questions focusing on how concerned we should be about the growth of surveillance in South Africa, and whether it is becoming routinised. I asked to what extent South Africa is becoming a surveillance society governed by a surveillance state, where surveillance becomes a key instrument of social control. I also sought to establish patterns in how surveillance is being practised, and the uses to which it is being put. I was interested to know if the uses of surveillance (to the extent that it was being used) were justifiable or whether they were leading to the major privacy violations that we've seen exposed by Snowden. These questions led me to map the different forms of state surveillance in South Africa, their interconnections (if any), and the democratic controls (or the lack of them) on these capabilities, and their social and political uses.

In Chapter 1, I considered some of the key theoretical debates about surveillance and privacy before and after the Snowden revelations. In this chapter, I made it clear that a political economy, and more specifically a Marxist, analysis made the most sense to me, as it linked the growth of surveillance to the continued reality of class domination, and provided a basis for defining surveillance as involving the collection and analysis of information and the accessing of a person's physical characteristics for the purposes of social control. Such a definition allowed surveillance to be separated out from other, more routine forms of information-processing. Unless the two were separated, surveillance could be normalised, making it less possible to conceive of an emancipated society that can free itself from surveillance. I also looked at whether privacy could be said to be dead in the post-Snowden era, drawing on some of the theoretical debates about privacy and how it should be defined.

In Chapter 2, I argued that there are powerful interests at work in promoting the expansion of the surveillance industry, as arms companies and supportive governments sought new markets because of the declining number of conventional wars. The incorporation of military practices and logics into domestic law enforce-ment and national security work has created an industrial base for surveillance, allowing for its rapid expansion and even universalisation. I argued that while there have been victories in the struggle against unaccountable mass surveillance, these practices are continuing and are even expanding, which suggests that resistance to surveillance in the wake of the Snowden revelations has not been as effective as it needs to be. Privacy, conceptualised as an individual right, is not an adequate concept. Resistance strategies led by NGOs and specialists are unlikely to be suc-cessful as they depoliticise the problem and fail to galvanise the social power that is necessary to confront the powerful interests at work in the spread of surveillance. I argued that if anti-surveillance activists are going to be successful, they need to 'do' their work differently, placing more emphasis on working in and through organ-ised social formations that are focused, not just on privacy and surveillance, but on transforming the exploitative and oppressive social relations that continue to be maintained by surveillance.

In Chapter 3, I analysed the shifting modes of state repression in South Africa, especially the shift from more reactive to pre-emptive forms of social control in the wake of the politically costly Marikana massacre. I argued here that South Africa is manifesting elements of a Gramscian organic crisis, which means that while the ruling hegemonic bloc cannot offer concessions very easily, neither can they repress very easily either. The fact that the state lacked the capacity to repress openly – and, ironically enough, the Marikana massacre had weakened its capacity even more, as it had solidified mass opposition rather than discouraged it – meant that it had to resort to less visible, more pre-emptive forms of social control, such as surveil-lance. That there were these shifts in the coercive capacities of the state attest to the hegemonic bloc's weakness, rather than its strength, and as a result it appears less unassailable.

In Chapter 4, I examined the practices of lawful interception for intelligence and criminal justice purposes in South Africa. I analysed the domestication of lawful interception practices, the uses to which they are being put, and their regulation. I found that while these practices were reasonably well regulated, there were lacu-nae in their accountability mechanisms that allowed them to be abused. While there was evidence of lawful interception being successful as a crime-fighting tool in particular cases, there was too little evidence to justify the conclusion that the state's growing thirst for intercept information was proving to be an effective inves-tigative tool.

In Chapter 5, I examined state mass surveillance, tactical surveillance and hack-ing in South Africa, and South Africa's position in the global mass surveillance regime. There was little evidence in the Snowden documents of South Africa being of great interest to the Five Eyes countries. Yet, in spite of the fact that South Africa faces no major threats to national security, there is evidence of South Africa becoming a user of mass surveillance, hacking and tactical surveillance tools, with a bias towards hacking as a form of surveillance. South Africa has also become a producer of mass surveillance tools. I concluded from the available evidence that South Africa's role in the global surveillance complex is sub-imperial in nature, as it operates as a middle power that reproduces rather than challenges the mass surveillance practices of the Five Eyes countries.

In Chapter 6, I examined privacy, surveillance and public spaces in South Africa, and looked more closely at the uses of CCTV cameras in crime-fighting and for automated road-tolling, as well as the regulation of drones. I argued that street-level surveillance has become increasingly normalised in South Africa with little public resistance, owing to high levels of crime. However, there is little evidence that street-level surveillance is having a consistently deterrent effect on serious contact crimes, and even property crimes. Success stories tend to be anecdotal. Furthermore, inaccurate information about people's travel habits reduced the effectiveness of these databases as surveillance tools. While CCTV camera systems in public spaces have been portrayed as a silver bullet for street crimes, in reality they divert public attention away from the far more basic policing interventions that are needed for effective crime prevention. While South Africa's drone regulations are completely silent on privacy and data protection issues, there is little reason to believe that their uses for law enforcement will yield different policing results from those achieved by CCTV.

In Chapter 7, I explored the uses of biometrics as a form of surveillance in South Africa. I did so by tracing the introduction of biometrically based identity systems in a variety of public functions, including the social security system, the new Department of Home Affairs ID 'smart card' and the use of biometrics in border control. I found that while biometric technologies were being used mainly for social welfare purposes rather than for social control, their potential surveillance purposes were most apparent in relation to border control. However, the full surveillant potential of biometrics was unlikely to be realised given the inability of the state to achieve the interoperability of its various biometric databases. However, the police had been provided with direct access to the Home Affairs database, which looked set to expand in time, and which was likely to play a more surveillant role in time to come.

In Chapter 8, I analysed what particularly vulnerable constituencies are doing to adapt to and resist communications surveillance (namely lawyers, journalists, academics, civic activists and trade unionists). Bearing in mind some of the strengths and weaknesses of resistance practices discussed in Chapter 2, I argued on the basis of interviews with representatives from these various constituencies that key elements needed to be present in the fightback against unaccountable surveillance, which needs to take place on the material/technological, cultural, institutional as well as political and economic levels. These elements provided a basic framework for effective resistance to surveillance, one that attempted to re-politicise struggles against unaccountable surveillance.

Returning to the analytical framework outlined in the introduction, I will address some of the questions posed by this framework. In relation to the *surveillance actors and interest groups*, I examined the main state surveillance 'clients' (the police, military and intelligence, and other state agencies), surveillance oversight bodies, communications companies, surveillance subjects, civil society and social movements, and their roles and responsibilities. I also considered whether there was any evidence of other actors becoming active in relation to surveillance. In relation to interest groups involved in surveillance, there is clearly a complex mix of actors. In relation to state actors, several state entities have access to the targeted interception capacities of the state, housed in the OIC and falling under the political control of the SSA and the legislative control of RICA. The number of surveillance actors has increased, with the traditional actors such as the police and the SSA being supplemented by the SANDF and the FIC, suggesting that the need for intercept information was increasing in state institutions. However, the SSA has its own, much more invasive capabilities, which are under-regulated. This is of concern as there are clear signs of the agency becoming the watchdog of legitimate political and journalistic activities for the dominant faction of the ruling party. The SAPS has become an increasingly important actor in the surveillance space, especially its CID. Much of this has to do with the fact that the SAPS has embraced intelligence-led policing as a policing model that is less likely to result in controversies than paramilitary policing, as abuses – when they occur – are much more visible in the latter case. There are also signs that Crime Intelligence has misused its intelligence-gathering powers.

Oversight actors include a range of bodies, from the RICA judge, the Inspector General of Intelligence and the JSCI, to the privacy/information regulator and the courts. Communications network service providers in South Africa are important actors in that they need to co-operate with the OIC to provide access to communications in line with interception directions authorised by the designated judge. No evidence is available of service providers being complicit in mass surveillance in the ways that they have been in the US. Local governments are emerging as increasingly important surveillance actors, especially in the major metropolitan areas, where there is relatively more money to fund technologies like CCTV on a public–private partnership basis. Cape Town appears to be more advanced than other metros in building a local surveillance state, deploying the 'ring of steel' approach to crime-fighting seen in various UK cities, using ANPR technologies in CCTV and testing drones for surveillance purposes. The City of Johannesburg is also beginning to experiment with facial recognition technologies in CCTV. The CAA has become a surveillance actor almost by default, in the sense that it had an opportunity to regulate the privacy impacts of drones, but has failed to do so, and rather has stayed silent on privacy questions.

Biometrics have been used for surveillance purposes by the police for many years now, as they have operated their own fingerprint database. Initially, they processed fingerprints manually, but computerisation allowed them to shift to automated analysis through the AFIS. Other departments that make use of biometrics – namely Home Affairs and Social Security – have focused on using biometrics for social welfare rather than surveillance purposes. In the case of Home Affairs, surveillance for the purposes of social sorting has always been an element of its mandate, and biometrics have been used increasingly for these purposes, especially in the wake of the introduction of the biometrically based smart ID cards. The department's integration into the security cluster, and closer co-operation with the police, meant that its surveillance role was likely to increase.

In relation to *surveillance interventions or actions*, I identified the *surveillance perpetrators*: who they were, how often they were undertaking surveillance (at least in relation to lawful interception), and what was motivating the surveillance. I also looked at what forms of surveillance they used, and how these were changing over time (if at all). There is evidence of the South African state changing its forms of surveillance over time; furthermore, the evidence points to these changes being broadly consistent with international trends. South Africa undertook physical surveillance, as well as surveillance of telephony in the analogue era, using technologies that intercepted circuit-switched landlines. As cellphones became more widespread, and communications networks changed from circuit-switched to digitised, packet-switched networks, South Africa changed its surveillance law and practices to bring them into line with CALEA, and CALEA and ETSI standards set the bases for lawful interception. South Africa then introduced mass surveillance technologies, housed in the NCC, and there is also evidence suggesting that in response to the growing use of encryption, the country is developing capacities to use malware to hack into computers, as well as to undertake tactical surveillance of devices belonging to people who communicate 'on the go'.

South Africa has been a user of CCTV cameras for a long time, although mainly in private contexts. The roll-out of CCTV in public spaces is a relatively new development, as is the introduction of tools like ANPR and facial recognition. ANPR has been used in the context of e-tolling and is now being experimented with in the context of law enforcement. Drones have also been tested for law enforcement purposes in at least one municipality. Biometrics have been used mainly for welfare purposes, although increasingly they are being deployed for surveillance purposes as well, especially when it comes to tracking the identities and movements of suspected non-nationals. The national state and, increasingly, the local state are establishing massive databases of perfectly innocent citizens, and using them to check for criminal suspects, with inadequate controls to prevent abuse of personal information. South Africa appears to be an active market for the diffusion of next-generation surveillance equipment, and consequently has become a customer of some of the biggest multinational technology firms in the world. In the case of some of these technologies, it enjoys the industrial capacity to make its own surveillance technologies, and even to export them.

As in other parts of the world, the surveillance capacities in South Africa that relate to national security appear to be the most invasive, yet are the least regulated. Other surveillance capacities that relate to more general forms of crime-fighting, or that are used to distinguish nationals from non-nationals, are not well regulated for privacy either, but their invasiveness is limited in scope. The democratic controls of the targeted communications interception capabilities of the state are inadequate, although they cannot be used with complete abandon. Yet the loopholes are large enough for the system to be very open to abuse. There has been a sharp rise in the use of these capabilities by a range of surveillance actors, although the police and the SSA dominate. The NCC's exact technological capabilities are unknown, but, on its own admission, it does undertake mass surveillance and is actively seeking to expand its ability to do so. A confidential source has also claimed that the NCC has the capabilities to hack as well. Certainly, assuming that the South African state was indeed the purchaser of FinFisher licences as evidence suggested, it has been a prominent user of one of the most invasive hacking tools in the world today, although it is not clear which government departments were licensed to use it. Crime Intelligence officers have expressed interest in hacking tools, but they are largely reliant on the OIC, of which they and the SSA are becoming more frequent users. So while the police are becoming intelligence-led, they remain tied to relatively targeted intelligence-led investigations.

One of the most well-recognised weaknesses of CCTV as surveillance devices is that they tend to displace crime, in that criminals move to areas that are not covered by CCTV. While the Cape Town municipality has attempted to address this problem by adopting a containment approach towards crime, where crime-fighting tools such as CCTV have been rolled out throughout the metro, the most effective cameras are confined to the CBD, as many are privately funded, whereas those that are publicly funded tend to be ineffective, are underutilised, and some have fallen into disrepair. However, the existence of CCTV does not necessarily result in reductions in crime as the SAPS appears incapable of putting its footage to use in investigations, limiting their effectiveness as panoptic devices. Street-level surveillance is also being implemented by some municipalities in the absence of functional privacy and data protection controls, and the lack of any controls on physical privacy whatsoever. The silence of the CAA on privacy matters meant that drones could be deployed by state actors for surveillance purposes with few controls on their activities if the director of the CAA authorised their use. With respect to the use of biometrics for surveillance purposes, their potential as full surveillance tools for criminal justice or national security purposes was thwarted by the fact that the different biometric and biographic databases across different government departments did not 'talk' to one another, or even within the Home Affairs department itself. Consequently, their documentary efforts were limited to their departmental efforts, or even discrete functions within departments, thereby constraining the ability of the state to use these capabilities for panoptic purposes.

I then looked at the *surveillance oversight bodies*, and considered what interventions they engaged in to keep surveillance actors under review, how they are set up, how independent and accountable they are, and how effective they are at holding actors to account if there are abuses. With respect to the RICA judge, much depended on the person who occupied the role; however, structural problems prevented this position from being truly effective at oversight, as the judge takes decisions about granting or refusing interception directions and writes the report about the decisions, conflating decision-making with oversight. The Inspector General did not seem to be involved in performing oversight of the state's surveillance capacities on a regular basis, and appeared to be mainly a complaints-driven body. The fact that both the Inspector General and the JSCI operated with secrecy as the default position made it difficult to assess their true effectiveness, but the many cases of intelligence excesses suggested that they were not being as effective as they should be. Another potentially important oversight body is the privacy/information regulator, but at the time of writing it was still in the process of being established, so its effectiveness had not been felt yet. Indeed, it is telling that the state has expanded its surveillance capacities in the absence of a functional data protection authority, which means that when the regulator finally begins work, it will have to contend with an already highly developed surveillance architecture. In fact, it could be surmised that state surveillance actors were served very well by not having the regulator in place for so long. In any event, privacy regulators have not proved to be particularly effective, as they tend to become mired in enforcing formalistic privacy notices on private companies, while failing to address broader developments that erode privacy. Large national security exclusions in privacy law mean that privacy regulators are often ineffective at addressing privacy violations on national security grounds, leaving the private sector far better regulated for privacy than the state. While privacy advocates have argued for data protection laws and regulators to protect privacy, too much faith has been placed in these mechanisms to stop systemic privacy violations. This is not to say that South Africa's information regulator should not be turned into a site of struggle. Some reforms are possible because POPI makes it clear that the Act may apply to criminal justice or national security matters if it can be shown that existing privacy protections are inadequate. There is little doubt that this is so with respect to a range of surveillance practices.

The Inspector General played a robust role at one point in history, when evidence emerged of the mass surveillance capacities of the state being abused to spy on journalists, business people and politicians, but since then there has been scant evidence of its being an effective oversight body. The kinds of exposure that have been made by the UK's IPT have not been forthcoming from the Inspector General's office, but this could be attributed in part to the fact that advocacy organisations have not pushed the office through well-targeted complaints, as their UK counterparts have done. The UK successes with the IPT, however modest, suggest that there are real gains to be made from complaints-driven legal advocacy; however, the courts need to be considered as a back-up if this tactic fails. In this regard, the role of the South African courts in holding surveillance actors to account was still unfolding at the time of writing, with one RICA-related case, where journalists had allegedly been spied on, having been decided in favour of the journalists. But the fact that the case arrived in court in the first place suggests that courts may be an important way of achieving accountability if information comes to light about surveillance abuses. The courts could also be used to hold private individuals to account for abusing surveillance technology. However, the courts remained untested as forums for systemic abuses by the state (as opposed to errant individuals), in ways that have been possible in the European court system and, to a much lesser extent, in the US court system.

With respect to the *surveillance subjects*, I considered how these subjects are chosen, and whether particular individuals, social groups or professions are more likely to become subjects of surveillance, and, if so, who they are. I also explored whether different categories of victim respond differently to surveillance or at least the threat of surveillance. I also considered whether the organisations and individuals being placed under surveillance are changing over time, why, and where they stand in relation to key power-holders in the state and society.

These were very difficult questions to answer as there is no user notification in relation to lawful interception practices, and certainly not in relation to mass surveillance. An additional problem is that not enough information is provided about the types of crimes that trigger surveillance, which would provide clues as to the types of surveillance subjects. Rightfully, information should also be provided about interception directions that have resulted in arrests and convictions, so that the public can assess whether RICA is meeting its stated purpose of bringing down crime or whether the directions are being used for speculative 'fishing expeditions' to ferret out intercept information that is not related to crime-fighting. Apart from criminal suspects, historical experiences have shown that there are particular groups and professions that are especially vulnerable to surveillance. These include people who by virtue of their actions or professions are in conflict with power on a fairly regular basis, namely journalists, political activists, lawyers and even academics. The possibility of these constituencies being considered subjects of interest has been strengthened by the fact that the SSA has gathered political intelligence, which has broadened its definition of potential criminality to include suspected crimes against the state (such as subversion). There is evidence that this category of crime has led the SSA and Crime Intelligence to include those engaged in political dissent, and their perceived supporters, in their definition of people of interest. Evidence has also emerged strongly suggesting and on occasion even proving that individuals within these constituencies are under surveillance.

However, in South Africa, responses to other, emerging surveillance technologies have been inadequate. South Africans have not risen up in their numbers against centralised biometrically based identity systems, as little public awareness-raising has taken place about their dangers. Much of this has to do with the fact that South Africans (and especially those who were politically active under apartheid) have historical memories of certain forms of surveillance, especially physical and communications surveillance, and consequently they are more tangible and easier to politicise and organise around. Largely, the technology press has been uncritical about the adoption of biometrics. Also, because the government has not compelled the carrying of identity cards, the issue has not been politicised in the way that it was for instance in Mauritius. A movement against state biometric surveillance is possible, given the high levels of discontent about the mismanagement of social grants, but this discontent has not yet been channelled in the direction of the privacy issues inherent in biometric identification.

I also looked at the roles of *surveillance intermediaries, such as communications network service providers,* and asked whether there have been shifts in their roles over time and, if so, why. I asked if they themselves engaged in surveillance, and, if they do, what technologies they used and how these were changing over time. Furthermore, I also asked under what conditions they enabled surveillance, and under what conditions they resisted it. Unlike in the US and Europe in the wake of the Snowden revelations, there is no evidence of communications service providers pushing back against unaccountable communications interception practices. For instance, they have failed to insist on the legal space for transparency reports in the way that Vodaphone did after the Snowden revelations. Perhaps this is because their users have not insisted on these companies protecting their privacy, and consequently they have not seen a business case for protecting their privacy rights yet. At the same time, there is a burgeoning industry in surveillance hardware and software applications.

The democratic South African state inherited a large security and arms industry from the apartheid regime, and its position of relative commercial strength in the region has created markets for the production and export of surveillance technologies. There is evidence that its industrial base is expanding, made possible by the lack of controls on former spies, who are able to commercialise their skills in the open marketplace, using the knowledge they gained inside state surveillance structures. These lax controls are allowing both South Africa and Israel to become increasingly important mid-level players in the surveillance industry, and both have identified Southern countries with few democratic controls of surveillance activities as possible markets for their wares. States that are truly serious about their surveillance capabilities custom-build their own surveillance tools, rather than buying them 'off the shelf' from surveillance companies like the HackingTeam and Gamma Group/FinFisher. However, South Africa appears to lack skills to manufacture the latest-generation malware and hacking tools used to circumvent encryption; consequently, as the HackingTeam leaks suggest, even a well-established actor like Vastech has had to seek a partnership to boost its offerings in this area. The fact that South Africa is importing surveillance equipment and expertise from more highly developed surveillance markets suggests that its state surveillance sector is not in a position to have its equipment custom-built entirely in the country.

In relation to *civil society and social movements*, which could be classified either as surveillance subjects or as non-official surveillance actors, I explored what the roles of these actors are in relation to surveillance, and whether their roles have been shifting over time. I also examined the conditions under which they take up advocacy around surveillance, and the main organising concepts they use. Civil society actors in highly developed surveillance societies like the UK and the US are well established and fairly well defined: they generally self-identify as non-governmental or non-profit organisations and are usually devoted to niche areas such as digital rights, privacy or human rights law. They often have considerable expertise in their chosen areas, and engage in a range of activities, such as making submissions to official committees, and becoming involved in litigation, publicity and general awareness-raising. Even when the work has been expanded to other countries, the actors there tend to be focused largely on digital rights; so the general trend appears to be towards specialisation rather than generalising issues relating to surveillance more broadly in organised social and political formations. While a number of specialist NGOs have been in existence for some time now, the Snowden revelations galvanised their work, leading to an explosion of actors and work in defence of privacy and information rights.

In South Africa, there has been an attempt to bring a broader range of actors into anti-surveillance work. Rather than establishing new specialist NGOs devoted to issues relating to privacy and surveillance as a primary strategy, the main focus has been on 'mainstreaming' privacy and surveillance issues in existing mass movements, bringing them together in a coalition around anti-surveillance work. The specialist NGOs that do exist provide technical support to the broader movement, but do not supplant it (at least they try not to supplant it, although complaints about NGO dominance abound).

Privacy has been possibly the most important organising concept for NGOs resisting surveillance. However, given that privacy is often understood as, and articulated as, a 'me, me, me' right, the utility of this concept is in question when it comes into conflict with broader societal concerns, such as national security. As a result, some theorists have made laudable attempts to develop a social theory of privacy, which focuses on the right's utility in enabling a broader set of rights, such as the right to organise and participate in a democracy. Anti-surveillance advocates could use this social content to argue that the denial of the right to privacy impacts not only on individuals, but on society as a whole. There is a need to politicise the concept as well, to focus on the ways in which privacy-eroding surveillance is used to discriminate against particular social groups or political formations, to prevent them from exercising power, claiming broader citizenship rights and fighting inequality. Politicising privacy also drives advocates towards analysing the political and economic interests at work in expanding surveillance, identifying the social forces that are most likely to confront these interests successfully, and developing a vision for a society that is organised differently.

I also examined the *relationships between different surveillance actors* and, more specifically, what the relationships are, if any, between private and state surveillance. I also considered whether decision-making among these different actors is static or changing over time, and, if so, why. I looked at whether the roles and responsibilities of these different actors are clear, and which actors seem to hold the power in relation to decision-making about surveillance. In relation to surveillance actors and their subjects, I examined why different actors support or resist surveillance, whether they act alone, or whether they build coalitions of interest around this issue. I also looked at the relationships between actors and the broader political environment, how these actors relate to this environment and what the uses of surveillance tell us about broader political shifts.

Surveillance has become widespread partly because governments have recruited private service providers to assist, at least in part. The shift to lawful interception around the world, ushered in by CALEA, has seen governments placing particular obligations on private sector actors to assist in surveillance efforts, and private sector roles in doing so have expanded a great deal recently, to the point where intelligence agencies compel communications companies to store huge amounts of data in case they need it for investigations. This increasing reliance on private sector involvement in surveillance has not been without its contradictions. As public outrage spread in the wake of the Snowden revelations, communications companies felt pressured to act to protect their users' privacy, and began to encrypt more of their activities. They began to see a business case for privacy, as communications risked drying up if people refrained from communicating out of fear of being subjected to surveillance. Some companies pushed back against state surveillance in more visible ways, leading to growing tensions between private actors and state actors. There has been no evidence of such a push-back taking place in South Africa. Companies have not, for instance, challenged the gag on their ability to speak about the prevalence of surveillance of their networks. Furthermore, there is evidence of private actors providing capacities to the state to run the state surveillance machinery, which raises serious questions not only about the security of the information being collected, but about potential conflicts of interest in private companies delivering surveillance services in one of the most sensitive areas of government. It is very possible that South African companies have not spoken out about surveillance because there are existing public–private partnerships in the provision of surveillance services, and great potential for even more lucrative partnerships.

However, there are not insignificant contradictions in the South African state, which make it unlikely that a full-blown surveillance state will come into being. Owing to the state's over-reliance on private companies to undertake various surveillance functions, a great deal of personal information is locked up in proprietary systems. Linkability is essential for a functioning, panoptic surveillance state: in other words, the state needs access to a number of databases that would allow it to track the movements, habits and relationships of persons of interest. However, there are indications that such linkability is not possible across a variety of state functions, at least at the moment, and some state databases contain inaccurate information and are therefore simply unreliable. Databases of personal information tend to operate in departmental silos, and databases that should be linked for the purposes of administrative efficiency are not being connected. The communication surveillance capacities of the state operated by the SSA are, however, much more centralised and tightly controlled. It is these surveillance capacities that threaten democracy the most, as their efforts become concentrated on spying on perceived political opponents.

In so much of the post-Snowden activism, rarely is there evidence of a broader range of social actors on the front line of anti-surveillance work. Trade unions or other social movements, such as the environmental movement, lack visibility in these struggles. This lack of visibility is in spite of the fact that, historically, such movements have been the targets of unaccountable surveillance, and therefore they have a direct and vested interest in becoming active on these issues. Furthermore, there is little evidence of the traditional surveillance actors in civil society broadening their advocacy work to include such movements or even place them at the centre of their work.

Conditions do exist in South Africa for the politicisation of surveillance. That is, it is becoming increasingly possible to move beyond specific concerns about surveillance and its impact on privacy as an individual right, to focus on the broader structural factors that are driving the expansion of state surveillance and the ways in which surveillance is being used to sustain powerful interests and inequality. Unless these factors are understood and addressed, it will be impossible to challenge unaccountable surveillance actors systematically. Certainly, isolated challenges may be successful, but they are unlikely to stem the long march towards a surveillance state. Globally, neoliberalism has created many more marginalised and alienated 'out' groups as it has intensified inequality; it has also dismantled older, corporatist arrangements that allowed concessions to be offered to groups that would ordinarily be in conflict with political and economic elites, such as the trade union movement. This has made resistance actors less knowable to the state, which has increased the need for surveillance. While computerisation has made mass surveillance more possible, this provides a technical explanation for the spread of surveillance practices, not a political one, but technical (as opposed to political) explanations for the spread of surveillance are inadequate. The arms industry's need to open up new avenues for profits – given the long-term decline in the number of wars, growing public antipathy to the human cost of war, and democratic limits on overt state violence – has been key in driving the shift away from more overt to less visible forms of repression. All of these factors have created conditions for a worldwide attack on privacy. One of the ways in which states have succeeded in expanding their surveillance capacities is to seize on crises, like the terrorist attacks, and use them to create moral panics and achieve public acquiescence in this expansion. They have prevented citizens from being able to assess the true value of surveillance in bringing down crime and fighting terrorism (not only in financial terms, but in social, political and cultural terms as well). If publics undertook these cost-benefit analyses, they might well conclude that the benefits of surveillance relative to their costs remain slight. In any event, societies should never allow democratic governments to enjoy certain powers, even if these powers have investigatory benefits (torture being one of these, although its value as an investigatory tool is the subject of considerable controversy). Mass surveillance is just such a power. Its invasiveness far outweighs its investigatory value. There can be no doubt that it is useful for national security purposes, but that does not automatically make it right. As Privacy International and other UK NGOs have argued, 'Not everything that is useful to a secret intelligence service is permissible in a democratic society'.[1] Once democracies draw lines in the sand about which powers they are willing to tolerate and which they find repugnant, security services simply need to make do with the powers they have.

South Africa is manifesting more elements of an organic crisis. Political divisions are opening up in the ANC hegemonic bloc, and the more people are being detached from it and forming alternative organisations, the more pervasive political surveillance is likely to become and, consequently, the more conditions are created for a mass movement against surveillance. Overt forms of state violence are hastening detachment from the hegemonic bloc – the Marikana massacre being a case in point – and this has forced the state to look for less visible forms of repression: surveillance provides it with just that. It allows the state to target its repressive interventions much more carefully. Ironically, though, the high cost of communication makes it less likely that communications surveillance will be an effective form of surveillance, as this problem reduces the penetration of communications technologies, especially the internet. Nevertheless, the threat of communication surveillance is leading to activists changing how they organise; rather than relying increasingly on 'slacktivism', activists are turning back to traditional, face-to-face forms of organising which typically promote strong ties relative to online forms of organising. The R2K Campaign has played a role as a 'network of networks', linking mass-based social movements and more traditional NGOs into a campaign against secrecy and, more recently, securitisation and surveillance, although there are criticisms that it is acting more like an NGO than a social movement. There are benefits to politicising surveillance, in that it becomes easier to identify and challenge the underlying drivers of surveillance, but unless such politicisation takes place on a non-sectarian basis, there is a danger that it will become impossible to build a broad-based alliance that resists surveillance irrespective of political affiliations. Key to doing so will be to emphasise those aspects of privacy that relate to lived working-class realities, and placing these at the centre of mobilising work. In South Africa, a key challenge is how to include members of the hegemonic bloc who themselves are concerned about surveillance, as there is evidence of the surveillance capacities of the state having been used to spy on internal contenders for power or internal dissenters.

I then explored the *outcomes and impacts of surveillance*, looking at how different actors have responded to surveillance or the threat of it, and what the impacts and consequences have been of surveillance or, at least, the threat of it. I also considered the impacts and consequences of resistance to surveillance, and what forms of resistance work. I tried to explore the broader political significance of surveillance, and how this significance (or lack of it) impacts on civil society and social movement responses. If surveillance is clearly being used for positive purposes, are positive impacts evident, and, if so, what are they? If surveillance is being used for negative purposes, are negative impacts evident, and, if so, what are they?

Widespread surveillance erodes trust between official actors and citizens; if people feel that they are being watched all the time, they may well feel that they are not trusted and are always under suspicion. Surveillance can make people fearful and withdrawn, as they do not know when their most private and intimate thoughts are going to be exposed. In such situations, surveillance can have a chilling effect on individuals, and a demobilising effect on organisations, activism and sensitive professions that rely on privileged communications. However, under certain conditions, surveillance can also have a galvanising effect, encouraging people to speak out and resist incursions into their personal and collective spaces.

The responses of sensitive professions to the threat in South Africa have been uneven. Journalists have been much more technically competent in protecting their communications, as the threats to their privacy and freedom of expression are pressing. They have implemented security measures to protect the confidentiality of their sources, some of which have involved shunning online communications altogether. However, perhaps because of the rampant individualism in the profession, journalists have not developed an organised response, relative to other vulnerable groups. Lawyers have been behind journalists in adopting security measures, but are beginning to take the need for these measures much more seriously. Academics who directly challenge power in a public fashion have implemented security measures, too, although perhaps because their numbers are small, they have not become involved in more organised responses. Political activists are the most likely to develop organised responses, as their experience in translating individual grievances into collective demands has stood them in good stead. One of the difficulties in organising against surveillance is that the public lacks 'victims' with whom they can identify: in other words, the problem remains largely abstract because there are few concrete examples of known surveillance abuses. While some cases have come to light of journalists being placed under surveillance, they could hardly be considered popular figures given the still relatively elite nature of the profession. As a result, it is difficult to organise around these cases. In order for surveillance to become a basis for popular organisation, the problem needs to be given a popular 'face' that ordinary people identify with, and are consequently more likely to organise around.

Organised responses that are social movement-led are more likely to politicise the uses of surveillance in South Africa, identifying its importance to the state in repressing political dissent. These attempts at developing mass-based responses to surveillance are important in avoiding the traps of engaging in NGO-led challenges to surveillance, where arguments are made about reining in unaccountable surveillance without ensuring that the social forces with the power to actually stop these practices are mobilised. UK civil society's struggle against the Investigatory Powers Act provides a salutary lesson in the drawbacks of challenging surveillance using NGO forms of activism, relying on assumptions that reasoned arguments alone will win the day, without paying sufficient attention to organising mass opposition to the Act.

Coming back to the overall question whether South Africa is becoming a surveillance society governed by a surveillance state, there are strong indications that surveillance is becoming routinised in a variety of different state functions. As part of a modernisation drive, various state institutions have embraced surveillant forms of governance, investing heavily in keeping track of people's movements, communication habits, banking practices and the like, and thereby making their habits, thoughts and even possible future actions more visible to the state. Elements of a surveillance state are manifesting themselves most strongly in relation to the intelligence services, although there are signs that the police have been increasing their intelligence-gathering activities and have at the very least been attempting to develop their own capabilities. There are signs of a massive expansion of powers and functions, and of these services being under-regulated, which predisposes them to abuse. Furthermore, South Africa is susceptible to becoming a surveillance state, as some of its most important documentation functions are centralised, such as the registration of births and deaths, the licensing of vehicles and drivers, and the issuing of identity documents and passports.[2] Forms of identification that have been used primarily for civil and social security purposes in the past are being increasingly securitised. However, a surveillance state requires a certain level of bureaucratic efficiency, and the available evidence points to the South African state not having the levels needed to realise this potential fully. Too much private sector involvement has frustrated the panoptic ambitions that the state may have held; as a result, the state has been unable to achieve a 'single view of the citizen'. Ironically enough, the commodification of information and communications has had contradictory effects: on the one hand, it has created more opportunities for surveillance and, on the other, it has thwarted attempts to achieve panoptic forms of surveillance. The criminal justice system cannot always rely on the information collected, and, where it can, it may not even use it, as in the case of CCTV evidence. While there are signs of the police becoming more intelligence-led, this form of policing is being pursued not necessarily as a complement to more overt forms of repression, but as an alternative to it, as overt state violence is hastening political shifts away from the ruling hegemonic bloc. Consequently, political repression is erratic and reversals are possible, as repression may not dampen political resistance, but in fact increase it.

However, the threats to democracy posed by the state's surveillance capacities should not be dismissed too quickly. In this regard, it is necessary to distinguish between core and peripheral state surveillance practices. Mass and tactical surveillance and, to a lesser extent, targeted surveillance lie at the core of state power, in that they provide technical support to the security cluster; as a result, they are much more likely to be abused than those that are still fairly peripheral, such as local street-level surveillance or biometrics. The emerging evidence strongly suggests that core surveillance capabilities are being used to maintain the hegemony of the ruling bloc, and have assisted them to concentrate executive power. However, while its capabilities for political surveillance are increasing, those for surveillance linked to crime-fighting are being run down. The predictable result is a growing crime wave, especially that of organised crime.

The authors of a recent report on state capture have invoked the concept of neopatrimonialism as an analytical framework to explain the relationship of the Zuma administration to various state institutions. For instance, they have accused his administration of weakening state institutions to enable state capture, and referred to seven broad areas of state capture, including the security cluster. The authors argued that the Zuma administration (or at least corrupt elements in it) had captured the cluster by removing people who were considered to be obstacles to the state capture project from the investigative and prosecutorial arms of the state, and replacing them with more pliant officials. The intention was to ensure that the agents of state capture would not be held to account. The authors also expressed concern about a growing shadow security state, where intelligence agents were being used to destabilise opposition and neutralise potential threats. Zuma acolytes pursued radical economic transformation by weakening state institutions. The report is anchored in the literature on neopatrimonialism, and draws on its key concepts, such as rent-seeking (the allocation of resources from one group to another by using the state) and the shadow state, where a small group of individuals act together secretly to extract rents from the state.[3] The available evidence does point to state surveillance enabling state capture, in that those aspects of the system that could be used to crack down on agents of state capture have been weakened, while those that could be used for political surveillance, including of political adversaries of the incumbent president, have been strengthened. But the available evidence also points to uses that extend far beyond the state capture project, to the containment of growing dissent against the ruling hegemonic bloc more broadly. In fact, that is what political economy analyses of surveillance point to: that surveillance has become increasingly important to capitalist efforts to redistribute resources upwardly, and to state strategies to manage inequality and resistance to it.

Neopatrimonialism emerges when patrimonial relations are grafted onto rational-legal systems of government, and state officials use their positions for the purposes of private accumulation. It has been used to explain why African societies are not modernising, and asserts that the problem originates from a marriage of tradition and modernity in these societies.[4] This marriage leads to governments encouraging bloated states to capture more state resources. Neopatrimonialism builds on methodological communalism, where the community is considered to be the primary building block of social relations, and it has problematic cultural undertones in that it could be used to argue that African societies are inherently less capable of clean government, as relationship-based transactions are bound to undercut bureaucratic functioning. But, in important respects, rather than being bloated, the state is under-funded.[5] In the case of the South African surveillance state, Zuma has been accused of grafting the ANC intelligence networks formed in exile onto the security cluster to ensure that individuals whom he trusts are in control. Thus, in terms of this frame-work, the neopatrimonial approach to intelligence is weakening the agencies, as it is undermining attempts to establish a professional culture.

However, neopatrimonialism is a simplistic narrative that ignores the leg-acy of apartheid and colonialism, placing full blame for these weaknesses on post-apartheid, post-colonial leaders. It assumes the universality of the Weberian (usually Western) ideal-type state based on a separation of political and civil capac-ities and rational-legal rule, and Africa's political formations and realities are por-trayed as being deviant departures from this ideal. The fact that such a state hardly ever exists in reality does not stop proponents of this state form from continuing to promote it.[6] In the case of state surveillance, the Snowden revelations have made it clear that this ideal state type does not exist even in the presumed heartlands of rational-legal authority, such as the US and the UK. Who and what is responsi-ble for the underdevelopment of South Africa's intelligence services? Intelligence capabilities in the colonies were deliberately stunted by colonial authorities, and, where they did exist, they were often tightly controlled by these authorities and were designed to facilitate private accumulation. In the case of South Africa, the country did not have an intelligence service until 1961, as the UK government pro-vided these services. Eventually, when they were established, they remained under the tutelage of the UK until it became politically impossible to continue, given the growing antipathy of the UK public towards apartheid.[7] In truth, the first real efforts to establish professional intelligence structures took place only after the 1994 tran-sition to democracy. It is therefore unsurprising that a professional intelligence cul-ture has failed to take root, as the historical basis for doing so did not exist. Rather than attributing the problem only to Zuma and his intelligence background (with all its baggage), what Zubairu Wai has referred to as the cultural and political past histories of domination also need to be acknowledged as factors.

In this regard, there are important and disturbing parallels between the uses of the intelligence services under apartheid and in the post-apartheid democracy so it cannot be argued that the 1994 transition represented a clean break with the intelligence practices of the past, as there are important indicators of continuity. In the case of the ANC, its intelligence capabilities were geared towards strategically mapping out future scenarios, and its tactical and operational intelligence capabil-ities focused on rooting out apartheid spies. But it also extended its role beyond counter-intelligence against its apartheid foe, to suppressing political dissent within the movement's own ranks. It should surprise no one that the movement has carried these practices over into government, as there were no significant consequences for these abuses. But what has changed is that the technical capabilities available to the agencies have increased massively, while legal regulations have not kept up with technological advances. In fact, legal reform of intelligence matters has been deliberately delayed to keep the most advanced surveillance capabilities under-regulated over a crucial period of South Africa's political history. What has also changed, is the extent to which the private sector has enabled state surveillance, vastly extending the capabilities of state spy agencies, and both public and private spy agencies have a vested interest in keeping these activities under-regulated when it serves them. As former RICA judge Yvonne Mokgoro argued in an interview, the real danger of the under-resourcing of the RICA process, and the consequent lack of technical capacity, is that communications surveillance may be driven underground, where the services rely increasingly on the private sector for their capabilities, leading to them operating on an extra-legal basis.[8] In other words, under-resourcing of lawful interception could facilitate private sector expansion in the surveillance industry. In that regard, a political economy analysis is more useful than a framework offered by neopatrimonialism, as it focuses on how public and private entities are colluding to use surveillance to reproduce inequality and limit resistance to it. This problem is not confined to 'less modern' African or Southern countries, but is to be found at the centre of the 'mature democracies'. In the case of the apartheid security services, they were highly operational in that they collected intelligence and acted on it. Under Zuma's presidency, there were signs that the civilian intelligence agency was becoming operational, attempting to influence the political course of events directly in the Zuma administration's favour. There are many continuities of practice between apartheid and democracy when it comes to corporate and state collusion in facilitating crimes that benefit small elites, and secrecy enables these continuities,[9] but the extent to which this is so in the state security sector needs further research.

However, when the broad array of South African state surveillance practices are taken into account – and not just those relating to intelligence-gathering on matters of national security – there is evidence of the state not acting as a unitary entity. Rather, there are signs of it acting as a site where different and, at times, even competing interests play out. This aligns more with a Gramscian view of the state than a Leninist view, which posited a unitary state acting in the interests of the capitalist class. For Gramsci, the state cannot be understood as a mere tool of the capitalist class, as there may well be competing factions and even contradictions in how it acts. Rather, the state is an outcome of concrete political struggles, and the agency of different political actors shapes and reshapes how the state is structured and how it operates. Furthermore, on a day-to-day basis, and by virtue of the logics of its own bureaucratic functions, the state is capable of exercising some autonomy from the dominant political class. However, it does not exercise complete autonomy, especially in respect of the coercive capacities of the state, as these are more likely to be mobilised to protect dominant interests in times of crisis. Furthermore, the state is not equally available to all social groups.[10] The unevenness in the surveillance capacities of the state makes resistance easier in some respects, as surveillance practices are not monolithic. This makes multiple forms of resistance not only possible, but more likely to be effective. South Africa has an unruly political class, and factions are opening up all the time.

Furthermore, the number of groups from which the state can obtain consent for repression is declining, which puts it in a very delicate position indeed. There is even evidence suggesting that surveillance is being used within the ruling hegemonic bloc to track the realignment of loyalties and the formation of alternative factions within it. The mass surveillance capacities of the state have been used by competing factions of the ruling party to track one another's movements in the past.[11] So, while the growing use of surveillance represents a more sophisticated attempt to contain mass struggles than merely resorting to overt violence, and undoubtedly these practices are having a demobilising effect, this is not to the extent that one can say that the levels of struggle have declined. To that extent, state surveillance has not been particularly successful in disassembling mass movements, although, at the same time, these struggles are still being waged in pockets, with little evidence of their coalescing into a national anti-systemic movement that poses a significant threat to the way power is organised in South African society. According to Foucault, surveillant forms of power are successful in maintaining social control when they allow for the automatic functioning of power; but in order for them to be successful, people need to know about their existence. If this is what the South African state is attempting to do – in other words, govern from a distance by coercing citizens into policing themselves – then the high levels of secrecy surrounding actual surveillance practices are self-defeating. Knowing so little about surveillance means that people are unlikely to check their actions out of fear of being watched.

Many people in South Africa have a visceral dislike of wealth and power, and the political experience to challenge them. Hence the message that surveillance is not about eroding privacy but about asserting dominance is an easy one to put across in campaign work. To that extent, it cannot be said that surveillance realism has established itself in the country. The country has a recent history of overcoming a coercive regime and these memories are still relatively fresh. These distinct features mean that struggles against surveillance do not necessarily have to be defensive: they could also be formative in that they could challenge the very foundations of surveillance practices. However, these struggles would need to be led by social forces focused on systemic change. While the activism of NGOs has been extremely important in the wake of Snowden's revelations, this activism has led to surveillance structures remaining basically the same. It will not help to engage in an uncritical celebration of civil society as a panacea for a growing surveillance state and society. Furthermore, while South Africa may well have developed elements of a surveillance state, the development of a surveillance society – where private companies drive surveillance rather than the state – has been made more difficult by the prohibitively high costs of communications in the country, which by 2016 saw low-income users often spending significant amounts of their income on relatively small data amounts.[12] Just over 50 per cent of households had at least one member with access to the internet.[13] The commodification of communications has led to a contradiction: high communications costs have caused large swathes of society, especially the working class, to become unknowable through surveillance.

With the global rise of right-wing parties and ideologies, especially in the centres of surveillance power in the North, there are signs that governments are intending to expand their surveillance powers or are actually doing so.[14] The growth of surveillance societies and states is made possible by the secrecy that surrounds their growth. They can get away with not having to justify their actions, as these are less visible than other elements of the security apparatus, like the police and the military. A US military intelligence officer has even described the growth of surveillance powers as a giant 'self-licking ice cream cone', which exists mainly to perpetuate itself.[15] As Reg Whitaker has argued, the surveillance industry is based on a 'remarkably self-sustaining growth model', as industry experts get to define the extent of the problem, and are then contracted to deliver the solution. There are in-built and relatively unchecked conflicts of interest in how these surveillance states operate. Watchdog bodies that may be privy to intelligence secrets become captured, as they are subjected to the very requirements of secrecy that have allowed executive agencies to continue rights-violating surveillance.[16] This is why these bodies have not accounted for the most significant disclosures of recent times; instead, whistleblowers have.

Gradually, a new form of state is coming into being, characterised by a decline of democracy and shrinking spaces for dissent.[17] The world appears to be moving into a post-democracy era as a global shift to the right delivers more and more conservative governments. However, it would be a mistake to see the spectre of fascism in this shift, as the new (or 'alt') right tends to tolerate the internationalisation of capital (but not necessarily of labour). Neoliberalism and moral panics around immigration and terrorism, and their subsequent securitisation, have boosted the cause of the political right, and the centre and the right (and even sections of the liberal-left) have converged on issues relating to security. As policing and security have been privatised, the right has also moved into these spaces, leading to the development of paramilitary 'pop-up armies'. As cities have become increasingly polarised, police forces have embraced authoritarian policing models designed to control unpredictable publics. As citizens in countries like the UK disavow multilateral institutions like the EU, authoritarian elements in the state can extend executive power beyond what would be acceptable in terms of international human rights norms and standards. Right-wing movements have argued that the state must protect what they consider to be 'legitimate' populations, and surveillance provides one of the tools to do just that. Hence, any forward-looking anti-surveillance movement must focus not only on the state and corporations, but on right-wing movements and their growing social power, as well.

In order to rise to the task of challenging the ever-expanding surveillance architecture, it is necessary to bring both the state and agency back into a picture that has often been dominated by structural analyses. In this regard, Cox and Nilsen's conception of the state as a movement from above is helpful.[18] They argue that conventional theory sees social movements as the fruits of collective actions by subaltern groups; but collective agency is not only practised by these groups alone. Recognising the state as a social movement from above helps to demystify social structures, and allows movements from below to see the state, not as an inevitable given of the order of things, but as a historical entity that has been made by human agency. Consequently, the state can be changed by human agency, too. Movements from below in the global South have been relatively successful at envisioning political alternatives to neoliberalism, especially in relating their particular, situated experiences to the structures that produce them. These movements' shift in focus from the particular to the general has allowed them to focus on the social totality and how it needs to change, as well as on the possibilities happening through political action. The ability of these movements to generalise particular struggles raises the stakes for the political elites.[19] The Marikana massacre was a catalytic event in recent South African history, and the subsequent fragmentation of the country's politics has broadened the possibilities for oppositional practices that generalise issues across what have been called 'militant particularisms', where struggles are embedded in local ways of life peculiar to particular communities.[20]

In the worldwide fight against expanding surveillance, too little attention has been paid to making this fight relevant to the social forces that have made the most gains (although modest) in challenging how society is organised, as they have the least to lose and the most to gain from doing do. If there is a relationship between austerity and surveillance, in that austerity creates more excluded groups that are more in need of surveillance, then it stands to reason that surveillance should become a platform of the anti-austerity protests. Links need to be drawn between the two phenomena. While the recent anti-austerity movement has been hetero-geneous in nature, the 'precariat' that formed a key component of its social base, for instance, has been a major loser in neoliberal restructuring. Its participants are likely to be young, underemployed or unemployed, and many may even be highly educated and technologically savvy. These social groups are more likely than others to transform discontent into grievances, and then into claims where personal prob-lems become collective ones and social conditions are politicised. However, it is not enough simply to politicise problems such as surveillance; to do so would be to imply that movements must focus primarily on transforming political institutions. Rather, the focus needs to be on interactions between these institutions and the market, or how political institutions sustain market power. Neoliberalism reduces the capacity of the state to respond to citizens' demands, and creates the social basis for a widespread condemnation of the power of big corporations.[21]

While mass mobilisation is key to sustained resistance to surveillance, it is important not to be dogmatic about the organisational forms it should take. In this regard, Giroux's suggestion of anti-capitalist parties becoming vanguards of anti-surveillance struggles appears somewhat outdated. The anti-austerity protests have displaced hierarchical forms of organisation, typical of old labour's approach to struggles. These struggles have highlighted the strengths of more networked models that are capable of bringing precarious workers into democratic politics, thereby socialising a new generation into political work. As institutions of formal democracy have become hollowed out, exposing them as relatively inept at granting and protecting rights, movements have moved beyond seeking recourse through institutions. Neoliberalism has also exposed the collusive relations between markets and politics, and more specifically between political and business elites.[22] In relation to surveillance, the growth of surveillance powers would not have been possible without such collusion, although this has not been without its challenges for both states and corporations. If movements expose the extent of this collusion, drawing on recent whistleblower leaks, and generalise them as being part of a broader trans-fer of power to economic elites (or the 'one per cent', in the language of sections of the anti-austerity movement), they can also lay the basis for movements pursuing prefigurative aims in relation to surveillance which may, in time to come, lead to paradigmatic changes in public policy.

In other words, activists should also be concerned with socialising the right to privacy, and making it available to all – not just to those with the money and power to defend their rights. In promoting the right as a positive right, activists would need to universalise the means of communications, including the internet, and promote it as a commons, rather than as increasingly privatised and commercialised space. If the evolution of communications networks is understood historically, then it becomes apparent that surveillance is not an inevitable consequence of the networked world in which we live, and things can be done differently. Widespread surveillance has been consciously produced; as a result, there is a need to re-envision a society that is not just technically possible, but socially possible too. In the 1990s, when the internet expanded across the world, its founders promoted it as the first truly global medium of communication. At the time, they established some important first principles to ensure collaboration across borders for a free and open internet, including the need to use freely available standards that everyone could build on, and ensure that the various components of the internet were interoperable. All data was supposed to be treated equally, irrespective of its contents, so that the internet remained a level playing field for all its users (the 'net neutrality' principle).

Since then, governments and internet corporations have chipped away at these foundational principles, eroding the internet's status as a global public resource. More governments have begun to filter and censor internet content, and some have even considered delinking from the internet to control information flows better: a move that would clearly undermine the global nature of the medium. While the existing global forums are promoting internet freedom, they are not being sufficiently robust about the thorny question of who controls the internet. Unless internet users ensure that the medium becomes what it is truly meant to be – a self-managed network of users, designed for communication and collaboration – then control is likely to remain in the hands of governments and corporations that are driven by interests other than the need to maintain the publicness of the internet.

Activists need to defend the free and open nature of the internet, which means opposing its commodification, including the increasing tendency for people to experience it within the walled gardens of corporate-controlled applications. As Snowden has argued, surveillance has become the business model of the internet. If this is so, then alternative models should be explored. In this regard, the non-profit model explored by Wikipedia, coupled with its crowdsourcing of information, is one example of a practical, albeit imperfect option. Privacy should be the default position for communications, rather than people having to opt out of more surveillant options and into more privacy-enhancing options. Communications providers should adopt the approach of 'privacy by design'; that is, privacy is taken into account when communications systems are built. IMSI catchers, for instance, exploit a well-known vulnerability in second-generation cellphone communications, where the cellphone is required to authenticate itself to the service provider's base towers, but the service provider is not required to authenticate itself to the cellphone. Newer-generation protocols can be jammed, forcing the cellphone back onto the 2G protocol.[23] But doing so should not be at the expense of a commonsing approach to the internet, foregrounding the public and shared nature of the communications resources. Opposing the securitisation and militarisation of the internet is also important, where the internet is treated increasingly as the fifth domain of warfare, after land, sea, air and space. By developing offensive cyber-warfare capabilities, countries risk entering into a cyber arms race, where their enemies develop similar or even superior capabilities, leading to the creation of a 'cyber-security dilemma' involving even more insecurity.[24] If principles such as these were taken up by mass movements – whose members, after all, have a vested interested in seeing them being realised – then perhaps another communications system may become possible, one that has human emancipation, rather than human enslavement, at its heart.

NOTES

INTRODUCTION

1   Angelique Chrisafis, Jessica Reed, Raya Jalabia and Nicky Woolf, 'Witness Accounts from across Paris: "I Saw My Final Hour Unfurl before Me"', *The Guardian*, 14 November 2015, https://www.theguardian.com/world/2015/nov/13/eyewitness-accounts-paris-attacks (accessed 23 August 2016).

2   British Broadcast Corporation, 'Paris Attacks: What Happened on the Night', BBC News, 9 December 2015, http://www.bbc.com/news/world-europe-34818994 (accessed 15 March 2017).

3   George Orwell, *Nineteen Eighty-Four* (London: Harvill Secker, 1949).

4   Michel Foucault, *Discipline and Punish: The Birth of the Prison* (Harmondsworth: Penguin Books, 1979), 201–16.

5   Article 12, United Nations Universal Declaration of Human Rights, United Nations General Assembly, Paris, 1948, http://www.un.org/en/universal-declaration-human-rights/.

6   Lee Rainie and Shiva Maniam, 'Americans Feel the Tensions between Privacy and Security Concerns', Pew Research Centre, http://www.pewresearch.org/fact-tank/2016/02/19/americans-feel-the-tensions-between-privacy-and-security-concerns/ (accessed 1 September 2016); Amnesty International, 'Global Opposition to USA Big Brother Mass Surveillance' (opinion poll), https://www.amnesty.org/en/press-releases/2015/03/global-opposition-to-usa-big-brother-mass-surveillance/ (accessed 1 September 2016); Centre for International Governance Innovation and IPSOS, 'Most Global Citizens Say Law Enforcement Agencies Should Have a Right to Access Online Communications of Its Citizens (70%), Especially Those Suspected of a Crime (85%)' (survey), 2 March 2016, https://www.cigionline.org/sites/default/files/factum_2016_cigiipsos_survey_securityprivacy.pdf (accessed 1 September 2016).

7   Alan Rusbridger, Janine Gibson and Ewen MacAskill, 'Edward Snowden: NSA Reforms in the USA Are Only the Beginning', *The Guardian*, 22 May 2015, https://www.theguardian.com/us-news/2015/may/22/edward-snowden-nsa-reform (accessed 23 August 2016).

8   Privacy International, 'The Five Eyes', undated blog, https://www.privacyinternational.org/node/51 (accessed 1 March 2017).

9   Amnesty International and Privacy International, 'Protecting Human Rights in an Era of Mass Surveillance' (report), 2015, https://www.privacyinternational.org/sites/default/files/Two%20Years%20After%20Snowden_Final%20Report_EN_0.pdf (accessed 23 August 2016).

10 Alfred W. McCoy, 'Surveillance and Scandal: Weapons in an Emerging Array for US Global Power', *Monthly Review* 66, no. 3 (2014), http://monthlyreview.org/2014/07/01/the-new-surveillance-normal/ (accessed 27 July 2016); David H. Price, 'The New Surveillance Normal: NSA and Corporate Surveillance in the Age of Global Capitalism', *Monthly Review* 66, no. 3 (2014), http://monthlyreview.org/2014/07/01/the-new-surveillance-normal/ (accessed 27 July 2016).

11 Elizabeth Goitein and Faiza Patel, 'What Went Wrong with the FISA Court?', Brennan Centre for Justice, New York School of Law, 2015, http://litigation.utahbar.org/assets/materials/2015FedSymposium/3c_What_Went_%20Wrong_With_The_FISA_Court.pdf (accessed 23 September 2016).

12 Aziz Choudry, 'Crackdown', *New Internationalist* no. 376 (1 March 2005), https://new-int.org/features/2005/03/01/targeting-activists/ (accessed 7 June 2016).

13 Peter Gill and Mark Phythian, *Intelligence in an Insecure World* (Cambridge: Polity Press, 2012), 24.

14 Luis Fernandez, *Policing Dissent: Social Control and the Anti-Globalisation Movement* (Toronto: Rutgers University Press, 2008); Choudry, 'Crackdown'; Jane Duncan, *The Rise of the Securocrats: The Case of South Africa* (Johannesburg: Jacana Media, 2014).

15 Gill and Phythian, *Intelligence in an Insecure World*, 79–101.

16 David Lyon, 'Surveillance, Snowden and Big Data: Capacities, Consequences, Critique', *Big Data and Society*, July 2014, http://bds.sagepub.com/content/1/2/2053951714541861 (accessed 24 August 2016).

17 Chatham House, 'Mass Surveillance, Counterterrorism and Privacy: The Way Forward' (transcript of seminar debate between Ben Emmerson, UN Special Rapporteur on Counterterrorism and Human Rights, and Malcolm Rifkind, Chairman, Intelligence and Security Committee), 28 October 2014, https://www.chathamhouse.org/sites/files/chathamhouse/field/field_document/20141028MassSurveillance.pdf (accessed 27 August 2017).

18 Ten Human Rights Organisations, '10 Human Rights Organisations vs. the United Kingdom: Applicants' Reply to Observations of the Government of the United Kingdom', application number 24960/15, 17–18, https://www.documentcloud.org/documents/3115985-APPLICANTS-REPLY-to-GOVT-OBSERVATIONS-PDF.html (accessed 27 August 2017).

19 Ten Human Rights Organisations, '10 Human Rights Organisations vs. the United Kingdom', 17–18.

20 Author's interview with Eric King, director, Don't Spy on Us, interview conducted by Skype, Johannesburg, 20 October 2016.

21 Author's interview with Eric King, 20 October 2016.

22 Matthew Harwood, 'The Terrifying Surveillance Case of Brandon Mayfield', *Al Jazeera*, 8 February 2014, http://america.aljazeera.com/opinions/2014/2/the-terrifying-surveillancecaseofbrandonmayfield.html (accessed 25 August 2016).

23 David Lyon's keynote presentation to the International Association for Media and Communications Research, 14 July 2015, https://www.youtube.com/watch?v=Vzgok-3kUl0o (accessed 7 June 2016).

24 Susan Landau, *Surveillance or Security? The Risks Posed by New Wiretapping Technologies* (Cambridge: MIT Press, 2010).

25 Landau, *Surveillance or Security?*

26 Landau, *Surveillance or Security?*

27   Directorate-General for External Policies, European Parliament, 'After the Arab Spring: New Paths for the Internet and Human Rights in European Foreign Policy', briefing paper, July 2012, http://www.academia.edu/1246989/After_the_Arab_Spring_New_Paths_for_Human_Rights_and_the_Internet_in_European_Foreign_Policy (accessed 23 November 2013).

28   Privacy International, 'What Communications Surveillance?', undated blog, https://www.privacyinternational.org/node/10 (accessed 22 February 2017).

29   Arne Hintz and Ian Brown, 'Enabling Digital Citizenship? The Reshaping of Surveillance Policy after Snowden', *International Journal of Communication* 11 (2017): 782–801.

30   Ewen MacAskill and Gabriel Dance, 'NSA Files Decoded: What the Revelations Mean to You', *The Guardian*, 1 November 2013, https://www.theguardian.com/world/interactive/2013/nov/01/snowden-nsa-files-surveillance-revelations-decoded#section/1 (accessed 22 February 2017).

31   Author's interview with Eric King, 20 October 2016. For a graphic depiction of the differences between targeted and mass interception, see the image at https://privacyinternational.org/sites/default/files/global_surveillance.pdf, 58.

32   Foucault, *Discipline and Punish*, 201–16.

33   Scarlet Kim, 'Privacy International's Work on Hacking', Privacy International (blog), 10 February 2016, https://medium.com/privacy-international/privacy-internationals-work-on-hacking-153a0565e1ce#.2p8ua25rs (accessed 22 February 2017).

34   Privacy International, 'Press Release: Privacy International and Five Internet and Communications Companies Challenge British Government's Bulk Hacking Abroad before the European Court of Human Rights' (press release), 5 August 2016, https://www.privacyinternational.org/node/915 (accessed 14 October 2016).

35   Heidi Swart, 'Secret State: How the Government Spies on You', *Mail & Guardian*, 14 October 2011, http://amabhungane.co.za/article/2011-10-14-secret-state (accessed 23 March 2017).

36   South African Press Association, 'Boeremag Members' Prison Cells Bugged, Says Spy', *Mail & Guardian*, 25 February 2013, http://mg.co.za/article/2013-02-25-boeremag-members-recorded-in-jail-says-spy (accessed 16 February 2018).

37   Zolile Ngcakani, 'Executive Summary of the Final Report of the Findings of an Investigation into the Legality of the Surveillance Operations of the NIA Carried Out on Mr. S Macozoma, Inspector General of Intelligence' (publicly available summary of confidential report), 23 March 2006, not available online.

38   Privacy International, 'South African Government Still Funding Vastech, Knows Previous Financing Was for Mass Surveillance', Privacy International blog, 30 January 2014, https://www.privacyinternational.org/node/305 (accessed 23 March 2017).

39   Vincent Mosco, *A Political Economy of Communications: Rethinking and Renewal* (London: Sage Publications, 2009), 49.

40   Janet Wasko, 'Studying the Political Economy of Media and Information', *Comunicação e Sociedade* 7 (2005): 44.

41   Graham Murdock and Peter Golding, 'Culture, Communications and Political Economy', in *Mass Media and Society*, ed. James P. Curran and Michael Gurevitch, 4th edn (London: Arnold, 2005), 60–83.

42   David Lyon, 'Surveillance Studies: Understanding Visibility, Mobility and Phonetic Fix' (editorial), *Surveillance and Society* 1, no. 1 (2002): 1–7.

43   Andrew Couts, 'State of the Web: Who Killed Privacy? You Did', *Digital Trends*, 7 August 2012, http://www.digitaltrends.com/opinion/state-of-the-web-who-killed-privacy/ (accessed 6 September 2016).

CHAPTER 1

1   Alan Sears, *A Good Book, in Theory: A Guide to Theoretical Thinking* (Orchard Park: Broadview Press, 2005).

2   Jeremy Bentham quoted in Armand Mattelart, *The Globalisation of Surveillance* (Cambridge: Polity Press, 2010), 7.

3   For the plan of Jeremy Bentham's panopticon, see the image available at http://files. libertyfund.org/pll/pdf/Bentham_0872-04_EBk_v7.0.pdf, 78.

4   Michel Foucault, *Discipline and Punish: The Birth of the Prison* (Harmondsworth: Penguin Books, 1979), 201.

5   Foucault, *Discipline and Punish*, 200–16.

6   Foucault, *Discipline and Punish*.

7   Nicholas Gane, 'The Governmentalities of Neoliberalism: Panopticism, Post-Panopticism and Beyond', *Sociological Review* 60 (2012): 611–34.

8   Ayse Ceyhan, 'Surveillance as Biopower', in *Routledge Handbook of Surveillance Studies*, ed. Kirstie Ball, Kevin D. Haggerty and David Lyon (London: Routledge, 2012), 39.

9   Ceyhan, 2012, 'Surveillance as Biopower', 39.

10   John Gaventa, 'Power after Lukes: A Review of the Literature', Institute of Development Studies, Brighton, 2003, http://www.powercube.net/wp-content/uploads/2009/11/ power_after_lukes.pdf (accessed 29 May 2015).

11   Roy Coleman and Joe Sim, '"You'll Never Walk Alone": CCTV Surveillance, Order and Neoliberal Rule in Liverpool City Centre', *British Journal of Sociology* 51, no. 4 (2000): 623–39.

12   Markus Kienscherf, 'Beyond Militarization and Repression: Liberal Social Control as Pacification', *Critical Sociology* 42, no. 7–8 (2016).

13   Steve Mann, Jason Nolan and Barry Wellman, 'Sousveillance: Inventing and Using Wearable Computing Devices for Data Collection in Surveillance Environments', *Surveillance and Society* 1, no. 3 (2003): 331–55.

14   Thomas Allmer, *Towards a Critical Theory of Surveillance in Informational Capitalism* (Peter Lang: Frankfurt, 2012), 24–31.

15   Kevin Haggerty, 'Tear Down the Walls: On Demolishing the Panopticon', in *Theorising Surveillance: The Panopticon and Beyond*, ed. David Lyon (London: Routledge, 2006), 23–45.

16   Christian Fuchs, 'How Can Surveillance Be Defined?', *Matrizes* 1, no. 5 (2011): 117.

17   Thomas Mathiesen, 'The Viewer Society: Michel Foucault's "Panopticon" Revisited', *Theoretical Criminology* 1, no. 2 (May 1997): 215–34.

18   David Lyon, *Surveillance after Snowden* (London: Polity Press, 2015), 79.

19   Kevin D. Haggerty and Richard V. Ericson, 2000, 'The Surveillant Assemblage', *British Journal of Sociology* 51, no. 4 (2000): 605–22.

20   David Lyon, 'Liquid Surveillance: The Contribution of Zygmunt Bauman to Surveillance Studies', *International Political Sociology* 4 (2010): 325–38.

21   Gilles Deleuze, 'Postscript on the Societies of Control', *October* 59 (Winter 1992): 3–7.

22   Deleuze, 'Postscript on the Societies of Control', 3–7.

23 Zachary Bruno, 'The PRISM Programme Panopticon: Foucault's Insights into the Era of Snowden' (unpublished paper), Occidental College, 24 March 2014.

24 Melina Sherman, 'New Panopticism: The Materiality of Surveillance in Society', https://melinasherman.files.wordpress.com/2014/06/panopticon-pic.jpg; Gilbert Caluya, 'The Post-Panoptic Society? Reassessing Foucault in Surveillance Studies', *Social Identities* 16, no. 5 (2010): 621–33.

25 Caluya, 'The Post-Panoptic Society?', 621–33.

26 Lyon, *Surveillance after Snowden*, 16.

27 Fuchs, 'How Can Surveillance Be Defined?'

28 Jason Koebler, 'James Clapper Finally Admitted the NSA Used PRISM to Spy on US Citizens', *Vice*, 1 April 2014, http://motherboard.vice.com/read/james-clapper-finally-admitted-the-nsa-used-prism-to-spy-on-us-citizens (accessed 13 September 2016).

29 Arjun Kharpal, 'Apple vs. FBI: All You Need to Know', CNBC, 29 March 2016, http://www.cnbc.com/2016/03/29/apple-vs-fbi-all-you-need-to-know.html (accessed 23 August 2016).

30 Ben Hayes, 'The Surveillance-Industrial Complex', in *Routledge Handbook of Surveillance Studies*, ed. Kirstie Ball, Kevin D. Haggerty and David Lyon (London: Routledge, 2012), 167.

31 Hayes, 'The Surveillance-Industrial Complex', 167–75.

32 Fuchs, 'How Can Surveillance Be Defined?'

33 Allmer, *Towards a Critical Theory of Surveillance in Informational Capitalism*, 24–31.

34 David Lyon, *The Electronic Eye: The Rise of the Surveillance Society* (Minneapolis: University of Minnesota Press, 1994), vii–x.

35 Gary Marx, '"Your Papers Please": Personal and Professional Encounters with Surveillance', in *Routledge Handbook of Surveillance Studies*, ed. Kirstie Ball, Kevin D. Haggerty and David Lyon (London: Routledge, 2012), xxv.

36 Roger Clarke, 'Information Technology and Dataveillance', *Communications of the ACM* 35, no. 5 (1988): 498–9.

37 Allmer, *Towards a Critical Theory of Surveillance in Informational Capitalism*, 42–3.

38 Christian Fuchs, *Reading Marx in the Information Age: A Media and Communications Studies Perspective on 'Capital Volume 1'* (London: Routledge, 2016), 165–70.

39 Fuchs, 'How Can Surveillance Be Defined?', 114.

40 Fuchs, 'How Can Surveillance Be Defined?', 109–33.

41 Lina Dencik and Jonathan Cable, 'The Advent of Surveillance Realism: Public Opinion and Activist Responses to the Snowden Leaks', *International Journal of Communication* 11 (2017): 763–81.

42 David Lyon, 'Surveillance Culture: Engagement, Exposure and Ethics in Digital Modernity', *International Journal of Communication* 11 (2017): 824–42.

43 David Lyon, 'Surveillance Culture', 824–42.

44 Colin Bennett, 2011, 'In Defence of Privacy', *Surveillance and Society* 8, no. 4 (2011): 487–8.

45 Article 12, United Nations Declaration of Human Rights, 1948, http://www.claiminghumanrights.org/udhr_article_12.html#at13 (accessed 12 August 2016).

46 David McQuoid-Mason, 'Privacy', in *Constitutional Law of South Africa*, ed. M. Chaskalson et al. (Cape Town: Juta, 2008), 18.1–18.16.

47 Alan Westin, *Privacy and Freedom* (New York: Atheneum, 1970), 7.

48 Westin, *Privacy and Freedom*, 7.

49   Valerie Steeves, 'Reclaiming the Social Value of Privacy', in *Lessons from the Identity Trail: Anonymity, Identity and Privacy in a Networked Society*, ed. Ian Kerr, Carole Lucock and Valerie Steeves (Oxford: Oxford University Press, 2009), 193.

50   Bennett, 'In Defence of Privacy', 487–8.

51   Elia Zureik and L. Lynda Harling Stalker, 'The Cross Cultural Study of Privacy: Problems and Prospects', in *Surveillance, Privacy and the Globalisation of Personal Information: International Comparisons*, ed. Elia Zureik, L. Lynda Harling Stalker, Emily Smith, David Lyon and Yolande E. Chan (Montreal: McGill-Queens University Press, 2010), 12.

52   Zureik and Stalker, 'The Cross Cultural Study of Privacy', 12.

53   See Bennett, 'In Defence of Privacy', 487; A. Etzioni, 'A Communitarian Perspective on Privacy', *Connecticut Law Review* 32, no. 3 (2000): 897–905; Zureik and Stalker, 'The Cross Cultural Study of Privacy', 8–30; Priscilla Regan, *Legislating Privacy* (Chapel Hill: University of North Carolina Press, 1995).

54   Steeves, 'Reclaiming the Social Value of Privacy', 203.

55   Bennett, 'In Defence of Privacy', 487–8.

56   Lyon, *Surveillance after Snowden*, 106.

57   Steeves, 'Reclaiming the Social Value of Privacy', 191–208.

58   Lyon, *Surveillance after Snowden*, 109.

59   Lyon, *Surveillance after Snowden*, 118.

60   Bruno, 'The PRISM Programme Panopticon'.

61   K. Marx and F. Engels, *The German Ideology*, Part 1, 1845, https://www.marxists.org/archive/marx/works/1845/german-ideology/ch01d.htm (accessed 23 May 2017).

62   Henry A. Giroux, 'Totalitarian Paranoia in the Post-Orwellian Surveillance State', *Cultural Studies* 29, no. 2 (2015): 108–40.

63   Christian Fuchs, 'Towards an Alternative Concept of Privacy', *Journal of Information, Communication and Ethics in Society* 9, no. 4 (2011): 220–37.

CHAPTER 2

1   'Obama on NSA Surveillance: Can't Have 100% Security and 100% Privacy', *RT*, 7 June 2014, https://www.rt.com/usa/obama-surveillance-nsa-monitoring-385/ (accessed 16 September 2016).

2   'Obama on NSA Surveillance'.

3   Vincent Boulanin, 'Arms Production Goes Cyber: A Challenge for Arms Control', Stockholm International Peace Research Institute, 30 May 2013, https://www.sipri.org/node/361 (accessed 27 October 2016).

4   Samuel Weigley, '10 Companies Profiting the Most from War', 24/7 Wall Street.com, 10 March 2013, http://www.usatoday.com/story/money/business/2013/03/10/10-companies-profiting-most-from-war/1970997/ (accessed 27 October 2016).

5   Robert B. Durham, *Supplying the Enemy: The Modern Arms Industry and the Military-Industrial Complex* (Morrisville: Lulu.com, 2015), 74.

6   Durham, *Supplying the Enemy*, 52; Susan Berfield, 'How Walmart Keeps an Eye on Its Massive Workforce', *Bloomberg Businessweek*, 24 November 2015, http://www.bloomberg.com/features/2015-walmart-union-surveillance/ (accessed 27 October 2016).

7   Carola Hoyos, 'Thales Chief Laments Group's International Market Prowess', 16 September 2013, https://www.ft.com/content/56d3d05c-1b03-11e3-b781-00144feab7de (accessed 2 March 2017).

8   John Bellamy Foster and Robert McChesney, 'Surveillance Capitalism: Monopoly-Finance Capital, the Military-Industrial Complex, and the Digital Age', *Monthly Review* 66, no. 3 (2014): 1–31, http://monthlyreview.org/2014/07/01/surveillance-capitalism/ (accessed 4 November 2016).

9   Foster and McChesney, 'Surveillance Capitalism'.

10   Edward Snowden in discussion with Kumi Naidoo at the 'Privacy Rights, Surveillance Wrongs: An Activists' Dialogue' conference, co-hosted by the Legal Resources Centre and the International Network of Civil Liberties' Organisations, 31 October 2016.

11   Foster and McChesney, 'Surveillance Capitalism'.

12   Peter Kraska, 'Militarisation and Policing: Its Relevance to 21st Century Policing', *Policing* 1, no. 4 (2007): 501; Foster and McChesney, 'Surveillance Capitalism'.

13   Peter Andreas and Richard Price, 'From War Fighting to Crime Fighting: Transforming the American National Security State', *International Studies Review* 3 (2001): 31–52.

14   Foster and McChesney, 'Surveillance Capitalism'.

15   Anriette Esterhuysen, executive director of the Association for Progressive Communications, speaking at the 'Privacy Rights, Surveillance Wrongs: An Activists' Dialogue' conference, co-hosted by the Legal Resources Centre and the International Network of Civil Liberties' Organisations, 31 October 2016.

16   Foster and McChesney, 'Surveillance Capitalism'.

17   James C. Scott. *Weapons of the Weak: Everyday Forms of Resistance* (New Haven: Yale University Press, 1985).

18   Miriam Posada Garcia, 'Mexico Will Shut Down 25.9 Million Cellphones', *La Jornada*, 11 April 2010, www.jornada.unam.mx/2010/04/11/index.php?section=economia&article=024n1eco (accessed 29 May 2013).

19   David Lyon, 'Surveillance Culture: Engagement, Exposure and Ethics in Digital Modernity', *International Journal of Communication* 11 (2017): 828.

20   Colin Bennett, *The Privacy Advocates: Resisting the Spread of Surveillance* (Cambridge: MIT Press, 2008), 58.

21   International Principles on the Application of Human Rights to Communications Surveillance, 14 May 2014, https://necessaryandproportionate.org/principles (accessed 9 January 2016).

22   Privacy International, 'Data Protection' (undated blog), https://www.privacyinternational.org/node/44 (accessed 1 December 2016).

23   David Banisar, 'National Comprehensive Data Protection/Privacy Laws and Bills' (map), 28 November 2016, https://papers.ssrn.com/sol3/papers.cfm?abstract_id=2876310&download=yes (accessed 29 November 2016).

24   Organisation for Economic Co-operation and Development, *The OECD Privacy Framework*, 2013, 14–15, http://www.oecd.org/sti/ieconomy/oecd_privacy_framework.pdf, (accessed 30 November 2016).

25   Fred H. Cate, 'The Failure of Fair Information Practice Principles', in *Consumer Protection in the Information Economy*, ed. Jane K. Winn (Aldershot: Ashgate, 2006), 341–78.

26   Michael Geist, 'Canada's Privacy Failure: My Appearance before the Standing Committee on Access to Information, Privacy and Ethics', Michael Geist (blog), http://www.michaelgeist.ca/2016/10/canadas-privacy-failure-my-appearance-before-the-standing-committee-on-access-to-information-privacy-ethics/ (accessed 1 December 2016).

27   Barton Gellman, 'NSA Broke Privacy Rules Thousands of Times per Year, Audit Finds', *Washington Post*, 15 August 2013.

28   Investigatory Powers Tribunal, 'Volume of Complaints' (updated website entry), http://www.ipt-uk.com/content.asp?id=30 (accessed 1 December 2016).

29   Privacy International, 'Press Release: Privacy International and Five Internet and Communications Providers Challenge British Government's Bulk Hacking Abroad before the European Court of Human Rights', 5 August 2016, https://www.privacyinternational.org/node/915 (accessed 1 December 2016).

30   Privacy International, 'GCHQ-NSA Intelligence-Sharing Unlawful, Says UK Surveillance Tribunal' (press release), https://www.privacyinternational.org/node/482 (accessed 1 December 2016).

31   Privacy International, 'GCHQ-NSA Intelligence-Sharing Unlawful'.

32   Ryan Gallagher, 'UK's Mass Surveillance Databases Were Unlawful for Seventeen Years, Court Rules', *The Intercept*, 17 October 2016, https://theintercept.com/2016/10/17/gchq-mi5-investigatory-powers-tribunal-bulk-datasets/ (accessed 1 December 2016).

33   Glyn Moody, 'Tired of Losing Legal Challenges to Its Surveillance, UK Government Secretly Changes Law So It Can Win', *TechDirt*, 15 May 2015, https://www.techdirt.com/articles/20150518/09360731037/tired-losing-legal-challenges-to-surveillance-uk-government-secretly-changes-law-so-it-can-win.shtml (accessed 1 December 2016).

34   Lorna Woods, 'Zakharov v Russia: Mass Surveillance and the European Court of Human Rights', EU Law Analysis (blog), 16 December 2015, http://eulawanalysis.blogspot.co.za/2015/12/zakharov-v-russia-mass-surveillance-and.html (accessed 1 December 2016);

35   *Roman Zakharov v Russia* [2015] Eur Court HR (No. 47143/06) (4 December 2015), http://hudoc.echr.coe.int/eng#{%22itemid%22:[%22001-159324%22]} (accessed 1 November 2016).

36   European Court of Human Rights, 'Hungarian Legislation on Secret Anti-Terrorist Surveillance Does Not Have Sufficient Safeguards against Abuse' (press release), 12 January 2016, http://www.statewatch.org/news/2016/jan/echr-case-SZAB-%20AND-VISSY-v-%20HUNGARY-prel.pdf (accessed 1 December 2016).

37   L'Association Européenne pour la Défense des Droits de l'Homme, 'Ambiguous Judgment of the European Court of Human Rights on Surveillance Issues' (blog), 28 January 2016, http://www.aedh.eu/Ambiguous-judgment-of-the-European.html (accessed 1 December 2016).

38   Orla Lyskey, 'Joined Cases C-293/12 and 594/12 Digital Rights Ireland and Seitlinger and Others: The Good, the Bad and the Ugly' (blog), European Law Blog, 8 April 2014, http://europeanlawblog.eu/?p=2289 (accessed 1 December 2016).

39   Court of Justice of the European Union, S.94, *Maximillian Schrems* versus *The Data Protection Commissioner of the Republic of Ireland*, Judgment in Case C-362/14; Court of Justice of the European Union, 'The Court of Justice Declares That the Commission's US Safe Harbour Decision Is Invalid' (press release), 6 October 2015, http://curia.europa.eu/jcms/upload/docs/application/pdf/2015-10/cp150117en.pdf (accessed 1 October 2016).

40   Adam Liptak, 'Justices Turn Back Challenge to Broader US Eavesdropping', *New York Times*, 26 February 2013, http://www.nytimes.com/2013/02/27/us/politics/supreme-court-rejects-challenge-to-fisa-surveillance-law.html (accessed 1 December 2016).

41   Supreme Court of the United States, '*Clapper, Director of National Intelligence et al.* v. *Amnesty International USA et al.*, No. 11-1025, 26 February 2013, https://www.supremecourt.gov/opinions/12pdf/11-1025_ihdj.pdf (accessed 1 December 2016).

42   Second Circuit Court of Appeals Ruling in *ACLU* v. *Clapper* (Docket No. 14-42-cv), https://www.aclu.org/files/assets/order_granting_governments_motion_to_dismiss_ and_denying_aclu_motion_for_preliminary_injunction.pdf (accessed 9 January 2016); Dan Roberts and Spencer Ackerman, 'NSA Mass Surveillance Revealed by Edward Snowden Ruled as Illegal', *The Guardian*, 7 May 2016, https://www.theguardian.com/ us-news/2015/may/07/nsa-phone-records-program-illegal-court (accessed 23 August 2016).

43   Dan Roberts, Sabrina Saddiqui and Spencer Ackerman, 'House Rejects NSA Collection of Phone Records with Vote to Reform Spy Agency', *The Guardian*, 13 May 2015, https://www.theguardian.com/us-news/2015/may/13/nsa-surveillance-congress-usa-freedom-act (accessed 23 August 2016).

44   Natasha Lomas, 'ACLU Calls for Tech Firms to Lobby for Surveillance Reforms', *Tech-Crunch*, 13 February 2017, https://techcrunch.com/2017/02/13/aclu-calls-for-tech-firms-to-lobby-for-surveillance-reform/ (accessed 4 March 2017).

45   Chad Squitieri, 'The Limits of the Freedom Act's Amicus Curiae', *Washington Journal of Law, Technology and Arts* 11, no. 3 (2015): 198.

46   European Commission for Democracy through Law, 'Update of the 2007 Report on Democratic Oversight of the Security Services and Report on the Democratic Oversight of Signals Intelligence Agencies', Strasbourg, 7 April 2015, http://www.venice.coe.int/ webforms/documents/default.aspx?pdffile=CDL-AD(2015)006-e (accessed 13 October 2017).

47   Squitieri, 'The Limits of the Freedom Act's Amicus Curiae', 198.

48   Sarah Johanna Eskens, O. van Daalen and Nico van Eijk, 'Ten Standards for Oversight and Transparency of National Intelligence Services', report for the Institute for Information Law, 2015, https://pure.uva.nl/ws/files/2664065/171187_1591.pdf (accessed 13 October 2017).

49   Squitieri, 'The Limits of the Freedom Act's Amicus Curiae', 197–210.

50   Arne Hintz and Ian Brown, 'Enabling Digital Citizenship? The Reshaping of Surveillance Policy after Snowden', *International Journal of Communication* 11 (2017): 788.

51   United Nations High Commissioner for Human Rights, 'The Right to Privacy in the Digital Age' (report), Twenty-Seventh Session of the Human Rights Council, 30 June 2014, http://www.ohchr.org/EN/HRBodies/HRC/RegularSessions/Session27/Documents/A. HRC.27.37_en.pdf (accessed 1 December 2016).

52   Joseph A. Cannataci, 'Report of the Special Rapporteur on the Right to Privacy Joseph A. Cannataci', 8 March 2016, http://www.ohchr.org/Documents/Issues/Privacy/A-HRC-31-64.doc (accessed 1 December 2016).

53   Cannataci, 'Report of the Special Rapporteur on the Right to Privacy Joseph A. Cannataci'.

54   Privacy International, 'The Global Surveillance Industry: An Explainer' (report), July 2016, https://privacyinternational.org/sites/default/files/global_surveillance.pdf (accessed 9 January 2017).

55   Amnesty International, 'Coalition against Unlawful Surveillance Exports' (blog), November 2014, https://www.amnesty.org/en/latest/news/2014/04/questions-and-answers-co-alition-against-unlawful-surveillance-exports-cause/ (accessed 9 January 2016).

56   Andy Greenberg, 'Hacking Team Breach Shows a Global Spying Firm Run Amok', *Wired*, 7 June 2015, https://www.wired.com/2015/07/hacking-team-breach-shows-global-spying-firm-run-amok/ (accessed 9 January 2016).

57   Colin Anderson, 'Considerations on Wassenaar Arrangement Control List Additions for Surveillance Technologies', *Access*, 2015, https://www.accessnow.org/cms/assets/uploads/archive/Access%20Wassenaar%20Surveillance%20Export%20Controls%20 2015.pdf (accessed 10 January 2017).

58   James Curran, Natalie Fenton and Des Freedman, eds., *Misunderstanding the Internet* (London: Routledge, 2012).

59   Prabir Purkayastha and Rishab Bailey, 'US Control of the Internet: Problems Facing the Movement to International Governance', *Monthly Review*, July/August 2014: 103–28.

60   Purkayastha and Bailey, 'US Control of the Internet'.

61   Lina Dencik and Jonathan Cable, 'The Advent of Surveillance Realism: Public Opinion and Activist Responses to the Snowden Leaks', *International Journal of Communication* 11 (2017): 776.

62   Arne Hintz and Lina Dencik, 'Expanding State Powers in Times of "Surveillance Realism": How the UK Got a "World Leading" Surveillance Law', *openDemocracy*, 23 December 2016, https://www.opendemocracy.net/digitaliberties/arne-hintz-lina-dencik/expanding-state-power-in-times-of-surveillance-realism-how-uk   (accessed 10 January 2017).

63   Author's interview with Gus Hosein, Privacy International Offices, London, 7 April 2017.

64   Author's interview with Scarlet Kim, Privacy International Offices, London, 7 April 2017.

65   Author's interview with Scarlet Kim, 7 April 2017.

CHAPTER 3

1   Christopher McMichael, 'Police Wars and State Repression in South Africa', *Journal of Asian and African Studies* 51, no. 1 (2016): 3–16; Richard Pithouse, *Writing the Decline: On the Struggle for South Africa's Democracy* (Johannesburg: Jacana Media, 2016), 1–5.

2   Sipho Hlongwane, 'This Brutal Police State in Which We Live', *Business Day*, 22 January 2014, http://www.bdlive.co.za/opinion/columnists/2014/01/22/this-brutal-police-state-in-which-we-live (accessed 15 April 2016); Ronnie Kasrils, 'To Spy or Not to Spy?', address by Ronnie Kasrils, MP, Minister for Intelligence Services Budget Vote, National Assembly, 23 May 2008, http://www.ssa.gov.za/Portals/0/SSA%20docs/Speeches/2008/Minister%20 Kasrils%20Budget%20Speech%2023%20May%202008.pdf (accessed 5 February 2017); Christiaan Bezuidenhout, 'The Nature of Police and Community Interaction alongside the Dawn of Intelligence-Led Policing', *Acta Criminologica*, CRIMSA conference special edition, no. 3 (2008): 59, http://repository.up.ac.za/bitstream/handle/2263/9445/Bezuid-enhout_Nature%282008%29.pdf?sequence=1 (accessed 20 May 2016).

3   Kevin O'Brien, *The South African Intelligence Services: From Apartheid to Democracy 1948–2005* (London: Routledge, 2011), 16–72.

4   O'Brien, 2011, *The South African Intelligence Services*, 53.

5   Thomas O'Toole, 'South Africa's Spying Seen as Painful Blow to West', *Washington Post*, 11 June 1984, https://www.washingtonpost.com/archive/politics/1984/06/11/south-africans-spying-seen-as-painful-blow-to-west/6d38779b-ebea-452a-9b67-607bc1c56fab/?utm_term=.1b6419e2d972 (accessed 10 August 2017).

6   Duncan Campbell and Patrick Forbes, 'UK's Listening Link with Apartheid', *New Statesman*, August 1986, http://www.duncancampbell.org/menu/journalism/newstates-

man/newstatesman-1986/uk%20listening%20link%20with%20apartheid.pdf (accessed 10 August 2017).

7   Truth and Reconciliation Commission, 'The Liberation Movements from 1960 to 1990', *Truth and Reconciliation Commission Final Report*, vol. 2, ch. 4, 373.

8   Stephen Ellis, *External Mission: The ANC in Exile* (Cape Town: Jonathan Ball Publishers, 2012), 151.

9   Ronnie Kasrils, *Armed and Dangerous: My Undercover Struggle against Apartheid* (Oxford: Heinemann, 1993), 84–91.

10   Andrew Curry, 'Piecing Together the Dark History of East Germany's Secret Police', *Wired*, 18 January 2008, https://www.wired.com/2008/01/ff-stasi/ (accessed 24 August 2017).

11   Truth and Reconciliation Commission, 'The Liberation Movements from 1960 to 1990', 361.

12   Chris Hani quoted in Skweyiya Commission, 'Report of the Commission of Enquiry into Complaints by Former African National Congress Prisoners and Detainees', 1992, African National Congress website, https://www.google.co.za/url?sa=t&rct=j&q=&esrc=s&sourc e=web&cd=1&ved=0ahUKEwj_1ofn993VAhXjBsAKHax0AsIQFggnMAA&url=http%3 A%2F%2Fwww.anc.org.za%2Fcontent%2Fskweyiya-commission-report&usg=AFQjCN GwGIDBvCRnlxmEDU31-QPSX-YZOA (accessed 23 August 2017).

13   O'Brien, *The South African Intelligence Services*, 78.

14   Ellis, *External Mission*, 155–7.

15   Ellis, *External Mission*, 158.

16   Bandile Ketelo, Amos Maxongo, Zamxolo Tshona, Ronnie Massango and Luvo Mbengo, 'A Miscarriage of Democracy: The ANC Security Department in the 1984 Mutiny in Umkhonto we Sizwe', *Searchlight South Africa* (July 1990): 35–68.

17   Stuart Commission, 'Commission of Enquiry into Recent Developments in the People's Republic of Angola', Lusaka, 14 March 1984, http://www.anc.org.za/content/stu-art-commission-report (accessed 17 August 2017).

18   Ellis, *External Mission*, 161–70.

19   Paul Trewhela, 'The Dilemma of Albie Sachs: ANC Constitutionalism and the Death of Thami Zulu', *Searchlight South Africa* (October 1993): 34–52.

20   Truth and Reconciliation Commission, 'The Liberation Movements from 1960 to 1990', 373.

21   Ellis, *External Mission*, 240.

22   Skweyiya Commission, 'Report of the Commission of Enquiry into Complaints by Former African National Congress Prisoners and Detainees', August 1992.

23   Skweyiya Commission, 'Report of the Commission of Enquiry into Complaints by Former African National Congress Prisoners and Detainees'.

24   Amnesty International, 'Torture, Ill-Treatment and Executions in African National Congress Camps', 2 December 1992, index number AFR 53/027/1992, https://www. amnesty.org/en/documents/afr53/027/1992/en/ (accessed 24 August 2017).

25   Rapule Tabane, 'Jacob Zuma: Crushing of the Mbokodo', *Mail & Guardian*, 1 September 2003, https://mg.co.za/article/2003-09-01-crushing-of-the-mbokodo (accessed 16 October 2017).

26   South African Government, White Paper on Intelligence, 1995, http://www.info.gov.za/ whitepapers/1995/intelligence.htm (accessed 22 April 2013).

27   South African Government, White Paper on Intelligence.

28   South African Government, White Paper on Intelligence.

29 Section 198, Constitution of the Republic of South Africa, http://www.saps.gov.za/const_framework/constitution/chap11.htm (accessed 25 April 2013).

30 Sections 209 and 210, Constitution of the Republic of South Africa, http://www.saps.gov.za/const_framework/constitution/chap11.htm (accessed 25 April 2013).

31 See the organogram of the State Security Agency, undated, available at https://www.documentcloud.org/documents/1672699-organogram-of-south-africa-state-security-agency.html.

32 Sandy Africa, 'The Policy Evolution of the South African Intelligence Services: 1994 to 2009 and Beyond', unpublished paper, 2012, 117, http://repository.up.ac.za/bitstream/handle/2263/20766/Africa_Policy(2012).pdf?sequence=1 (accessed 25 May 2016).

33 Kasrils, 'To Spy or Not to Spy?'

34 Ministerial Review Commission on Intelligence, 'Intelligence in a Constitutional Democracy', final report to the Minister for Intelligence Services, the Honourable Mr Ronnie Kasrils, MP, 2008, http://www.lse.ac.uk/internationalDevelopment/research/crisisStates/download/others/ReviewCommSept08.pdf (accessed 25 May 2016).

35 Email correspondence with Dale McKinley, 24 April 2013. Also see Anti-Privatisation Forum, 'The APF Condemns the Persecution of Its Members' (press statement), 22 September 2006.

36 South African Government, White Paper on Intelligence.

37 Parliamentary Monitoring Group, 'General Intelligence Laws Amendment Bill: State Security Agency Briefing', minutes of the Ad Hoc Committee on the General Intelligence Laws Amendment Bill, 14 May 2013, https://pmg.org.za/committee-meeting/15852/ (accessed 29 August 2017).

38 Ministerial Review Commission on Intelligence, 'Intelligence in a Constitutional Democracy', final report to the Minister for Intelligence Services, the Honourable Mr Ronnie Kasrils, MP, 2008, http://www.lse.ac.uk/internationalDevelopment/research/crisisStates/download/others/ReviewCommSept08.pdf (accessed 25 May 2016).

39 Parliamentary Monitoring Group, 'General Intelligence Laws Amendment Bill [B25-2011]', minutes of the Ad Hoc Committee on the General Intelligence Laws Amendment Bill, https://pmg.org.za/committee-meeting/15616/ (accessed 29 August 2017).

40 'Information Report: Planned WASP Actions in Limpopo', 4 October 2013.

41 Author's discussion with Mametlwe Sebei (telephonic), 19 December 2013.

42 Right2Know Campaign, *Big Brother Exposed: Stories of the South African Intelligence Agencies' Monitoring and Harassing Activist Movements* (handbook), 2015, http://bigbrother.r2k.org.za/wp-content/uploads/Big-Brother-Exposed-R2K-handbook-on-surveillance-web.pdf (accessed 20 May 2016).

43 Heidi Swart, 'You Always Feel Like Somebody's Watching You? They Probably Are', *Daily Maverick*, 2016, http://www.dailymaverick.co.za/article/2016-06-03-you-always-feel-like-somebodys-watching-you-they-probably-are./#.V1UzsTV97IU (accessed 6 June 2016).

44 Swart, 'You Always Feel Like Somebody's Watching You?'

45 Evgeny Finkel and Yitzhak M. Brudny, 'No More Colour! Authoritarian Regimes and Colour Revolutions in Eurasia', *Democratisation* 19, no. 1 (2012): 4.

46 Finkel and Brudny, 'No More Colour!', 1–14.

47 David Mahlobo, 'Input by the South African Minister of State Security Honourable David Mahlobo on National Security and Development at the 7th BRICS Meeting of High Representatives for Security Issues, Beijing, China', speech given on 28 July 2017.

48   Marc Davies, 'The Agents Are Coming: Four Phases of a "Colour Revolution" According to the ANC', *Huffington Post*, 6 July 2017, http://www.huffingtonpost.co.za/2017/07/05/the-agents-are-coming-four-phases-of-a-colour-revolution-acco_a_23017225/ (accessed 3 October 2017).

49   Parliament of the Republic of South Africa, *Annual Report of the Joint Standing Committee on Intelligence for the Financial Year Ending 31 March 2016*, 8–19.

50   Privacy International, 'Switching Hats: Why South Africa's Surveillance Industry Needs Scrutiny', blog post, 14 December 2016, https://www.privacyinternational.org/node/1031 (accessed 7 March 2017).

51   Parliamentary Monitoring Group, 'Inspector General of Intelligence Appointment: Interviews', Parliamentary Joint Standing Committee on Intelligence, 8 November 2016, https://pmg.org.za/committee-meeting/23645/ (accessed 23 March 2017).

52   David Mahlobo, 'State Security Agency Budget Vote 2017/18', 16 May 2017, http://www.gov.za/speeches/minister-david-mahlobo-state-security-agency-budget-vote-201718-16-may-2017-0000 (accessed 27 August 2017).

53   'Sex, SARS and Rogue Spies', *City Press*, 29 April 2015, http://www.news24.com/Archives/City-Press/Sex-Sars-and-rogue-spies-20150429 (accessed 25 August 2017). Also see Pieter-Louis Myburgh and Poloko Tau, 'Zuma, Spooks and the Bogus Union', *City Press*, 8 May 2016, http://city-press.news24.com/News/zuma-spooks-and-the-bogus-union-20160508 (accessed 25 August 2017).

54   Marianne Thamm, 'Analysis: SARS Official on Trial for Corruption Was State Security Spy', *Daily Maverick*, 24 May 2017, https://www.dailymaverick.co.za/article/2017-05-24-analysis-sars-official-on-trial-for-corruption-was-state-security-spy.-the-question-is-why/#.WZ_f9fgjHIV (accessed 25 August 2017).

55   'Sex, SARS and Rogue Spies', *City Press*, 29 April 2015.

56   Helmoed Heitman, *The Battle in Bangui: The Untold Story* (Johannesburg: Mampoer Shorts, 2013), 36.

57   Bianca Capazorio, 'New Crime Intelligence Chief Denies Wife Is His PA', *Times Live*, 27 June 2017, https://www.timeslive.co.za/politics/2017-06-27-new-crime-intelligence-chief-denies-claims-wife-is-his-pa/ (accessed 25 August 2017).

58   Rahima Essop, 'Commission to Probe Richard Mdluli's Protracted Disciplinary Process', *Eyewitness News*, 7 August 2017, http://ewn.co.za/2017/07/07/commission-agrees-to-probe-mdluli-s-protracted-disciplinary-process (accessed 25 August 2017).

59   Kwanele Sosibo, 'Xenophobia: What Did We Learn from 2008?', *Mail & Guardian*, 24 April 2015, https://mg.co.za/article/2015-04-23-xenophobia-what-did-we-learn-from-2008 (accessed 29 August 2017).

60   Ockert de Villiers, 'Xenophobia: South Africa Seeks to Reassure African States', *News24*, 17 April 2015, http://www.news24.com/SouthAfrica/News/Xenophobia-SA-seeks-to-reassure-African-states-20150417 (accessed 7 March 2017).

61   Jane Duncan, 'Are Secrecy Obsessed Spooks Putting State before Citizens?', *Sunday Times*, 18 February 2015, 21.

62   Gareth Newham, 'Why SAPS Needs Better Crime Intelligence', Institute for Security Studies, 7 September 2016, https://issafrica.org/iss-today/why-saps-needs-better-crime-intelligence (accessed 1 September 2017).

63   Jessica Bezuidenhout and Phillip de Wet, '#Guptaleaks: The Eight Big Cheeses Who Must Be Grilled', *Mail & Guardian*, 15 June 2017, https://mg.co.za/article/2017-06-15-00-guptaleaks-the-eight-big-cheeses-who-must-be-grilled (accessed 1 September 2017).

64 Kyle Cowan, 'Guptas Tipped Off on Thuli's "Spy" Claims', *Times Live*, 3 July 2017, https://www.timeslive.co.za/politics/2017-07-02-guptas-tipped-off-on-thuli-spy-claims/ (accessed 1 September 2017).

65 Pieter-Louis Myburgh, *The Republic of Gupta: A Story of State Capture* (Cape Town: Penguin Publishers, 2017), 87–93.

66 Duncan, 'Are Secrecy Obsessed Spooks Putting State before Citizens?', 21.

67 Frontline, 'Interview with David Kay', undated interview, Public Broadcasting Services, http://www.pbs.org/wgbh/pages/frontline/darkside/themes/nie.html (accessed 7 March 2017).

68 Jane Duncan, *The Rise of the Securocrats: The Case of South Africa* (Johannesburg: Jacana Media, 2014), 2–5.

69 Greg Nicolson, 'Military Is the New Normal: The Army's Extended Fiela Deployment', *Daily Maverick*, 8 July 2015, http://www.dailymaverick.co.za/article/2015-07-08-military-is-the-new-normal-the-armys-extended-fiela-deployment/#.V0gYcjV97IU (accessed 27 May 2016).

70 Michel Foucault, *Discipline and Punish: The Birth of the Prison* (Harmondsworth: Penguin Books, 1979), 200–16.

71 Bezuidenhout, 'The Nature of Police and Community Interaction'.

72 Ten Human Rights Organisations, '10 Human Rights Organisations v the United Kingdom', Applicants' Reply to Observations of the Government of the United Kingdom, Application no. 24960/15, 81, https://www.ilsa.org/jessup/jessup16/Batch%201/WEBER%20AND%20SARAVIA%20v.%20GERMANY.pdf (accessed 1 September 2017).

73 Luis Fernandez, *Policing Dissent: Social Control and the Anti-Globalisation Movement* (Toronto: Rutgers University Press, 2008).

74 Rosamunde van Brakel and Paul de Hert, 'Policing, Surveillance and Law in a Pre-Crime Society: Understanding the Consequences of Technology Based Strategies', *Cahiers Politiestudies* 20 (2011): 163–92, http://www.vub.ac.be/LSTS/pub/Dehert/378.pdf (accessed 4 March 2017).

75 South African Police Service, 'South African Police Service Strategic Plan 2010–2014', 2010, 8, http://www.saps.gov.za/saps_profile/strategic_framework/strategic_plan/2010_2014/strategic_plan_2010_2014_2.pdf.

76 Johan Burger, 'A Dysfunctional Crime Intelligence Division Has Severe Implications for Reducing Crime', *Institute for Security Studies Today*, 8 October 2013, https://www.issafrica.org/iss-today/a-dysfunctional-saps-intelligence-division-has-severe-implications-for-reducing-crime (accessed 17 May 2016).

77 Bezuidenhout, 'The Nature of Police and Community Interaction', 48–9.

78 The following municipalities were studied: the Rustenburg municipality, the Nelson Mandela metro, Lukhanji, Makana and Blue Crane (all Eastern Cape), Breede Valley, Witzenberg and Langeberg (all municipalities falling into the Cape Winelands District Municipality), Mbombela (Mpumalanga), eThekwini (KwaZulu-Natal) and the Greater Johannesburg Metropolitan Council (Gauteng).

79 Jane Duncan, *Protest Nation: The Right to Protest in South Africa* (Durban: University of KwaZulu-Natal Press, 2016).

80 According to SAPS's IRIS records for the period, the largest number of unrest-related crowd management incidents, relative to peaceful incidents, took place in Mpumalanga in the following areas: KaNyamazane, Tonga, Kabokweni, Calcutta, Masoi, Leslie.

81 'KaNyamazane Unrest-Related Crowd Management Incidents, 24/01/2012, 26/01/2012, 26/01/2012, 26/01/2012, 27/01/2102/ 27/01/2012,11/02/2012', IRIS-BIS information

released by SAPS to South African Research Chair in Social Change, University of Johannesburg, 2014.

82 Jane Duncan, 'Thabo Mbeki and Dissent', in *Mbeki and After: Reflections on the Legacy of Thabo Mbeki*, ed. Daryl Glaser (Johannesburg: Wits University Press, 2010), 105–27.

83 Department of Cooperative Governance, 'Guidelines for Managing Service Delivery Protests and Public Marches', 19 June 2012, unpublished memo to the heads of department responsible for local government and the South African Local Government Association.

84 Lehlohonolo Majoro's discussion with Mr Heunis, responsible officer in terms of the Regulation of Gatherings Act, Mbombela Municipality, 2 February 2014.

85 Pamela Oliver and Daniel Myers, 'Diffusion Models of Cycles of Protest as a Theory of Social Movements', unpublished paper, July 1998, http://www.ssc.wisc.edu/~oliver/PROTESTS/ArticleCopies/diffusion_models.pdf (accessed 20 May 2016).

86 Hélène Combes, and Olivier Fillieule, 'Repression and Protests: Structural Models and Strategic Interactions', *Revue Française de Science Politique* (English) 61, no. 6 (2011): 1047–1072.

87 Laurence Cox, 'Changing the World without Getting Shot: How Popular Power Can Set Limits to State Violence', in *State of Peace Conference*, ed. Australia Study Centre for Peace and Conflict Resolution (Vienna and Berlin: LTI-Verlag, 2013).

88 Markus Kienscherf, 'Beyond Militarization and Repression: Liberal Social Control as Pacification', *Critical Sociology* 42, no. 7-8 (2016): 1179–94.

89 Kienscherf, 'Beyond Militarization and Repression'.

90 Laurence Cox, 'Waves of Protest and Revolution: Elements of a Marxist Analysis', unpublished paper, 2014, http://eprints.maynoothuniversity.ie/4867/ (accessed 1 February 2015).

91 Patrick Bond, 'Protests and Repression in South Africa', *Counterpunch*, 17 July 2012, http://www.counterpunch.org/2012/07/17/protest-and-repression-in-south-africa/ (accessed 26 January 2015).

92 Sydney Tarrow, *Democracy and Disorder: Protest and Politics in Italy, 1965–1975* (Oxford: Oxford University Press, 1989).

93 Colin Beck, 'The World-Cultural Origins of Revolutionary Waves: Five Centuries of European Contention', *Social Science History* 35, no. 2 (2011): 167–207.

94 Cox, 'Changing the World'; Cox, 'Waves of Protest and Revolution'.

95 Cox, 'Waves of Protest and Revolution'.

96 Susan Booysen, *The African National Congress and the Regeneration of Political Power* (Johannesburg: Wits University Press, 2011), 126–73.

97 Ebrahim Fakir, 'Circling the Square of Protests: Democracy, Development, Delivery and Discontent in Bekkersdal', Ruth First Memorial Lecture, University of the Witwatersrand, 13 August 2014, http://witsvuvuzela.com/wp-content/uploads/2014/08/Final-RuthFirstLecture2014.EF_.pdf (accessed 14 January 2015).

98 Cox, 'Changing the World'.

99 Gia Nicolaides, 'Marikana Tragedy Enquiry Is a Witch-Hunt, Says Phigeya', *Eyewitness News*, 2016, http://ewn.co.za/2016/02/03/Marikana-tragedy-investigation-is-a-witch-hunt-says-Phiyega (accessed 19 April 2016).

100 Charles Molele, Matuma Letsoalo and Sam Sole, 'Minister versus Top Spooks', *Mail & Guardian*, 16 September 2011, http://mg.co.za/article/2011-09-16-minister-vs-top-spooks (accessed 19 April 2016).

101 Albie Sachs, Concurring Judgment, *South African National Defence Union* v. *Minister of Defence and Chief of the South African National Defence Force*, 26 May 1999, Constitutional Court of South Africa judgment CCT/27/98, 33.
102 Duncan, *The Rise of the Securocrats*.
103 Graeme Hosken, 'They Would've Been Shot for Mutiny', *Independent Online*, 5 September 2009, http://www.iol.co.za/news/south-africa/they-wouldve-been-shot-for-mutiny-457509 (accessed 19 April 2016).
104 Cox, 'Changing the World'.
105 Duncan, *The Rise of the Securocrats*.
106 Taschica Pillay, 'Durban Councillors Found Guilty for Hit on Activist', *Times Live*, 20 May 2016, http://www.timeslive.co.za/local/2016/05/20/Durban-councillors-found-guilty-for-hit-on-activist (accessed 20 May 2016).
107 Cox, 'Changing the World'.
108 Cox, 'Changing the World'.

CHAPTER 4

1   Centre for International Governance Innovation and IPSOS, 'Most Global Citizens Say Law Enforcement Should Have a Right to Access Online Communications of its Citizens (70%), Especially Those Suspected of a Crime (85%)' (survey results), 2 March 2016, https://www.cigionline.org/sites/default/files/factum_2016_cigiipsos_survey_securityprivacy.pdf (accessed 11 January 2016).
2   Amnesty International, 'Global Opposition to USA Big Brother Mass Surveillance' (survey results), 18 March 2015, https://www.amnesty.org/en/press-releases/2015/03/global-opposition-to-usa-big-brother-mass-surveillance/ (accessed 11 January 2016).
3   Jane Duncan, *The Rise of the Securocrats: The Case of South Africa* (Johannesburg: Jacana Media, 2014), 9.
4   Author's interview with former RICA judge Yvonne Mokgoro, Constitutional Court, Johannesburg, 22 September 2017.
5   Regulation of Interception of Communications and Provision of Communication-Related Information Act 70 of 2002, http://www.justice.gov.za/legislation/acts/2002–070.pdf, (accessed 15 October 2015).
6   Yvonne Mokgoro, 'Annual Report on Interception of Private Communications, period 2014/15', Annual Report of the Joint Standing Committee on Intelligence for the Financial Year Ending 31 March 2016, 15 October 2015, 35, https://mail.google.com/mail/u/0/#search/Mokgoro/15902b1de4582e01?projector=1 (accessed 8 January 2018).
7   Heidi Swart, 'Big Brother Is Listening: On Your Phone', *Mail & Guardian*, 13 November 2015, http://mg.co.za/article/2015-11-12-big-brother-is-listening-on-your-phone (accessed 13 January 2017); Heidi Swart, 'Communications Surveillance by the South African Intelligence Services', report commissioned by the Media Policy and Democracy Project, February 2016, 20–5, http://www.mediaanddemocracy.com/uploads/1/6/5/7/16577624/comms-surveillance-nia-swart_feb2016.pdf (accessed 24 February 2017).
8   Heidi Swart, 'Big Brother Is Watching Your Cellphone Records', *Daily Maverick*, 10 May 2017, https://www.dailymaverick.co.za/article/2017-05-10-op-ed-big-brother-is-watching-your-phone-call-records/#.WhVvtdKWbIU (accessed 22 May 2017).

9   Author's interview with former RICA judge Yvonne Mokgoro, 22 September 2017.

10   International Principles on the Application of Human Rights to Communications Surveillance, 10 July 2013, https://necessaryandproportionate.org/text (accessed 22 May 2014).

11   US Code §2518: Procedure for Interception of Wire, Oral, or Electronic Communications, www.law.cornell.edu/uscode/text/18/2518 (accessed 22 May 2014).

12   Ministry of State Security, Office for Interception Centres, National Communications Centre and State Security Agency, '*AmaBhungane Centre for Investigative Journalism and Stephen Patrick Sole* v *The Minister of Justice and Correctional Services and Nine Others*: Second, Seventh, Eighth and Tenth Respondent's Answering Affidavit', case number 25078/2017, 24–5, paras. 474–5.

13   Privacy International, 'Submission to the Parliamentary Committee on Justice and Constitutional Development', 14 August 2001.

14   Nazreen Bawa, 'The Regulation of Interception of Communications and Provision of Communication-Related Information Act', in *Telecommunications Law in South Africa*, 320, ed. Lisa Thornton, Yasmin Carrim, Patric Mtshaulana and Pippa Reburn, http://link.wits.ac.za/papers/tele-law.html (accessed 5 June 2013).

15   Ministry of State Security, Office for Interception Centres, National Communications Centre and State Security Agency, '*AmaBhungane Centre for Investigative Journalism and Stephen Patrick Sole* v *Minister of Justice and Correctional Services and Nine Others*: Second, Seventh, Eighth and Tenth Respondent's Answering Affidavit', case number 25078/2017, 45–6.

16   Oxford Pro Bono Publico, 'Legal Opinion on Intercept Communication', University of Oxford, 2006, http://www2.law.ox.ac.uk/opbp/OPBP%20Intercept%20Evidence%20Report.pdf (accessed 18 January 2017).

17   Kevin P. Donovan and Aaron K. Martin, 'The Rise of African SIM Registration: Mobility, Identity, Surveillance and Resistance', Information Systems and Innovation Group Working Paper no. 186, London School of Economics and Political Science, London, 2012.

18   Heidi Swart, 'Missed Call: SIM Card Registration "Useless" for Crime Fighting Purposes', *Daily Maverick*, 10 November 2016, https://www.dailymaverick.co.za/article/2016-11-10-missed-call-rica-registration-useless-for-crime-prevention-purposes/#.WHY1e-9J97IU (accessed 11 January 2016).

19   David Lyon, *Surveillance after Snowden* (London: Polity Press, 2015), 109.

20   Sam Sole, 'Booysen Attacks NPA "Abuse"', amaBhungane Centre for Investigative Journalism', 13 May 2016, http://amabhungane.co.za/article/2016-05-13-00-booysen-attacks-npa-abuse (accessed 5 November 2017).

21   Discussion with Stephan Hofstatter and Mzilikazi wa Afrika, Rosebank, 20 March 2014.

22   Discussion with Stephan Hofstatter and Mzilikazi wa Afrika, 20 March 2014.

23   Affidavit by Stephan Hofstatter, 24 March 2012.

24   Affidavit by Brian Padayachee, 14 March 2012.

25   Discussion with Stephan Hofstatter and Mzilikazi wa Afrika, 20 March 2014.

26   Author's email correspondence with Stephan Hofstatter, 25 October 2017.

27   AmaBhungane Centre for Investigative Journalism, '*AmaBhungane Centre for Investigative Journalism and Stephen Patrick Sole* v *Minister of Justice and Correctional Services and Nine Others*', Case number 25078/2017.

28   National Strategic Intelligence Act 39 of 1994, https://www.acts.co.za/national-strategic-intelligence-act-1994/1__definitions (accessed 27 August 2017).

29 AmaBhungane Centre for Investigative Journalism, '*AmaBhungane Centre for Investigative Journalism and Stephen Patrick Sole* v *Minister of Justice and Correctional Services and Nine Others*', Case number 25078/2017, 30.

30 Ministry of State Security, Office for Interception Centres, National Communications Centre and State Security Agency, '*AmaBhungane Centre for Investigative Journalism and Stephen Patrick Sole* v *Minister of Justice and Correctional Services and Nine Others*: Second, Seventh, Eighth and Tenth Respondent's Answering Affidavit', case number 25078/2017, 53–6.

31 S.I. Dintwe, 'Complaint: Alleged Unlawful Interception of Confidential Communications', letter from the Office of the Inspector General of Intelligence to Sam Sole, amaBhungane Centre for Investigative Journalism, 17 August 2017.

32 Joshua Khumalo, 'Report to Joint Standing Committee on Intelligence for the Period 1 April 2010 to 31 October 2011', report to the National Assembly of the Joint Standing Committee on Intelligence, http://pmg-assets.s3-website-eu-west-1.amazonaws.com/140306jscireport.pdf (accessed 12 October 2017).

33 Author's correspondence with the amaBhungane Centre for Investigative Journalism, 30 October 2017.

34 Joshua Khumalo, 'Statistical Briefing by Designated Judge for the Period 1 April 2009 to 31 March 2010', report to the National Assembly of the Joint Standing Committee on Intelligence.

35 Author's interview with former RICA judge Yvonne Mokgoro, 22 September 2017.

36 Author's interview with Dennis Dlomo, National Intelligence Coordinating Committee offices, Pretoria, 18 December 2013.

37 Joint Standing Committee on Intelligence, 'Annual Report of the Joint Standing Committee on Intelligence for the Financial Year Ending 31 March 2016', National Assembly and National Council of Provinces Committee Reports, 13 December 2016, http://pmg-assets.s3-website-eu-west-1.amazonaws.com/intelligence.pdf (accessed 1 September 2017).

38 Author's interview with former RICA judge Yvonne Mokgoro, 22 September 2017.

39 Joint Standing Committee on Intelligence, 'Annual Report of the Joint Standing Committee on Intelligence for the Financial Year Ending 31 March 2013 Including the Period up to February 2014', http://pmg-assets.s3-website-eu-west-1.amazonaws.com/140410jscireport.pdf (accessed 12 October 2017).

40 Author's interview with Charles Nqakula, University of Johannesburg, Johannesburg, 13 November 2017.

41 Author's email correspondence with Ant Brooks, 26 September 2017.

42 Author's interview with former RICA judge Yvonne Mokgoro, 22 September 2017.

43 Author's interview with former RICA judge Yvonne Mokgoro, 22 September 2017.

44 Author's interview with Charles Nqakula, 13 November 2017.

45 Yvonne Mokgoro, 'Annual Report on Interception of Private Communications, Period 2014/2015', report for the Joint Standing Committee on Intelligence, 15 October 2015, 52, http://pmg-assets.s3-website-eu-west-1.amazonaws.com/intelligence.pdf (accessed 3 July 2017).

46 Mokgoro, 'Annual Report on Interception of Private Communications, Period 2014/2015', 48.

47 Mokgoro, 'Annual Report on Interception of Private Communications, Period 2014/2015', 339–40.

48   Sarel Robbertse, Supporting Affidavit, *AmaBhungane Centre for Investigative Journalism and Another* v *Minister of Justice and Correctional Services and Others*, case no. 2598/2017, 28 November 2017.

49   Tsepo Ndwalaza, 'Satisfied with the Sentence Handed Down to the Murderer', *Khasho*, October–November 2014, 6, https://www.npa.gov.za/sites/default/files/newsletters/NPA%20Khasho%20October%20-%20November%202014.pdf (accessed 1 March 2017).

50   *The State* v *Peter Michael Roberts and Others*, High Court of South Africa (Eastern Cape, Port Elizabeth), case no. CC20/2011.

51   Megan Baadjies, 'Cellphone Links Man to Wife's Murder', *Independent Online*, 1 October 2015, http://www.iol.co.za/news/crime-courts/cellphone-links-man-to-wifes-murder-1923905 (accessed 1 March 2017).

52   *The State* v *Thulani Mtoto*, in the High Court of South Africa (Western Cape Division, Cape Town), case no. A488/14.

53   *The State* v *Selwyn Winston de Vries and Others*, in the High Court of South Africa, Cape of Good Hope Provincial Division', case no. 67/ 2005, Judgment delivered 10 June 2008.

54   State vs. Agliotti, (SS 154/2009) [2010] ZAGPJHC 129; 2011 (2) SACR 437 (GSJ) (25 November 2010), http://www.saflii.org/za/cases/ZAGPJHC/2010/129.html (accessed 28 February 2018).

55   Swart, 'Communications Surveillance by the South African Intelligence Services', 20–5, http://www.mediaanddemocracy.com/uploads/1/6/5/7/16577624/comms-surveillance-nia-swart_feb2016.pdf (accessed 24 February 2017).

56   Right2Know Campaign's Submission to Parliament of the Republic of South Africa on the Cybercrime and Cyersecurity Bill, 10 August 2017, http://www.r2k.org.za/2017/08/11/r2k-submission-on-the-cybercrimes-bill-2017/ (accessed 24 October 2017).

CHAPTER 5

1   See the Boundless Informant heat map, undated, available at https://edwardsnowden.com/wp-content/uploads/2014/05/hm.pdf.

2   Wayne Madsen, 'America's Expanding Aggressive Signals Intelligence Operations', Strategic Culture Foundation, 6 August 2014, http://www.strategic-culture.org/news/2014/08/06/americas-expanding-aggressive-signals-intelligence-operations.html (accessed 13 January 2017).

3   Andy Müller-Maguhn, Laura Poitras, Marcel Rosenbach, Michael Sontheimer and Christian Grothoff, 'Map of the Stars', *The Intercept*, 14 September 2014, https://theintercept.com/2014/09/14/nsa-stellar/ (accessed 17 January 2017).

4   James Risen and Laura Poitras, 'NSA Report Outlined Goals for More Power', *New York Times*, 22 November 2013, http://www.nytimes.com/2013/11/23/us/politics/nsa-report-outlined-goals-for-more-power.html?pagewanted=all (accessed 17 January 2017).

5   Jan Vermeulen, 'Secret NSA Online Spying Node in South Africa: Report', *MyBroadband*, 15 September 2015, https://mybroadband.co.za/news/security/109882-secret-nsa-online-spying-node-in-south-africa-report.html (accessed 17 January 2017).

6   See the image of the National Security Agency Treasure Map PG-Server locations, undated, available at https://theintercept.com/document/2014/09/14/treasure-map-presentation/. See also an image of the five 'classes of access' that the NSA uses in its worldwide signal

intelligence operations, 2012, available at https://www.nrc.nl/nieuws/2013/11/23/nsa-in-fected-50000-computer-networks-with-malicious-software-a1429487.

7   Adam Oxford, 'Why Is XKeyscore in Zambia and the Sudan ?', *HTXT*, 3 August 2013, http://www.htxt.co.za/2013/08/03/why-is-xkeyscore-in-zambia-and-the-sudan/ (accessed 11 August 2016).

8   Oxford, 'Why Is XKeyscore in Zambia and the Sudan?'

9   Foreign Intelligence Surveillance Court, 'Exhibit F: In the Matter of Foreign Governments, Foreign Factions, Foreign Entities and Foreign Based Political Organisations', Certification 2010 A, https://search.edwardsnowden.com/docs/ExhibitF2014-06-30nsa-docs (accessed 11 August 2016). See the image of the XKeyscore locations by 25 February 2008, available at https://www.theguardian.com/world/interactive/2013/jul/31/nsa-xkeyscore-program-full-presentation.

10   Jeremy Scahill and Josh Begley, 'The Great SIM Heist: How Spies Stole the Keys to the Encryption Castle', *The Intercept*, 19 February 2015, https://theintercept.com/2015/02/19/great-sim-heist/ (accessed 11 August 2016).

11   Government Communications Head Quarters, 'DAPINO GAMMA Target Personalisation Centres' (wiki page), 2011, https://search.edwardsnowden.com/docs/DAPINOG-AMMATargetPersonalisationCentres2015-02-19nsadocs (accessed 11 August 2016).

12   Investigatory Powers Tribunal, 'Amended Open Determination in the Matter between Liberty and Others and GCHQ and Others, 22 June 2015, http://www.ipt-uk.com/docs/Final_Liberty_Ors_Open_Determination_Amended.pdf (accessed 13 January 2017).

13   Alex Kane, 'How Israel Became a Hub for Surveillance Technology', *The Intercept*, 17 October 2016, https://theintercept.com/2016/10/17/how-israel-became-a-hub-for-surveillance-technology/ (accessed 25 November 2016).

14   Kane, 'How Israel Became a Hub for Surveillance Technology'.

15   Jenna McLaughlin, 'South African Spy Company Used by Gaddafi Touts Its NSA-Like Capabilities', *The Intercept*, 31 October 2016, https://theintercept.com/2016/10/31/south-african-spy-company-used-by-gadaffi-touts-its-nsa-like-capabilities/ (accessed 25 November 2016).

16   Responses provided to Heidi Swart by the Innovation Hub, updated document, in Heidi Swart, 'Communications Surveillance by the South African Intelligence Services', report commissioned by the Media Policy and Democracy Project, February 2016, http://www.mediaanddemocracy.com/uploads/1/6/5/7/16577624/comms-surveillance-nia-swart_feb2016.pdf (accessed 24 February 2017), 32.

17   Siyabonga Mchunu, 'DTI "Funded Gaddafi Spyware"', *Mail & Guardian*, 22 November 2013, http://mg.co.za/article/2013–11-22-dti-funded-gaddafi-spyware (accessed 24 February 2017).

18   Sam Vaknin quoted in Swart, 'Communications Surveillance by the South African Intelligence Services', 10.

19   Privacy International, 'South African Government Still Funding Vastech, Knows Previous Financing Was for Mass Surveillance' (blog), 30 January 2014, https://www.privacy-international.org/node/305 (accessed 24 February 2017).

20   Author's correspondence with Leon Labuschagne, Manager: Marketing and Technology Research, Vastech, 6 April 2017.

21   Privacy International, 'Monitoring Centres: Force Multipliers from the Surveillance Industry', Privacy International blog, 29 April 2014, https://www.privacyinternational.org/node/439 (accessed 9 January 2016).

22   Vastech, 'Zebra Strategic Network Communication Monitoring', undated product brochure, https://www.documentcloud.org/documents/711299-brochure484.html#document/p4/a119774 (accessed 9 January 2016).

23   Yolandi Groenewald, 'SA Firm "Helped" Gaddafi Spy on the People of Libya', *Mail & Guardian*, 2 September 2011, http://mg.co.za/article/2011-09-02-sa-firm-helped-gaddafi-spy (accessed 9 January 2016).

24   Ewan McAskill, Julian Borger, Nick Hopkins, Nick Davies, and James Ball, 'GCHQ Taps Fibre Optic Cables for Secret Access to World's Communications', *The Guardian*, 21 June 2013, https://www.theguardian.com/uk/2013/jun/21/gchq-cables-secret-world-communications-nsa (accessed 27 October 2017). For a map of African undersea cables, 2017, see the image available at https://manypossibilities.net/african-undersea-cables/.

25   Author's email correspondence with Lasse Skou Andersen, journalist with *Information*, 16 January 2017.

26   Author's email correspondence with Lasse Skou Andersen, 27 October 2017.

27   Collin Anderson, 'Considerations on Wassenaar Arrangement Control List Additions for Surveillance Technologies', paper published by Access, https://cda.io/r/ConsiderationsonWassenaarArrangementProposalsforSurveillanceTechnologies.pdf, pp. 21–23 (accessed 27 October 2017).

28   Erhvervsstyrelsen [Danish Business Authority], 'End User Certificate, AKT 515288, BILAG 2 [11750], 15 July 2016', released in response to Freedom of Information Request in Denmark.

29   Author's email correspondence with Lasse Skou Andersen, 16 January 2017.

30   Erhvervsstyrelsen, 'End User Certificate, AKT 515288, BILAG 2 [11750], 15 July 2016'.

31   Nawal al-Maghafi, 'Weapons of Mass Surveillance' (documentary), British Broadcasting Corporation Arabic, 7 July 2017, http://www.bbc.com/news/av/world-middle-east-40531967/weapons-of-mass-surveillance (accessed 24 October 2017).

32   'How BAE Systems Sold Cyber-Surveillance Tools to Arab States', *BBC News*, 5 June 2017, http://www.bbc.com/news/world-middle-east-40276568 (accessed 27 September 2017).

33   ETI Group, 'Evident', product brochure, undated, https://www.privacyinternational.org/sites/default/files/Letter%20from%20PI%20re%20Information%20DBA.pdf (accessed 29 September 2017).

34   ETI Group, 'Evident Investigator', product brochure, undated, 'The Spy Files', WikiLeaks, https://wikileaks.org/spyfiles/docs/ETIGROUP_2011_Evid_en.html, 4 September 2013, 6–7 (accessed 24 October 2017).

35   ETI Group, 'Evident Investigator'.

36   ETI Group, 'Evident: Decode and Render Target Communication', product brochure, undated, 'The Spy Files', WikiLeaks, https://wikileaks.org/spyfiles/docs/ETIGROUP_2011_Evid_en.html, pg. 6, 4 September 2013 (accessed 24 October 2017).

37   See the product brochure for ETI's Evident System, 2011, at https://wikileaks.org/spyfiles/document/etigroup/ETIGROUP-2011-Evid-en/page-1/#pagination, (accessed 24 October 2017).

38   'How BAE Systems Sold Cyber-Surveillance Tools to Arab States', *BBC News*, 5 June 2017.

39   Jenna McLaughlin, 'BAE Systems Sells Internet Surveillance Gear to United Arab Emirates', *The Intercept*, 26 August 2016, https://theintercept.com/2016/08/26/bae-systems-sells-internet-surveillance-gear-to-united-arab-emirates/ (accessed 16 January 2017).

40   Lasse Skou Andersen, 'Demark Is a Major Exporter of Internet Surveillance', *Information*, 27 August 2016, https://www.information.dk/indland/2016/08/danmark-storeksportoer-internetovervaagning (accessed 15 January 2017).

41   Author's interview with Charles Nqakula, University of Johannesburg, Johannesburg, 13 November 2017.

42   International Procurement Services, 'Searchlight GSM TX Locator', undated product brochure, http://intpro.co.uk/product/searchlight-gsm-tx-locator/ (accessed 23 February 2017).

43   National Conventional Arms Control Committee, '2012 Annual Report', report submitted to Parliament in February 2013; National Conventional Arms Control Committee, '2013 Annual Report', report submitted to Parliament in April 2014.

44   National Conventional Arms Control Committee, '2014 Annual Report', report submitted to Parliament in February 2015.

45   National Conventional Arms Control Committee, '2015 Annual Report', report submitted to Parliament in February 2016.

46   National Conventional Arms Control Committee, '2016 Annual Report', report submitted to Parliament in February 2017.

47   Ministry of State Security, Office for Interception Centres, National Communications Centre and State Security Agency, '*AmaBhungane Centre for Investigative Journalism and Stephen Patrick Sole* v *Minister of Justice and Correctional Services and Nine Others*: Second, Seventh, Eighth and Tenth Respondent's Answering Affidavit', case number 25078/2017, 57–63.

48   Ministry of State Security, Office for Interception Centres, National Communications Centre and State Security Agency, '*AmaBhungane Centre for Investigative Journalism and Stephen Patrick Sole* v *Minister of Justice and Correctional Services and Nine Others*: Second, Seventh, Eighth and Tenth Respondent's Answering Affidavit', 58, para. 132.

49   Eric King, 'In the Investigatory Powers Tribunal between Privacy International and the Secretary of State for Foreign and Commonwealth Affairs and Government Communication Headquarters', witness statement of Eric King, 8 June 2014, 22–7.

50   Ministry of State Security, Office for Interception Centres, National Communications Centre and State Security Agency, '*AmaBhungane Centre for Investigative Journalism and Stephen Patrick Sole* v *Minister of Justice and Correctional Services and Nine Others*: Second, Seventh, Eighth and Tenth Respondent's Answering Affidavit', 59, para. 135.

51   Author's interview with Dennis Dlomo, National Intelligence Coordinating Committee offices, Pretoria, 18 December 2013.

52   Ten Human Rights Organisations, '10 Human Rights Organisations v the United Kingdom', Applicants' Reply to Observations of the Government of the United Kingdom, Application no. 24960/15, undated, https://www.ilsa.org/jessup/jessup16/Batch%201/ WEBER%20AND%20SARAVIA%20v.%20GERMANY.pdf (accessed 1 September 2017).

53   Ten Human Rights Organisations, '10 Human Rights Organisations v the United Kingdom', 72–7.

54   Chatham House, 'Mass Surveillance, Counterterrorism and Privacy: The Way Forward' (transcript of seminar debate between Ben Emmerson, UN Special Rapporteur on Counterterrorism and Human Rights, and Malcolm Rifkind, Chairman, Intelligence and Security Committee), 28 October 2014, https://www.chathamhouse.org/sites/files/ chathamhouse/field/field_document/20141028MassSurveillance.pdf, 6 (accessed 27 August 2017).

55 Ten Human Rights Organisations, '10 Human Rights Organisations v the United Kingdom', 83.

56 Government of the United Kingdom, '10 Human Rights Organisations v the United Kingdom', the United Kingdom's Observations on the Merits, Application no. 58170/13, undated, https://privacyinternational.org/sites/default/files/United%20Kingdom%E2%80%99s%20Observations%20on%20the%20Merits.pdf, 154 (accessed 1 September 2017).

57 Ten Human Rights Organisations, '10 Human Rights Organisations v the United Kingdom', 84.

58 Zolile Ngcakani, Executive Summary of the Final Report of the Findings of an Investigation into the Legality of the Surveillance Operations of the NIA Carried Out on Mr S. Macozoma, Inspector General of Intelligence, 23 March 2006.

59 Ministerial Review Commission on Intelligence, 'Intelligence in a Constitutional Democracy', final report to the Minister for Intelligence Services, the Honourable Mr Ronnie Kasrils MP, 2008.

60 South African Government, White Paper on Intelligence, 1995, http://www.info.gov.za/whitepapers/1995/intelligence.htm (accessed 22 April 2013).

61 Ad Hoc Committee on General Intelligence Laws Amendment Bill, 'General Intelligence Law Amendment Bill [B25-2011] Deliberations Continued', 26 March 2013, https://pmg.org.za/committee-meeting/15643/ (accessed 27 February 2017).

62 Ad Hoc Committee on General Intelligence Laws Amendment Bill, 'General Intelligence Law Amendment Bill [B25-2011] Deliberations Continued', 26 March 2013.

63 Gareth van Zyl, 'Data the New Voice as Telkom Shifts Focus', Fin24Tech, 22 May 2016, http://www.fin24.com/Tech/Companies/data-the-new-voice-as-telkom-shifts-focus-20160722 (accessed 21 January 2017).

64 Christopher Soghoian, 'The Next Crypto-Wars 6: Obstacles to Dragnet Surveillance' (blog), Privacy PC, 8 August 2014, http://privacy-pc.com/articles/the-next-crypto-wars-6-obstacles-to-dragnet-surveillance.html (accessed 20 February 2017).

65 Anne Johnson, Emily Grumbling, and Jon Eisenberg, 'Exploring Encryption and Potential Mechanisms for Authorised Government Access to Plaintext: Proceedings of a Workshop' (Washington: National Academies Press, 2016), 4–5, http://cryptome.org/2016/08/nap-encryption-gov-access.pdf (accessed 20 February 2017).

66 Johnson, Grumbling, and Eisenberg, 'Exploring Encryption and Potential Mechanisms for Authorised Government Access to Plaintext', 4–5.

67 Christopher Soghoian, 'The Next Crypto-Wars 5: Government Contractors' Activity Revealed' (blog), Privacy PC, 3 August 2014, http://privacy-pc.com/articles/the-next-crypto-wars-5-government-contractors-activity-revealed.html (accessed 20 February 2017).

68 Soghoian L, 'The Next Crypto-Wars 6'.

69 Citizen Lab, 'About', undated, https://citizenlab.org/about/ (accessed 16 January 2017).

70 Bluecoat, 'WAN Optimization: PacketShaper' (undated), https://www.bluecoat.com/products-and-solutions/wan-optimization-packetshaper (accessed 16 January 2017); Christian Fuchs, 'Implications of Deep Packet Inspection Internet Surveillance for Society', Privacy and Security Research Paper Series, no. 1, Department of Informatics and Media, Uppsala University, http://fuchs.uti.at/wp-content/uploads/DPI.pdf (accessed 17 January 2017).

71 See the global map of Bluecoat on public networks, 2013, available at https://citizenlab.org/storage/bluecoat/CitLab-PlanetBlueCoatRedux-FINAL.pdf, 10.

72   Chris Szabo, 'US Intelligence Analyst Thinks That SA Government Is Likely Spying on Citizens', *Defenceweb*, 22 July 2015, http://www.defenceweb.co.za/index.php?option=com_content&view=article&id=39998:us-intelligence-analyst-thinks-sa-government-likely-spying-on-citizens-&catid=49:National%20Security&Itemid=115 (accessed 16 January 2017).

73   WikiLeaks, 'FinFisher: Documents', Spyfiles 4 (database of leaked documents), 15 September 2014, https://wikileaks.org/spyfiles4/documents.html (accessed 24 February 2017).

74   FinFisher, 'FinSpy PC', Remote Monitoring Solutions, product brochure, WikiLeaks Spyfiles 4 (database of leaked documents), https://wikileaks.org/spyfiles4/documents/FinSpy-Catalog.pdf (accessed 24 February 2017).

75   Wikileaks, 'Spyfiles 4: FinFisher Customers' (database of leaked FinFisher customer files), 15 September 2014, https://wikileaks.org/spyfiles4/customers.html (accessed 23 February 2017).

76   FinFisher, 'Tactical IT Intrusion Portfolio: FinIntrusion Kit', October 2011, https://wikileaks.org/spyfiles/docs/gamma/300_tactical-it-intrusion-portfolio-finintrusion-kit.html (accessed 24 February 2017).

77   Heidi Swart, 'Cyberspying: The Ghost in Your Machine', *Daily Maverick*, 21 February 2017, https://www.dailymaverick.co.za/article/2017-02-21-cyberspying-the-ghost-in-your-machine/#.WK7gM9J97IU (accessed 24 February 2017).

78   Swart, 'Cyberspying'.

79   Privacy International, 'Government Hacking and Surveillance: Ten Recommendations' (unpublished leaflet), London, September 2017.

80   Author's interview with former RICA judge Yvonne Mokgoro, Constitutional Court, Johannesburg, 22 September 2017.

81   For an image of suspected FinFisher government users that were active at some point in 2015, see https://citizenlab.org/2015/10/mapping-finfishers-continuing-proliferation/. For an image of HackingTeam and FinFisher clients around the world, see https://www.eff.org/deeplinks/2015/07/hacking-team-leaks-reveal-spyware-industrys-growth.

82   Bill Marczak, Claudio Guarnieri, Morgan Marquis-Boire and John Scott-Railton, 'Mapping HackingTeam's "Untraceable" Spyware', *Citizenlab* blog, 17 February 2014, https://citizenlab.org/2014/02/mapping-hacking-teams-untraceable-spyware/ (accessed 17 January 2017).

83   Internal HackingTeam email from David Vincenzetti, 20 May 2012, https://wikileaks.org/hackingteam/emails/emailid/611864 (accessed 21 January 2017).

84   Marczak, Guarnieri, Marquis-Boire and Scott-Railton, 'Mapping HackingTeam's "Untraceable" Spyware'.

85   Jon Tullett, 'HackingTeam Failed to Crack SA', *IT Web*, 14 July 2015, http://www.itweb.co.za/index.php?option=com_content&view=article&id=144683:Hacking-Team-failed-to-crack-SA&catid=234 (accessed 21 January 2017).

86   Clarence Walker, 'New Hi-Tech Police Surveillance: The "Stingray" Cellphone Spying Device', Global Research, Centre for Research on Globalisation, 19 May 2015, http://www.globalresearch.ca/new-hi-tech-police-surveillance-the-stingray-cell-phone-spying-device/5331165 (accessed 13 January 2017).

87   Jane Duncan, 'Spies Are All Set to Grab Your Metadata', *Mail & Guardian*, 11 September 2015, http://mg.co.za/article/2015-09-10-spies-are-all-set-to-grab-your-metadata (accessed 17 January 2017).

88   Duncan, 'Spies Are All Set to Grab Your Metadata'.

89   Duncan, 'Spies Are All Set to Grab Your Metadata'.

90 Nate Raymond, 'In First, U.S. Judge Throws Out Cell Phone "Stingray" Evidence', *Reuters*, 13 July 2016, http://www.reuters.com/article/us-usa-crime-stingray-idUSKCN-0ZS2VI (accessed 20 February 2017).

91 Department of Justice and Constitutional Development, 'Notice in Terms of Section 44(1)(a) of the Regulation of Interception of Communications and Provision of Communication-Related Information Act', 2002, *Government Gazette* 28371 (29 December 2005), https://mail.google.com/mail/u/0/#inbox/15f15ec0e0bfebd4?projector=1 (accessed 18 October 2017).

92 Solly Maphumulo, 'Beware Superspy "Grabber"', 27 August 2015, http://www.iol.co.za/capetimes/beware-superspy-grabber-1906372 (accessed 20 February 2017).

93 Swart, 'Communications Surveillance by the South African Intelligence Services', 16–7.

94 'In the Matter of the State versus Paul Scheepers' (charge sheet), 21 April 2016.

95 Forensic Telecommunications Services, 'An Overview of FTS Products and Services', 31 January 2011, 11, https://wikileaks.org/spyfiles/docs/FORENSICTELECOMMUNICATIONS-2011-Anoverof-en.pdf (accessed 24 February 2017).

96 Verint, 'Tactical Off-Air Intelligence Solutions', undated product brochure, uploaded to Document Cloud by Privacy International, https://www.documentcloud.org/documents/885760-1278-verint-product-list-engage-gi2-engage-pi2.html (accessed 24 February 2017).

97 'In the Matter of the State versus Willem Mattheus Johannes Lotter, Joseph Lebone Pooe, Johannes Jacobus Cronje and Willem Johannes Willemse' (charge sheet), case no. 14/725/15, 19 August 2016; Sam Sole and Sally Evans, 'The Smuggler, the Spook and the Grabber', amaBhungane Centre for Investigative Journalism, 27 August 2016, http://amabhungane.co.za/article/2016-08-27-the-smuggler-the-spook-and-the-grabber (accessed 24 February 2017).

98 Duncan, 'Spies Are All Set to Grab Your Metadata'.

99 Simnikiwe Mzekandaba, 'Grabber Used for "National Security"', *ITWeb*, 8 September 2015, http://www.itweb.co.za/index.php?option=com_content&view=article&id=146019 (accessed 24 February 2017).

100 Duncan, 'Spies Are All Set to Grab Your Metadata'.

101 Duncan, 'Spies Are All Set to Grab Your Metadata'.

102 Author's interview with former RICA judge Yvonne Mokgoro, 22 September 2017.

103 Author's interview with Charles Nqakula, 13 November 2017.

104 Joint Standing Committee on Intelligence, 'Annual Report of the Joint Standing Committee on Intelligence for the Financial Year Ending 31 March 2016', National Assembly and National Council of Provinces Committee Reports, 13 December 2016, http://pmg-assets.s3-website-eu-west-1.amazonaws.com/intelligence.pdf (accessed 1 September 2017).

105 Duncan, 'Spies Are All Set to Grab Your Metadata'.

106 United Nations Human Rights Committee, 'Concluding Observations on the Initial Report of South Africa' (report of the committee in terms of the International Covenant on Civil and Political Rights), 27 April 2016, http://tbinternet.ohchr.org/_layouts/treatybodyexternal/Download.aspx?symbolno=CCPR%2fC%2fZAF%2fCO%2f1&Lang=en (accessed 27 February 2017).

107 United Nations Human Rights Committee, 'Concluding Observations on the Initial Report of South Africa'.

108 United Nations Human Rights Committee, 'Concluding Observations on the Initial Report of South Africa'.

109 News24, 'SA Votes against Internet Freedoms in UN Resolution', *Daily Maverick*, 4 July 2016, http://www.dailymaverick.co.za/article/2016-07-04-sa-votes-against-internet-freedoms-in-un-resolution/#.V6sFUFt97IU (accessed 10 August 2016).

110 Gareth van Zyl, 'Why South Africa Voted against Internet Freedoms at the UN', *Fin-24Tech*, 7 May 2016, http://www.fin24.com/Tech/News/why-sa-voted-against-internet-freedoms-at-the-un-20160705 (accessed 17 January 2017).

111 Rebecca Davis, 'What's South Africa's Anti-Human Rights Game at the UN?', *Daily Maverick*, 29 March 2015, http://www.dailymaverick.co.za/article/2015-03-29-analysis-whats-south-africas-anti-human-rights-game-at-the-un/#.V6sG8Ft97IU (accessed 10 August 2016).

112 Davis, 'What's South Africa's Anti-Human Rights Game at the UN?'

113 Swart, 'Communications Surveillance by the South African Intelligence Services', 10.

114 Patrick Bond, 'Subimperialism as Lubricant of Neoliberalism: South African "Deputy Sheriff" Duty within BRICS', *Third World Quarterly* 34, no. 2 (2013): 251–70.

CHAPTER 6

1   Electronic Frontier Foundation, 'The Problem with Mobile Phones', Surveillance Self Defence (web-based resource), https://ssd.eff.org/en/module/problem-mobile-phones (accessed 12 June 2015).

2   Privacy Commission of New Zealand, 'Privacy and CCTV: A Guide to the Privacy Act for Businesses, Agencies and Organisations' (booklet), 2009, https://www.privacy.org.nz/assets/Files/Brochures-and-pamphlets-and-pubs/Privacy-and-CCTV-A-guide-October-2009.pdf (accessed 12 June 2015).

3   Robert Ellis Smith, 'Sometimes What's Public Is Private: Legal Rights to Privacy in Public Spaces', in *Eyes Everywhere: The Global Growth of Camera Surveillance*, ed. Aaron Doyle, Randy Lippert and David Lyon (London: Routledge, 2012), 370–9.

4   Office of the Information Commissioner of Queensland, 'Camera Surveillance and Privacy', undated web page, https://www.oic.qld.gov.au/guidelines/for-government/guidelines-privacy-principles/applying-the-privacy-principles/camera-surveillance-and-privacy (accessed 25 January 2017); Privacy Commissioner of New Zealand, 'Privacy and CCTV'.

5   Will Knight, 'CCTV Footage Shows London Suicide Bombers', *New Scientist*, 13 July 2005, https://www.newscientist.com/article/dn7669-cctv-footage-shows-london-suicide-bombers/ (accessed 22 January 2017).

6   Patrick Derby, 'Policing in the Information Age: Automated Number Plate Recognition', in *Eyes Everywhere: The Global Growth of Camera Surveillance*, ed. Aaron Doyle, Randy Lippert and David Lyon (London: Routledge, 2012), 157.

7   Derby, 'Policing in the Information Age', 157.

8   Liberty, 'CCTV and ANPR', undated web page, https://www.liberty-human-rights.org.uk/human-rights/privacy/cctv-and-anpr (accessed 22 January 2017).

9   No CCTV, 'What's Wrong with ANPR?' (booklet), October 2013, http://www.no-cctv.org.uk/docs/Whats%20Wrong%20With%20ANPR-No%20CCTV%20Report.pdf (accessed 21 January 2017).

10   Aaron Doyle, Randy Lippert and David Lyon, eds., *Eyes Everywhere: The Global Growth of Camera Surveillance* (London: Routledge, 2012), 1–20.

11 'Axing CCTV in London Is a "Crazy Idea", Counter-Terrorism Expert Tells RT', *RT*, 25 August 2016, https://www.rt.com/uk/357160-cctv-cameras-london-terrorism/ (accessed 25 January 2017).

12 'CCTV Cameras Could Be Axed by Westminster Council to Save 1.7 Million Pounds', *BBC News*, 1 June 2016, http://www.bbc.com/news/uk-england-london-36425885 (accessed 24 January 2017).

13 Clive Norris, 'There's No Success Like Failure and Failure's No Success at All: Some Critical Reflections on Understanding the Global Growth of CCTV Surveillance', in *Eyes Everywhere: The Global Growth of Camera Surveillance*, ed. Aaron Doyle, Randy Lippert and David Lyon (London: Routledge, 2012), 33–40.

14 Norris, 'There's No Success Like Failure', 37.

15 Norris, 'There's No Success Like Failure', 33–40.

16 Derby, 'Policing in the Information Age', 167.

17 Derby, 'Policing in the Information Age', 161.

18 Robert Gurney, Michael Rhead, Soodamani Ramalingam and Vivienne Lyons, 'The Effect of ANPR Camera Settings on System Performance', 5th International Conference on Imaging for Crime Detection and Prevention, 1 January 2013, http://researchprofiles.herts.ac.uk/portal/files/2684800/The_effect_of_ANPR_Camera_Settings_on_System_Performance_RG_MR.pdf (accessed 23 January 2017).

19 Mike Rhead, Robert Gurney, Soodamani Ramalingam and Neil Cohen, 'Accuracy of Automatic Number Plate Recognition (ANPR) and Real World UK Number Plate Problems', Proceedings of the 46th IEEE International Carnahan Conference on Security Technology, Boston, United States, 15–18 October 2012, https://pdfs.semanticscholar.org/d529/3335eb75e4b3898c6e6d428570e0583c4db9.pdf (accessed 23 January 2017).

20 No CCTV, 'What's Wrong with ANPR?'

21 Independent Police Complaints Commission, 'IPCC Publishes Findings from Investigation into Police Responses to ANPR Intelligence on Peter Chapman' (media release), 11 February 2011, https://www.ipcc.gov.uk/news/ipcc-publishes-findings-investigation-police-response-anpr-intelligence-peter-chapman (accessed 23 January 2017).

22 James Bridle, 'How Britain Exported Next Generation Surveillance', *Medium*, 18 December 2013, https://medium.com/matter/how-britain-exported-next-generation-surveillance-d15b5801b79e#.2diooz7ix (accessed 23 January 2017).

23 Derby, 'Policing in the Information Age', 165.

24 Matthew Wall, 'Is Facial Recognition Tech Really a Threat to Privacy?', *BBC News*, 19 June 2015, http://www.bbc.com/news/technology-33199275 (accessed 23 January 2017).

25 Office of the Privacy Commissioner of Canada, 'Automated Facial Recognition in the Public and Private Sectors' (report), March 2013, 4, https://www.priv.gc.ca/media/1765/fr_201303_e.pdf (accessed 23 January 2017).

26 Clare Garvie, Alvaro Bedoya and Jonathan Frankle, 'The Perpetual Line-Up: Unregulated Police Face Recognition in America', Georgetown Law Center on Privacy and Technology, 18 October 2016, https://www.perpetuallineup.org/ (accessed 24 January 2017).

27 Brendan Klare, Mark J. Burge, Joshua C. Klontz, Richard W.V. Bruegge and Anil K. Jain, 'Face Recognition Performance: Role of Demographic Information', *IEEE Transactions on Information Forensics and Security* 7 (December 2012): 1789–1801, https://assets.documentcloud.org/documents/2850196/Face-Recognition-Performance-Role-of-Demographic.pdf (accessed 24 January 2017).

28   Garvie, Bedoya and Frankle, 'The Perpetual Line-Up'.

29   Anthony Minnaar, 'The Growth and Further Proliferation of Camera Surveillance in South Africa', in *Eyes Everywhere: The Global Growth of Camera Surveillance*, ed. Aaron Doyle, Randy Lippert and David Lyon (London: Routledge, 2012), 100–21.

30   Anthony Minnaar, 'The Implementation and Impact of Crime Prevention/Crime Control Open Street Closed Circuit Television Surveillance in South African Central Business Districts', *Surveillance and Society* 4, no. 3 (2007): 174–207.

31   Minnaar, 'The Growth and Further Proliferation of Camera Surveillance in South Africa', 103–4.

32   Minnaar, 'The Implementation and Impact of Crime Prevention', 174–207.

33   Lorraine Glanz and Fatima Nacerodien, 'An Assessment of Closed-Circuit Television Surveillance with Reference to the Benoni Project', Directorate: Policy Monitoring, South African Police Service (undated report), http://www.policesecretariat.gov.za/downloads/reports/cctv.pdf (accessed 12 June 2015).

34   Masa Kekana, 'City of JHB Installs Smart Cameras around City', *EyeWitness News*, 26 June 2016, http://ewn.co.za/2016/06/26/City-of-JHB-installs-smart-cameras-around-city (accessed 24 January 2017).

35   Johannesburg Metropolitan Police Department, 'CCTV Surveillance Project', City of Johannesburg website (undated), http://www.joburg.org.za/index.php?option=com_content&id=702&limitstart=2 (accessed 24 January 2017).

36   Adam Wakefield, 'Multi-Million Rand CCTV System Hits Crime Hard in CBD, *News24*, 14 August 2015, http://www.news24.com/SouthAfrica/News/Multi-million-rand-CCTV-system-hits-crime-hard-in-Joburg-CBD-20150814 (accessed 24 January 2017).

37   Jo'burg City Safety Strategy Programme (JCSP), 'Evaluation of the Impact of the CoJ Surveillance System on Safety and Security in the Johannesburg Inner City. Johannesburg City Safety Programme', 2012.

38   City of Johannesburg, 'Camera Positions in Johannesburg', list of CCTV cameras provided by the city in response to a Promotion of Access to Information Act request by the South Africa History Archive, 22 September 2017.

39   Thembisa Zwane, 'Affidavit of Deputy Information Officer, City of Johannesburg', affidavit released in response to Promotion of Access to Information Act request from the South African History Archive, 22 September 2017.

40   Discussion with Wayne Minnaar, JMPD CCTV control room, Sophiatown, Johannesburg, 26 October 2017.

41   'Forensic Investigation into Jo'burg's R1.3bn Fibre Network', *Business Day*, 10 March 2017, https://www.businesslive.co.za/bd/national/2017-03-10-forensic-investigation-into-joburgs-r13bn-fibre-network/ (accessed 27 October 2017).

42   Discussion with Wayne Minnaar, 26 October 2017.

43   Discussion with Wayne Minnaar, 26 October 2017.

44   Discussion with Wayne Minnaar, 26 October 2017.

45   Discussion with Wayne Minnaar, 26 October 2017.

46   Discussion with Wayne Minnaar, 26 October 2017.

47   Ridwan Wagiet, 'City of Cape Town Metropolitan Police Department, Master Plan for an Integrated Closed Circuit Television (CCTV) System for the City of Cape Town', revised, http://www.khayelitshacommission.org.za/bundles/category/29-10-city-of-cape-town-documents-coi.html?download=554:cctv%20master%20plan%20ammended%202012jan, 2011.

48   Catherine O'Regan and Vusumzi Pikoli, 'Towards a Safer Khayelitsha', August 2014, http://www.saflii.org/khayelitshacommissionreport.pdf (accessed 24 January 2017).

49   Nora Ní Loideain, 'Cape Town as a Smart and Safe City: Implications for Governance and Data Privacy' (2017) 7(4) *International Data Privacy Law* 314.

50   Murray Williams, 'Cape Town's CCTV Ring of Steel', *Independent Online*, 16 October 2014, http://www.iol.co.za/news/crime-courts/cape-towns-cctv-ring-of-steel-1766209 (accessed 25 January 2017).

51   City of Cape Town, 'Regulation of External and Privately Owned CCTV Cameras on City Property', Policy Number 21207, approved by Council, 25 June 2014, http://resource.capetown.gov.za/documentcentre/Documents/Bylaws%20and%20policies/Regulation%20of%20External%20and%20Privately%20Owned%20CCTV%20Cameras%20on%20City%20Property%20-%20(Policy%20number%2021207)%20approved%20on%2025%20June%202014.pdf (accessed 25 January 2017).

52   Anel Lewis, 'Cape Mulls Policy on CCTV Footage', *Independent Online*, 9 June 2014, http://www.iol.co.za/news/crime-courts/cape-mulls-policy-on-cctv-cameras-1700602 (accessed 24 January 2017).

53   O'Regan and Pikoli, 'Towards a Safer Khayelitsha'.

54   'SA Police Not Using CCTV Footage to Catch Criminals', *BusinessTech*, 5 February 2016, https://businesstech.co.za/news/technology/111529/sa-police-not-using-cctv-footage-to-catch-criminals-da/ (accessed 25 January 2017).

55   Minnaar, 'The Implementation and Impact of Crime Prevention', 174–207.

56   Emma Thelwell, 'Police Not Using Khayelitsha CCTV to Catch Criminals', *News24*, 27 August 2014, http://www.news24.com/SouthAfrica/News/Police-not-using-Khayelitsha-CCTV-to-catch-criminals-20140827 (accessed 25 January 2017).

57   Ní Loideain, 'Cape Town as a Smart and Safe City'.

58   Ní Loideain, 'Cape Town as a Smart and Safe City'.

59   Ní Loideain, 'Cape Town as a Smart and Safe City'.

60   Erin Hommes and Marlene Holmner, 'Intelligent Transport Systems: Privacy, Security, and Societal Considerations within the Gauteng Case Study', *Innovation* 46 (June 2013): 192–206.

61   Andrew J. Blumberg and Peter Eckersley, 'On Location Privacy, and How to Avoid Losing It Forever', blog post, 3 August 2009, https://www.eff.org/wp/locational-privacy (accessed 7 March 2017).

62   Blumberg and Eckersley, 'On Location Privacy'.

63   Advisory Panel Appointed by Gauteng Premier Mr David Makhura, 'The Socio-Economic Impact of the Gauteng Improvement Project and E-Tolls Report', 30 November 2014, http://www.gautengonline.gov.za/Campaign%20Documents/Report%20of%20eToll%20Panel.pdf (accessed 7 March 2017).

64   Advisory Panel, 'The Socio-Economic Impact of the Gauteng Improvement Project and E-Tolls Report'.

65   Raluca A. Popa, Hari Balakrishnan and Andrew J. Blumberg, 'VPriv: Protecting Privacy in Location-Based Vehicular Services', *Proceedings of the 18th Conference on USENIX Security Symposium*, Montreal, Canada, 10–14 August 2009, 335–50, http://math.stanford.edu/~blumberg/traffic/vpriv.pdf (accessed 7 March 2017); Andrew J. Blumberg and Robin Chase, 'Electronic Tolling and Locational Privacy: How to Make EX-Pass Preserve Locational Privacy', unpublished paper, http://math.stanford.edu/~blumberg/traffic/secureEZ.pdf (accessed 7 March 2017).

66 Josep Balasch, Carmela Tronsoco and Alfredo Rial, 'Privacy Preserving Road Charging', undated blog, https://cosic.esat.kuleuven.be/road_charging/pretp.html (accessed 7 March 2017).

67 Blumberg and Eckersley, 'On Location Privacy'.

68 Jan Vermeulen, 'E-Toll Website Flaw a Cyber-attack', MyBroadband.com, 8 January 2014, https://mybroadband.co.za/news/security/94554-e-toll-website-flaw-a-cyber-attack-sanral.html (accessed 25 January 2017).

69 Dale McKinley, 'New Terrains of Privacy in South Africa' (monograph), Right2Know Campaign and Media Policy and Democracy Project, 2016, 11, http://www.r2k.org.za/wp-content/uploads/Monograph_New_Terrains_of_Privacy_in_South_Africa_2016.pdf (accessed 25 January 2017); Nicola Mawson, 'Millions Wasted on eNatis', ITWeb, 29 January 2013, http://www.itweb.co.za/index.php?option=com_content&view=article&id=61386 (accessed 25 January 2017).

70 McKinley, 'New Terrains of Privacy in South Africa', 11.

71 Shain Germaner, 'E-Toll Data Too Flawed for Court', Independent Online, 25 November 2014, http://www.iol.co.za/motoring/industry-news/e-toll-data-too-flawed-for-court-1785813 (accessed 25 January 2017).

72 Jessica Purkiss and Jack Searle, 'Obama's Covert Drone Wars in Numbers: Ten Times More Strikes than Bush', Bureau of Investigative Journalism, 17 January 2017, https://www.thebureauinvestigates.com/2017/01/17/obamas-covert-drone-war-numbers-ten-times-strikes-bush/ (accessed 26 January 2017).

73 Jay Stanley and Catherine Crump, 'Protecting Privacy from Aerial Surveillance: Recommendations for Government Use of Drone Aircraft' (report), American Civil Liberties Union, December 2011, https://www.aclu.org/files/assets/protectingprivacyfromaerialsurveillance.pdf (accessed 28 January 2017).

74 Devin Coldeway, 'Drone outside Window Spooks Seattle Woman but Cops Say No Law Broken', NBC News, 24 June 2014, http://www.nbcnews.com/tech/tech-news/drone-outside-window-spooks-seattle-woman-cops-say-no-law-n139626 (accessed 26 January 2017).

75 Stanley and Crump, 'Protecting Privacy from Aerial Surveillance'.

76 Electronic Frontier Foundation, 'Public Comments of the Electronic Frontier Foundation Regarding Proposed Privacy Requirements for the Unmanned Aircraft System Test Site Programme' (submission), submitted on 23 April 2013 to the Federal Aviation Administration, https://www.eff.org/document/effs-comments-faa (accessed 28 January 2017).

77 Daneel Knoetze, 'Game of Drones: City Tests Underway', GroundUp, 3 December 2014, http://www.groundup.org.za/article/game-drones-city-tests-underway_2497/ (accessed 28 January 2017).

78 Knoetze, 'Game of Drones'.

79 Mark Rotenberg, 'Civil Society Letter to Michael P. Huerta, Acting Administrator, United States Federal Aviation Administration', 24 February 2012, https://epic.org/privacy/drones/FAA-553e-Petition-v-1.1.pdf (accessed 27 January 2017).

80 Civil Aviation Authority, 'Proposed Amendment of the Civil Aviation Regulations, 2011', 11 December 2014, http://www.uasvision.com/wp-content/uploads/2014/12/SA-CAA-101-DECEMBER-2014-publication.pdf (accessed 27 January 2017).

81 Department of Transport, 'Civil Aviation Act, 2009 (Act no. 13 of 2009), Eighth Amendment of the Civil Aviation Regulations, 2015', no. 38830, 27 May 2015, http://www.gov.za/sites/www.gov.za/files/38830_rg10437_gon444.pdf (accessed 29 January 2017).

82   Department of Transport, 'Civil Aviation Act, 2009'.

83   McKinley, 'New Terrains of Privacy in South Africa', 13.

84   McKinley, 'New Terrains of Privacy in South Africa', 13.

85   David Smith, 'Pepper-Spray Drones Offered to South African Mines for Strike Control', *The Guardian*, 20 June 2014, https://www.theguardian.com/world/2014/jun/20/pepper-spray-drone-offered-south-african-mines-strike-control (accessed 28 January 2017).

86   South African Civil Aviation Authority, 'Request for Access to Records: List of All Organisations and Individuals That Have Applied for Licences to Operate Remotely Piloted Aircrafts (or Drones) in Terms of the 2015 Amendments to the Civil Aviation Regulations', 9 June 2017, record released in response to a Promotion of Access to Information Act request from the South African History Archive.

CHAPTER 7

1   Hillary Clinton, 'Reporting and Collection Needs: The United Nations' (leaked diplomatic communiqué), 31 July 2009, WikiLeaks, https://wikileaks.org/plusd/cables/09STATE80163_a.html#efmJZLJeM (accessed 25 January 2017).

2   James Risen and Laura Poitras, 'NSA Collecting Millions of Faces from Web Images', *New York Times*, 31 May 2014, https://www.nytimes.com/2014/06/01/us/nsa-collecting-millions-of-faces-from-web-images.html?_r=1 (accessed 25 January 2017).

3   Keith Breckenridge, *Biometric State: The Global Politics of Identification and Surveillance* (Cambridge: Cambridge University Press, 2014), 12.

4   Tomer Zarchin, 'Population Database Hacked in 2006 Reached the Internet', *Haaretz*, 25 October 2011, http://www.haaretz.com/population-database-hacked-in-2006-reached-the-internet-1.391812 (accessed 7 March 2017).

5   Dini Lallah, 'The Slippery National Identity Card', *Le Mauricien*, 14 October 2015, http://www.lemauricien.com/article/slippery-national-identity-card (accessed 7 March 2017).

6   Privacy International, 'State of Privacy: India' (monograph), 4 November 2016, https://www.privacyinternational.org/node/975#toc-6 (accessed 30 January 2017).

7   Kevin P. Donovan, 'The Biometric Imaginary: Bureaucratic Technopolitics in Posta-partheid Welfare', *Journal of Southern African Studies* 41, no. 4 (2015): 815–33.

8   Constitutional Court of South Africa, 'AllPay Consolidated Investment Holdings (Pty) Ltd', Case CCT 48/13, 17 April 2014, http://www.saflii.org/za/cases/ZACC/2014/12.pdf (accessed 2 February 2017).

9   Craig McKune, '"Name Your Price" Bribe Offer for R7 Billion Tender', amaBhungane Centre for Investigative Journalism, http://amabhungane.co.za/article/2012-02-24-name-your-price-bribe-offer-for-r7billion-rand-tender (accessed 2 February 2017).

10   George Tillmann, 'Stolen Fingers: The Case against Biometric Identity Theft Protection', *Computerworld*, 27 October 2009, http://www.computerworld.com/article/2528553/it-management/opinion–stolen-fingers–the-case-against-biometric-identity-theft-protection.html (accessed 7 May 2017).

11   Siyabonga Mdodi, 'SASSA's Biometric Requirements Too Onerous: SACP Eastern Cape' (press release), 29 April 2014, http://www.politicsweb.co.za/politics/sassas-biometric-requirements-too-onerous–sacp-ec (accessed 30 January 2017).

12   Ratula Beukman, 'SASSA's New Technology Fails Grant Beneficiary', undated blog, Black Sash, http://www.blacksash.org.za/index.php/media-and-publications/

in-our-opinion/1528-sassa-s-new-technology-fails-grant-beneficiary (accessed 30 January 2017).

13 Natasha Vally, 'Insecurity in South African Social Security: An Examination of Social Grant Deductions, Cancellations and Waiting', *Journal of Southern African Studies* 42, no. 5 (2016): 965–82.

14 Parliamentary Monitoring Group, 'Grant Payment Insourcing: SASSA Progress Report, with Minister', minutes of meeting of Parliamentary Portfolio Committee on Social Development, 30 November 2016, https://pmg.org.za/committee-meeting/23795/?via=cte-menu (accessed 30 January 2017).

15 Parliamentary Monitoring Group, 'Grant Payment Insourcing: SASSA Progress Report, with Minister'.

16 Department of Social Development, 'Biometrics Makes Grants Easy and Fraud Free', *Vukuzenzele*, July 2012, http://www.vukuzenzele.gov.za/biometrics-makes-grants-easy-and-fraud-free (accessed 3 February 2017).

17 Kgomoco Diseko, 'SASSA Statement on Pressing Charges against Financial Service Providers' (press statement), 15 June 2016, http://www.sassa.gov.za/index.php/newsroom/207-sassa-statement-on-pressing-charges-against-financial-services-providers (accessed 3 February 2017).

18 Ben Stanwix, 'Social Grants: State Decides Not to Award Tender', *GroundUp*, 16 October 2015, http://www.groundup.org.za/article/social-grants-state-decides-not-award-tender_3407/ (accessed 3 February 2017).

19 Donovan, 'The Biometric Imaginary', 815–33.

20 David Lyon and Özgün E. Topak, 'Promoting Global Identification: Corporations, IGOs and ID Card Systems', in *Routledge Handbook of Surveillance Studies*, ed. Kirstie Ball, Kevin D. Haggerty and David Lyon (London: Routledge, 2012), 27–43.

21 Simnikiwe Mzekandaba, 'Possible Delays in Smart ID Rollout', *IT Web*, 24 July 2015, http://www.itweb.co.za/index.php?option=com_content&view=article&id=144937:Possible-delay-in-smart-ID-rollout&catid=234 (accessed 7 February 2017).

22 Keith Breckenridge, 'The Elusive Panopticon: The HANIS Project and the Politics of Standards in South Africa', in *Playing the Identity Card: Surveillance, Security and Identification in Global Perspective*, ed. Colin J. Bennett and David Lyon (London: Routledge, 2008), 39–56.

23 Nicolas Pejout, 'World Wide Weber: Formalise, Normalise, Rationalise: E-Government for Welfare State – Perspectives from South Africa', in *Electronic Constitution: Social, Cultural and Political Implications*, ed. Francesco Amoterri (New York: Information Science Reference, 2009), 99–114.

24 Selene Brophy, "Digitising SA: DHA and Stats SA Partner to Modernise 286+ Million Civil Records', 23 November 2016, http://traveller24.news24.com/TravelPlanning/VisaInfo/digitising-sa-dha-and-stat-sa-partner-to-modernise-289-million-civil-records-20161123 (accessed 7 February 2017).

25 Lallah, 'The Slippery National Identity Card'.

26 Breckenridge, *Biometric State*, 12.

27 Internal Question Paper no. 17 of 2012, asked by Mr M.S.F. de Freitas (DA) to the Minister of Home Affairs, reply received on August 2012, published on 1 June 2012.

28 Chantall Presence, 'Four Million South Africans Have Smart IDs', *Independent Online*, 22 April 2016, http://www.iol.co.za/news/south-africa/four-million-south-africans-have-smart-ids-2013360 (accessed 3 February 2017).

29   Lee Rondganger, 'Home Affairs ID Frustration', 19 January 2016, http://www.iol.co.za/news/south-africa/kwazulu-natal/home-affairs-id-frustration-1973108 (accessed 3 February 2017).

30   Parliamentary Monitoring Group, 'Using Banks for Smart ID Card Applications', Parliamentary Portfolio Committee on Home Affairs minutes of briefing by the Department of Home Affairs, 21 April 2015, https://pmg.org.za/committee-meeting/20712/ (accessed 7 February 2017).

31   Author's interview with Thulani Mavuso, Deputy Director of Institutional Planning and Support, Department of Home Affairs, Pretoria, 28 November 2017.

32   Jan Vermeulen, 'Anonymous Taking a Long Hard Look at South Africa: SAPS Hacker', *MyBroadband.com*, 17 June 2013, https://mybroadband.co.za/news/security/78979-anonymous-taking-a-long-hard-look-at-south-africa-saps-hacker.html (accessed 3 February 2017); Jan Vermeulen, 'Anonymous Hacks SA Government Database', *MyBroadband.com*, 12 February 2016, https://mybroadband.co.za/news/security/155030-anonymous-hacks-sa-government-database.html (accessed 3 February 2017).

33   Ian Steadman, 'Anonymous Hacks Police Site, Releases List of South African Whistleblowers', *Wired*, 22 May 2013, http://www.wired.co.uk/article/south-africa-whistleblower-leak (accessed 3 February 2017).

34   Nico Gous, 'Private Records of 31.6 Million South Africans Removed from the Internet', *The Times*, 18 October 2017, https://www.timeslive.co.za/news/south-africa/2017-10-18-private-information-of-around-316m-south-africans-breached-still-online/ (accessed 28 November 2017).

35   Author's interview with Thulani Mavuso, 28 November 2017.

36   Lyon and Topak, 'Promoting Global Identification', 27–43.

37   Duncan Alfreds, 'New SA ID Card Is at Risk of Theft, Expert Warns', *News24*, 17 October 2013, http://www.news24.com/Technology/News/New-SA-ID-card-is-at-risk-of-theft-expert-warns-20131007 (accessed 7 February 2017).

38   Project Losika, 'Asylum at a Price: How Corruption Impacts Those Seeking Asylum in South Africa' (report), Corruption Watch, 2 December 2016, https://www.corruptionwatch.org.za/wp-content/uploads/2016/12/Project-Lokisa-Digital-FINALRRU-Logo-2Dec2016.pdf (accessed 7 February 2017).

39   S.21(1), Identification Act 68 of 1997, *Government Gazette* no. 18485, http://www.gov.za/sites/www.gov.za/files/a68-97.pdf (accessed 7 February 2017).

40   Deneesha Pillay, 'ID and Passport Fraud Likely to Increase', *Herald*, 29 July 2015, http://www.heraldlive.co.za/news/2015/07/29/id-passport-fraud-likely-increase/ (accessed 7 February 2017).

41   Parliamentary Monitoring Group, 'Criminal Justice System (CJS) Modernisation: Follow-Up Meeting with SAPS and Its Stakeholders' (minutes of meeting), Portfolio Committee on Police, 10 June 2015, http://dnaproject.co.za/new_dna/wp-content/uploads/2015/06/Meeting-minutes-10-June-2015.pdf (accessed 7 February 2017).

42   Breckenridge, 'The Elusive Panopticon', 50–3.

43   Selene Brophy, 'Home Affairs Modernised: Data Intelligence with Far Reaching Effects', *Traveller24*, 19 May 2016, http://traveller24.news24.com/TravelPlanning/VisaInfo/home-affairs-modernised-data-intelligence-with-far-reaching-effects-20160519 (accessed 7 February 2017).

44   Author's interview with Thulani Mavuso, 28 November 2017.

45   Author's interview with Thulani Mavuso, 28 November 2017.

46 Centre on Privacy and Technology, 'The Perpetual Line-Up: Unregulated Police Face Recognition in America', Georgetown Law, 18 October 2016, 3, https://www.perpetuallineup.org/sites/default/files/2016-12/The%20Perpetual%20Line-Up%20-%20Center%20on%20Privacy%20and%20Technology%20at%20Georgetown%20Law%20-%20121616.pdf (accessed 28 November 2017).

47 Centre on Privacy and Technology, 'The Perpetual Line-Up'.

48 Gabi Falanga, 'No ID Card – and No Vote – for Irate SA Man', *Independent Online*, 2 August 2016, http://www.iol.co.za/news/politics/no-id-card–and-no-vote–for-irate-sa-man-2052444 (accessed 7 February 2017).

49 Author's interview with Thulani Mavuso, 28 November 2017.

50 Liesl Muller, 'ID Blocking: A Growing Threat to Nationality' (blog), Lawyers for Human Rights, 5 September 2013, http://www.lhr.org.za/blog/2013/9/id-blocking-growing-threat-nationality (accessed 7 February 2017).

51 Peter Adey, 'Borders, Identification and Surveillance: New Regimes of Border Control', in *Routledge Handbook of Surveillance Studies*, ed. Kirstie Ball, Kevin D. Haggerty and David Lyon (London: Routledge, 2012), 194–5.

52 Malusi Gigaba, 'Statement by Home Affairs Minister Malusi Gigaba during the Inspection of the Pilot Project on Biometric Capturing at Ports of Entry: OR Tambo International Airport' (speech), Ministry of Home Affairs of South Africa, 15 December 2015, http://www.home-affairs.gov.za/index.php/statements-speeches/721-statement-by-home-affairs-minister-malusi-gigaba-during-the-inspection-of-the-pilot-project-on-biometric-capturing-at-ports-of-entry-or-tambo-international-airport (accessed 25 January 2017).

53 Masa Kekana, 'South Africans Exempt from International Airports Biometric System', 7 July 2016, http://ewn.co.za/2016/07/07/South-Africans-exempt-from-international-airports-biometric-system (accessed 25 January 2017).

54 Admire Moyo, 'Home Affairs Blames Biometrics Glitch for Airport Chaos', 12 July 2016, http://www.defenceweb.co.za/index.php?option=com_content&view=article&id=44233:home-affairs-blames-biometrics-glitch-for-airport-chaos&catid=87:border-security&Itemid=188 (accessed 27 January 2017).

55 Guy Friday, 'The Only Way to Protect South Africa's Borders Is to Develop a Clear Border Control Policy: Expert', *DefenceWeb*, 4 March 2011, http://defenceweb.co.za/index.php?option=com_content&view=article&id=13932:the-only-way-to-protect-south-africas-borders-is-to-develop-a-clear-border-control-policy–expert&catid=87:border-security&Itemid=188 (accessed 20 August 2013).

56 'Border Management Agency Supersized?', *Defence Web*, 8 June 2011, http://www.defenceweb.co.za/index.php?option=com_content&view=article&id=16057:border-management-agency-supersized-&catid=87:border-security&Itemid=188 (accessed 20 August 2013).

57 Kim Helfrich, 'SANDF Border Protection Paying Dividends', *DefenceWeb*, 13 March 2014, http://www.defenceweb.co.za/index.php?option=com_content&view=article&id=33974:sandf-border-protection-deployment-paying-dividends&catid=111:-sa-defence (accessed 26 January 2017).

58 TMG Digital, 'Immigration Officials Intercepted IS Suspect at OR Tambo, Says Gigaba', 18 January 2017, http://www.dispatchlive.co.za/news/2017/01/18/update-immigration-officers-intercepted-suspect-tambo-says-gigaba/ (accessed 26 January 2017).

59 Loyiso Sidimba and Candice Bailey, 'Gwede's Swedish Diplomatic Row', *Independent Online*, 23 March 2013, http://www.iol.co.za/news/politics/gwedes-swedish-diplo-

matic-row-1536159 (accessed 7 March 2017); Genevieve Quintal, 'SA Needs Refugee Camps: Mantashe', 13 April 2015, http://www.news24.com/SouthAfrica/News/SA-needs-refugee-camps-Mantashe-20150412 (accessed 7 March 2017).

60   Bongani Hans, 'King's Anti-Foreigner Speech Causes Alarm', *Independent Online*, 23 March 2015, http://www.iol.co.za/news/politics/kings-anti-foreigner-speech-causes-alarm-1835602 (accessed 7 March 2017).

61   South African Broadcasting Corporation, 'SA Troops to Be Deployed at Border Posts', *SABC Online*, 16 April 2016, http://www.sabc.co.za/news/a/e96d780048094de-9a605e678423ca9af/%28Over-350-army-officers-set-to-be-deployed-at-border-posts-20151604 (accessed 7 March 2017).

62   Greg Nicholson, 'Operation Fiela: Thousands of Arrests, Doubtful Impact', *Daily Maverick*, 8 September 2015, https://www.dailymaverick.co.za/article/2015-09-08-operation-fiela-thousands-of-arrests-doubtful-impact/#.WItIp9J97IU (accessed 25 January 2017).

63   'Mapisa-Nqakula Wishes for a Defence Budget That Is Two Percent of GDP', *DefenceWeb*, 25 May 2015, http://www.defenceweb.co.za/index.php?option=com_content&view=article&id=39213:mapisa-nqakula-wishes-for-a-defence-budget-that-is-two-percent-of-gdp&catid=111:sa-defence&Itemid=242 (accessed 7 March 2017).

64   Kate Wilkinson, 'Are Foreigners Stealing Jobs in South Africa?', *Africa Check*, 8 February 2015, https://africacheck.org/2015/02/08/analysis-are-foreigners-stealing-jobs-in-south-africa-2/ (accessed 7 March 2017).

65   Moipone Malefane, 'ANC Favours Opening Up SA Borders', *Sowetan Live*, 31 May 2013, http://www.sowetanlive.co.za/news/2013/05/31/anc-favours-opening-up-sa-borders (accessed 7 March 2017).

66   Selene Brophy, 'Biometric Data Bottleneck to Cause OR Tambo "Festive Season Havoc"', *Traveller24*, 24 October 2016, http://traveller24.news24.com/TravelPlanning/VisaInfo/biometric-data-bottleneck-expected-to-cause-festive-season-delays-havoc-20161024 (accessed 25 January 2017).

67   Donovan, 'The Biometric Imaginary', 815–33.

68   Breckenridge, *Biometric State*.

CHAPTER 8

1   American Association of University Professors, 'Academic Freedom and Electronic Communications' (report), 2013, https://www.aaup.org/report/academic-freedom-and-electronic-communications-2014 (accessed 30 May 2016).

2   Bar Council and Law Society, 'Investigatory Powers and Legal Professional Privilege', position paper developed in response to the Draft Investigatory Powers Bill, October 2015, file:///C:/Users/jduncan/Downloads/position-paper-investigatory-powers-legal-professional-privilege-october-2015.pdf (accessed 27 June 2016); Michelle Stanistreet, 'The Government Is Using Terrorism as an Excuse to Spy on Journalists', *The Guardian*, 14 March 2016, file:///C:/Users/jduncan/Downloads/position-paper-investigatory-powers-legal-professional-privilege-october-2015.pdf (accessed 27 June 2016).

3   British Government, 'Investigatory Powers Bill: Protections for Communications Involving Sensitive Professions' (factsheet), 2015, https://www.gov.uk/government/uploads/system/uploads/attachment_data/file/530562/Protections_for_Sensitive_Professions_Factsheet.pdf (accessed 27 June 2016).

4   Lyon, D, 'National IDs in a Global World: Surveillance, Security and Citizenship', *Case Western Reserve Journal of International Law* 42, no. 3 (2010): 607–23 http://scholarly-commons.law.case.edu/cgi/viewcontent.cgi?article=1247&context=jil, 607 (accessed 20 July 2016).

5   Admire Mare's interview with *Sunday Times* journalist, *Sunday Times* offices, Rosebank, Johannesburg, 7 October 2015.

6   Admire Mare's interview with *Sunday Times* journalist, 7 October 2015.

7   Admire Mare's interview with *Sunday Times* journalist, 7 October 2015.

8   Admire Mare's email interview with journalist, 20 October 2015.

9   Admire Mare's email interview with journalist, 27 October 2015.

10   Sarah Evans, 'Marikana Service Delivery Researchers Spooked', *Mail & Guardian*, 7 March 2014, http://mg.co.za/article/2014-03-06-marikana-service-delivery-researchers-spooked (accessed 27 July 2016).

11   Admire Mare's interview with three academics attached to the South African Research Chair in Social Change, University of Johannesburg, Bunting Road campus, 9 October 2015.

12   Admire Mare's interview with three academics attached to the South African Research Chair in Social Change, 9 October 2015.

13   Admire Mare's interview with three academics attached to the South African Research Chair in Social Change, 9 October 2015.

14   Admire Mare's interview with three academics attached to the South African Research Chair in Social Change, 9 October 2015.

15   Admire Mare's interview with three academics attached to the South African Research Chair in Social Change, 9 October 2015.

16   Admire Mare's interview with three academics attached to the South African Research Chair in Social Change, 9 October 2015.

17   Admire Mare's email interview with academic, 18 October 2015.

18   The Right2Know Campaign is an activist-driven campaign focusing on the rights of access to information, freedom of expression and the right to protest. Formed in 2010 to campaign against the Protection of Information Bill, the campaign opposes state secrecy and promotes a culture of openness and transparency. It has a focus group on secrecy and securitisation, and has recently launched a campaign for reforms to South Africa's communications surveillance policies and practices. See http://www.r2k.org.za/about/.

19   Admire Mare's email interview with academic, 18 October 2015.

20   Right2Know Campaign, 'Big Brother Exposed: Stories of South Africa's Intelligence Structures Monitoring and Harassing Activist Movements' (handbook), 2015, 22, http://bigbrother.r2k.org.za/ (accessed 2 September 2016).

21   Phillip de Wet, 'Why the SSA Is After AMCU's Leader', *Mail & Guardian*, 13 March 2015, http://mg.co.za/article/2015-03-12-why-the-ssa-is-after-amcus-leader (accessed 2 September 2016).

22   Phillip de Wet, 'Why the SSA Is After AMCU's Leader'.

23   Right2Know Campaign, 'Big Brother Exposed', 21.

24   Admire Mare's interviews with civic activists, at the offices of the Socio-Economic Rights Institute, 19–20 October 2015.

25   Admire Mare's interviews with civic activists, 19–20 October 2015.

26   Admire Mare's interviews with civic activists, 19–20 October 2015.

27   Admire Mare's interviews with civic activists, 19–20 October 2015.

28 Admire Mare's interviews with civic activists, 19–20 October 2015.

29 Admire Mare's interviews with lawyers from the Legal Resources Centre, 14 October 2015.

30 A network that consists of nine domestic civil liberties and human rights organisations: the American Civil Liberties Union, the Association for Civil Rights in Israel, the Canadian Civil Liberties Association, Centro de Estudios Legales y Sociales, the Egyptian Initiative for Personal Rights, the Hungarian Civil Liberties Union, the Kenyan Human Rights Commission, the Legal Resources Centre, and Liberty.

31 Admire Mare's interviews with lawyers from the Legal Resources Centre, 14 October 2015.

32 G. Caluya, 'The Post-Panoptic Society? Reassessing Foucault in Surveillance Studies', *Social Identities* 16, no. 5 (2010): 621–33.

33 Laurence Cox and Alf Nilsen, *We Make Our Own History: Marxism and Social Movements in the Twilight of Neoliberalism* (London: Pluto Press, 2014).

34 David Lyon's keynote presentation to the International Association for Media and Communications Research, 14 July 2015, https://www.youtube.com/watch?v=Vzgok3kUl0o (accessed 7 June 2016).

CHAPTER 9

1 Ten Human Rights Organisations, '10 Human Rights Organisations v the United Kingdom', Applicants' Reply to Observations of the Government of the United Kingdom, Application no. 24960/15, undated, 51, https://www.ilsa.org/jessup/jessup16/Batch%201/WEBER%20AND%20SARAVIA%20v.%20GERMANY.pdf (accessed 1 September 2017).

2 Keith Breckenridge, 'The Elusive Panopticon: The HANIS Project and the Politics of Standards in South Africa', in *Playing the Identity Card: Surveillance, Security and Identification in Global Perspective*, ed. Colin J. Bennett and David Lyon (London: Routledge, 2008), 39–56.

3 Mark Swilling, Haroon Bhorat, Mbongiseni Buthelezi, Ivor Chipkin, Sikhulekile Duma, Lumkile Mondi, Camaren Peter, Mzukisi Qobo and Hannah Friedenstein, 'Betrayal of the Promise: How South Africa Is Being Stolen' (research report), State Capacity Research Project, May 2017.

4 Thandika Mkandiware, 'Neopatrimonialism and the Political Economy of Economic Performance in Africa: Critical Reflections', *World Politics* 67, no. 3 (2015): 563–612.

5 Zubairu Wai, 'Neo-Patrimonialism and the Discourse of State Failure in South Africa', *Review of African Political Economy* 39, no. 131 (2012): 27–43.

6 Zubairu Wai, 'Neo-Patrimonialism and the Discourse of State Failure in South Africa'.

7 Kevin O'Brien, *The South African Intelligence Services: From Apartheid to Democracy 1948–2005* (London: Routledge, 2011), 13–19.

8 Author's interview with former RICA judge Yvonne Mokgoro, Constitutional Court, Johannesburg, 22 September 2017.

9 Open Secrets, 'Declassified: Apartheid Profits: The Sanction Busters' Toolkit', *Daily Maverick*, 17 August 2017, https://www.dailymaverick.co.za/article/2017-08-17-declassified-apartheid-profits-the-sanctions-busters-toolkit/#.WdH_F4-CzIU (accessed 2 October 2017).

10   Laurence Cox, 'Changing the World without Getting Shot: How Popular Power Can Set Limits to State Violence', in *Political Power Reconsidered: State Power and Civic Activism between Legitimacy and Violence. Peace Report 2013*, ed. M. Lakitsch (Berlin and Vienna: LIT-Verlag, 2014).

11   African News Agency, 'State Resources Used to Spy on SACP', *Independent Online*, 17 November 2015, http://www.iol.co.za/capetimes/state-resources-used-to-spy-on-sacp-1946746 (accessed 14 February 2017).

12   Research ICT Africa, 'Update: State of Prepaid Market in South Africa: Submission to the Parliament of South Africa on "The Cost to Communicate in South Africa"', 2016, http://www.researchictafrica.net/polbrf/Research_ICT_Africa_Policy_Briefs/2016_Policy_Brief_4_South_Africa_Cost_to_Communicate.pdf (accessed 15 February 2017).

13   Simnikiwe Mzekandaba, 'SA Internet User Numbers Surge', *ITWeb*, 3 June 2016, http://www.itweb.co.za/index.php?option=com_content&view=article&id=153224 (accessed 15 February 2017).

14   Asaf Lubin, 'A New Era of Mass Surveillance Is Emerging across Europe', *Just Security* 9 (January 2017), https://www.justsecurity.org/36098/era-mass-surveillance-emerging-europe/ (accessed 14 February 2017); James Bamford, 'Donald Trump Has Keys to the Most Invasive Surveillance State in History', *Foreign Policy*, 6 January 2017, http://foreignpolicy.com/2017/01/06/donald-trump-has-the-keys-to-the-most-invasive-surveillance-state-in-history-nsa-cia/ (accessed 14 February 2017).

15   Reg Whitaker, 'The Surveillance State', in *The Politics of the* Right, ed. Leo Panitch and Greg Albo (London: Merlin Press, 2015), 350.

16   Whitaker, 'The Surveillance State', 350.

17   Bill Fletcher Jr, '"Stars and Bars": Understanding Right-Wing Populism in the USA', in *The Politics of the Right*, ed. Leo Panitch and Greg Albo (London: Merlin Press, 2015), 297.

18   Laurence Cox and Alf Nilsen, *We Make Our Own History: Marxism and Social Movements in the Twilight of Neoliberalism* (London: Pluto Press, 2014), 59–61.

19   Cox and Nilsen, *We Make Our Own History*, 145–52.

20   Cox and Nilsen, *We Make Our Own History*, 76.

21   Donatella della Porta, *Social Movements in Times of Austerity* (Cambridge: Polity Press, 2015).

22   Della Porta, *Social Movements in Times of Austerity*.

23   Stephanie Pell, 'We Must Secure America's Cell Networks: From Criminals and Cops', *Wired*, 27 August 2014, https://www.wired.com/2014/08/we-must-secure-americas-cell-networks-from-criminals-and-cops-alike/ (accessed 23 March 2017).

24   Myriam Dunn Cavelty, 'The Militarisation of Cyberspace: Why Less May Be Better', 4th International Conference on Cyber-conflict, North Atlantic Treaty Organisation Cooperative Cyber Defence Centre of Excellence, Tallinn, 2012.

SELECT BIBLIOGRAPHY

Adey, Peter. 'Borders, Identification and Surveillance: New Regimes of Border Control'. In *Routledge Handbook of Surveillance Studies*, edited by Kirstie Ball, Kevin D. Haggerty and David Lyon, 194–5. London: Routledge, 2012.

Africa, Sandy. 'The Policy Evolution of the South African Intelligence Services: 1994 to 2009 and Beyond'. Unpublished paper, 2012. http://repository.up.ac.za/bitstream/handle/2263/20766/Africa_Policy(2012).pdf?sequence=1 (accessed 25 May 2016).

Allmer, Thomas. *Towards a Critical Theory of Surveillance in Informational Capitalism*. Peter Lang: Frankfurt, 2012.

Andreas, Peter, and Richard Price. 'From War Fighting to Crime Fighting: Transforming the American National Security State'. *International Studies Review* 3 (2001): 31–52.

Bawa, Nazreen. 'The Regulation of Interception of Communications and Provision of Communications Related Information Act'. In *Telecommunications Law in South Africa*, edited by Lisa Thornton, Yasmin Carrim, Patric Mtshaulana and Pippa Reburn (2006), 296–332. http://link.wits.ac.za/papers/tele-law.html (accessed 5 June 2013).

Beck, Colin. 'The World-Cultural Origins of Revolutionary Waves: Five Centuries of European Contention'. *Social Science History* 35, no. 2 (2011): 167–207.

Bennett, Colin. *The Privacy Advocates: Resisting the Spread of Surveillance*. Cambridge: MIT Press, 2008.

Bennett, Colin. 'In Defence of Privacy'. *Surveillance and Society* 8, no. 4 (2011): 487–8.

Bezuidenhout, Christiaan. 'The Nature of Police and Community Interaction alongside the Dawn of Intelligence-Led Policing'. *Acta Criminologica*, CRIMSA conference special edition, no. 3 (2008). http://repository.up.ac.za/bitstream/handle/2263/9445/Bezuidenhout_Nature%282008%29.pdf?sequence=1 (accessed 20 May 2016).

Bond, Patrick. 'Subimperialism as Lubricant of Neoliberalism: South African "Deputy Sheriff" Duty within BRICS'. *Third World Quarterly* 34, no. 2 (2013): 251–70.

Booysen, Susan. *The African National Congress and the Regeneration of Political Power*. Johannesburg: Wits University Press, 2011.

Brakel, Rosamunde van, and Paul de Hert. 'Policing, Surveillance and Law in a Pre-Crime Society: Understanding the Consequences of Technology Based Strategies'. *Cahiers Politiestudies* 20 (2011): 163–92. http://www.vub.ac.be/LSTS/pub/Dehert/378.pdf (accessed 4 March 2017).

Breckenridge, Keith. 'The Elusive Panopticon: The HANIS Project and the Politics of Standards in South Africa'. In *Playing the Identity Card: Surveillance, Security and Identification in Global Perspective*, edited by Colin J. Bennett and David Lyon, 39–56. London: Routledge, 2008.

Breckenridge, Keith. *Biometric State: The Global Politics of Identification and Surveillance.* Cambridge: Cambridge University Press, 2014.

Bruno, Zachary. 'The PRISM Programme Panopticon: Foucault's Insights into the Era of Snowden'. Unpublished paper, Occidental College, 24 March 2014.

Caluya, Gilbert. 'The Post-Panoptic Society? Reassessing Foucault in Surveillance Studies'. *Social Identities* 16, no. 5 (2010): 621–33.

Cate, Fred H. 'The Failure of Fair Information Practice Principles'. In *Consumer Protection in the Information Economy,* edited by Jane K. Winn, 341–78. Aldershot: Ashgate, 2006.

Cavelty, Myriam Dunn. 'The Militarisation of Cyberspace: Why Less May Be Better'. 4th International Conference on Cyber-Conflict, North Atlantic Treaty Organisation Cooperative Cyber Defence Centre of Excellence, Tallinn, 2012.

Ceyhan, Ayse. 'Surveillance as Biopower'. In *Routledge Handbook of Surveillance Studies,* edited by Kirstie Ball, Kevin D. Haggerty, and David Lyon. London: Routledge, 2012.

Clarke, Roger. 'Information Technology and Dataveillance'. *Communications of the ACM* 35, no. 5 (1988): 498–9.

Coleman, Roy, and Joe Sim. '"You'll Never Walk Alone": CCTV Surveillance, Order and Neoliberal Rule in Liverpool City Centre'. *British Journal of Sociology* 51, no. 4 (2000): 623–39.

Combes, Hélène, and Olivier Fillieule. 'Repression and Protests: Structural Models and Strategic Interactions'. *Revue Française de Science Politique* 61, no. 6 (2011): 1047–72.

Cox, Laurence. 'Changing the World without Getting Shot: How Popular Power Can Set Limits to State Violence', in *Political Power Reconsidered: State Power and Civic Activism between Legitimacy and Violence. Peace Report 2013,* ed. M. Lakitsch (Berlin and Vienna: LIT-Verlag, 2014).

Cox, Laurence. 'Waves of Protest and Revolution: Elements of a Marxist Analysis'. Unpublished paper, 2014. http://eprints.maynoothuniversity.ie/4867/ (downloaded 1 February 2015).

Cox, Laurence, and Alf Nilsen. *We Make Our Own History: Marxism and Social Movements in the Twilight of Neoliberalism.* London: Pluto Press, 2014.

Curran, James, Natalie Fenton, and Des Freedman, eds. *Misunderstanding the Internet.* London: Routledge, 2012.

Deleuze, Gilles. 'Postscript on the Societies of Control'. *October* 59 (Winter 1992): 3–7.

Della Porta, Donatella. *Social Movements in Times of Austerity.* Cambridge: Polity Press, 2015.

Dencik, Lina, and Jonathan Cable. 'The Advent of Surveillance Realism: Public Opinion and Activist Responses to the Snowden Leaks'. *International Journal of Communication* 11 (2017): 763–81.

Derby, Patrick. 'Policing in the Information Age: Automated Number Plate Recognition'. In *Eyes Everywhere: The Global Growth of Camera Surveillance,* edited by Aaron Doyle, Randy Lippert and David Lyon, 156–73. London: Routledge, 2011.

Donovan, Kevin P. 'The Biometric Imaginary: Bureaucratic Technopolitics in Postapartheid Welfare'. *Journal of Southern African Studies* 41, no. 4 (2015): 815–33.

Donovan, Kevin P., and Aaron.K. Martin. 'The Rise of African SIM Registration: Mobility, Identity, Surveillance and Resistance'. Information Systems and Innovation Group Working Paper no. 186, 2012, London School of Economics and Political Science, London.

Doyle, Aaron, Randy Lippert, and David Lyon, eds. *Eyes Everywhere: The Global Growth of Camera Surveillance.* London: Routledge, 2012.

Duncan, Jane. 'Thabo Mbeki and Dissent'. In *Mbeki and After: Reflections on the Legacy of Thabo Mbeki*, edited by Daryl Glaser, 105–27. Johannesburg: Wits University Press, 2010.

Duncan, Jane. *The Rise of the Securocrats: The Case of South Africa*. Johannesburg: Jacana Media, 2014.

Duncan, Jane. *Protest Nation: The Right to Protest in South Africa*. Durban: University of KwaZulu-Natal Press, 2016.

Durham, Robert B. *Supplying the Enemy: The Modern Arms Industry and the Military-Industrial Complex*. Morrisville: Lulu.com, 2015.

Ellis, Stephen. *External Mission: The ANC in Exile*. Cape Town: Jonathan Ball Publishers, 2012.

Etzioni, A. 'A Communitarian Perspective on Privacy'. *Connecticut Law Review* 32, no. 3 (2000): 897–905.

Fernandez, Luis A. *Policing Dissent: Social Control and the Anti-Globalisation Movement*. Toronto: Rutgers University Press, 2008.

Finkel, Evgeny, and Yitzhak M. Brudny, 'No More Colour! Authoritarian Regimes and Colour Revolutions in Eurasia'. *Democratisation* 19, no. 1 (2012): 1–14.

Fletcher, Bill Jr. '"Stars and Bars": Understanding Right-Wing Populism in the USA'. In *The Politics of the Right*, edited by Leo Panitch and Greg Albo, 296–311. London: Merlin Press, 2015.

Foster, John Bellamy, and Robert McChesney. 'Surveillance Capitalism: Monopoly-Finance Capital, the Military-Industrial Complex, and the Digital Age'. *Monthly Review* 66, no. 3 (July–August 2014): 1–31. http://monthlyreview.org/2014/07/01/surveillance-capitalism/ (accessed 4 November 2016).

Foucault, Michel. *Discipline and Punish: The Birth of the Prison*. Harmondsworth: Penguin Books, 1979.

Fuchs, Christian. 'Towards an Alternative Concept of Privacy'. *Journal of Information, Communication and Ethics in Society* 9, no. 4 (2011): 220–37.

Fuchs, Christian. 'How Can Surveillance Be Defined?' *Matrizes* 1, no. 5 (2011): 109–36.

Fuchs, Christian. *Reading Marx in the Information Age: A Media and Communications Studies Perspective on Capital, Volume 1*. London: Routledge, 2016.

Gane, Nicholas. 'The Governmentalities of Neoliberalism: Panopticism, Post-Panopticism and Beyond'. *Sociological Review* 60 (2012): 611–34.

Gill, Peter, and Mark Phythian. *Intelligence in an Insecure World*. Cambridge: Polity Press, 2012.

Giroux, Henry A. 'Totalitarian Paranoia in the Post-Orwellian Surveillance State'. *Cultural Studies* 29, no. 2 (2015): 108–40.

Goitein, Elizabeth, and Faiza Patel. 'What Went Wrong with the FISA Court?' Brennan Centre for Justice, New York School of Law, 2015. http://litigation.utahbar.org/assets/materials/2015FedSymposium/3c_What_Went_%20Wrong_With_The_FISA_Court.pdf (accessed 23 September 2016).

Gurney, Robert, Michael Rhead, Soodamani Ramalingam, and Vivienne Lyons. 'The Effect of ANPR Camera Settings on System Performance'. 5th International Conference on Imaging for Crime Detection and Prevention, 1 January 2013. http://researchprofiles.herts.ac.uk/portal/files/2684800/The_effect_of_ANPR_Camera_Settings_on_System_Performance_RG_MR.pdf (accessed 23 January 2017).

271

Haggerty, Kevin. 'Tear Down the Walls: On Demolishing the Panopticon'. In *Theorising Surveillance: The Panopticon and Beyond*, edited by David Lyon, 23–45. London: Routledge, 2006.

Haggerty, Kevin D., and Richard V. Ericson. 'The Surveillant Assemblage'. *British Journal of Sociology* 51, no. 4 (2000): 605–22.

Hayes, Ben. 'The Surveillance-Industrial Complex'. In *Routledge Handbook of Surveillance Studies*, edited by Kirstie Ball, Kevin D. Haggerty, and David Lyon, 167–75. London: Routledge, 2012.

Heitman, Helmoed. *The Battle in Bangui: The Untold Story*. Johannesburg: Mampoer Shorts, 2013.

Hintz, Arne, and Ian Brown. 'Enabling Digital Citizenship? The Reshaping of Surveillance Policy after Snowden'. *International Journal of Communication* 11 (2017): 782–801.

Hommes, Erin, and Marlene Holmner. 'Intelligent Transport Systems: Privacy, Security, and Societal Considerations within the Gauteng Case Study'. *Innovation* 46 (June 2013): 192–206.

Kasrils, Ronnie. *Armed and Dangerous: My Undercover Struggle against Apartheid*. Oxford: Heinemann, 1993.

Kienscherf, Markus. 'Beyond Militarization and Repression: Liberal Social Control as Pacification', *Critical Sociology* 42, no. 7–8 (2016).

Kraska, Peter. 'Militarisation and Policing: Its Relevance to 21st Century Policing'. *Policing* 1, no. 4 (2007): 501–13.

Landau, Susan. *Surveillance or Security? The Risks Posed by New Wiretapping Technologies*. Cambridge: MIT Press, 2010.

Lyon, David. *The Electronic Eye: The Rise of the Surveillance Society*. Minneapolis: University of Minnesota Press, 1994.

Lyon, David. 'Surveillance Studies: Understanding Visibility, Mobility and Phonetic Fix'. *Surveillance and Society* 1, no. 1 (2002): 1–7.

Lyon, David. 'Liquid Surveillance: The Contribution of Zygmunt Bauman to Surveillance Studies'. *International Political Sociology* 4 (2010): 325–38.

Lyon, David. 'National IDs in a Global World: Surveillance, Security and Citizenship'. *Case Western Reserve Journal of International Law* 42, no. 3 (2010): 607–23. http://scholarly-commons.law.case.edu/cgi/viewcontent.cgi?article=1247&context=jil (accessed 20 July 2016).

Lyon, David. 'Surveillance, Snowden and Big Data: Capacities, Consequences, Critique'. *Big Data and Society*, July 2014. http://bds.sagepub.com/content/1/2/2053951714541861 (accessed 24 August 2016).

Lyon, David. *Surveillance after Snowden*. London: Polity Press, 2015.

Lyon, David. 'Surveillance Culture: Engagement, Exposure and Ethics in Digital Modernity'. *International Journal of Communication* 11 (2017): 824–42.

Lyon, David, and Özgün E. Topak. 'Promoting Global Identification: Corporations, IGOs and ID Card Systems'. In *Routledge Handbook of Surveillance Studies*, edited by Kirstie Ball, Kevin D. Haggerty, and David Lyon, 27–43. London: Routledge, 2012.

Mann, Steve, Jason Nolan, and Barry Wellman. 'Sousveillance: Inventing and Using Wearable Computing Devices for Data Collection in Surveillance Environments'. *Surveillance and Society* 1, no. 3 (2003): 331–55.

Marx, Gary. '"Your Papers Please": Personal and Professional Encounters with Surveillance'. In *Routledge Handbook of Surveillance Studies*, edited by Kirstie Ball, Kevin D. Haggerty, and David Lyon, xx–xxxi. London: Routledge, 2012.

Mathiesen, Thomas. 'The Viewer Society: Michel Foucault's "Panopticon" Revisited'. *Theoretical Criminology* 1, no. 2 (1997): 215–34.

Mattelart, Armand. *The Globalisation of Surveillance*. Cambridge: Polity Press, 2010.

McCoy, Alfred W. 'Surveillance and Scandal: Weapons in an Emerging Array for US Global Power'. *Monthly Review* 66, no. 3 (July–August 2014): 70–81. http://monthlyreview. org/2014/07/01/the-new-surveillance-normal/ (accessed 27 July 2016).

McMichael, Christopher. 'Police Wars and State Repression in South Africa'. *Journal of Asian and African Studies* 51, no. 1 (2016): 3–16.

McQuoid-Mason, David. 'Privacy'. In *Constitutional Law of South Africa*, edited by M. Chaskalson et al. Cape Town: Juta, 2008.

Minnaar, Anthony. 'The Implementation and Impact of Crime Prevention/Crime Control Open Street Closed Circuit Television Surveillance in South African Central Business Districts'. *Surveillance and Society* 4, no. 3 (2007): 174–207.

Minnaar, Anthony. 'The Growth and Further Proliferation of Camera Surveillance in South Africa'. In *Eyes Everywhere: The Global Growth of Camera Surveillance*, edited by Aaron Doyle, Randy Lippert, and David Lyon, 100–21. London: Routledge, 2012.

Mkandiware, Thandika. 'Neopatrimonialism and the Political Economy of Economic Performance in Africa: Critical Reflections'. *World Politics* 67, no. 3 (2015): 563–612.

Mosco, Vincent. *A Political Economy of Communications: Rethinking and Renewal*. London: Sage Publications, 2009.

Murdock, Graham, and Peter Golding. 'Culture, Communications and Political Economy'. In *Mass Media and Society*, edited by James P. Curran, and Michael Gurevitch, 4th edn, 60–83. London: Arnold, 2005.

Myburgh, Pieter-Louis. *The Republic of Gupta: A Story of State Capture*. Cape Town: Penguin Publishers, 2017.

Ní Loideain, Nora. 'Cape Town as a Smart and Safe City: Implications for Governance and Data Privacy'. *International Data Privacy Law* 7 no. 4 (2017): 314–334.

Norris, Clive. 'There's No Success Like Failure and Failure's No Success at All: Some Critical Reflections on Understanding the Global Growth of CCTV Surveillance'. In *Eyes Everywhere: The Global Growth of Camera Surveillance*, edited by Aaron Doyle, Randy Lippert, and David Lyon, 33–40. London: Routledge, 2012.

O'Brien, Kevin. *The South African Intelligence Services: From Apartheid to Democracy 1948–2005*. London: Routledge, 2011.

Orwell, George. *Nineteen Eighty-Four*. London: Harvill Secker, 1949.

Pejout, Nicolas. 'World Wide Weber: Formalise, Normalise, Rationalise: E-Government for Welfare State – Perspectives from South Africa'. In *Electronic Constitution: Social, Cultural and Political Implications*, edited by Francesco Amoterri, 99–114. New York: Information Science Reference, 2009.

Pithouse, Richard. *Writing the Decline: On the Struggle for South Africa's Democracy*. Johannesburg: Jacana Media, 2016.

Popa, Raluca A., Hari Balakrishnan, and Andrew J. Blumberg. 'VPriv: Protecting Privacy in Location-Based Vehicular Services'. In *Proceedings of the 18th Conference on USENIX Security Symposium*, Montreal, 10–14 August 2009, 335–50. http://math.stanford. edu/~blumberg/traffic/vpriv.pdf (accessed 7 March 2017).

Price, David H. 'The New Surveillance Normal: NSA and Corporate Surveillance in the Age of Global Capitalism'. *Monthly Review* 66, no. 3 (2014): 43–53. http://monthlyreview. org/2014/07/01/the-new-surveillance-normal/ (accessed 27 July 2016).

Regan, Priscilla. *Legislating Privacy*. Chapel Hill: University of North Carolina Press, 1995.

Rhead, Mike, Robert Gurney, Soodamani Ramalingam, and Neil Cohen. 'Accuracy of Automatic Number Plate Recognition (ANPR) and Real World UK Number Plate Problems'. In *Proceedings of the 46th IEEE International Carnahan Conference on Security Technology*, Boston, 15–18 October 2012, 286–91. https://pdfs.semanticscholar.org/d529/3335eb75e4b3898c6e6d428570e0583c4db9.pdf (accessed 23 January 2017).

Scott, James C. *Weapons of the Weak: Everyday Forms of Resistance*. New Haven and London: Yale University Press, 1985.

Sears, Alan. *A Good Book, in Theory: A Guide to Theoretical Thinking*. Orchard Park: Broadview Press, 2005.

Smith, Robert Ellis. 'Sometimes What's Public Is Private: Legal Rights to Privacy in Public Spaces'. In *Eyes Everywhere: The Global Growth of Camera Surveillance*, edited by Aaron Doyle, Randy Lippert, and David Lyon, 370–9. London: Routledge, 2012.

Squitieri, Chad. 'The Limits of the Freedom Act's Amicus Curiae'. *Washington Journal of Law, Technology and Arts* 11, no. 3 (2015): 197–210.

Steeves, Valerie. 'Reclaiming the Social Value of Privacy'. In *Lessons from the Identity Trail: Anonymity, Identity and Privacy in a Networked Society*, edited by Ian Kerr, Carole Lucock, and Valerie Steeves, 191–208. Oxford: Oxford University Press, 2009.

Tarrow, Sydney. *Democracy and Disorder: Protest and Politics in Italy, 1965–1975*. Oxford: Oxford University Press, 1989.

Trewhela, Paul. 'The Dilemma of Albie Sachs: ANC Constitutionalism and the Death of Thami Zulu'. *Searchlight South Africa* 11 (October 1993): 34–52.

Vally, Natasha. 'Insecurity in South African Social Security: An Examination of Social Grant Deductions, Cancellations and Waiting'. *Journal of Southern African Studies* 42, no. 5 (2016): 965–82.

Wai, Zubairu. 'Neo-Patrimonialism and the Discourse of State Failure in South Africa'. *Review of African Political Economy* 39, no. 131 (2012): 27–43.

Wasko, Janet. 'Studying the Political Economy of Media and Information'. *Comunicação e Sociedade* 7 (2005): 25–48.

Westin, Alan. *Privacy and Freedom*. New York: Atheneum, 1970.

Whitaker, Reg. 'The Surveillance State'. In *The Politics of the Right*, edited by Leo Panitch and Greg Albo, 347–73. London: Merlin Press, 2015.

Zureik, Elia, and L. Lynda Harling Stalker. 'The Cross Cultural Study of Privacy: Problems and Prospects'. In *Surveillance, Privacy and the Globalisation of Personal Information: International Comparisons*, edited by Elia Zureik, L. Lynda Harling Stalker, Emily Smith, David Lyon, and Yolande E. Chan, 8–30. Montreal: McGill-Queens University Press, 2010.

INDEX

Printed and bound by CPI Group (UK) Ltd, Croydon, CR0 4YY

16/04/2025

14658448-0001